INSIDE

JAVASCRIPT™

BILL BERCIK

JILL BOND

Contributions by Craig Olague

New Riders

New Riders Publishing, Indianapolis, Indiana

CW00796671

Inside JavaScript

By Bill Bercik and Jill Bond

With contributions by Craig Olague

Published by:
New Riders Publishing
201 West 103rd Street
Indianapolis, IN 46290 USA

Printed in the United States of America 1 2 3 4 5 6 7 8 9 0

Library of Congress Cataloging-in-Publication Data

```
Bercik, Bill, 1964-
    Inside JavaScript / Bill Bercik, Jill Bond.
        p.  cm.
    Includes index.
    ISBN 1-56205-593-3
    1.  JavaScript (Computer program language)
    I. Bond, Jill, 1962-  II. Title: Inside
    JavaScript
    QA76.73.J38B47   1996
    005.2--DC20
    96-42687
    CIP
```

Warning and Disclaimer

Publisher *Don Fowley*

Publishing Manager *Julie Fairweather*

Marketing Manager *Mary Foote*

Managing Editor *Carla Hall*

Product Development Specialist
Julie Fairweather

Acquisitions Editor
Nancy Maragioglio

Senior Editor
Sarah Kearns

Development Editor
Ami Frank

Project Editor
Ami Frank

Copy Editors
Keith Cline
Greg Pearson

Technical Editor
Craig Olague

Associate Marketing Manager
Tamara Apple

Acquisitions Coordinator
Tracy Turgeson

Administrative Coordinator
Karen Opal

Cover Designer
Michael Wilson

Cover Illustration
©Vadim Vahrameer/SIS

Cover Production
Aren Howell

Book Designer
Sandra Schroeder

Production Manager
Kelly D. Dobbs

Production Team Supervisor
Laurie Casey

Graphics Image Specialists
Dan Harris

Production Analysts
Jason Hand
Bobbi Satterfield

Production Team
Tricia Flodder
Janelle Herber
Christopher Morris
Eric L. Puckett
Daniela Raderstorf
Beth Rago
Elizabeth San Miguel
Scott Tullis
Megan Wade

Indexer
Ginny Bess

About the Authors

Bill Bercik has a diverse background in computer technology, ranging from programming flight simulators to visualization of satellite data. During his spare time, Mr. Bercik maintains his very popular "Dippy Bird" Web site, and keeps an active interest in recumbent bicycles and railbikes. Mr. Bercik has a BS in Computer Engineering from Clemson University and has done graduate work at California State University at Chico.

Jill Bond has been involved in the computer book publishing industry since 1989. She worked in-house at Macmillan as an indexer and editor, and left in 1992 to work as a freelance editor, developer, and author. Her most recent work is *Java API Reference* (New Riders Publishing, 1996) as a co-author with Colin Frazier. Jill received her degree from Purdue University in English and Sociology.

In addition to writing and developing books for Macmillan, Jill also teaches and writes music for the Catholic Church and enjoys reading, bicycling, and cooking. Jill lives in Columbus, Indiana with her husband Joel and her two daughters, Ashley and Alecia.

Trademark Acknowledgments

All terms mentioned in this book that are known to be trademarks or service marks have been appropriately capitalized. New Riders Publishing cannot attest to the accuracy of this information. Use of a term in this book should not be regarded as affecting the validity of any trademark or service mark. OS/2 is a registered trademark of International Business Machines Corporation.

Dedication

For KPIG, the best damn radio station in the world — Bill Bercik

For Ashley, Alecia, and Joel — Jill Bond

Acknowledgments

I appreciate all the help and support from the following people and pets, without whom this book would have been history.

From Bill Bercik:

Jill D. Bond, co-author, for being so cool, positive, and tolerant of my weird ways. Jill is really what saved this book.

Nancy Maragioglio and Ami Frank for doing such a good job of managing the unmanageable.

Gus, for being such a good little bird, sitting on my shoulder, and pooping on me only when I deserve it.

My sweety, Brigette Cawiezell for the back rubs and encouragement and for not leaving me during the two months I didn't have a life.

Todd Conners, for convincing me to quit my old job and write this book instead (Ha!).

Production and Editorial ~~staff who should get a day off work after this book.~~ (Sorry, I guess I'm not allowed to say that.) who do the REAL work in putting together a book.

From Jill Bond:

Books are projects created by many people, not just one or two. Thank you to Bill Bercik, my co-author, whose patience and knowledge seems to be unending (also thanks for the new experiences in Monterey!). As always, my heartfelt gratitude goes to Carla Hall, Managing Editor at NRP, who continually gives me more time, and to Nancy Maragioglio at NRP, my Acquisitions Editor and dear friend. Also, thanks to Ami Frank (Development Editor), Craig Olague (Technical Editor), Greg Pearson (Copy Editor), and all those wonderful folks in the Production Department who made this book better.

Also, a special thank you and mention goes to Basil Hashem of Netscape, who came to the rescue to provide screen shots and helpful comments regarding Chapter 12. Most of all, my appreciation goes to all those who love me and are patient with my absence while writing: my parents, Betty and Chet Bomaster, for their confidence in me, and to my family, Joel, Ashley, and Alecia, for their patience and continual support.

Contents at a Glance

Chapters:

Appendices:

Table of Contents

4 JavaScript Objects and Properties   63

Introduction

*I*nside JavaScript is for developers and programmers who develop environments and applications for the Internet. Information you will find here can help you create and develop applications and environments that are easier to use, provide more user interaction, and are visually appealing. By using JavaScript, you can script smarter and faster, thus saving time and money. Using LiveWire, LiveConnect, and LivePayment, the possibilities for creating and enhancing awesome Web sites are limitless. In this book, you will find information on the following:

◆ Using JavaScript to script browser applications for Netscape Navigator

◆ Controlling the flow of your programs

◆ Creating and using Navigator objects and methods, and using JavaScript's built-in functions and methods to simplify application development

◆ Using Navigator objects, such as windows and frames, to create great-looking and functional HTML documents that will be guaranteed to catch the eye

◆ LiveWire's built-in objects on the server side

◆ The many advantages of the Application Manager, which enables you to manage your LiveWire applications, including tasks such as starting, stopping, restarting, and running applications

◆ Database access, how to use cursors, about database types, and how to handle database errors

◆ Files on the server and calling external libraries

◆ LiveConnect, a new Internet technology developed by Netscape to enable interoperability between client Web applications

◆ Using JavaScript and Java to communicate with plug-ins

◆ Commerce on the Internet using LivePayment

◆ Intranet environments—putting Web basics to work in your organization

Chapter Overview

This book consists of 13 chapters and five appendices. Following are overviews for each chapter.

Chapter 1, "The Internet Application Framework," guides you through the different phases of the Internet, such as TCP/IP, the World Wide Web, plug-ins, Java, and JavaScript, giving you background information on how the Internet, HTML, and scripting languages have evolved over the last 10 years.

Chapter 2, "Presenting JavaScript," discusses how scripting languages, such as JavaScript, play an important role in the interplay that occurs between applications and documents. Just as we need MS-DOS scripting and Visual Basic for Applications (VBA) scripting in Windows 95, JavaScript is an important scripting language for the World Wide Web. It also discusses the differences between JavaScript and Java and how you can use JavaScript to script browser applications for Netscape Navigator.

Chapter 3, "JavaScript Language Fundamentals," provides the basics of the JavaScript language. You will learn how to JavaScript in your HTML documents, the JavaScript program structure, and commenting scripts. You will also learn how to declare and manipulate JavaScript variables, how to control the flow of your programs, and the basics about JavaScript functions.

Chapter 4, "JavaScript Objects and Properties," discusses how JavaScript objects differ from OOP Objects, about Navigator objects and properties (including the JavaScript Object Model), how to create and use Navigator objects and methods, and how to use JavaScript's built-in functions and methods.

Chapter 5, "Netscape Navigator Objects," discusses how Netscape Navigator objects work and how to use them in detail. You will learn about the object hierarchy, how to use the window and frame objects, the importance of location and history objects, and the numerous ways you can use form objects and their properties to create helpful forms that are easy to use.

Chapter 6, "Netscape LiveWire Objects," provides detailed information about LiveWire's built-in objects on the server side: request, client, project, and server. You will also learn about their properties and techniques used for maintaining these objects.

Chapter 7, "Introduction to LiveWire, LiveConnect, and LivePayment," takes you into the second half of this book and provides introductory information about the basics of LiveWire, including Site Manager and the LiveWire compiler. You will learn about server extension provided by LiveWire and more about LiveWire's use of a SQL database. You also will learn about the advantages of LiveConnect—an add-on communication technology to the JavaScript, Java, and plug-in technologies—and LivePayment, an extension to LiveWire, which is an open cross-platform server and online payment software that enables you to perform transactions and collect payments over the Internet.

Chapter 8, "Getting Familiar with LiveWire's Application Manager," discusses how to use Application Manager to manage your LiveWire applications, including tasks such as starting, stopping, restarting, and running applications. You put to use one of LiveWire's sample applications, Hello World, and get to work on the provided hands-on examples.

Chapter 9, "Using Client and Server Scripts," provides information about client and server scripts, including when to use them, communication between client and server scripts, using files on the server, and calling external libraries.

Chapter 10, "Creating Database Applications Using LiveWire Pro," discusses how to install database components using LiveWire Pro, how to access a database, and how to use cursors. This chapter also covers database types, and how to handle database errors.

Chapter 11, "Using LiveConnect with JavaScript," provides information about LiveConnect, a new Internet technology developed by Netscape to enable interoperability between client Web applications. You will learn how to use JavaScript and Java to communicate with plug-ins. You also will learn about the LiveConnect plug-ins that work with JavaScript, such as LiveAudio, LiveVideo, and Live3D.

Chapter 12, "Internet Commerce (LivePayment) with JavaScript," presents material on Netscape's LivePayment software. It discusses hardware and software requirements, those who can use LivePayment and their roles in the transaction process, and LivePayment features. It also covers developing applications with LivePayment, security features, and the LivePayment utility commands.

Chapter 13, "Intranet Solutions with JavaScript," features an overview of an Intranet system and compares protocol and uses to the Internet. It also includes a real-life example of an employee directory that you can put to use in your organization.

Be sure to check out the appendices for a quick reference to JavaScript authoring, the color values chart, additional WWW resources, and technical insight into the development of plug-ins and Java applets with JavaScript in mind.

How to Use This Book

This book is intended to be an easy-to-use, easy-to-read reference tutorial on JavaScript. As you read it, be sure to go through the examples (which are all provided on the CD-ROM that is included with this book). There are the regular notes, tips, and warnings designed to draw your attention to information that is useful and important, but might otherwise be overlooked.

In this *Inside* book, you will also notice two new features: the jargon note and the "Did you know..." section. Jargon notes are there to highlight new terms as you come across them. All new terms are also located in the glossary at the back of the book. "Did you know..." sections are a feature for the less experienced users. People who are already familiar with JavaScript and programming will probably not need to read those, but people who are new to the concept will find the information contained in the "Did you know..." sections helpful.

Lastly, there is one caveat regarding the code: please note that some code is numbered along the left margin. These numbers are NOT part of the code—they are placed there to make the explanations that follow easier to understand. For instance, the authors will refer to a number that corresponds with the line of code when speaking of the function performed by that line of code. Also when the lines of code were wrapped to the next line, a special character was used. It looks like ➡.

Once you've read the book and gone through the examples, dive into a whole new world of developing and programming that will utilize your new knowledge and abilities! You will be able to make your Web applications sparkle with new functionality. Go to it!

CHAPTER 1

The Internet Application Framework

Technically speaking, the Internet is just a bunch of computers all over the world connected by routers that communicate using a common protocol.

Routers are devices that forward data traffic between networks.

 Protocol relates to a set of formal rules describing how to transmit data.

The compelling aspect of the Internet has little to do with what the Internet is, but rather what you can do with it. You can now use the Internet for a wide range of purposes, including the sharing of research data, online shopping, joining discussions in chat rooms, and participating in three-dimensional virtual worlds.

This opening chapter guides you through the different phases of Internet development. Due to a basic principal called open standards, the Internet took off from being a networking system used exclusively by computer specialists to becoming an actual application framework used for distributing applications to a corporate and consumer market. Following are the three phases of the Internet this chapter looks at:

◆ First generation: Open standards and TCP/IP

◆ Second generation: The birth and growth of World Wide Web document-centered communication

◆ Third generation: Interactive Internet applications take off

It is in the third generation of Internet popularity that JavaScript was born. This chapter explains in detail the interactive nature of the third-generation Internet and how JavaScript functionality relates to it.

Did you know...

The old IBM PC operating system was called DOS, which stood for Disk Operating System. As the DOS operating system evolved and applications that ran on top of DOS became more widely used, the focus of enthusiasm shifted away from the original prospect of doing disk operations to the more exciting prospect of working with applications that run on top of DOS. The Internet has evolved in a similar fashion as DOS, in which it is the killer apps, not the Internet in itself, that make it important.

Open Standards

The leading principle that made the Internet so popular during its onset and is making the Internet even more popular today is the Internet's adoption of open standards. Before the Internet, a networking protocol called TCP/IP was bundled in the Berkeley distribution of the Unix operating system. As freeware, TCP/IP (and Berkeley Unix) was on just about every workstation and became the de facto protocol for communicating between workstations. Because of its freedom and openness, TCP/IP was adopted early on by the Internet. After the success of TCP/IP (and Unix), it became apparent that open standards are a good thing, and from that point on, the powers that guide the Internet have embraced one new open standard after another.

 Open standards can be used openly without requiring payment.

First Generation: Open Standards and TCP/IP

It was not long after the widespread use of TCP/IP throughout the Internet that a nation of universities and research centers with interconnected workstations suddenly flourished. Bundled with these workstations was a common set of programs that sat on top of TCP/IP. These bundled programs gave a network user a common set of commands to work from for network communication. It was no longer important what type of machine a person used—the same set of commands worked on all of them. Like TCP/IP, the protocols used by these programs were non-proprietary. The basic set of programs that almost every workstation was and still is packaged with today is ftp, Telnet, a SMTP-based e-mail service, and an NNTP-based Usenet service. These programs are generally terse, command-line-oriented Unix programs that are difficult to use and not designed with the casual user in mind. This state of maturity of the Internet, whereby the typical user is highly computer literate and the content is non-graphical (see fig. 1.1), is generally considered to be the Internet's first generation. Following is an examination of the basic Internet programs and protocols.

Figure 1.1

A first-generation Internet application.

ftp, Telnet, SMTP-based e-mail, and NNTP-based Usenet

File Transfer Protocol is a program named after the protocol it uses, ftp. This protocol enables users to download files from another workstation on the Internet. Users also can transfer their own files to other workstations. Some common uses of ftp include getting software from public sites and transferring work files or school assignments completed at home.

Public ftp sites usually require "Anonymous" as the login and the user's e-mail for a password. Users cannot transfer files to or from any computer system—they can only access computers that are set up as ftp servers.

Telnet is another program named after its protocol. The non-proprietary protocol Telnet uses is called Telnet. Telnet enables users to perform a remote login through a character-based terminal emulator. With Telnet, an administrator of a workstation can remotely administer the computer from clear across the country. Telnet also makes it possible for a seemingly endless number of terminal connections to be simultaneously connected to a workstation.

E-mail was likely the first killer app on the Internet. Although several e-mail programs were competing initially, the protocol for sending and receiving e-mail became standard. This protocol is called SMTP, or Simple Mail Transfer Protocol. This protocol was not exclusive to just the Internet; however, it was the Internet that made possible a standard means of exchanging e-mail on a global scale.

Usenet is a distributed bulletin board system based on an open protocol called NNTP (Network News Transfer Protocol). Originally implemented in 1979 to 1980 by Steve Bellovin, Jim Ellis, Tom Truscott, and Steve Daniel at Duke University, it swiftly grew to become international in scope and, likely, the largest decentralized collaboration utility in existence.

Usenet grew to encompass government agencies, universities, high schools, businesses of all sizes, and home computers of all descriptions. By 1993, Usenet hosted well over 1,200 newsgroups and an average of 40 megabytes (the equivalent of several thousand paper pages) of new technical articles, news, and discussions.

Not all Internet hosts subscribe to Usenet, and not all Usenet hosts are on the Internet; but, like e-mail, there is a large overlap of Internet and Usenet users.

Note   Although the technologies of transferring files, remote login sessions, and e-mail were available on many mainframe and microcomputers at the time, it was the non-proprietary, openness of the underlying Internet protocols that brought these technologies to such a wide global acceptance.

The first generation of the Internet provided an incredible amount of networking functionality; however, you had to be a computer expert to take advantage of it.

Furthermore, the documents on the Internet were either in a boring plain-text format or in a proprietary document format. The next phase, the Internet's second generation, fixed these exact problems.

Second Generation: The Birth and Growth of World Wide Web Document-Centered Communication

The birth and growth of the World Wide Web has changed the way people communicate all over the globe. Through its simple, yet elegant, document-centered architecture, the Web has grown at enormous speed. This new global medium has gained popular acceptance faster than any other communication medium in history. In the following sections, you will be exposed to the following topics:

◆ Introduction to the World Wide Web

◆ HyperText Transfer Protocol (HTTP)

◆ HyperText Markup Language (HTML)

◆ Wide Area Information Server (WAIS) and Common Gateway Interface (CGI)

Introduction to the World Wide Web

In March 1989, Tim Berners-Lee of Geneva (Switzerland) European Particle Physics Laboratory (which is abbreviated as CERN, based on the laboratory's French name) distributed a proposal to build a hypertext system for the purpose of enabling efficient and easy collaboration among geographically separated teams of researchers in the high-energy physics community. Important qualities of this proposed system included the following:

◆ A consistent user interface

◆ The ability to incorporate a wide range of document types

◆ A common interface so that anyone reading the document views it in a similar fashion

 Hypertext is a term coined around 1965 by Ted Nelson meaning a collection of documents, or *nodes*, containing cross-references, or *links*, that, with the aid of an interactive browser program, enable the reader to move easily from one document to another.

About three years after his proposal, in 1992, the ideas of Tim Berners-Lee became reality in the form of what was called the WWW (World Wide Web) project. A

rudimentary WWW browser was made available via ftp from CERN, and a variety of organizations and audiences got its first look at it. By January 1993, 50 WWW servers supported the non-proprietary WWW protocol called HTTP (HyperText Transfer Protocol), and a graphical WWW browser for Unix systems, Viola, was made available. Viola offered the first glimpse of the graphical, point-and-click hypertext system originally conceived by Tim Berners-Lee.

 HyperText Transfer Protocol (HTTP) is the client-server TCP/IP protocol used on the World Wide Web for the exchange of HTML documents.

CERN got the World Wide Web up and running, but soon other organizations joined in the action. Most notably was NCSA (the National Center for Supercomputing Applications, in Champaign, Illinois) which released in February 1993 the first alpha version of Mosaic for Unix platforms. Developed by Marc Andreessen, this WWW browser was soon ported by his colleagues at NCSA to the Macintosh and Windows platforms.

Commercialization of the Web was the big focus in 1994. Important developments in secure Web access took place that year, developments that paved the road for corporate acceptance of the Web after corporations realized that credit card transactions would be possible with this new technology. In addition, Mosaic source code was licensed to commercial developers, leading to many commercial-quality Web browsers. Commercialization, although great for the Web community, was not so great for NCSA Web development—Marc Andreessen and others departed to form the Mosaic Communication Corporation (now Netscape Communications Corporation).

The new not-so-humble Web project had soon outgrown CERN, and the project was turned over to a group called the W3 Organization, a joint venture between CERN and MIT (the Massachusetts Institute of Technology) to guide the Web's future. The Web was obviously becoming the core information distribution system of the Internet, and the responsibility for its development and growth required more human and financial resources than one research laboratory could handle.

Within the course of a few months in 1994 and early 1995, the W3 Organization was transformed into a conglomerate of organizations called the World Wide Web Consortium. This organization is led by Web pioneer Tim Berners-Lee and operates with funding from memberships. The Consortium expanded in April 1995 when MIT was joined by the French National Institute for Research in Computer Science and Control (INRIA) as cohost of the Consortium. Even with this expansion, CERN still remains an important collaborator in the consortium. You can go to the Consortium's Web site (http://www.w3.org) if you are interested in official statements or standards produced by the organization.

As you can see, just as TCP/IP was made a huge success by the openness and collaboration that went into the freeware Berkeley Unix operating system, similar openness and collaboration demonstrated by CERN, the W3 Organization, and now the World Wide Web Consortium have led to the Web's success, extending the Internet's domain even further to embrace the previously excluded corporate and consumer market.

If you had to describe the Web with only two words (well, technically six words as two acronyms), they would be HTTP and HTML (HyperText Markup Language). HTTP is the network protocol that provides a common method of transferring HTML documents from Web servers to Web browsers. HTML is the standard for creating content-rich documents that can be viewed similarly regardless of the Web browser or the platform the Web browser is running on.

HyperText Transfer Protocol

You would expect that with the astonishing functionality that HTTP brings, you would get as a side effect a matching complexity that comes along with it. This expectation does not hold up, however, because an HTTP transaction consists of only the following four basic phases:

◆ Connection

◆ Request

◆ Response

◆ Close

During the connection phase, a Web browser such as Netscape Navigator attempts to establish a connection with the server. When this phase is processing, you might see a line in the status bar of your browser that says something such as "Connecting to http://www.newriders.com." If the browser can't perform the connection, nothing further happens until the browser times out. After timing out, the browser displays a message explaining the failed connection.

If a connection to the HTTP server is established, the browser sends a request to the server. The request specifies which protocol is being used, what object it is looking for, and how the server should respond. The protocol is likely HTTP, but it can also be ftp, NNTP(remember Network News Transfer Protocol), or some other protocol. Included in the request is the browser's command to the server (commonly called a method). A likely command to the server would be "Get," which is basically a request to retrieve a specific object from the server.

If the HTTP server can fulfill the request, it executes a response. Otherwise, it sends error messages. Similar to the first phase, you may see a description of the transaction in the status bar of your browser that looks something like "Reading Response." Like the request, the response describes the protocol being used, and it offers a *reason line,* which shows up on the browser's status bar. From the status bar, you can tell what is going on at that point, usually seeing a message that looks something like "Transferring example.gif."

After the server has fulfilled the request, the connection between the Web client and the Web server is closed. It's time now for the browser to either load and display the selected object, save the object to a file, or launch an associated viewer. The browser displays text file objects as a plain text document. The browser displays graphics such as GIFs and JPEGs, or if it isn't capable of displaying a specific type of graphic, launches a viewer specified in its configuration settings. Usually, however, the Web browser simply displays an HTML document that contains the text, graphics, links, and formatting that the Web has become so famous for.

HyperText Markup Language

HTML is a relatively standard hypertext page description language. HTML is intended as a common medium for tying together information from widely different sources, a means to rise above the interoperability problems of existing document formats, and a means to provide a truly open interface to proprietary platforms. HTML is derived from non-proprietary SGML (Standard Generalized Markup Language), which uses tags to make documents readable across a variety of platforms and software. Notice once again how the Internet community picked a format that is platform and software neutral. Similar to SGML, HTML operates through a series of tags placed within an ASCII (plain text) document. These tags are translated by Web browsers into special kinds of formats to be displayed on the screen. An example of a tag is the bold markup tag. When a start and end bold markup tag surround a block of text, that block of text is displayed in a bold format by the Web browser.

 Tags are used for the purpose of creating descriptive markup in a document. There are two kinds of tags: start tags and end tags. They appear in the form of <StartTag> and </EndTag>.

Other HTML tags include links, lists, headings, titles, images, forms, and maps. As would be expected, growth in the HTML standard has coincided with the growth of the Internet.

The original HTML standard allowed only text, and soon inline images and several types of lists and link types were added. It was only later that such element types as fill-in forms and clickable image maps were possible. The reason for the initial simplicity of HTML was to make it simpler to write browsers for this document type. This simplicity has played a major role in the incredibly rapid growth of the World Wide Web. The new HTML 3.0 provides a clean superset of HTML 2.0, adding high value features such as tables, text flow around figures, and math, while still remaining a simple document format.

Inline images are graphics that appear on a document instead of requiring a separate viewer.

As mentioned previously, HTML is platform-independent. HTML is designed to enable rendering on a wide array of devices, from old teletypes to terminals, DOS, Windows, Macs, and high-end workstations, as well as non-visual media such as speech and Braille. In other words, HTML enables users to exploit the legacy of older equipment as well as the latest and best of new machines. HTML 3.0 provides for improved support of non-graphical clients, allowing for rich markup text in place of the figures shown on graphical clients. HTML can be rendered by a browser on a wide variety of screen sizes by using a scrolling or paged model. The fonts and presentation can be adjusted to suit the resources available in the host machine and the user's preferences. A person with poor eyesight can increase the size of his browser's default fonts.

The World Wide Web is all about content—not presentation markup; however, content providers are used to having tight control over the final look of documents. The need for platform independence weighs against this, but there is still strong pressure to find an appropriate means for content providers to express their intentions. History has shown the dangers of mixing presentation markup with content (or structural) markup. First, it becomes difficult to apply different presentation styles. Second, it becomes painful to incorporate material from different sources (with different presentation styles). And finally, it becomes difficult to be truly platform-independent. As a result, HTML 3.0 is designed for use with linked style information that defines the presentation style that was intended for each element. You will be able to use style sheets to be expressive in a platform-independent fashion or to provide a more detailed control for particular classes of client browsers or output media. With cascading style sheets, it will soon be possible to create professional-grade page layout and design with HTML documents. For example, an author will be able to specify the exact font and point size that some text should be rendered. If the Web browser does not have that font, it just displays the text with the font it has.

Most documents you run across with Web browsers such as Netscape Navigator are HTML documents. Of course, Web browsers can display ASCII text files, but these are just plain old text files that can be downloaded and viewed in any text editor. The compelling aspect of an HTML file is its markup tag. A link appears as a highlighted item, a list appears with associated bullets or numbers, and a graphic appears as the image it references. To put it another way, the World Wide Web would be pretty boring without HTML.

Wide Area Information Server and Common Gateway Interface

In October 1991, a CGI gateway script for a WAIS search was added to Mosaic. This demonstrated how a site could provide advanced server-side search and retrieval capabilities. You could now use the Mosaic Web browser as a front-end client and

WAIS as a back-end server to provide your users with a friendly, yet powerful, window into your information universe along with sophisticated query, retrieval, and indexing capabilities.

 WAIS, or *Wide Area Information Server*, is the service you use if you want to locate a document on the Internet.

 CGI, or *Common Gateway Interface*, is the format and syntax for passing information from browsers to servers via forms or document-based queries in HTML.

With this introduction, the Web evolved from being a mechanism for tying together information from widely different sources to having the additional functionality as the world's most powerful search tool.

Third Generation: Interactive Internet Applications Take Off

The first generation of the Internet could be regarded as a time when networking was the focus. Built tightly on top of TCP/IP, a few bundled Berkeley Unix programs were widely used by computer experts to communicate data back and forth.

The second generation of the Internet could be regarded as the birth of the World Wide Web, and as a byproduct of this invention, the dynamic growth of document-centric network communication. No longer restricted to computer experts, the Web was now in the hands of everybody, and instead of users focusing on the mechanics of transferring data, a much higher importance was placed on the authoring of data and data searching. The second generation was also the era of widespread acceptance for the Internet in the corporate and consumer marketplace.

The third generation of the Internet is where the real excitement begins. No longer is the Internet community satisfied with simply sharing documents across the Web; it now wants to share *applications* across the Web. In addition, the Internet community wants the documents that are shared to be as content-rich as they would be on a multimedia CD-ROM title. Some of the Internet technologies that make this possible are:

◆ Java

◆ JavaScript

◆ Netscape Plug-Ins

◆ VRML 2.0

◆ LiveConnect

◆ ActiveX

Just as the second generation of the Internet paved the way for corporate involvement in the Internet, the third generation heralded the repurposing of Internet framework for use in corporate intranets.

 Intranets are networks that use the same protocols, software applications, and technology as the Internet outside it; however, an intranet is not necessarily even connected to the Internet—a company might just set up a World Wide Web server on an internal network for distribution of information within the company.

Java

Java is defined by Sun Microsystems as a simple, object-oriented, distributed, interpreted, robust, secure, architecture-neutral, portable, multithreaded, dynamic, buzzword-compliant, general-purpose programming language. If that sentence has you confused, don't worry. To sum it up, Java is a very powerful language, yet it is simple to use. Java supports programming for the Internet in the form of platform-independent Java "applets." Java applets can be executed as attachments in World Wide Web documents by using either Sun's HotJava browser, Netscape Navigator version 2.0 or later, Internet Explorer 3.0, or Oracle PowerBrowser 2.5.

 Applets are programs written in Java that can be distributed as an attachment in an HTML document.

Java is similar to the overwhelmingly popular object-oriented language C++, but without many of the complexities associated with it, such as operator overloading, multiple inheritance, and pointer arithmetic. Unlike C++, Java has automatic garbage collection, reducing a large programming overhead in having to manually allocate and deallocate memory storage.

Java comes with an extensive library of routines for TCP/IP protocols such as HTTP and ftp. Java applications can access objects across the Internet via URLs as easily as on the local file system.

 URLs, or *Uniform Resource Locators*, are a standard syntax for specifying an object on the Internet, such as a file or newsgroup. URLs are used extensively on the World Wide Web to specify the target of a hyperlink.

Java is the first general purpose programming language that supports the creation of virus-free, tamper-free systems.

The Java compiler generates an architecture-neutral object file. This object file is then executable on any processor supporting the Java run-time system. The object code consists of bytecode instructions designed to be both easy to interpret on any machine and easily translated into native machine code at load time. The programs that translate the Java bytecode to machine code at load time are called *just-in-time compilers.*

The Java libraries provide for portable interfaces across platforms. For example, there is an abstract Windows class that has separate implementations on the Unix, Microsoft Windows, and Macintosh platform.

JavaScript

Formerly called LiveScript, JavaScript is Sun Microsystem's and Netscape Communication Corporation's simple cross-platform World Wide Web scripting language that has been adopted by Netscape Navigator 2.0 and later Internet Explorer 3.0. JavaScript is an easy-to-use object-based scripting language designed for creating live Internet applications that link objects and resources on both clients and servers. While Java is used by programmers to create new objects and applets, JavaScript is designed for use by HTML page authors and enterprise application developers to dynamically script the behavior of objects running on either the client or the server. JavaScript has a simplified C-like syntax. Its functionality is more geared toward scripting commercial Web applications rather than toward developing commercial applications. Netscape Navigator 2.0 currently interprets JavaScript statements embedded directly in an HTML page, and Netscape LiveWire and LiveWire Pro enable you to create server-based applications similar to common gateway interface (CGI) programs.

With JavaScript, an HTML page may contain an interactive form that permits loan payment or currency exchange calculations right on the client in response to user input. A server-side JavaScript script might pull data out of a relational database and format it in HTML on the fly. A page might contain JavaScript scripts that run on both the client and the server. On the server, the scripts might dynamically compose and format HTML content based on user preferences stored in a relational database; and on the client, the scripts might integrate an assortment of Java applets and HTML form elements into a live interactive user interface. JavaScript will be explained in finer detail in subsequent chapters.

Netscape Plug-Ins

Netscape plug-ins extend Netscape to include a wide range of interactive and multi-media functionality not available with standard Netscape. Like Web browser helper applications, plug-ins are platform-specific external applications that extend a browser. Unlike helper applications though, Netscape plug-ins can be embedded inline within a World Wide Web document, permitting the user to see the interactive data without being encumbered by an extra helper window on the desktop.

It is worth noting, however, that plug-ins, unlike helper applications, are currently only compatible with Netscape 2.0 or better. Also, plug-ins are specific to a particular operating system (Microsoft Windows 3.1, NT, and Macintosh are available). Popular commercial plug-ins include Shockwave, RealAudio, Adobe PDF, and Corel CMX (vector graphics). The file to be displayed is included in a Web page using an <EMBED...> HTML tag. Plug-ins, both commercially and independently authored, are usually downloaded for free and stored locally.

Unlike Java applets, plug-ins are not guaranteed to be virus-free. What makes plug-ins so popular is that they can run up to 10 times faster than a Java applet, they have free realm to access the client operating system, and they can easily leverage already existent C++ code.

VRML 2.0 Overview

The Virtual Reality Modeling Language (VRML) 2.0 (formerly called Moving Worlds) is a language that enables a Web developer to embed a virtual reality scene (.WRL file) describing multi-participant, hyperlinked, interactive virtual worlds. You can specify all aspects of virtual world display, interaction, and internetworking with the VRML language. As VRML authoring environments become more freely available, interactive virtual reality worlds will likely flourish on the Web, and VRML will become the standard language for interactive simulation within the World Wide Web.

Although for now VRML works under Netscape via a plug-in and Internet Explorer 3.0 via an ActiveX control, this will likely change. In the near future, VRML will probably go the route of inline GIF's, while most browsers will come off the shelf with VRML support. VRML is much more important than just another browser data type.

LiveConnect Overview

LiveConnect is a feature built into Netscape 3.0 and, to some degree, into Internet Explorer 3.0 that makes it possible to design Web pages with a dynamic level of interactivity between JavaScript, Java, and plug-in objects.

With Netscape's LiveConnect, a Netscape plug-in loaded on a page may interact with JavaScripts running on the same page. What this means is that a developer can write a custom interface to control a Java applet or a plug-in with simple-to-write HTML form elements and JavaScript.

In addition, LiveConnect provides the functionality for Java applets loaded on a page to communicate with JavaScripts running on the same page, and vice versa.

The principle behind LiveConnect is pretty simple. Any Java applet that Netscape 3.0 downloads becomes an object. The attributes of the Java applet (now an object) that were defined as public in the Java program can be referenced from a JavaScript embedded in an HTML document.

Communicating with a plug-in by using LiveConnect takes a bit more effort on the plug-in programmer's part—you need to develop your plug-in as a program that is linked with Netscape's plug-in API as well as the Java run-time interface in order to use LiveConnect. The Java run-time interface is a template library that lets developers define Java classes in their C++ plug-in code. The end result is that you can now add Java public classes to your plug-ins, classes that can be referenced from both JavaScript scripts as well as Java applets.

Microsoft ActiveX

ActiveX is an Internet and Windows technology created by Microsoft that enables Web developers to take advantage of Microsoft's operating system as it homogenizes itself with the Internet. One way this is done is through a new dual development role that enables a person to write a program for a control (library program) to be used on the desktop that doubles as an object that can be embedded inside an HTML document and viewed with Microsoft's Internet Explorer. From a browser standpoint, ActiveX technology has features similar to Netscape plug-ins in that it is based on fast native compiled C++ code. Like Netscape plug-ins, ActiveX is desirable to Web developers that want to take advantage of their existing C++ code base. The added advantage of ActiveX is that a developer can develop for the Internet and still maintain a tight integration with Microsoft desktop development environments, such as Visual Basic, that will support ActiveX in the future.

A major disadvantage of Web application development using ActiveX technology is that your embedded ActiveX object will not be compatible with the Netscape browser in the foreseeable future. Another disadvantage of ActiveX is the notion that this technology steps apart from the Internet Application Framework ideal, where standards are collaborations created in public by committees with representatives from diverse organizations. Although Microsoft is striving to make ActiveX more open to standards bodies, many developers regard ActiveX as somewhat of a self-serving technology created by Microsoft to be used as a promotion of Microsoft platform development.

Third Generation Technologies

At your disposal are several new technologies to aid in the development of Web-based applications:

- **Java**—the best technology for the development of cross-platform Web applications (applets) that do not need access to the client's local operating system.

- **JavaScript**—a great technology for scripting applications and for preprocessing user input. JavaScript is also a good alternative to writing server-side CGI scripts.

- **Plug-in development**—the way to go should you want to build a Web application that runs quickly and has free realm to access the local operating system.

- **Off the shelf plug-ins such as Shockwave**—a good option if you want to develop media-rich content on your Web site and if your clients are willing to download the plug-in.

- **VRML**—the technology of choice for interactive simulation, endorsed by Silicon Graphics, Netscape, Microsoft, and Sony.

- **LiveConnect**—the technology to use for communicating between Java, JavaScript, and plug-ins.

- **ActiveX**—an option for building Web applications for clients that use Internet Explorer 3.0.

Summary

The Internet has developed through three generational stages. In the first generation, the development of the TCP/IP infrastructure marked the beginning of a useful worldwide network. The problem was that a user would spend more time in touch with the network system than with the actual data or document of interest. This tended to bar the casual user from the Internet. The second generation marked the beginning of the World Wide Web, where casual users feel at home and documents—not networking systems—are the main focal point. The second generation also marked the beginning of the Internet being used for searching rather than just browsing. The third generation is when the Internet is becoming more than just a distribution mechanism for documents, but rather a distribution mechanism for applications. The third generation is also witnessing the birth of the intranet.

Chapter 2, "Presenting JavaScript," further introduces you to the scripting language JavaScript. There you will learn the importance of JavaScript as a scripting language and its role as a language for creating scripts both for Netscape Navigator and Netscape LiveWire Pro.

Presenting JavaScript

As you learned in Chapter 1, the Internet has evolved from being merely a network of computers linked together with a common protocol into something much more. The Internet now enables developers to build platform-independent, large-scale client/server applications.

Platform independence means that your application is not dependent on any specific hardware platform. Creating platform-independent programs gives you a major advantage in that your application is able to run on almost any system.

Platform independence means that your application is not dependent on any specific hardware platform.

The capability to be platform-independent has changed the direction of focus for developers. For a large portion of application programming, it now makes better sense to focus on developing for the Internet rather than developing for an operating system or specific chip set that might be extinct in a few years.

Figure 2.1 is the Netscape LiveWire Application Manager, which is an example of an application developed for the Internet rather than an operating system. The Application Manager also is an example of a JavaScript Web application that works the same way running on Unix or Windows NT. The advantages to the developers of the Application Manager program are obvious. Instead of writing two separate Application Manager programs, one for Unix and another for NT, as they would do when developing a typical desktop application, developers can write Application Manager once for an Internet application, and the same code base can be used on both the Unix and NT platforms.

Figure 2.1

The Netscape LiveWire Application Manager.

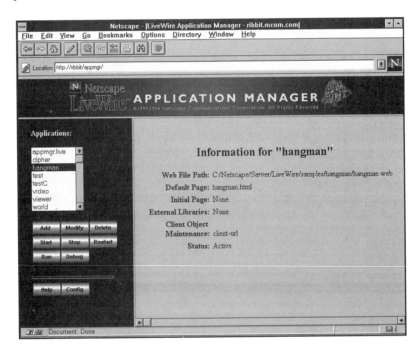

This chapter introduces the JavaScript language. Specifically, you will learn about the following:

◆ The need for scripting languages

◆ Scripting WWW browser applications for Netscape Navigator

◆ Scripting WWW servers applications with LiveWire

Why Scripting Languages are Essential

Now that you can look at the Internet as being a true platform, take a look at how it compares to other platforms. Because it is one of the most popular, Windows 95 is a good platform to compare to the Internet platform with respect to interplay between documents and applications. Following are several comparisons of the two platforms.

Documents launching an application:

◆ **Win 95**—Double-clicking on a document brings up an application (see fig. 2.2).

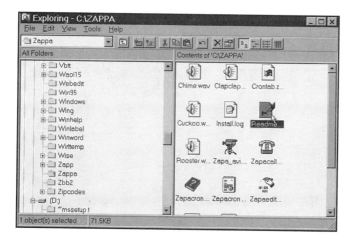

Figure 2.2

Documents launching an application in Windows 95.

◆ **Internet**—Documents found by browsers such as Netscape Navigator launch helper applications or plug-ins. Helper applications and plug-ins are used by a Web browser to interpret files that it has retrieved but is unable to read. For helper applications, the file is loaded into the window of the helper application; for plug-ins, the file is loaded into the plug-in application. Unlike the helper application, a plug-in application is embedded inside the browser's window (see fig. 2.3).

Figure 2.3

A plug-in for a video file in Netscape Navigator 3.0.

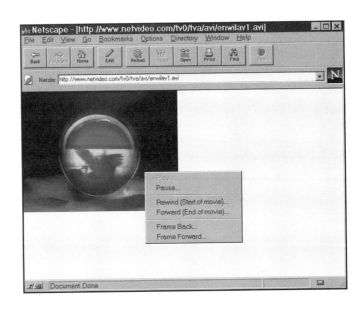

Application reading/writing to a document:

◆ **Win 95**—Reads/writes file based on drive, directory, and file name (see fig. 2.4).

◆ **Internet**—Reads/writes file based on URL.

Figure 2.4

Opening a file in Windows 95.

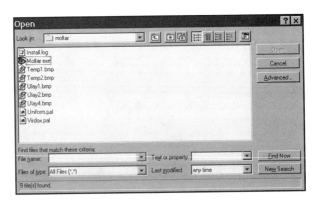

 URLs, or *Uniform Resource Locators*, are used for specifying objects on the Internet, such as files or newsgroups. URLs are used extensively on the World Wide Web. They are used in HTML documents to specify the target of a hyperlink (see fig. 2.5).

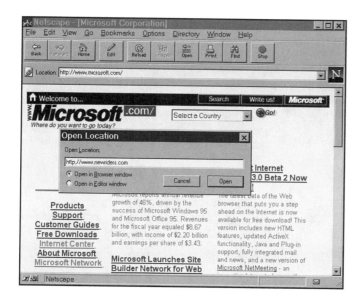

Figure 2.5

Opening an URL in Netscape Navigator 3.0.

Application controlling another application:

◆ **Win 95**—Programs (usually C++) written with OLE (Object Linking and Embedding) Automation in mind can be controlled by Visual Basic scripts (see fig. 2.6).

C++ is one of the most-used object-oriented languages. C++ is a superset of C developed primarily by Bjarne Stroustrup at AT&T Bell Laboratories in 1986. OLE Automation enables applications and components to expose data and functionality in a form that virtually any Windows application development language can access and use. OLE automation programs are most often controlled by scripts written in Visual Basic.

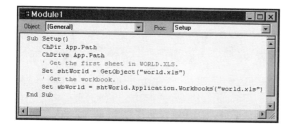

Figure 2.6

OLE Automation scripting in Visual Basic.

◆ **Internet**—Java programs and plug-ins written with JavaScript in mind can be controlled by JavaScript scripts (see fig. 2.7).

Figure 2.7

Controlling a Java application with JavaScript.

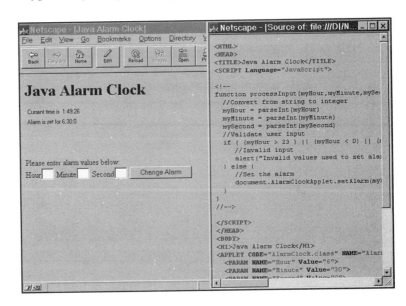

Application that uses commercial components:

◆ **Win 95**—Components are DLLs (Dynamically Linked Library), VBXs (Visual Basic Controls), or OCX (OLE Custom Controls) controls. An application programmer creates a custom program in Visual Basic or Delphi that takes advantage of these OCX controls in a manner that best suits the problem at hand. The Microsoft Multimedia Control is an example of a commercial component that can be used in a custom program written in Visual Basic (see fig. 2.8).

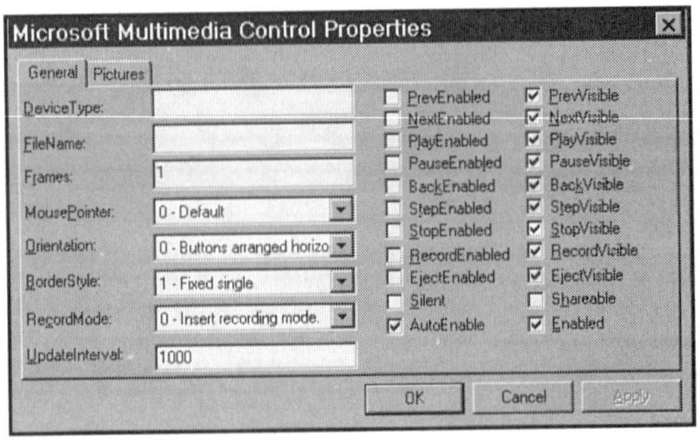

Figure 2.8

Using the Microsoft Multimedia Control component.

◆ **Internet**—Components are plug-ins or Java applets. An application programmer creates a custom program in JavaScript that takes advantage of these components in a manner that best suits the problem at hand. Netscape's Live3D, LiveVideo, and LiveAudio multimedia plug-ins are examples of commercial components that can be used in a custom Internet application written with JavaScript (see fig. 2.9).

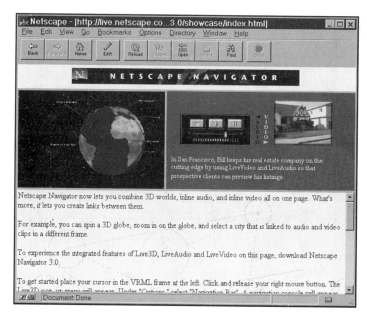

Figure 2.9

Using Netscape's Live3D, LiveAudio, and LiveVideo.

 An *applet* is a program written in Java that can be distributed as an attachment in a World Wide Web document and then be executed.

While plug-ins and applets both have Internet connectivity in mind, the traditional DLL, VBX, and OCX Windows components have the MS Windows operating system in mind. Microsoft, however, is rapidly changing this differentiation with its new Active-X component, which has both the Windows and Internet operating systems in mind. In addition, future versions of Windows 95 will have the World Wide Web integrated as a component of the operating system.

Running several applications sequentially:

◆ **Win95**—Creates a batch (.BAT) file, such as the AUTOEXEC.BAT file that uses MS-DOS scripting (see fig. 2.10).

◆ **Internet**—Uses JavaScript programming (see fig. 2.11).

Figure 2.10

A Windows 95 batch file.

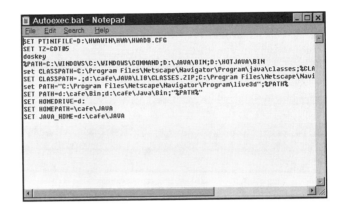

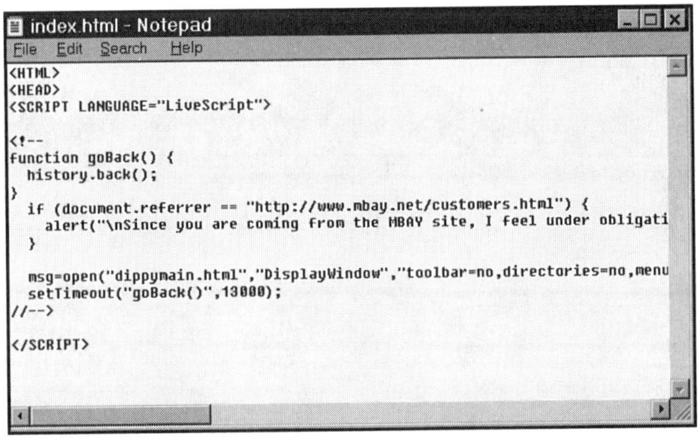

Figure 2.11

A JavaScript file.

As you can see from the preceding comparisons, scripting options such as JavaScript play an important role in the interplay that occurs between applications and documents. Just as you need MS-DOS scripting and Visual Basic for Applications (VBA) scripting in Windows 95, JavaScript is an important scripting language for the World Wide Web.

Differences Between Java and JavaScript

JavaScript, like MS-DOS scripting, is simple—it does not require a special development system, just a text editor to embed the script in plain old HTML.

Before going further, this chapter is going to clarify the meaning of the JavaScript name. It is a false assumption that JavaScript competes as a dummied-down Java. JavaScript was never meant for writing programs, just as Java was never meant for scripting programs. JavaScript is easier to program with than Java is, but that is only a consequence of how you can be more productive programming scripts in a simple language rather than with a full-featured, object-oriented programming language. The following contrasts Java and JavaScript:

Compilation:

- ◆ Java is compiled on the server before being executed by the client.
- ◆ JavaScript is interpreted, not compiled, by the client.

Object support:

- ◆ Java is object-oriented. Java applets consist of object classes that support inheritance.
- ◆ JavaScript is object-based. JavaScript code makes use of built-in, extensible objects, but no classes or inheritance are supported in JavaScript.

Integration with HTML:

- ◆ Java applet logic is distinct from HTML, although Java applets are accessed from HTML pages.
- ◆ JavaScript code, with a few exceptions, is integrated with and embedded in HTML pages.

Variable data types:

- ◆ Java is a strongly typed language. Java variables must be declared.
- ◆ JavaScript is a loosely typed language. JavaScript variable types are not declared.

Binding:

- ◆ Java uses static binding. Java object references must exist at compilation time.
- ◆ JavaScript uses dynamic binding. JavaScript object references are not checked until the execution of the script.

Writing to disk:

- ◆ Java does not directly support writing to the hard disk.
- ◆ JavaScript does not directly support writing to the hard disk.

Scripting WWW Browser Applications for Netscape Navigator

Netscape Navigator 2.0 was the first browser to support JavaScript. Navigator 3.0 is a JavaScript-capable browser, as well. Unlike Netscape's Java support, JavaScript runs on all Netscape Navigator 2.0 (or higher) versions. The level of support of the JavaScript language, however, varies between 2.0 and 3.0, with the major difference being that version 2.0 does not support a feature called LiveConnect (see Chapter 11, "Using Live Connect with JavaScript," for more information). Microsoft Internet Explorer 3.0 (included on the CD with this book) also supports JavaScript, almost as well as Netscape Navigator.

 In addition to Netscape Navigator supporting JavaScript, Microsoft has already released a stand-alone version of a JavaScript engine, which for trademark reasons is called JScript. Although the JScript engine can be integrated into any application, it does not yet include source code which would enable developers to further customize the JScript engine and port it to other platforms. The source code is supposed to be available near the end of 1996.

The Internet is designed as a client/server type of architecture. On the client side are Web browsers such as Netscape Navigator. These programs run on your computer at home or work. They spend much of their time requesting Internet objects and displaying them. On the server side are Web servers and server programs. Web servers and server programs spend much of their time satisfying requests from the client Web browsers.

JavaScript programs that are interpreted by Netscape Navigator are called *client-side JavaScript scripts* because they are operated on a computer (an Internet client) that is running Netscape Navigator. Client-side JavaScript scripts are free to communicate with objects that are made available by Navigator. These objects include Navigator objects, as well as Java applets, plug-ins, and other JavaScript scripts.

 Client-side JavaScript scripts are JavaScript programs that are operated on a computer (an Internet client) that is running Netscape Navigator and are interpreted by Netscape Navigator.

You typically use client-side scripts to enhance existing HTML content. Following are examples of uses for client-side scripts:

◆ Creating custom Netscape windows in which style properties (width, height, no button-bar, and so on) are set to give the browser an appropriate look

◆ Detecting whether the browser supports a certain plug-in

◆ Displaying information in the Netscape status bar

◆ Validating user form input

◆ Controlling a plug-in

◆ Prompting a user for confirmation

◆ Alerting the user of errors or information

◆ Conditionalizing HTML so that the content displayed is customized

◆ Performing post-processing of information retrieved from server-side JavaScript scripts

◆ Communication between different frames

◆ Communication between Java applets, plug-ins, and HTML files

WWW Server Application Scripting (LiveWire)

JavaScript programs that run on the server often are referred to as *LiveWire applications* because they utilize the Netscape LiveWire online development environment.

For now, Netscape LiveWire is the only system that supports server-side JavaScript development and deployment.

Netscape LiveWire

Netscape LiveWire runs on Windows NT and Unix workstations. You must have a Netscape HyperText Transfer Protocol (HTTP) server running on the workstation to run LiveWire applications.

 Note   A version of LiveWire for the Macintosh also is available; however, because a Netscape server for the Mac OS is not available, you currently cannot run the LiveWire JavaScript applications on the Mac OS.

continues

But there is nothing keeping you from developing LiveWire applications on the Macintosh and deploying them on a Unix or NT platform with a Netscape server. Just use the LiveWire product Site Manager and the LiveWire compiler to create the applications on your Macintosh system, and then run the applications on a Netscape server.

Server-Side JavaScript

Like CGI programs, *server-side JavaScripts* (LiveWire) applications play a role in providing interactive World Wide Web pages. Unlike CGI programs, however, LiveWire applications are more closely integrated to the HTML pages that control them. For example, with a LiveWire application, you can have a Web page that accepts credit card payments and gives the user immediate feedback concerning whether the card was accepted. For a CGI program that has similar functionality, the user's feedback would consist of a new Web page loaded in his or her browser—not immediate feedback on the same page as with server-side JavaScript. Then, if the user wanted to retype the credit card information, he or she would have to use the Back button. LiveWire applications can range from internal corporate intranet-based, information-sharing to mass-market, Internet-based electronic transactions and commerce. Following are examples of uses for server-side scripts:

◆ Handling information that needs to be stored by using a series of Netscape Navigator sessions. This information could be anything from a user ID to an item that a user is waiting to purchase.

◆ Handling data shared among several users concurrently running Netscape Navigator on your Web site.

◆ Accessing databases or files on the server.

Creating Client-Side Versus Server-Side JavaScripts

Developing server-side JavaScript applications is a bit different than developing client-side JavaScript applications. Although the JavaScript language basically is the same on both the server and client side, a server-side JavaScript application likely will have a different implementation than a client-side application.

It depends on the circumstance when deciding which parts of your JavaScript implementation should be on the client-side and which JavaScript implementation should be on the server-side. You can use several programming blocks to partition an application between the server and client. Although for certain programming tasks implementation can be done only on the client or the server, but not both, other programming tasks can be implemented either on the client-side or the server-side. Table 2.1 shows you the general guidelines to help you determine when to implement JavaScript as server-side code.

TABLE 2.1

When to use server scripts	When to use client scripts
To maintain data shared among applications or clients	To display error or information boxes
To maintain information during client accesses	To validate user input
To access a database	To display confirmation boxes
To access server files	To process server data, such as aggregate calculations
To call server C libraries	To add simple programmable logic to HTML
To customize Java applets	To perform functions that do not require information from the server

The reason for the difference in implementation is that the majority of the objects with which your server-side JavaScripts communicate are different than the object with which your client-side JavaScripts communicate. Recall the discussion about client-side JavaScripts communicating with Java applets, Netscape plug-ins, and the Netscape Navigator objects: server-side JavaScripts communicate instead with Java, C libraries, databases, and files on the server and LiveWire objects.

Another difference between client-side JavaScript and server-side JavaScript development is the method by which the scripts are deployed. You embed the JavaScript inside an HTML file for both client-side and server-side scripting; but after you create the HTML file that contains the embedded server-side JavaScript, you compile the HTML filewith the LiveWire compiler. Although client-side and server-side scripting both involve embedding JavaScript inside an HTML file, the deployment of the file after you have authored it is different. When you deploy a server-side script you *must* compile the HTML file with the LiveWire compiler. An HTML file that does not contain server-side JavaScript does not need to be compiled by the LiveWire compiler. It can be deployed as is.

This compilation creates a file that is in a platform-independent and compiled bytecode format. If you were to look at this compiled file with a text editor, it would be unreadable; however, the Netscape server can read this file and display it to the user as if it were straight HTML.

Notice the extra steps involved for a server-side JavaScript as shown in in figure 2.12, compared to deploying a client-side JavaScript, as shown in figure 2.13. Also note that although all the client-side JavaScript utilizes is Netscape Navigator and a standard HTML server, server-side JavaScript entails the LiveWire Compiler, the LiveWire Application Manager, and a Netscape HTML server that supports the LiveWire server extension. LiveWire will be discussed in much more detail in subsequent chapters.

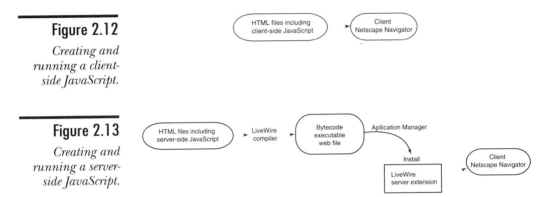

Figure 2.12

Creating and running a client-side JavaScript.

Figure 2.13

Creating and running a server-side JavaScript.

Summary

This chapter has provided an introduction to both client-side and server-side JavaScript development. You have learned the general requirements for creating Internet applications that take advantage of the JavaScript language. You also have learned implementation differences between JavaScript programming on the client-side versus server-side.

Chapter 3, "JavaScript Language Fundamentals," teaches the basics of the JavaScript language, including how to embed JavaScript in HTML, JavaScript program structure, and JavaScript language syntax.

CHAPTER 3

JavaScript Language Fundamentals

In the beginning, there was HTML (HyperText Markup Language), which is the language you use to create Web pages. Using HTML enables you to embed sound, images, and video snippets into a Web page or browser. In the beginning, this was great. Now, however, users want to be able to perform more than one task at a time; they want the capability to interface HTML with applications so that they can create applications that enable user interaction, such as forms you can submit over the Internet rather than just present information. Hence, the beauty of JavaScript. Although JavaScript is a scripting language rather than a programming language, you still apply programming rules when scripting. This chapter addresses some of those rules and terms. Specifically, this chapter teaches you about the following:

◆ Using JavaScript in HTML documents

◆ JavaScript program structure

◆ Commenting scripts

◆ Declaring and manipulating JavaScript variables

◆ Controlling the flow of your programs using JavaScript

◆ JavaScript functions

JavaScript and Your HTML Document

JavaScript does not enable you to write commercial, shrink-wrapped quality programs. What it does enable you to do, however, is script programs—in other words, coordinate and orchestrate the ways in which other programs work together to achieve the effect you want. You can use JavaScript code in HTML documents by using the <SCRIPT> tag or loading a file that contains JavaScript source code.

 HTML (HyperText MarkUp Language) is the programming language you use to create Web pages.

The <SCRIPT> Tag

To embed JavaScript code within an HTML document, you use <SCRIPT> tags to indicate where the code begins and ends. Place the code you want to embed between the <SCRIPT> and </SCRIPT> tags, as in the following:

```
<SCRIPT>
     JavaScript statements...
</SCRIPT>
```

Did you know...

You use tags to denote the various elements in an HTML document. HTML tags consist of a left angle bracket (<), a tag name, and a right angle bracket (>).Tags usually are paired (such as <H1> and </H1>) to start and end the tag instruction. The end tag looks just like the start tag, except that a slash (/) precedes the text within the brackets.

When embedding JavaScript code, you must indicate the scripting language you are using (JavaScript in this case). You use the <SCRIPT> tags and can include the scripting language when embedding your statements, as in the following:

```
<SCRIPT LANGUAGE="JavaScript">
    JavaScript statements...
</SCRIPT>
```

Note Unlike HTML, JavaScript is case sensitive. In HTML code, you can use all upper- or lowercase letters, or you can mix cases. The results of typing lookatme, LOOKATME, or Lookatme will be the same because HTML doesn't discriminate among upper- and lowercase letters. JavaScript, however, is reactive to the case you use in code.

The following exercise shows you how to create embedded code using the <SCRIPT> tags.

Embedding Simple Code

Start with an existing document, such as the following, and add the JavaScript code. Note that <p></p> tags are used to keep all necessary text on one line.

```
1. <HTML>
2. <HEAD>
3. </HEAD>
4. <BODY>
5. <p>That's it, baby. </p>
6. </BODY>
7. </HTML>
```

The following code has JavaScript code added.

```
1.  <HTML>
2.  <HEAD>
3.  <SCRIPT LANGUAGE="JavaScript">
4.  document.write("Hello World Wide Web.")
5.  </SCRIPT>
6.  </HEAD>
7.  <BODY>
8.  <p>That's it, baby. </p>
9.  </BODY>
10. </HTML>
```

Lines 1 and 10 are used to indicate to the browser that lines 1–10 will contain HTML elements.

Lines 2 and 6 mark the beginning and end of the HEAD tag block. The <HEAD> tag block usually contains general information about the document.

Just as lines 1 and 10 are used to indicate to the browser that this document contains <HTML> elements, lines 3 and 5 indicate that lines 3–5 contain <SCRIPT> code. Notice that inside the <SCRIPT> tag of line 3, it is specified that JavaScript is the intended language. Line 4 is the actual line of JavaScript code executed when the page is loaded.

Lines 7 and 9 indicate that lines 7–9 are the BODY portion of the document that contains the information that composes the visible portion of the document, rather than information that is about the document (such as in the <HEAD></HEAD> section).

Line 8 contains the content for this document. You may notice the <p> and </p> tags that surround "That's it, baby." These tags are used to identify this text as a new paragraph. In line 10, <HTML> indicates the HTML document into which you want to embed the JavaScript code.

You can see the result of the preceding code in figure 3.1.

Figure 3.1

The results of embedding simple code.

Hiding Embedded JavaScript Code from Non-Supporting Browsers

You can hide embedded code from old browsers that do not support JavaScript code (do not recognize the <SCRIPT></SCRIPT> tag), such as CompuServe's Web browser, by using the comment tag. According to HTML specification, if a browser runs across an HTML tag that it does not recognize, it should simply ignore it.

Knowing this, you easily could jump to the wrong conclusion that older browsers would simply ignore an HTML script that is embedded inside a start and end <SCRIPT> tag, as in the following example:

```
1.  <HTML>
2.  <HEAD>
3.  <TITLE>Code Hiding Example</TITLE>
4.  </HEAD>
5.  <BODY>
6.  Below is a script
7.  <P>
8.  <SCRIPT>
9.  document.write("Text generated by JavaScript")
10. </SCRIPT>
11. </BODY>
12. </HTML>
```

The rub is that although almost all browsers do not have a problem ignoring the actual HTML tags, many browsers still insist on displaying the information that lies between the start and end tag.

For the preceding script, a person using Netscape 3.0 would see what is shown in figure 3.2, while a person using a browser that does not support JavaScript might see something similar to what is shown in figure 3.3.

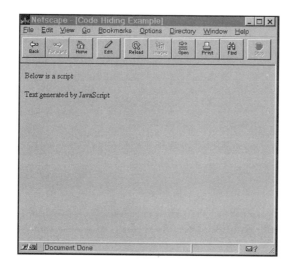

Figure 3.2

You can't see the hidden code when using a JavaScript supported browser.

Figure 3.3

Code you want to hide is not really hidden at all in a non-JavaScript supported browser.

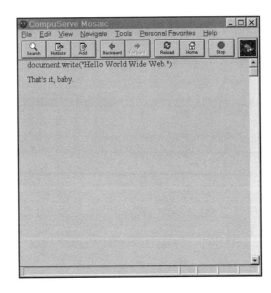

To remedy an older browser displaying text you want to hide, you can use the HTML comment tag, as in the following example, to effectively block out your script from older browsers.

```
 1.  <HTML>
 2.  <HEAD>
 3.  <TITLE>Code Hiding Example</TITLE>
 4.  </HEAD>
 5.  <BODY>
 6.  Below is a script
 7.  <P>
 8.  <SCRIPT>
 9.  <!--
10.  document.write("Text generated by JavaScript")
11.  //-->
12.  </SCRIPT>
13.  </BODY>
14.  </HTML>
```

The comment tag (line 9) consists of the start tag, which is <!--, and an end tag, which is -->. What are those additional double slashes before the comment end tag, you ask?

Double slashes (//) are one method of indicating a comment in JavaScript. They are required before the comment end tag because if you don't, the computer tries to read the end tag as a JavaScript command. If you leave out the double slashes (//), you will get an error, as in figure 3.4.

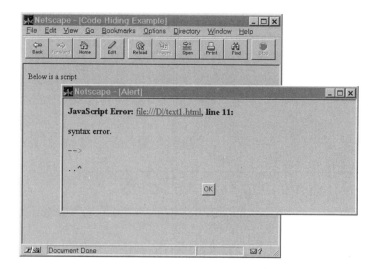

Figure 3.4

Omitting the double forward slashes (//) results in a JavaScript error message.

The following exercise shows you how to hide JavaScript code from older browsers.

Hiding JavaScript Code

1. Insert a new line after the <SCRIPT> tag.

2. Type <!-- into the new line.

3. Insert a new line before the </SCRIPT> tag.

4. Type //-->.

 If you use Netscape Navigator 3.0 Gold to edit your HTML files, watch out! At the time of this writing, Netscape Navigator 3.0 Gold does not take advantage of using the comment tag to hide scripts from older browsers.

External Scripts

External scripts are another way you can use JavaScript code within an HTML document. Apply external scripts when you are reusing the same bit of code in several (or many) HTML documents. This saves you from repeatedly embedding the same code into each HTML document. External scripts also give you the capability to change JavaScript code without having to touch the HTML source file, thus reducing the chance of accidentally corrupting the HTML file while working on the JavaScript code.

An external script acts as a file to which you refer a program or application. When a browser sees an external script tag, it reads the tag (which refers the program to the referenced code or file) as if it were reading from the actual HTML. Following is an example of an external script:

```
<SCRIPT LANGUAGE="JavaScript" SRC="JavaScriptCode.js">
</SCRIPT>
```

The following exercise shows how you can use external scripts in everyday HTML life.

Implementing External Scripts

1. Insert the following code snippet in a new line that is located one line above the end body tag </BODY>:

```
<SCRIPT LANGUAGE="JavaScript" SRC="JavaScriptCode.js">
</SCRIPT>
```

2. Create a new text file called "JavaScriptCode.js".

3. Insert the following code in "JavaScriptCode.js":

```
document.writeln("This page was written by Fred Farkle")
document.writeln("Fred is a world-famous web author")
document.writeln("Copyright 1996, All rights reserved")
```

When the browser sees the <SRC> property in the <SCRIPT> tag, the browser continues to parse within the file JavaScriptCode.js. When the browser reaches the end of that file, it returns to the file with the <SCRIPT> tag and continues to parse the remainder of the file.

Processing of the Script by the Browser

Processing refers to the way a browser reads plain text directives of HTML and then interprets the directives into on-screen graphical displays. This usually happens in sequential order—that is, from the top of the page down, determining the on-screen display as it moves down the page.

Processing refers to the way a browser reads plain text directives of HTML and then interprets the directives into on-screen graphical displays.

The browser interprets embedded JavaScript code within the HTML page *after* the entire page loads but *before* the page is displayed. When processing pages that contain external scripts, the browser processes the external script code as if it were embedded inside the script container.

Placement of Scripts in the <HEAD> Portion of the Document

The browser processes the HTML code and embedded or external scripts in sequential order, beginning with the <HEAD> portion of the document. Because the <HEAD> portion is the first to load, it's best to define the functions for a page in this part of the document. Doing this ensures that functions actually are loaded before you try to call a function in the <BODY> part of the HTML document.

> **Did you know...**
>
> Defining a function is not the same as calling a function. *Defining* refers to naming the function and specifying what you want the function to do when it is called. *Calling* the function actually invokes the actions you specified when defining.

JavaScript Program Structure

JavaScript programs you write are event-driven in that functions are called when an event takes place. When an event, such as a mouse click or a page load, takes place, the corresponding JavaScript code executes. JavaScript program code consists of the following, which is discussed in detail in the following sections.

◆ Main body

◆ Event handlers

◆ Functions

Main Body

In JavaScript, any code that is between the <SCRIPT> and </SCRIPT> tags that is not a function definition is considered to be part of the main body. This code commonly is found in the BODY section of an HTML document. Script code in the main body is interpreted in the sequential order by the browser as soon as the page is loaded.

It is a good programming practice to keep the main body code size as small as possible and to outsource most functionality to several modular JavaScript functions. The concept of modular functions is similar to hardware components in your computer. It's much easier to work with components rather than large complex systems. This is the same with code. It's much easier to work with modular sections than a large monolithic block of code. These functions commonly are defined in the HEAD section of the HTML file. You only need to define the function once to be able to call the function numerous times. For example, you can define a single function in the head and call it twice within the body, as in the following:

```
1.   <HEAD>
2.   <SCRIPT LANGUAGE="JavaScript">
3.   <!--
4.   function bugUser() {
5.      alert("I wrote this JavaScript myself")
6.   }
7.   //-->
8.   </SCRIPT>
9.   </HEAD>
10.  <BODY>
11.  <SCRIPT LANGUAGE="JavaScript">
12.  <!--
13.  bugUser()     //Call the function for the first time
14.  bugUser()     //Call the function again
15.  //-->
16.  </SCRIPT>
15.  </BODY>
```

 Note   Putting the main body JavaScript code in the BODY of the HTML file and the function JavaScript code in the HEAD section is not a rule; it is merely a style convention.

Event Handlers

Events are actions that usually occur in response to something the user does, such as clicking the mouse or re-sizing a window. *Event handlers* are scripts you define that enable you to link events (actions) to JavaScript functions in HTML. You embed event handlers in HTML documents as attributes of HTML tags. Following is the general syntax:

```
<TAG eventHandler="JavaScript Code">
```

TAG indicates an HTML tag and *eventHandler* is the name of the event handler you define.

 JavaScript uses mixed case in scripting. Using a lowercase letter for the first word and an initial capital letter for the second word makes it easy for the developer to differentiate variable names that have compound words.

 Event handlers are scripts you define that enable you to link events (actions) to JavaScript functions in HTML.

To help you better understand how event handlers work, go through the following exercise.

Defining a Simple Event Handler

1. In Notepad or a similar text editor, create a new file called "bugMe.html" and enter the following code:

```
1.  <HTML>
2.  <HEAD>
3.  <SCRIPT LANGUAGE="JavaScript">
4.  <!--
5.  function bugUser() {
6.    alert("I wrote this JavaScript myself")
7.  }
8.  //-->
9.  </SCRIPT>
10. </HEAD>
11. <BODY>
12. <FORM NAME="myForm">
13.   <INPUT TYPE="button" VALUE="Bug Me" ONCLICK="bugUser()">
14. </FORM>
15. </BODY>
16. </HTML>
```

2. Open the file with Netscape Navigator and see what happens each time you click the button (see fig. 3.5).

Figure 3.5

A simple event handler.

Functions

JavaScript also supports *functions*. Functions are sections of JavaScript code that just sit around and wait to be executed by other sections of JavaScript code. When you define a JavaScript function, you are telling the interpreter to make this section of code available to be called (executed) by script code in either the main body, the event-handler sections, or by other functions.

Functions are synonymous to tasks or chores on a list. When you want to perform each task, you refer to the chore list. JavaScript does the same thing. It refers to the functions you define in the <HEAD> portion of the HTML document, so you only need to define the function once (in the <HEAD> section); however, JavaScript can refer to that function many times throughout the program. Following is an example of defining a function in the <HEAD> of an HTML document.

A *function* is an action or purpose achieved by a program or section of code within a program.

A *property* is an element you can modify, such as color.

Defining a Function in an HTML Document

1. The following is a simple function definition:

```
<SCRIPT LANGUAGE="JavaScript">
<!--
   function WriteName() {
      document.writeln("My name is Fred Farkle")
   }
//-->
</SCRIPT>
```

2. The following is the definition of a function that accepts one argument:

```
<SCRIPT LANGUAGE="JavaScript">
<!--
   function WriteName(userName) {
      document.write("My name is ")
      document.writeln(userName)
   }
//-->
</SCRIPT>
```

3. The following is the definition of a function that accepts one argument and returns a value:

```
<SCRIPT LANGUAGE="JavaScript">
<!--
   function Times10(value) {
     return 10*value
   }
//-->
</SCRIPT>
```

Using Comments in Scripts During Application Development

Adding comments to scripts enables you to insert explanations into your code. This is useful for other users when you write code because you can include notes (comments) that remind you or tell another user why you used a particular command or what you want it to accomplish. The comments are for you and other users to see and do not interfere with the JavaScript code. JavaScript provides two comment styles you can use.

// comment

The // comment is from the C++ programming language. This style comment begins and ends with double forward slashes (//) and is good to use when comments will fit on one line. Following is an example:

```
return 10*value       //return 10 times the value//
```

The comment at the end of the code reminds you that this function, when called, will return 10 times the value of the initial amount you indicate.

Did you know...

C++ is one of the most used object-oriented languages. C++ is a superset of C developed primarily by Bjarne Stroustrup at AT&T Bell Laboratories in 1986. OLE (Object Linking and Embedding) Automation enables applications and components to expose data and functionality in a form that virtually any Windows application development language can access and use. OLE automation programs are most often controlled by scripts written in Visual Basic.

/*comment*/

Taken from the C programming language, you use /*comment*/ to document code blocks or major functions. Comments using this style can extend over several lines and are useful for detailed discussion of code. This style comment begins and ends with a single forward slash (/), as in the following example:

```
/*************************************************
*    This function multiplies a given value by 10 *
*    Written by Fred Farkle                        *
*************************************************/
```

Declaring JavaScript Variables

JavaScript variables enable you to store data type values for future use. JavaScript variables do not have explicit data types; you can create variables that contain any type of data, such as string literals, numbers, or Boolean values. Using variables enable you to assign a name that is easy to remember to a value that might be difficult to remember.

 A *variable* is a named piece of data to which you can refer when defining functions. You can change the value of a variable while the name of the variable remains the same.

To use a variable, you need to declare it. After you declare the variable, you can assign a new value to it and still continue to refer to the variable. To declare a variable, you use the var command, as in the following example:

```
var example;
```

In the preceding line, you defined the variable example. Now you need to declare it and assign a string value, as in the following:

```
var example="Show me an example";
```

The following exercise shows you how to declare and assign a variable and invoke the result.

Using Variables

1. In Notepad or a similar text editor, create a file called "beers.html" and insert the following code:

```
1.   <HTML>
2.   <HEAD><TITLE>Bottles of Beer</TITLE></HEAD>
3.   <BODY>
4.   How many bottles of beer?
5.   <p>
6.   <SCRIPT LANGUAGE="JavaScript">
7.   <!--
8.   var beerCount
9.   document.write(beerCount + " bottles of beer on the wall")
10.  //-->
11.  </SCRIPT>
12.  </BODY>
13.  </HTML>
```

2. Save this file and load it in Netscape Navigator. Notice how the number of bottles of beer on the wall is undefined, as in figure 3.6.

Figure 3.6

*JavaScript result
with variable
undefined.*

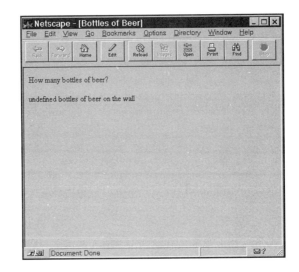

3. Define the beerCount variable. Change line 8 from the following:

```
var beerCount
```

to

```
var beerCount = 687
```

4. The variable named beerCount now is defined to the integer value of 687. Save the file and click the Reload button on Netscape. The variable now is defined, and the page will look similar to the page shown in figure 3.7.

Figure 3.7

*JavaScript result
with variable
defined as an
integer.*

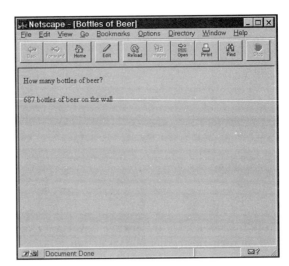

5. Define the beerCount variable as a character string. Insert the following new line after line 8.

```
var beerCount = "Six hundred and eighty seven"
```

The beerCount variable now is defined to the character string value of "six hundred and eighty seven."

6. Save the file and click the Reload button on Netscape. The page will look similar to the page shown in figure 3.8. Notice how the JavaScript language is loosely typed, allowing a variable to be redefined from an integer to a character string.

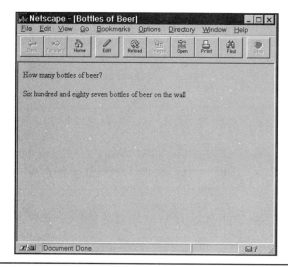

Figure 3.8

JavaScript result with variable redefined to a character string.

Did you know...

When you *declare* a variable, you are telling JavaScript about that particular variable so that the interpreter will be able to connect references to that variable throughout the script.

Valid Variable Names (Identifiers)

Variable names are case sensitive in JavaScript. Variable names also must start with a letter or an underscore (_). After the letter or underscore you can include other characters and numbers. JavaScript variables have meaningful names, which means that you can assign and even combine words so that the name of the variable applies to its purpose. A common convention is for the first word to be in lowercase, and subsequent words to have initial uppercase letters, as in the following:

```
var shoppingDaysUntilChristmas = 27
```

JavaScript uses identifiers, which are names given to functions and variables so that the interpreter can identify them. All identifiers must begin with a letter or the underscore (_) character. Identifiers can consist of alphabetical letters that are upper- and lowercase. Subsequent characters can include digits (0–9). The following, for example, would be incorrect:

```
123ereiam
```

however, the following example of an identifier is correct:

```
_123ereiam
```

or

```
ereiam123
```

 Note   JavaScript uses reserved keywords (identifiers) within the language that you cannot assign to your variables when creating scripts. Following is the list of JavaScript keywords:

abstract	double	import	public	try
boolean	else	in	return	var
break	extends	instanceof	short	void
byte	false	int	static	while
case	final	interface	super	with
catch	finally	long	switch	
char	float	native	synchronized	
class	for	new	this	
const	function	null	throw	
continue	goto	package	throws	
default	if	private	transient	
do	implements	protected	true	

Variable Scope

The scope of a variable refers to the place in which a variable exists. A local variable is one that cannot be referred to or manipulated outside of that function. A global variable is one that is declared outside of the function and is available throughout a script.

Did you know...

When you declare a local variable (a variable inside a function) inside the same scope as a global variable of the same name, the local variable takes precedence. Changing the value of the variable inside the function does not affect the value of the global variable.

JavaScript Data Types and Literals

JavaScript contains several data types:

◆ Numbers,

◆ Boolean Values, and

◆ String literals.

Numbers refer to any number, such as 1 or 5.25. Boolean values are either True or False. String literals usually are zero or more characters you enclose in single or double quotes, such as "Hello Net", '12345', or " ".

Note The set of double quotes that contains no text is referred to as an empty string, and is not to be confused with a null value. A null value represents nothing. If you reference an undefined value, null is returned.

Numbers (Numerical Values)

JavaScript uses two types of numerical values: floating-point numbers and integers. You can specify integers as whole numbers that have nothing following the decimal point and can be positive (+) or negative (–) numbers. You can specify integers in base 10 (decimal) such as 42, base 8 (octal) such as 010, or base 16 (hexadecimal) such as 0xFF.

An *integer* is a whole number that does not include any portion after the decimal point. Integers can be positive or negative numbers.

You can specify floating point numbers, which are fractions, in standard decimal point format (such as 5.25) or by using the engineering E-notation, such as (1.2e34). Floating point numbers also can contain a plus (+) or minus (–) sign (such as +5.25 or –1.2e34).

 Floating point numbers are values that can include a fraction. The fraction can be expressed as a decimal number or an exponential number and can be positive or negative.

Logical or Boolean Data Type

Logical data type (also called Boolean data type) returns two possible values: True or False. You use Boolean data type when you want to ensure that a criterion is met before continuing to the next action or step. (For example, if A is True, then move to the next action. If A is False, however, then the next action is not taken.) JavaScript converts True and False values into numeric values, as in 1 = True and 0 = False. JavaScript also converts non-zero integers into True.

Strings

Strings are zero or more characters (letters, numbers, or symbols) that you enclose in single or double quotes. You also can use zero-length strings by not including any characters between the single or double quotes (such as " " or ' '). When you specify strings using single or double quotes, you must end the string with the same type of quotation mark you used to begin the quote, such as the following:

```
'This is wrong"

"This also is wrong'

"This is right"
```

JavaScript currently enables you to use strings that contain special combinations of characters that denote certain special characters. These strings are known as *escape sequences*. You probably will not use these sequences often because of using formatting directives of HTML. Currently, the following sequences are supported:

- ◆ \b equals backspace

- ◆ \f equals form feed (vertical tab)

◆ \n equals return

◆ \r equals line feed

◆ \t equals tab

To use the \t string to indicate a tab space between words, for example, you could use the following:

```
See \t ya
```

for which the output would be

```
See   ya
```

null

A null value represents nothing. If you reference an undefined value, null is returned. The value null is returned when you try to reference a variable that you have not defined. Do not confuse null with an empty string or zero, which have actual values.

```
var beerCount       //beerCount is now null
beerCount = 687     //beerCount is no longer null
```

Datatype Conversion

Conversion takes place when JavaScript changes, or converts, a string of text to a number or vice versa. Depending on what you are trying to convert, this automatic conversion sometimes does not work. When JavaScript cannot perform a conversion, it returns an error message.

Variable Coercion and Casting

Once in a while, JavaScript cannot convert one type of data to another type of data. Because JavaScript does not have a compiler that checks the accuracy of assignments before they run, additional pressure is on the programmer when writing scripts. For example, if a string represents a number, the conversion is not a problem. But what happens when the string represents a series of letters? The result is conversion failure and an error, as in the following example:

```
intValue = 3 * "Fred Farkle"   //results in a run time error
intValue = 3 + "one"           //is OK
```

To avoid run-time errors, it is recommended as a good programming practice to perform the variable type conversion yourself, rather than letting the interpreter do it. When you let the interpreter handle the conversions, it is called *coercion*. When you let your programming logic handle the conversion, it is called *casting*. Casting gives you the capability to add a safety net to your script where you provide handler code that gracefully takes care of conversions that fail.

JavaScript now provides the parseInt() and parseFloat() functions to help in casting. These two functions convert strings into integers or floating point numbers, as in the following:

```
parseInt("34")
```

which returns 34

```
parseFloat("34.9")
```

which returns 34.9

Manipulating Variables

Variables are named locations in memory to which you associate values. You then can manipulate (vary) the value of the variable while the location of the variable remains the same. You also can combine, or concatenate, two or more variables to form an expression.

Expressions

Expressions are a collection of variables, operators, that return a single value. JavaScript uses several types of expressions. Assignment expressions enable you to assign a value to a variable. Arithmetic expressions enable you to calculate a particular number. String expressions enable you to use the addition operator to create and concatenate strings. Conditional expressions rely on the logic that *if* such-and-such is true, then JavaScript executes the first action; *else*, JavaScript performs the other action. Following is a simple example of an expression:

```
2+2+myVariableName
```

 Expressions are a collection of variables, operators, that return a single value.

Operators

Operators enable you to assign values to variables, make changes to variables, and perform calculations. When performing multiple operations, you use *precedence*, which refers to the order in which multiple operations are computed. Following is a simple example of an operator:

```
2+2
```

where the plus sign is the operator in this instance.

 Operators enable you to assign values to variables, make changes to variables, and perform calculations.

Precedence refers to the order in which multiple operations are computed, which can determine the total value of an expression.

Assignment Operators

You use *assignment operators* with assignment expressions to designate value to a variable. The operator assigns a value to a variable by performing an operation on the expression. Table 3.1 lists assignment operators. Suppose that you want a result from an expression stored in a variable. You would use the assignment operator to accomplish this task.

 Assignment operators enable you to use assignment expressions to designate a value to a variable.

TABLE 3.1
Assignment Operators

Operator	Description
=	Enables you to assign the value of the right operand to the left operand.
+=	Enables you to add the left and right operands and assign the result to the left operand.
.=	Enables you to subtract the right operand from the left operand and assign the result to the left operand.
*=	Enables you to multiply the two operands and assign the result to the left operand.
/=	Enables you to divide the left operand by the right operand and assign the value to the left operand.
%=	Enables you to divide the left operand by the right operand and assign the remainder to the left operand.

Arithmetic operators are the same as those operators on a basic calculator. Table 3.2 lists arithmetic operators.

TABLE 3.2
Arithmetic Operators

Operator	Description
+	For addition and string concatenation
-	For subtraction or negation (to make a positive value negative or vice versa)
*	For multiplication
/	For division
%	For modulus, which computes the remainder when performing division
++	For preincrementing and postincrementing a value by 1
--	For predecrementing and postdecrementing a value by 1

Note Some operators require only a single operand, such as ++, which adds 1 to its operand. These are referred to as unary operators. Other operators that demand two operands, such as +, are referred to as binary operators.

The addition operator (+) also enables you to create and concatenate strings. This operator (when used with strings and other objects) enables you to create a single string that contains the concatenation of all its operands. That is, operands in string concatenation that are not strings are converted automatically to strings.

Tip You can use the shorthand assignment operator (+=) to concatenate strings. For example, if the variable named myName = Fred (has the value of Fred), after this statement you could use myName+= " Farkle" where the result would be Fred Farkle.

Logical Operators

Logical operators (also referred to as Boolean operators) include binary and unary operators (refer to Table 3.2) and take Boolean values (True and False) as operands and return Boolean values. You use logical operators to carry out a test or combine the results of more than one test. Table 3.3 lists logical operators.

TABLE 3.3
Logical (Boolean) Operators

Operators	Description
== !=	Indicate equality and inequality.
< <= => >	Used for arithmetic and string comparisons.
!	Indicates the logical NOT.
&& ||	Indicate logical AND and logical OR, respectively.
?	Indicates conditional selection (trinary).
'	Indicates logical concatenation.

Note Following are the operators discussed in this chapter, in precedence order:

Comma ,

assignment = += -= *= /= %= <<= >>= >>>= &= ^= |=

Conditional ?:

Logical OR ||

Logical AND &&

Equality ==!=

relational <<= > >=

shift <<>> >>>

addition/subtraction +-

multiply/divide/modulus * / %

negation / increment !~-++—

call, member () []

Controlling Program Flow

For your program to move smoothly through the correct steps, you must use some sort of technique that enables you to indicate the order in which you want steps to take place. Programs generally must go through several series of steps to respond to input, perform calculations, and determine responses. When using JavaScript, you will want to use the JavaScript conditional statements that support control flow of the programming blocks of statements. These are discussed in the following sections.

 A *block* of statements is made up of several or many statements that behave as a single statement. You introduce a block with a left brace ({) and end the block with the right brace (}).

Conditional Statements (if Statement)

Conditional statements rely on the logic that *if* such-and-such is true, then JavaScript executes the first action; or *else*, JavaScript performs the other action, as in the following example:

```
if (myvariable != null) {
    document.write (myVariable)    //Write variable to page if it is initialized
}
else {
    alert("myVariable has not been initialized")
}
```

 When you do not want JavaScript to perform an action when the if statement is not true, you can omit the else expression.

You also can string together a series of conditional statements using nested if-else statements, as in the following:

```
if (temperature <= 32) {
    if (sky == "cloudy") {
        forecast = "snow"
    }
    else {
        forecast = "fair"
    }
}
```

```
else
   if (sky == "cloudy") {
       forecast = "rain"
   }
   else {
       forecast = "fair"
   }
}
alert("Today's forecast is " + forecast)
```

Creating a Simple Program Using Conditional Statements

1. Open a new HTML file in a text editor, such as NotePad, and insert the following
   function created from the preceding code, which accepts two parameters—
   temperature and sky.

```
function myForecast(temperature,sky)
{
  if (temperature <= 32) {
     if (sky == "cloudy") {
        forecast = "snow"
     }
     else {
        forecast = "fair"
     }
  }
  else{
     if (sky == "cloudy") {
        forecast = "rain"
     }
     else {
        forecast = "fair"
     }
  }
  alert("Today's forecast is " + forecast)
}
```

2. Add the following code that defines the input form to the HTML file:

```
<FORM>
Temperature:<INPUT TYPE="text" NAME="temperatureBox" SIZE="3"><p>
Sky Status:<INPUT TYPE="text" NAME="skyBox" SIZE="10"><p>
```

```
<INPUT TYPE="button" NAME ="buttonControl"
VALUE="Forecast"onClick="myForecast(form.temperatureBox.value,form.skyBox.value)">
</FORM>
```

3. Bring up this page in Netscape, and experiment by entering different values for sky and temperature.

Figure 3.9 shows the results of using if-else in a short program.

Figure 3.9

Using if-else in a short program.

Loop Statements

The loop statements (for, while, break, and continue) enable you to manipulate blocks of JavaScript statements. These statements are similar; however, each contains its own format and particular uses. This section discusses the following types of loop statements and when to use them:

◆ for

◆ while

◆ break

◆ continue

for Statement

Use the for statement to repeat a block of statements until a limit you specify is reached. When the limit is reached, the loop is broken. You use the for statement when working with arrays, which are discussed in Chapter 4, "JavaScript Objects and Properties." The for clause consists of three parts that are separated by two semicolons, as in the following example:

```
for (i=0;i < 10;i++) {
  functionCall(i)
}
```

The first expression (i=0), known as the initial expression, indicates to the for loop where to begin the variable. For this example, i is set to 1. The expression i<10, referred to as a conditional expression, indicates to the for loop when the loop should stop. In this example, the statement is True and the loop should continue for all values, 0–9. The expression i++, referred to as an update expression, tells the loop what action to perform on the variable. In this example, the expression instructs the JavaScript interpreter to increase the value of i by 1 every time the loop runs, which causes i to go from 0 to 9 through all the intervening integers.

while Statement

Use the while statement to execute a block of code when a certain condition is True. The block of code continues to execute while the condition remains True, and until the time the condition becomes false or until another statement ends the block. You use the while statement in situations where you need an easy way to exit a block of looping code as in the following example:

```
i = 20
while (i > 0) {
  functionCall(i)
  i = i - 2
}
```

break Statement

Use the break statement when you want to immediately exit a looping statement, such as for or while. When JavaScript encounters the break statement inside the while or for block, the loop terminates immediately. Following is an example:

```
i = 40
while (i > 0) {
     if (i == 4)
        break
     i = i - 2
  }
```

continue Statement

You use the continue statement inside while and for loops to force the control back to the top of the loop. This suppresses the remainder of the block and moves to the top of the block into the next iteration, as in the following example:

```
i = 20
n = 0
while (i > 0) {
   i = i - 2
   if (i == 6)
      continue //Go to top of loop
   n = n + i
}
```

The preceding statement indicates, assuming that the continue statement is executed, to skip over code inside the loop that follows the continue statement.

JavaScript Functions

JavaScript functions serve two purposes. You can use functions to organize recurring blocks of code, or you can use functions to handle actions or events on a Web page that uses JavaScript. When a user clicks a PlaySound button, for example, most likely the code that handles the functionality of playing the sound would be found in a function. When using functions in JavaScript, in order for your code to work properly, you must adhere to the following rules:

◆ The name of the function must immediately follow the function keyword.

◆ Function names must be unique. You cannot have two functions with the same name.

◆ You cannot use reserved key words, such as while or true, as function names.

Functions contain *parameters* (or *arguments*), which are values separated by commas, that are passed into the function. To create functions with JavaScript, you first must define the function and then call it.

A *function* is a block of code that has a name. When the function is called, the code within that block executes.

Parameters (or *arguments*) are values, separated by commas, that are passed into the function.

Defining a Function

Earlier in this chapter, you learned what functions are and where to place them. This section discusses "defining" a function, which means specifying what you want the function to accomplish. Defining a function in the head portion of your HTML document ensures that the function is read, interpreted, and loaded into memory before the rest of the HTML document. As mentioned earlier in this chapter, you define functions in the HEAD portion of your HTML document, as in the following example:

```
function dayOfWeek(myMonth,myDay,myYear) {
...
}
```

Naming conventions for functions are similar to the naming conventions you use for variables. Function names are case sensitive in JavaScript. Function names also must begin with a letter or an underscore (_). After the letter or underscore, you can include other characters and numbers.

Defining a function does not, however, cause a function to execute. To cause a function to execute, you must call it.

Calling a Function

A place you might call a function is within the BODY portion of your HTML document. You do this by including the name of the function within the body, along with its related arguments. Calling a function causes the specified actions to be executed or the result to be obtained. Look at the following example, which uses a function to print the day of week on the document:

```
<SCRIPT>
myDayOfWeek = dayOfWeek(myMonth,myDay,myYear)
document.write("Thank God it is " + myDayOfWeek)
</SCRIPT>
```

Summary

This chapter has provided the basics of the JavaScript language. You have learned about using JavaScript in your HTML documents, the JavaScript program structure, and commenting scripts. You also have learned how to declare and manipulate JavaScript variables, how to control the flow of your programs, and the basics about JavaScript functions.

In Chapter 4, "JavaScript Objects and Properties," you will learn about Navigator objects and properties, including the JavaScript Object Model, how to create and use Navigator objects and methods, and how to use JavaScript's built-in functions and methods.

CHAPTER 4

JavaScript Objects and Properties

avaScript is an object-oriented scripting language based on an object-oriented model. In object-oriented programming, an *object* is a unique instance of a data structure, defined by the template provided by its class. You can think of objects as containers that hold information and specific pieces of data. The data collected in the object are referred to as *properties*, which also can be other objects. Objects also contain functions, and when associated with objects, are referred to as the object's methods.

Confused? Don't worry. In this chapter, you are going to learn specifically about the following:

- ◆ How to use JavaScript objects
- ◆ How to create objects and properties
- ◆ JavaScript's built-in objects
- ◆ JavaScript's built-in functions

The JavaScript Object Model

The combination of objects, properties, methods, variables, and functions that comprises the Netscape universe makes up what is called the *JavaScript Object Model*. *Objects* enable you to organize data in much the same way that functions enable you to organize code. Objects also enable you to easily perform repetitive, event-invoked tasks. A JavaScript object, often referred to as a class or data structure in other programming languages, consists of a set of elements called *properties*, which are variables.

Properties enable you to store datatype values for later use. You assign each property a unique name so that you can later refer to that value by its name. When using properties in scripting, it is much easier to refer to that data by its name rather than trying to remember its specific value.

Objects also contain functions that, when contained in an object, are referred to as *methods*. These methods are procedures or routines that, when called, perform particular tasks.

 An *object* is a software entity that is described both by its composition and its function. JavaScript uses objects to store and organize specific pieces of data.

A *property* is similar to a variable—it contains or stores information an object needs to perform its specific task.

A *method* is similar to a function—it enables you to define the way you want the associated object to behave. The term *method* refers to both the named operation and the code that a specifc class provides to perform that operation.

A function is set of statements that performs a specific task. Functions are contained within objects.

JavaScript Objects Versus OOP Objects

Historically, object-oriented programming has used objects that contain a set of routines (methods) that operate on data. The operations can be performed by only the particular methods contained within the object.

The way JavaScript carries out the use of objects is considered to be *object-based* programming rather than *object-oriented* programming—the JavaScript programming capabilities do not provide many of the basics of OOP, such as inheritance, encapsulation, and abstraction. The goal of JavaScript is not to reinvent the wheel, so to speak, but rather to script together programs and applications you can use in your HTML documents.

Exploring Navigator and LiveWire Objects

Built-in objects enable you to get information about the HTML document and its contents. Many of JavaScript's built-in objects are Navigator objects and LiveWire objects that enable you to create interesting and visually appealing HTML documents. The built-in objects also get information about the current Navigator session and loaded Web page.

When creating or using client-side JavaScript programs, the objects you use most often are Navigator objects; LiveWire offers built-in objects for server-side. Client-side scripting is used to accomplish the following tasks:

◆ To display error or information boxes

◆ To validate user input

◆ To display confirmation boxes

◆ To process server data, such as aggregate calculations

◆ To add simple, programmable logic to HTML

◆ To perform functions that do not require information from the server

You typically use server-side scripting to accomplish the following tasks:

◆ To maintain data shared among applications or clients

◆ To maintain information during client access

◆ To access a database

◆ To access server files

◆ To call server C libraries

◆ To customize Java applets

For detailed information about client-side versus server-side scripting, see Chapter 9, "Using Client and Server Scripts."

Objects Created by Netscape Navigator When a Page Loads

When creating or using client-side JavaScript programs, the objects you use most often are Navigator objects. The built-in objects in Navigator are referred to as the *Navigator Object Hierarchy*, and they are built from the window object. The following objects are part of the Navigator Object Hierarchy and are available when you load an HTML page in Navigator:

◆ Window objects—Reflect the properties that apply to the entire on-screen window, such as the document, location, and so on.

◆ Location objects—Contain properties about the current URL (Uniform Resource Locator), such as the protocol part, host name, path name, and so on.

◆ History objects—Contain properties that represent the URLs the user visited previously.

◆ Document objects—Mirror attributes of the HTML document tag so they can be accessed in JavaScript. These attributes include the color of the active links, the background color of the document, and so on.

For detailed information, see Chapter 5, "Netscape Navigator Objects."

Objects Created by LiveWire When a Page Is Requested

Just as Navigator objects offer assistance in writing client-side JavaScripts, LiveWire objects enable you to write server-side scripts. These objects are collectively referred to as the *LiveWire object framework*. The framework consists of the following objects available when you request a Web page:

◆ request

◆ client

◆ project

◆ server

One of the major features of these objects is that they give you an easy way on your Web server to retain important program information gathered during separate runs of the program. For detailed information, see Chapter 6, "Netscape LiveWire Objects."

Using Objects

As stated earlier in this chapter, objects provide a way to categorize, organize, and store data and the routines (methods) that behave on these data. JavaScript provides built-in objects that work with HTML elements and offers other built-in objects that perform tasks such as mathematical calculations, text creation, and date calculations.

Objects contain properties that enable you to store data type values for later use. You assign each property a unique name so you can later refer to that value by its name.

Object Properties

Object properties, just like variables, are used to store values. These values can be set or retrieved, depending on whether the object property reference is located to the left or right side of an equals (=) assignment operator. You use properties to hold data that describes the behavior or form of an object. If you create a beer object, for example, its properties might be temperature (warm or cold), container (bottle or can), and number of ounces (10, 12, 16).

You access the properties of an object with a simple notation involving the dot (.) operator in the following syntax:

```
objectName.propertyName
```

You could refer to the properties in the beer object, for example, in the following manner:

```
beer.temperature="cold"
beer.container="bottle"
beer.numberOfOunces=32
```

Note The dot operator (.) is the standard method used for accessing properties in Java.

Note the change in case in the code. Unlike HTML, JavaScript is case sensitive; thus, the object name and the property name are case sensitive. (In HTML code, you can use all upper- or lowercase letters, or you can mix cases. For example, the results of typing dogboy, DOGBOY, or Dogboy in HTML is the same because HTML doesn't discriminate among upper- and lowercase letters. JavaScript, however, is reactive to the case you use in code.)

The values of properties (like with variables) can be assigned or retrieved, depending on whether the property reference is on the left or right side of the equals (=) assignment operator. The previous example contained an assignment of several properties of the beer object. To retrieve these properties into a variable, the code would look like the following:

```
var beerTemperature
var beerContainer
var beerNumberOfOunces
beerTemperature = beer.temperature
beerContainer = beer.container
beerNumberOfOunces = beer.numberOfOunces
```

Creating Instances of JavaScript Objects

For objects to be of any use to you, it is necessary to create instances of them. When you create an instance of an object, you in effect make an object alive. It is just like if you were to run Notepad by double-clicking on the icon, creating an instance of the Notepad program. If you run another copy of Notepad by double-clicking the icon again, you then have two instances of the Notepad program running—you are creating an instance by double-clicking on the Notepad icon.

In JavaScript, you create an instance of an object with the *new* operator:

```
myBeer = new beer("cold","can",12)
```

Here, myBeer is created and is assigned the specified values for its properties. You can create as many beer objects as you want by using the *new* operator:

```
yourBeer = new beer("warm","paper cup",10)
```

The properties warm, paper cup, and 10 tell about the beer—they describe the temperature, the container in which the beer is held, and the number of ounces of warm beer in the paper cup.

In addition to accessing object properties, you also can create instances of JavaScript objects by using functions. To create the objects, you need to define the properties of the object you want to create.

Scoping of Navigator and LiveWire Objects

The *scope* of an object refers to the place in a script at which the object is accessible. The objects you create in JavaScript that are to be used on the client-side by Netscape Navigator have a scope that is available only to the current HTML page on which the script resides. When programming server-side JavaScripts, however, you can create objects whose scope encompasses several HTML pages of scripts.

Using the *with* Statement

When you call methods and access properties, JavaScript enables you, via the *with* statement, to indicate which object you are referring to. When using the *with* statement, JavaScript considers the object you specify to be the default object. After you indicate the default object, any references to properties that do not specify an object are assumed to be for the default object. Like many tasks in JavaScript, using the *with* statement saves the programmer time and keystrokes. Following is the syntax for the *with* statement:

```
with (object){
    statements
}
```

The statements you place within the brackets assume that the object is appended to the front of the property. Following is an example of using the *with* statement:

```
with yourBeer {
  temperature="cold"
  numberOfOunces=15
}
```

The statements temperature and numberOfOunces tell you more about the beer— the temperature is cold and the number of ounces is 15.

Object Methods

As mentioned earlier in this chapter, objects can be composed of methods as well as properties. The methods are JavaScript functions that, when called, perform particular tasks on that object. To use methods within a built-in object, call the method by using the dot operator (.):

```
objectName.propertyName()
```

Suppose that the beer object has a method called drink that takes as an argument the number of ounces of beer to drink. You would call the drink method in the following way:

```
myBeer.drink(2)
```

Here a drink of two ounces of beer is taken.

Static Objects

You do not need to create an instance of a *static object* in order to use the methods and properties it contains. Because the object does not change, it is considered to be static. To access properties of a static object, just use the object name and the required property or method.

Following is an example of a static object method:

```
var x = 10*Math.random()                    //Math is a static object
document.write("A random number between 0 and 10 is " + x)
```

To see what this code would look like if a normal non-static math object named myMath were used, take a look at the following code:

```
myMathObject = new myMath()           //myMath is not a static object.
                                      //A create is required
```

```
var x = 10*myMathObject.random()
document.write("A random number between 0 and 10 is " + x)
```

Notice the extra step involved in creating the myMathObject instance.

Although many times you need to define properties to create objects, several objects are available to you for which you do not need to create an instance of the object to be able to use its methods and properties. These objects are considered to be static—the Math object, for example, already provides properties and methods that enable you to perform mathematical calculations with arithmetic operators. To access a property of a static object, use the following syntax:

```
objectName.propertyName
```

Or:

```
objectName.methodName
```

Using the *this* Keyword

To refer to the current object, JavaScript provides the *this* keyword. Suppose that you have a function called changeColor that, given an object as an argument, changes the value of that object's color property, as in the following:

```
function changeColor(obj,Color) {
  obj.color = Color
}
```

An object with a color property could change the value of that property with the following code:

```
changeColor(this,"red")
```

 Note Because *this* is a keyword, it is a reserved word and cannot be used as a JavaScript variable, function, method, or object name.

Creating Your Own Objects

As well as using pre-existing and built-in objects, JavaScript also enables you to create your own objects by using a constructor function that acts as a container to all the properties and method functions.

To create an object in JavaScript, you need to define the properties of the object you want to create, create new instances of that object, and add methods to the object. To define the properties of an object and methods, JavaScript provides a means that is similar to defining a function. Defining an object enables you to define not only the name of the function, but the properties as well. The following exercise shows you how to use the constructor function to create a new object.

Defining and Creating an Object

1. For the beer object, the properties are "temperature," "container," and "number of ounces." The beer object also contains the method "drink()," which accepts an argument of how many ounces to drink.

2. With knowledge of the properties for your beer object, you can define the object containing the desired properties by using the *this* statement:

```
function beer(temperature,container,numberOfOunce) {
    this.container = container
    this.temperature = temperature
    this.numberOfOunces = numberOfOunces
}
```

The parameters in this definition are used so that when you create an instance of this object, you can additionally initialize the properties, as in the following object creation:

```
myBeer = new beer("warm","bottle",16)
```

This method of defining an object may seem obscure to those of you who are more accustomed to defining objects in other programming languages such as C++ and Java, but after working with it a while, you will get used to it.

3. To add the drink method to the beer object, add a line of code to define the beer object method so that the object definition looks like the following:

```
function beer(temperature,container,numberOfOunce) {
    this.container = container
    this.temperature = temperature
    this.numberOfOunces = numberOfOunces
    this.drink = drink
}
```

4. In the previous object definition, an association with the drink method was defined in the object; however, the method itself has not been defined yet. To define a method, use the same syntax as you would for defining a function:

```
function beer(temperature,container,numberOfOunce) {
```

```
        this.container = container
        this.temperature = temperature
        this.numberOfOunces = numberOfOunces
        this.drink = drink
    }
    function drink(howMuch) {
        this.numberOfOunces = this.numberOfOunces - howMuch
    }
```

5. Then, to create a 16-ounce can of cold beer and then drink a big gulp from it, you would use the following code:

```
myBeer = new beer("cold","can",16)
myBeer.drink(6)_   //drink 6 ounces
```

Adding Properties to Objects

In addition to defining properties when you define an object, you also can later add properties to object definitions. This is a useful tool—you can add properties you initially forgot to include or had not anticipated needing.

When adding properties to an existing object, define a single parameter for the function of each property you want to add to the new object definition. To assign each property to one of the incoming parameters, use the *this* keyword in the body of the function, as in the following example:

Suppose you had been using an object named human. The definition of the human object would currently look like the following:

```
function human(name, age, socialSecurityNumber) {
    this.name = name
    this.age = age
    this.socialSecurityNumber = socialSecurityNumber
}
```

Your requirements now change where you suddenly need a human object with a personality. By adding the personality property, the code looks like the following:

```
function human(name, age, socialSecurityNumber, personality) {
    this.name = name
    this.age = age
    this.socialSecurityNumber = socialSecurityNumber
    this.personality = personality
}
```

Adding Methods to Objects

When adding a method to an object, you don't insert the entire function definition. Instead, you insert the name of the function, thus referencing it within the object definition. When the method is called, the statements within the function definition are executed. Look at the following example:

```
1. function human(name, age, socialSecurityNumber, personality) {
2.    this.name = name
3.    this.age = age
4.    this.socialSecurityNumber = socialSecurityNumber
5.    this.personality = personality
6.    this.play = play
7. }
8. play() {
9. ...
10.}
```

The play function is defined in lines 8 through 10. The play function is made into a method of the human object in line 6. Notice how in the parameter list in line 1 you do not need to add the play method like you do when adding object properties.

Creating Array Objects

An *array* is a set of two or more values in a particular order that you can refer to as one item through an index. Most programming languages include arrays as built-in data types. For example, in C, you can define an array of integer with the following statement:

```
int myIntValue[25];
```

This defines a set of 25 integers. Because C uses zero-based indexing, you would reference the first integer in this set with myIntValue[0] and the last integer in this set with myIntValue[24]. Languages such as Visual Basic and Fortran use one-based indexing, whereby the elements in the array start at 1 and progress on up to the item count (length) for the array. JavaScript happens to be one of those languages that use zero-based indexing.

JavaScript has no explicit array data type; however, arrays and properties in JavaScript are closely related—both offer different ways to access the same information. Every object property can be accessed as an array entry, and likewise, array entries can be represented as object properties. For a further demonstration, examine the following object definition:

```
function human(name, age, socialSecurityNumber, personality) {
    this.name = name
    this.age = age
    this.socialSecurityNumber = socialSecurityNumber
    this.personality = personality
}
```

A typical method of referencing the previous object is by the named properties of the human object:

```
myHuman.name="Fred Farkle"
myHuman.age=32
myHuman.socialSecurityNumber="555-55-5555"
myHuman.personality="Criminally insane"
```

In addition, the human object can be referenced by array index values, as in the following code:

```
myHuman[0]="Fred Farkle"
myHuman[1]=32
myHuman[2]="555-55-5555"
myHuman[3]="Criminally insane"
```

Referencing an object property by its index value rather than by its property name is a pretty obscure naming method—that is, unless you wish to access the properties sequentially inside a *for* loop. The following demonstrates how it is possible to print all the properties of the human object by using a *for* loop (see fig. 4.1):

```
<HTML>
<HEAD><TITLE>Fred Farkle's Properties</TITLE></HEAD>
<BODY>
<H1>Description of Fred Farkle</H1>
<SCRIPT Language="JavaScript">
<!--
function human(name, age, socialSecurityNumber, personality) {
    this.name = name
    this.age = age
    this.socialSecurityNumber = socialSecurityNumber
    this.personality = personality
}
```

```
var myHuman = new human()
myHuman[0]="Fred Farkle"
myHuman[1]=32
myHuman[2]="555-55-5555"
myHuman[3]="criminally insane"
for (var i = 0; i < 4; i++) {
    document.write("<BR>Human is " + myHuman[i])
}
//-->
</SCRIPT>
</BODY>
</HTML>
```

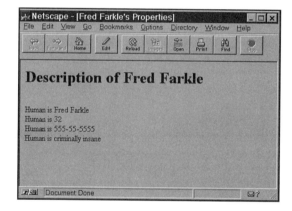

Figure 4.1

Printing out properties of Fred Farkle.

It is easy to add an additional property to an instance of an object by simply setting a new property name or property index to a value. Following are two methods of adding a fifth property to the myHuman object instance:

```
myHuman.eyeColor="blue"
myHuman[4]="blue"
```

With the capability to reference object properties as indices and to dynamically add properties to object instances, it is possible to spin your own array objects. Following is an object, mkArray that is used to define an array for a user-defined number of elements.

```
function mkArray(itemCount) {
  this.size = itemCount
  for (var I = 0; I < itemCount; I++) {
   this[I] = ""    //Initialize to blank
  }
}
```

This function creates an array with the number of items specified in the itemCount parameter. Each item, after being created, is initialized to a blank value. After you call the mkArray function, you then can use the *identifier[n]* statement to assign values and access the individual properties. The following code demonstrates how you might use the mkArray function to create an array and then access its elements.

```
var beerArray = new mkArray(4)
beerArray[0]="Budweiser"
beerArray[1]="Schaeffer"
beerArray[2]="Mickeys"
```

You will likely use a built-in JavaScript object called Array, which saves you from having to spin your own array object definition every time you want to use an array object. Following is what the previous code would look like if the built-in JavaScript Array object were used:

```
var beerArray = new Array(4)
beerArray[0]="Budweiser"
beerArray[1]="Schaeffer"
beerArray[2]="Mickeys"
```

 An *array* is a set of two or more values in a particular order that you can refer to as one item through an index. For example, you could have an array named beer that contains different types of domestic beers to which you assign numbers. If Samuel Adams were 1 and Killian's were 2, you could then refer to them as beer[1], beer[2], and so on.

Event Handlers as Functions

In addition to performing specific tasks, functions can also be used as event handlers for objects such as focus, blur, and so on. Table 4.1 shows the specific events JavaScript handles and the objects the events are associated with.

TABLE 4.1
Objects JavaScript events are associated with

Event	Object
Blur	Text fields, text areas, selections
Change	Text fields, text areas, selections

Event	Object
Click	Buttons, radio buttons, check boxes, submit buttons, reset buttons, links
Focus	Text fields, text areas, selections
MouseOver	Links
Select	Text fields, text areas

To process an event caused by a user interfacing with a form element, you need to add an event handler to the field tag. Following is an example of an OnClick event handler that has been added to a button form element.

```
<INPUT TYPE="button" NAME="FredsButton" VALUE="Click Me"
OnClick="processInput('Fred')">
```

When the button is clicked, the processInput function defined in your JavaScript code is executed. The processInput function is passed the character string value of Fred. Notice how Fred is enclosed in single quotes rather than double quotes, which normally are used to enclose JavaScript character strings. The single quotes differentiate the processInput argument from the double quotes inside the HTML field tag. The browser sees the single quotes and knows that what you mean are double quotes.

 Note   To differentiate HTML tag attributes from function arguments, you can add single quotes to your code.

Of the four Navigator objects (window, location, history, and document), the document object, which is associated with each window, is the only one that contains event handlers. (Navigator objects are discussed in detail in Chapter 5, "Netscape Navigator Objects.")

The onLoad and onUnload event handlers perform functions when a user loads or exits an HTML page. The load event onLoad occurs when a window or frames within a <FRAMESET> tag complete the load process. The load event onUnload takes place when a user exits a document. These event handlers are located inside the HTML <BODY> tag.

To alert the user when your Web page is loaded and unloaded, use the following code:

```
<BODY onLoad="alert('Hello my friend')" onUnload="alert('So long sucker!')">
```

navigator Object

Although you can count on event handlers being implemented in all versions of Netscape Navigator from 2.0 on up, some JavaScript functionalities, such as LiveConnect, work only in later versions of Netscape Navigator. For these occasions, it is a good idea to inspect your version of the Netscape Navigator Web browser before you attempt to perform operations that may not be implemented with the client's browser. In JavaScript, you can inspect the version of Navigator with the navigator object. The navigator object enables you to get information about the version of Navigator you are using. To use the navigator object, apply the following code:

```
navigator.propertyName
```

Table 4.2 shows the properties and descriptions of the navigator object. Note, however, that all properties of the navigator object are read-only.

TABLE 4.2
Properties of the navigator object

Property	Description
appCodeName	Specifies the code name of the browser
appName	Specifies the name of the browser
appVersion	Specifies version information for Navigator. The appVersion property specifies version information in the releaseNumber (platform; country) format. Following are the values contained in this format:
	releaseNumber is the version number of the Navigator. For example, 2.0b4 specifies Navigator 2.0, beta 4.
	platform is the platform upon which the Navigator is running. Win16, for example, specifies a 16-bit version of Windows, such as Windows 3.11.
	country is either "I" for the international release or "U" for the domestic U.S. release. Note that the domestic release has a stronger encryption feature than the international release.
userAgent	Represents the value of the user-agent header sent in the HTTP protocol from client to server.

JavaScript's Built-In Objects

JavaScript provides three built-in objects that come bundled with the JavaScript language and that are implemented by all JavaScript interpreters. You can use these objects—string, Math, and Date—both in client applications with Netscape Navigator and server applications with LiveWire.

string Object

The properties and methods of the string object enable you to work with string literals and variables. Following are two lines of syntax you can use for the string object:

```
stringName.propertyName
```

```
stringName.methodName(parameters)
```

Use stringName to indicate the name of the string variable with which you want to work. The only property available for propertyName is length, which is an integer you specify to indicate the length-related feature of the string object. Table 4.3 shows the methods available for the string object:

TABLE 4.3
Methods available for the string object

Method	Description
anchor	Used with the write or writeln methods to create and display an HTML anchor in a document that is used as a hypertext target. To display the anchor in a document after you create it, call write or writeln.
big	Specifies that a string appear on-screen in a large font, as though it were in a <BIG> tag.
blink	Specifies that a string blink, as though it were in a <BLINK> tag.
bold	Applies bold formatting to a string that appears on-screen, as though it were in a <B> tag.
charAt	Gets a character at an index you specify.

continues

Table 4.3, Continued
Methods available for the string object.

Method	Description
fixed	Specifies that a particular string appear on-screen in a fixed-pitch font as though it were in a <TT> tag.
fontcolor	Makes a string appear on-screen in a color you specify, as in the <FONT COLOR=color> tag. You can express the color as a hexadecimal RGB (red, green, blue) triplet; however, you must use the rrggbb format. For example, the hexadecimal values for red are red=FF, green=00, and blue=00. Note that this method overrides any value set in the fgColor property.
fontsize	Specifies that a string appear on-screen as though it were in a <FONTSIZE=size> tag. Note that when specifying size as an integer, you set the size of the stringName to one of the seven defined sizes. If you specify the size as a string as –3, for example, the font size of the stringName is relative to the size set in the <BASEFONT> tag.
indexOf	Gets the index within the calling string object of the first occurrence of the value you specify, beginning the search at fromIndex. Note that characters in a string are indexed from left to right, with the index of the first character as 0 and the index of the last character as stringName.length –1.
italics	Applies italic formatting to a string that appears on-screen, as though it were in an <I> tag.
lastIndexOf	Gets the index within the calling string object of the last occurrence of the value you specify. Note that JavaScript searches the calling string backwards, starting at fromIndex.
link	Creates an HTML hypertext link that moves to another URL you specify.
small	Specifies that a string appear on-screen in a small font, as though it were in a <SMALL> tag.
strike	Specifies that a string appear on-screen as struck-out or strike-through text, as though it were in a <STRIKE> tag.
sub	Specifies that a string appear on-screen as subscript text, as though it were in a <SUB> tag.

Method	Description
substring	Gets the subset of a string object. Note that if indexA is less than indexB, the substring method returns the subset starting with the character at indexA and ending with the character before indexB. If indexA is greater than indexB, the substring method returns the subset starting with the character at indexB and ending with the character before indexA. If indexA is equal to indexB, the substring method returns the empty string.
sup	Specifies that a string appear on-screen as superscript text, as though it were in a <SUP> tag.
toLowerCase	Converts the calling string value to lowercase. Note, however, that this method does not affect the value of stringName itself.
toUpperCase	Converts the calling string value to uppercase. Note, however, that this method does not affect the value of stringName itself.

The following JavaScript code uses the string object to produce the formatted output seen in figure 4.2.

```
<HTML>
<HEAD><TITLE>Built-in String Object</TITLE></HEAD>
<BODY>
<SCRIPT Language="JavaScript">
<!--
myString = "Great googly moogly"
document.write(myString+"<BR>")
document.write("The length of "+myString+" is "+myString.length+" characters
<BR>")
document.write(myString.anchor("AnchorHere")+"<BR>")
document.write(myString.big()+"<BR>")
document.write(myString.blink()+"<BR>")
document.write(myString.bold()+"<BR>")
document.write("The 6th character in "+myString+" is
"+myString.charAt(6)+"<BR>")
document.write(myString.fixed()+"<BR>")
document.write(myString.fontcolor("FF00FF")+"<BR>")
document.write(myString.fontcolor("Red")+"<BR>")
document.write(myString.fontsize(16)+"<BR>")
document.write("The string 'googly' begins in "+myString+" at position " +
myString.indexOf("googly")+"<BR>")
document.write(myString.italics()+"<BR>")
```

```
document.write("The last occurence of the string 'oogly' is found in
"+myString+" at position " + myString.lastIndexOf("oogly")+"<BR>")
document.write(myString.link("#AnchorHere")+"<BR>")
document.write(myString.small()+"<BR>")
document.write(myString.strike()+"<BR>")
document.write(myString.sub()+"<BR>")
document.write("Characters 6 to 12 make up " + myString.substring(6,12)+"<BR>")
document.write(myString.sup()+"<BR>")
document.write(myString.toLowerCase()+"<BR>")
document.write(myString.toUpperCase()+"<BR>")
//-->
</SCRIPT>
</BODY>
</HTML>
```

Figure 4.2

Printing formatted output with the string object.

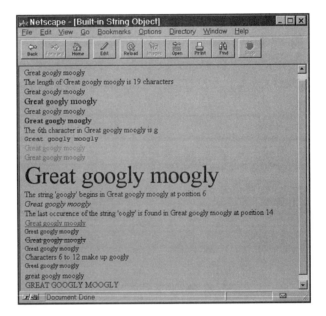

 Note Because many of the string methods do not take arguments, it is easy to accidentally leave off the parentheses in the call to the method. Keep in mind that these are methods, and that all methods need parentheses to differentiate themselves from properties.

In addition to producing formatted output, the string methods also provide an excellent means for a programmer to manipulate, parse, and validate strings input by the user.

Math Object

The Math object enables you to perform advanced calculations with its properties and methods. You can use either of the following two lines of syntax:

```
Math.propertyName
```

```
Math.methodName(parameters)
```

The Math object offers eight properties, as described in table 4.4.

TABLE 4.4
Math object properties

Property	Description
E	Returns the value of Euler's constant, which is approximately 2.718, and the base of natural logarithms. Note that because E is a constant, this is a read-only property.
LN2	Returns the natural logarithm of two, which is approximately 0.693. Note that because LN2 is a constant, this is a read-only property.
LN10	Returns the natural logarithm of ten, which is approximately 2.302. Note that because LN10 is a constant, this is a read-only property.
LOG2E	Returns the base 2 logarithm of e, which is approximately 1.442. Note that because LOG2E is a constant, this is a read-only property.
LOG10E	Returns the base 10 logarithm of e, which is approximately 0.434. Note that because LOG10E is a constant, this is a read-only property.
PI	Returns the ratio of the circumference of a circle to its diameter, which is approximately 3.14159. Note that because PI is a constant, this is a read-only property.
SQRT1_2	Returns the square root of one-half, which is approximately 0.707. Note that because SQRT1_2 is a constant, this is a read-only property.
SQRT2	Returns the square root of two, which is approximately 1.414. Note that because SQRT2 is a constant, this is a read-only property.

The following code demonstrates the use of the Math object properties to produce the output shown in figure 4.3.

```
<HTML>
<HEAD><TITLE>Built-in Math Object</TITLE></HEAD>
<BODY>
<SCRIPT Language="JavaScript">
<!--
document.write("Euler's constant = "+Math.E + "<BR>" )
document.write("Natural log of 2 = "+Math.LN2 + "<BR>")
document.write("Natural Log of 10 = "+Math.LN10 + "<BR>")
document.write("Base 2 log of e = "+Math.LOG2E + "<BR>")
document.write("Base 10 log of e = "+Math.LOG10E + "<BR>")
document.write("PI = "+Math.PI + "<BR>")
document.write("Square root of one half = "+Math.SQRT1_2 + "<BR>")
document.write("Square root of two = "+Math.SQRT2 + "<BR>")
//-->
</SCRIPT>
</BODY>
</HTML>
```

Figure 4.3

Printing Math constants using the Math object.

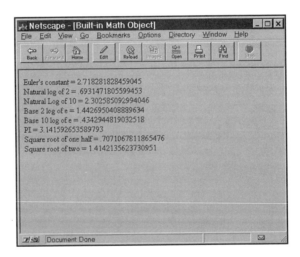

The Math object also provides 17 methods to help you perform advanced mathematical operations. Table 4.5 lists and describes these methods.

TABLE 4.5
Methods of the Math object

Method	Description
abs	Returns the absolute value of a number, where *number* can be any numeric expression or a property of an existing object.
acos	Returns the arc cosine (in radians) of a number, where *number* can be a numeric expression between –1 and 1 or a property of an existing object. If the value of number is outside the suggested range, the return value is always 0.
asin	Returns the arc sine (in radians) of a number, where *number* is a numeric expression between –1 and 1 or a property of an existing object. If the value of number is outside the suggested range, then the return value always is 0.
atan	Returns the arc tangent of a number between –pi/2 and pi/2 radians, where *number* is a numeric expression or a property of an existing object, representing the tangent of an angle.
ceil	Returns the lowest integer greater than or equal to a number, where *number* is any numeric expression or a property of an existing object.
cos	Returns the cosine of a number between –1 and 1, where *number* is a numeric expression representing the size of an angle in radians or a property of an existing object.
exp	Returns enumber, where *number* is the argument, a numeric expression or a property of an existing object; and e is Euler's constant, which is the base of the natural logarithms.
floor	Returns the greatest integer less than or equal to a number, where *number* is any numeric expression or a property of an existing object.
log	Returns the natural logarithm (base e) of a number, where *number* is any positive numeric expression or a property of an existing object. Note that if the value of number is outside the suggested range, then the return value is always –1.797693134862316e+308.
max	Returns the greater of two numbers, where *number1* and *number2* are any numeric arguments or the properties of existing objects.
min	Returns the lesser of two numbers, where *number1* and *number2* are any numeric arguments or the properties of existing objects.

continues

TABLE 4.5, CONTINUED
Methods of the Math object

Method	Description
pow	Returns base to the exponent power; that is, base exponent where base is any numeric expression or a property of an existing object. *exponent* is any numeric expression or a property of an existing object. If the result includes an imaginary number (for example pow(1,0.5)), the value returned is 0.
random	Available only on Unix platforms, this method returns a pseudo-random number between zero and one.
round	Returns the value of a number rounded to the nearest integer, where *number* is any numeric expression or a property of an existing object. Note that if the fractional portion of the number is .5 or greater, then the argument is rounded to the next highest integer. If the fractional portion of the number is less than .5, the argument is rounded to the next lowest integer.
sin	Returns a numeric value between −1 and 1, which represents the sine of the angle, where *number* is a numeric expression or a property of an existing object that represents the size of an angle in radians.
sqrt	Returns the square root of a number, where number is any non-negative numeric expression or a property of an existing object. Note that if the value of number is outside the suggested range, the return value always is 0.
Tan	Returns a numeric value that represents the tangent of the angle, where *number* is a numeric expression that represents the size of an angle in radians, or a property of an existing object.

The following code demonstrates how to use Math methods with Math properties to evaluate expressions (see fig. 4.4).

```
<HTML>
<HEAD><TITLE>Built-in Math Object</TITLE></HEAD>
<BODY>
<SCRIPT Language="JavaScript">
<!--
document.write("Euler's constant rounded = "+Math.round(Math.E) + "<BR>" )
document.write("Sine of natural log of 2 = "+Math.sin(Math.LN2) + "<BR>")
document.write("Square root of natural log of 10 = "+Math.sqrt(Math.LN10) +
```

```
"<BR>")
document.write("Tangent of square root of two = "+Math.tan(Math.SQRT2) +
"<BR>")
//-->
</SCRIPT>
</BODY>
</HTML>
```

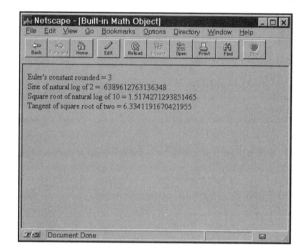

Figure 4.4

Using Math methods.

Note

Note that because the Math object is a static object, you never need to use the new statement to create a Math object instance. Also note that with the use of the *with* statement, the previous math code can be cleaned up as in the following:

```
<HTML>
<HEAD><TITLE>Built-in Math Object</TITLE></HEAD>
<BODY>
<SCRIPT Language="JavaScript">
<!--
with (Math){
  document.write("Euler's constant rounded = "+round(E) + "<BR>" )
  document.write("Sine of natural log of 2 = "+sin(LN2) + "<BR>")
  document.write("Square root of natural log of 10 = "+sqrt(LN10) + "<BR>")
  document.write("Tangent of square root of two = "+tan(SQRT2) + "<BR>")
}
//-->
</SCRIPT>
</BODY>
</HTML>
```

Date Object

The built-in Date object enables you to work with dates and times in JavaScript, such as displaying the date and time on a Web page. You can use form 1 of the syntax to create the current date and time. Note that if you omit hours, minutes, or seconds from form 2 or 4 of the syntax, the value will be set to 0. Also note that dates prior to 1970 are not allowed.

Although the Date object has no properties, it does provide 20 methods to help you work with dates and time. Table 4.6 describes the methods for the Date object.

TABLE 4.6
Methods for the Date object

Method	Description
getDate	Returns the day of the month for the specified date (an integer between 1 and 31), where *dateObjectName* is either the name of a date object or a property of an existing object.
getDay	Returns the day of the week for the date you specify, where dateObjectName is either the name of a date object or a property of an existing object. Note that the value returned by getDay is an integer corresponding to the day of the week: zero for Sunday, one for Monday, two for Tuesday, and so on.
getHours	Returns the hour (an integer between 0 and 23) for the date you specify, where *dateObjectName* is either the name of a date object or a property of an existing object.
getMinutes	Returns the minutes (an integer between 0 and 59) in the date you specify, where *dateObjectName* is either the name of a date object or a property of an existing object.
getMonth	Returns the month in the date you specify, where *dateObjectName* is either the name of a date object or a property of an existing object. Note that the value returned is an integer between zero and eleven. Zero corresponds to January, one to February, and so on.
getSeconds	Returns the seconds (an integer between 0 and 59) in the current time, where *dateObjectName* is either the name of a date object or a property of an existing object.
getTime	Returns the numeric value corresponding to the time for the specified date, where *dateObjectName* is either the name of a date

Method	Description
	object or a property of an existing object. Note that the value returned by this method is the number of milliseconds since 1 January 1970 00:00:00. You also can use this method to help assign a date and time to another date object.
getTimezoneOffset	Returns the time zone offset in minutes for the current locale, where *dateObjectName* is either the name of a date object or a property of an existing object. The time zone offset is the difference between local time and GMT. Note that daylight saving time prevents this value from being a constant.
getYear	Returns the year in the date you specify, where *dateObjectName* is either the name of a date object or a property of an existing object. The value returned by this method is the year minus 1900. If the year is 1980, for example, the value returned is 80.
parse	Returns the number of milliseconds in a date string since 1 January 1970 00:00:00 local time, where *dateString* is a string representing a date or a property of an existing object. The parse method takes a date string (such as "April 5, 1995"), and returns the number of milliseconds since January 1, 1970 at 00:00:00 local time. This function is useful for setting date values based on string values, such as in conjunction with the setTime method and the Date object.
	Given a string representing a time, parse returns the time value. It accepts the IETF standard date syntax: Mon, 4 Apr 1995 13:30:00 GMT. It understands the continental U.S. time zone abbreviations. For general use, however, use a time zone offset, such as "Mon, 5 Apr 1995 13:30:00 GMT+0430" (which indicates 4 hours, 30 minutes west of the Greenwich meridian). Note that if you do not specify a time zone, the local time zone is assumed; and that JavaScript considers GMT and UTC to be equivalent.
	Because the parse function is a static method of Date, you always use it as Date.parse() rather than as a method of a Date object you created.
setDate	Sets the day of the month for a date you specify, where *dateObjectName* is the name of a date object or a property of an existing object. Note that dayValue is an integer from 1 to 31 or a property of an existing object, representing the day of the month.

continues

TABLE 4.6, CONTINUED
Methods for the Date object

Method	Description
setHours	Sets the hours for a specified date, where dateObjectName is either the name of a date object or a property of an existing object. Note that *hoursValue* is an integer between 0 and 23 or a property of an existing object that represents the hour.
setMinutes	Sets the minutes for a date you specify, where *dateObjectName* is the name of a date object or a property of an existing object. Note that *minutesValue* is an integer between 0 and 59 or a property of an existing object that represents the minutes.
setMonth	Sets the month for a date you specify, where *dateObjectName* is either the name of a date object or a property of an existing object. Note that monthValue is an integer between 0 and 11 (representing the months January through December), or a property of an existing object.
setSeconds	Enables you to set the seconds for a date you specify, where *dateObjectName* is the name of a date object or a property of an existing object. Note that *secondsValue* is an integer between 0 and 59 or a property of an existing object.
setTime	Sets the value of a date object, where *dateObjectName* is the name of a date object or a property of an existing object. Note that *timevalue* is an integer or a property of an existing object that represents the number of milliseconds since the epoch (1 January 1970 00:00:00). You can use this method to help assign a date and time to another date object.
setYear	Sets the year for a date you specify, where *dateObjectName* is the name of a date object or a property of an existing object. Note that *yearValue* is an integer greater than 1900 or a property of an existing object.
toGMTString	Converts a date to a string by using the Internet GMT conventions, where *dateObjectName* is the name of a date object or a property of an existing object. Note that the exact format of the value returned by toGMTString varies according to the platform.
toLocaleString	Converts a date to a string by using the conventions of the current locale, where *dateObjectName* is the name of a date object or a property of an existing object. Note that if you are trying to

Method	Description
	pass a date by using toLocaleString, be aware that different locales assemble the string in different ways. Using methods such as getHours, getMinutes, and getSeconds provides more portable results.
UTC	Returns the number of milliseconds in a date object since January 1, 1970 at 00:00:00 Universal Coordinated Time (GMT), where *year* is a year after 1900, *month* is a month between 0 and 11, *date* is a day of the month between 1 and 31, *hrs* indicates hours between 0 and 23, *min* indicates minutes between 0 and 59, and sec indicates seconds between 0 and 59. Note that because UTC is a static method of Date, you always use it as Date.UTC() rather than as a method of a Date object you created

As demonstrated in figure 4.5, the following JavaScript code uses the built-in Date object to evaluate date values for the current date and time.

```
<HTML>
<HEAD><TITLE>Built-in Date Object</TITLE></HEAD>
<BODY>
<SCRIPT Language="JavaScript">
<!--
rightNow = new Date()
document.write("Right now's month is "+rightNow.getMonth()+"<BR>")
document.write("Right now's day of the month is "+rightNow.getDate()+"<BR>")
document.write("Right now's year is "+rightNow.getYear()+"<BR>")
document.write("Right now's day of the week is "+rightNow.getDay()+"<BR>")
document.write("Right now's hour is "+rightNow.getHours()+"<BR>")
document.write("Right now's minute is "+rightNow.getMinutes()+"<BR>")
document.write("Right now's second is "+rightNow.getSeconds()+"<BR>")
document.write("Number of milliseconds since Jan 1, 1970 is
"+rightNow.getTime()+"<BR>")
document.write("Difference in hours for the browser's time zone from GMT is
"+Math.round(rightNow.getTimezoneOffset()/60)+"<BR>")

//-->
</SCRIPT>
</BODY>
</HTML>
```

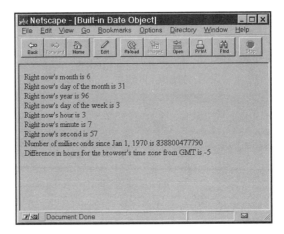

Figure 4.5

Using the Date object.

JavaScript's Built-in Functions

In addition to its built-in objects, JavaScript has built-in functions. The functions, eval, parseInt, parseFloat, escape, and unescape, return the numerical values for strings that represent numerical values. Because these functions are stand-alone and are not attached to any object, they can be called without reference to a particular instance or static reference to an object.

 Note   Note also that because the functions discussed in this section are not methods, you do not apply them to an instance by using the dot operator.

eval

Following is the syntax for the eval function:

```
eval(string)
```

Use the eval function to evaluate its string argument as a JavaScript expression. The string can be any string that represents a JavaScript expression (including variables and properties of existing objects), statement, or succession of statements. The function then returns the value of that string. Use the eval function to evaluate expressions, including variable substitution. That the eval function evaluates all JavaScript expressions makes it an extremely powerful and useful function for converting strings to numerical values, for example. To help you better understand this built-in function, look at the following code (and see fig. 4.6):

```
<HTML>
<HEAD><TITLE>eval function</TITLE></HEAD>
<BODY>
<SCRIPT Language="JavaScript">
<!--
var myValue = Math.PI
//-->
</SCRIPT>
<FORM NAME="myForm">
<INPUT TYPE="text" NAME="userValue" SIZE=40>
<INPUT TYPE="button" Value="Evaluate expression"
onClick="alert(eval(myForm.userValue.value))")
</FORM>
</BODY>
</HTML>
```

Here, the variable myValue is set to PI, and the user is able to apply the myValue variable when typing in a JavaScript expression in the form's text field. In this example, the eval function returns the results obtained from evaluating the expression, and the alert function displays the results in the alert box.

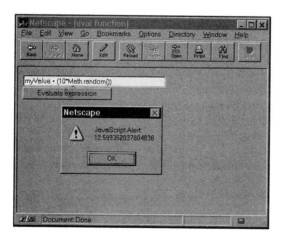

Figure 4.6

Using the eval function.

parseInt

Following is the syntax for the parseInt function:

```
partseInt(string, radix)
```

Use the parseInt function to get the numerical equivalent of the integer string, which is based on the radix you provide. The radix parameter is the base of the number to which you want to convert, such as 8 for octal, 16 for hexadecimal, and 10 for decimal. Radixes greater than ten are represented by letters of the alphabet to indicate numerals greater than 9. For hexadecimal numbers (base 16), for example, this function uses letters A through F.

Because parseInt expects an integer, it truncates decimal portions of a number without rounding. In cases where this function cannot parse the string you specify, it truncates the number where the number ends. If the first character of the string cannot be converted to a number in the radix you specify, NaN is returned.

To better understand how to use this function, look at the following example:

```
<HTML>
<HEAD><TITLE>parseInt function</TITLE></HEAD>
<BODY>
<SCRIPT Language="JavaScript">
<!--
function processInput(userEnteredValue) {
  if (userEnteredValue == "0") {
    alert("Result is 0")
    return
  }
  if (parseInt(userEnteredValue) != 0) {
    alert("Result is "+2*parseInt(userEnteredValue))
  } else {
    alert("Please enter a numeric value")
  }

}
//-->
</SCRIPT>
<FORM NAME="myForm">
<INPUT TYPE="text" NAME="userValue" SIZE=10>
<INPUT TYPE="button" Value="Multiply by two"
onClick="processInput(myForm.userValue.value)">
</FORM>
</BODY>
</HTML>
```

In this example, the parseInt function is used to validate that the data typed in by the user is actually numeric data. If the user types in data that is not numeric, that person receives an error message (see fig. 4.7). Otherwise, the user receives the value that was entered multiplied by two.

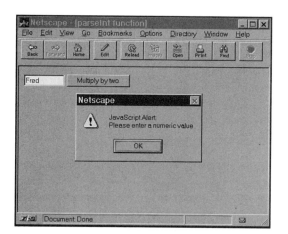

Figure 4.7

Using the parseInt function.

parseFloat

Following is the syntax for the parseFloat function:

```
parseFloat (string)
```

Use this function to get a floating point equivalent from a string you specify, where *string* is the value you want to parse. If this function comes upon a character other than a sign (+ or 0), numeral (0-9), exponent, or decimal, only the value up to that point is returned, and that character and all succeeding characters are ignored. If the first character cannot be converted to a number, to indicate that the value is not a number, this function returns 0 on Windows platforms or NaN on all other platforms.

escape

Following is the syntax for the escape function:

```
escape(string)
```

Use this function to convert strings to codes that map to the ISO Latin-1 character set. Escaping a character string is useful should you ever need to store data in a cookie file or URL that normally does not accept special characters such as tabs, slashes, and so on. Then, use the unescape function when you wish to retrieve the data. The escape and unescape functions save you the trouble of performing character conversions yourself. The following code is used to demonstrate how using the escape function works. The results from this code are displayed in figure 4.8.

```
<HTML>
<HEAD><TITLE>escape function</TITLE></HEAD>
<BODY>
<H1>escape function</H1>
<SCRIPT Language="JavaScript">
<!--
document.write("The escape code for the right bracket(]) character is  "+
escape("]"))
//-->
</SCRIPT>
</BODY>
</HTML>
```

Figure 4.8

Using the escape function.

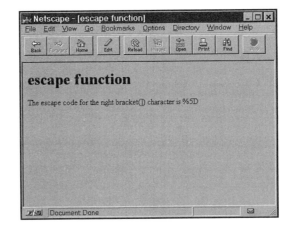

unescape

By using the unescape function, you can unencode those characters you encoded with the escape function. Following is the syntax for the unescape function:

```
unescape("string")
```

Use this function to get the ASCII value for the ISO Latin-1 character string you specify. This function is similar to the escape function—it performs character conversions; however, this function converts ISO Latin-1 characters characters to ASCII values rather than ASCII values to ISO Latin-1 characters.

Following is an example of the unescape function:

```
<HTML>
<HEAD><TITLE>unescape function</TITLE></HEAD>
<BODY>
<H1>unescape function</H1>
<SCRIPT Language="JavaScript">
<!--
document.write("The Copyright symbol is "+ unescape("%A9")+" and the Registered
Trademark symbol is "+ unescape("%AE"))
//-->
</SCRIPT>
</BODY>
</HTML>
```

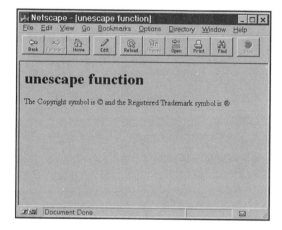

Figure 4.9

Using the unescape function.

Summary

In this chapter, you learned about Navigator objects and properties, including the JavaScript Object Model, how to create and use Navigator objects and methods, and how to use JavaScript's built-in functions and methods.

Chapter 5, "Netscape Navigator Objects," discusses objects in JavaScript and how to use Netscape Navigator objects. Specifically, it discusses Navigator objects, the Navigator object hierarchy, and how to implement the Window and Frame objects, Location and History objects, Document objects, and Form objects.

CHAPTER **5**

Netscape Navigator Objects

T he most important feature of the JavaScript language probably is its capability to use and create objects. For a scripting language, this is a pretty radical notion. Although many application programming languages, such as C++, Java, and Smalltalk, support the use of objects, very few scripting languages were designed with objects in mind.

Objects enable you to organize data in much the same way that functions enable you to organize code. A JavaScript object, often referred to as a class or data structure in other programming languages, consists of a set of elements called *properties* or *members*. Navigator objects are those elements and components you see on a loaded and displayed HTML document; they include the window, the URL text box, and the actual document.

The way JavaScript carries out the use of objects is considered to be *object-based* programming rather than *object-oriented* programming because the JavaScript programming capabilities do not provide many of the basics of OOP, such as inheritance, encapsulation, and abstraction. The goal of JavaScript is not to reinvent the wheel, so to speak, but rather to script together programs and applications you can use in your HTML documents to create more interesting, functional, and fun Web pages.

In this chapter, you will learn about objects in JavaScript and how to use Netscape Navigator objects. Specifically, you will learn about the following:

◆ Using Navigator objects

◆ The Navigator object hierarchy

◆ How to implement the Window and Frame objects by opening and closing windows, displaying alert boxes, and so on

◆ Location and History objects

◆ Document objects and their properties, forms, attributes, and event handlers

◆ Form objects and how their properties enable you to create interesting and easy-to-use forms that further enable user interaction

What Is an Object?

An *object* is a software entity that is described both by its composition and its function. A button, for example, is an object because it has both properties and methods. You can describe the properties of a button with one or more variables. You also can describe the actions a button can perform by one or more functions or methods. The value "property" refers to the caption that appears on the button. The button object is also composed of a "click" method, which describes an action that a button object is capable of performing.

A JavaScript object (whether created by JavaScript or made available to JavaScript) is based on a simple structure. Each object can be composed of two types of elements: properties and methods.

Properties are like variables in that they store information that objects need to perform a specific task. Continuing with the button object example, the text that appears on the button needs to be stored in a variable that is associated with this button. Methods are similar to functions; they enable you to define the way you want the object to behave. The method for the button object example happens to be "click."

 An *object* is a software entity that is described both by its composition and its function.

A *property* is similar to a variable—it contains or stores information an object needs to perform its specific task.

An *object property* is the variable in which you store the text that is on the button.

A *method* is similar to a function—it enables you to define the way in which you want the associated object to behave.

Using Navigator Objects

Imagine that the scripting language you use to give commands to your operating system (such as MS-DOS commands or Unix shell commands) supports the use of objects. If this were so, instead of running programs with esoteric command-line parameters, such as the following MS-DOS command line:

```
c:\> DIR  /S /P /W c:\dos
```

to give a directory listing (DIR) of the directory C:\DOS, including subdirectories (/S) one page at a time (/P) in wide (/W) format, you probably would perform the same operation using objects, similar to the following:

```
c:\> dir.directory="c:\dos"
c:\> dir.subDirectories=True
c:\> dir.onePage=True
c:\> dir.WideFormat=True
c:\> dir.printToScreen
```

As mentioned previously, you can use JavaScript for creating objects; however, these objects are less likely to take on the complexity and scale of an object you might create in C++ or Java. More likely, you will be using JavaScript to use objects rather than create objects.

For client-side JavaScript programs, the most commonly used objects are those made available by Netscape Navigator. Each time an HTML page is loaded by Netscape Navigator, the following objects are made available to you:

◆ Window objects—reflect the properties that apply to the entire on-screen window, such as the document, location, and so on

◆ Location objects—contain properties about the current URL (uniform resource locator), such as the protocol part, hostname, pathname, and so on

◆ History objects—contain properties that represent the URLs the user visited previously

◆ Document objects—mirror attributes of the HTML document tag so that you can gain access to them in JavaScript. These attributes include the color of the active links, the background color of the document, and so on

To demonstrate this concept, consider an example. Suppose that you create a page named forecast.html that contains the following HTML code:

```
<HTML>
<HEAD><TITLE>Forecast Example</TITLE></HEAD>
<BODY>
This is the body test
</BODY>
</HTML>
```

Each time these HTML pages load, they provide the window, location, history, and document objects. These objects would have properties, such as the following:

```
location.href = "http://www.newriders.com/forecast.html"
document.title = "Forecast Example"
document.fgColor = #FFFFFF
document.bgColor = #000000
history.length = 12
```

In practice, the preceding values would be based on the document's actual location, its title, foreground, and background colors, and so on.

Continuing with this example, Navigator also would create the following objects, based on the contents of the page:

```
document.forecastForm
document.forecastForm.buttonControl
document.forecastForm.temperatureBox
```

The preceding objects would have properties, such as the following:

```
document.forecastForm.action = http://www.newriders.com/forecast()
document.forecastForm.method = get
document.forecastForm.length = 3
document.forecastForm.buttonControl.value = "Forecast"
document.forecastForm.buttonControl.name = "buttonControl"
document.forecastForm.temperatureBox.value = "32"
document.forecastForm.temperatureBox.name = "temperatureBox"
document.forecastForm.skyBox.value = "cloudy"
document.forecastForm.skyBox.name = "skyBox"
```

Did you know...

Some of the document object and property names in the previous list contain more than one element. These elements are connected by dots (.).

Netscape Navigator uses an object hierarchy to reflect the structural placement of the elements within the HTML page itself. For the preceding objects, the sequence starts with document, followed by the name of the form, myform, and then the property name (for form properties) or the name of the form element. Netscape Navigator's object hierarchy is discussed in the next section.

Navigator Object Hierarchy

The Navigator object hierarchy helps organize the various HTML elements exposed by Netscape by using windows and frames. As you can see in figure 5.1, the window object is the top-level object in the hierarchy.

Note that parent, frames, self, and top are on the same line. The top property is synonymous with the top-most Navigator window (the browser). The parent property is synonymous with the window or frame that contains the current frame. Because these objects sometimes are interchangeable, the hierarchy can lead to confusion.

To help you understand this sometimes puzzling hierarchy, look at figure 5.2, which shows a single document loaded into a Navigator window.

Because everything is contained within a single window, you don't need to worry about the frame, top, or parent objects. Now take a look at a view with two frames, as shown in figure 5.3.

Here you have a parent window and two child frames. The window object (frameset) contains the HTML code that defines the two frames, and the two frames (each of which are window objects) contain a document.

The object hierarchy is made up of more than just window and frame objects. To learn more, continue with the following sections.

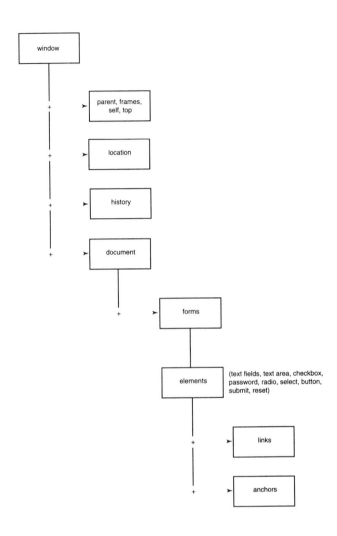

Figure 5.1

*The Navigator
object hierarchy.*

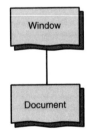

Figure 5.2

*A single
document in the
object hierarchy.*

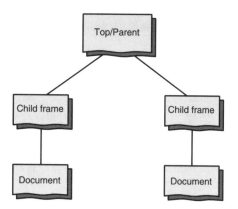

Figure 5.3
A view with two frames.

Did you know...

As shown in the Navigator object hierarchy, the window object is the parent object for each loaded document. For this reason, when using the dot notation to refer to window properties and methods, you can omit the window object name.

If an object is a descendant of another object, for example, it is represented using the *dot notation* as a property of its parent object. A form named *form1* is an object, but also is a property of *document*, and thus, is referred to as *document.form1*.

Dot notation enables you to indicate hierarchy and shows that an object is made up of two parts—the object to the left of the dot and the object to the right of the dot, such as *document.form1*.

Window and Frame Objects

JavaScript enables you to create, open, scroll, and close windows that contain HTML documents, text, form objects, and frames. The window object contains properties that apply to the entire on-screen window, and is the top-level object for the document, location, and history objects (refer to fig. 5.1). By using methods of the window object, you can specify messages in dialog boxes, determine the value of text in the status bar, open and close windows, and so on.

Opening and Closing Windows

To create an open window, use the open() method of the window object. To close a window, use the close() method of the window object. The open() method uses two required arguments and an optional feature list. The feature list includes options, such as toolbar, which enables you to create a standard toolbar, and status, which enables you to create the status bar. The two required arguments are URL and windowName, which enable you to specify the address and name of the window to open.

To create an open window and then close it using the open() and close() methods of the window object, complete the following steps.

Creating and Closing Windows

1. Create a new HTML file in a text editor, such as Notepad, and then add the following script code to it. This code, when executed, will open a new, menu-bar absent, blank window:

   ```
   helloWindow=window.open("","HelloWindow","menubar=no")
   ```

2. Load this file in Netscape Navigator and look at the results. Notice how the first parameter is blank. This parameter normally would contain the URL of an HTML document; however, for this example, you want the window to be blank. The return value from this function is the object reference name for your newly created window—helloWindow.

3. Write a message to your new window. Add the following code to your current script, and then reload the document into Netscape:

   ```
   helloWindow.document.write("<CENTER><B><I>Hello, World Wide Web!</B>
   </I></CENTER>")
   ```

4. Close the window. Add the following code to your script and then reload Netscape to see the results:

   ```
   helloWindow.open()
   ```

   Figure 5.4 shows an open window created using the open method of the window object.

5. To close an open window, just use close(), as in the following example:

   ```
   window.close();
   ```

Note   Note that the close() method only closes windows that have been opened with the JavaScript open() method. When attempting to close other windows, you are prompted to choose whether you actually want to close those windows.

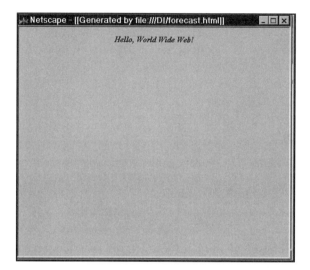

Figure 5.4

An open window using the open method.

You can use *self* or *window*, which are synonymous, to close the current window, as in the following:

```
window.close()
```

or

```
self.close()
```

As mentioned in Chapter 3, however, LiveWire objects and their properties are not accessible from within functions. Because of this, when opening or closing a window within an event handler, you must specify the name of the window with the event name so that HTML can distinguish between the entire document and a particular window. If you issue close() without specifying a particular window, you will close the entire document rather than one window in the document. The following, for example, indicates that you want to close the window "billsWindow":

```
billsWindow.close()
```

To close without specifying an object name, use a call to close, as in the following:

```
close()
```

This is interpreted as if you want to close the document, and would thus would be read as the following:

```
document.close()
```

Finally, you also can just omit the current window name. When calling the methods and properties of the current window, you do not need to reference the name of the window because HTML presumes the existence of the current window. The following, for example, closes the current window:

```
close()
```

Scrolling Windows

The new scroll method of the window object enables you to specify the number of pixels you want a particular window to scroll. You can specify vertical and horizontal scrolling. Following is the syntax for this method:

```
windowReference.scroll(x-coordinate,y-coordinate)
```

Use windowReference to refer to the window for which you want to set scrolling. The x-coordinate requires an integer you use to specify the horizontal offset in pixels. The coordinates for the upper left corner of a document, for example, are (0,0). The y-coordinate requires an integer you use to specify the vertical offset in pixels.

Popping up an Alert Window

Using the alert() method of the window object, you can display a specific message in a dialog box that contains an OK button. Following is an example of how to use the alert() method and figure 5.5 showing the results.

```
alert("You must be 21 or older to view this web page.")
```

Popping up a Confirm Window

A confirm window enables you to offer users the choice to proceed or cancel using OK and Cancel buttons. Because the buttons are Boolean, clicking OK returns True and clicking Cancel returns False. To display a confirm window, you use the confirm() method of the window object, as in the following example:

```
if (confirm("Are you sure you wish to buy this hammer?")) {
     buyItem(hammer)
  }
```

Figure 5.6 shows the results.

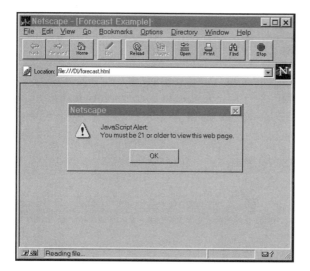

Figure 5.5

Displaying an alert window using the alert() method.

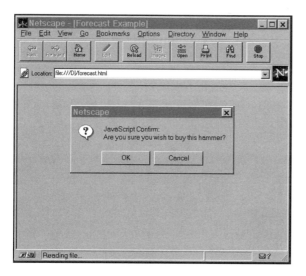

Figure 5.6

Displaying a confirm window using the confirm() method.

Referring to a Window or Frame

The windows you create can have two names. Use the first name to refer to the properties, methods, and containership of the window. The second name is optional, but if you want to refer to a window as a target for a hypertext link, you must assign the second name.

Containership is type of a hierarchical method that describes a component in terms of what it is contained in. For document.myForm.myButton, for example, the button named myButton is located in the form myForm.

Frames are different from windows in that they are individual rectangular spaces that contain separate files (see fig. 5.7). Use frames to specify multiple, independent, scrollable regions within a display window. Each frame can contain a separate HTML document that, when linked, can update other frames. Users can scroll and resize frames at the discretion of the page creator. Each frame can also be given NAME values so that it can be targeted by links in other documents or other frames.

 Frames are rectangular areas that enable you to specify multiple, independent, scrollable regions within a display window. Users can scroll and resize frames at the discretion of the page creator.

Creating a Frame or Frameset

In HTML, frames are organized into sets of frames that are referred to as *framesets*. To create a frameset in an HTML document, use the <FRAMESET> tag to determine the layout of frames on a page. To create a frame in a frameset, use the <FRAME> tag to determine the layout of the frame within the frameset.

Figure 5.7

Frames in a browser.

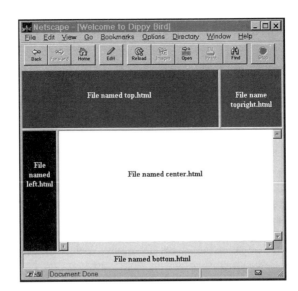

A *frameset* is a set of organized frames you use in an HTML document to display on one screen mutltiple rectangular areas that are individually scrollable and have discrete URLs.

The following exercise shows you how to create the frame shown in figure 5.7.

Creating Frames

1. Create five HTML files named "top.html," "topright.html," "left.html," "center.html," "bottom.html." For each of these files, include some content in them that describes their identity, such as "File named top.html."

2. Create a new file called "master.html" that contains the following frame information, specifying a window with a top, center, and bottom frame.

```
<HTML>
<FRAMESET ROWS="122,*,35">
<FRAME SRC="top.html" NAME="topFrame" MARGINHEIGHT=1 NORESIZE
➥SCROLLING="no" >
<FRAME SRC="center.html" NAME="topFrame" MARGINHEIGHT=1 NORESIZE
➥SCROLLING="yes" >
<FRAME SRC="bottom.html" NAME="topFrame" MARGINHEIGHT=1 NORESIZE
➥SCROLLING="no" >
</FRAMESET>
<HTML>
```

Notice how in the first line you specify the top frame to be 122 pixels high, the bottom frame as 35 pixels high, and the middle frame to use up the remaining space in the window. If you open "master.html" with Netscape, you should see a window with a top, center, and bottom frame.

3. Add some complexity to your frameset by dividing the top and center rows into two columns. You accomplish this by nesting an additional columns-frameset inside the current rows-frameset for each section you want to divide, as in the following code:

```
<FRAMESET ROWS="122,*,35">
<FRAMESET COLS="408,*">
<FRAME SRC="top.html" NAME="topFrame" MARGINHEIGHT=1 NORESIZE
➥SCROLLING="no" >
<FRAME SRC="topright.html" MARGINHEIGHT=2 NAME="topRightFrame" NORESIZE
➥SCROLLING="no">
</FRAMESET>
```

```
<FRAMESET COLS="80,*">
<FRAME SRC="left.html" MARGINHEIGHT=1 NAME="leftFrame" NORESIZE
➥SCROLLING="no">
<FRAME SRC="center.html" MARGINHEIGHT=1 NAME="centerFrame" NORESIZE
➥SCROLLING="yes">
</FRAMESET>
<FRAME SRC ="bottom.html" MARGINHEIGHT=1 NAME="bottomFrame" NORESIZE
➥SCROLLING="no">
</FRAMESET>
```

Frames are organized in a hierarchical fashion that utilizes parent/child relationships, framesets, and windows. Figure 5.8 shows the hierarchical relationship.

Figure 5.8

*A simple frame
hierarchy.*

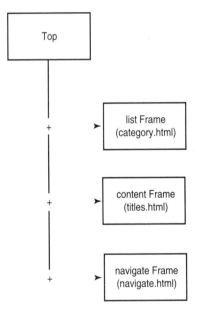

When dividing a document window into frames, use the top-level document (the
HTML document) to define the frames in the frameset. The window in which you
place the first frameset (A) is the parent of that frameset. In instances where you
place another frameset (B) within the initial frameset (A), the initial (A) frameset is
considered the parent of the second frameset (B).

Referring to a Frame

To refer to a frame, use the name of the frame or the frame array. The order in which frames appear in the HTML source code is the same order in which they appear in the array. To get from one frame to another document that contains more than one frame, your reference needs to start at the point in the hierarchy that includes both frames, which is the parent. Your reference also must include the actual frame.

 An *array* is a set of two or more values in a particular order that you can refer to as one item through an index. For example, you could have an array named beer that contains different types of domestic beers to which you assigned numbers. If Samuel Adams was 1 and Killian's was 2, you then could refer to them as beer[1], beer[2], and so on.

Referring to a Window and Its Elements

In addition to referring to frames, you can refer to a window and elements within that window. To successfully refer to the properties, event handlers, and methods of a window, you can only use certain keywords, such as in the following:

◆ The keywords *self* or *window*

◆ The top or parent keyword

◆ The name of the window stored in a variable

◆ Omission of the window name

In place of the window name, you can use the keywords *top* or *parent*, which also are synonymous. The parent keyword refers to a window that contains a frameset. The top keyword refers to the top-level Navigator window. To refer to the top frame in a window, for example, you could use the following:

```
parent.top.document.bgColor="black"
```

You also can refer to a window using the name of the window variable, which is the variable specified when you open a window, such as billsWindow.

When referring to a window as the target of a hypertext link or form submit, use the name of the window because the window you specify is the window into which the link or form is loaded, as in the following example:

```
<a href="newDocument.html" target="billsWindow">Load a document into window
named billsWindow</a>
```

To change the focal point, or focus, from one window to another, as you often will want to do, give focus to the window as the target of a hyperlink or to the object in a particular window.

Did you know...

Bringing focus to a window forces the window to become the active window. Focus also means that the active window will change visually in some way, such as the color of the title bar changing or the window superimposing other windows.

To give focus to another window using a hypertext link, for example, you would use the following code:

```
<a href="newDocument.html" target="billsWindow">Changes focus to a window named
billsWindow</a>
```

If billsWindow did not exist, it would be created.

You also can give focus to a window (or bring it forward) using the new focus method, which has the following syntax:

```
windowReference.focus()
```

The use of windowReference here is a valid way of referring to a window.

To remove focus from a window (or send it to the background), use the new blur method, as in the following sytax:

```
windowReference.blur()
```

The use of windowReference here is again a valid way of referring to a window.

Location and History Objects

As you learned earlier in this chapter, location objects contain properties about the current URL (uniform resource locator), such as the protocol part, hostname, pathname, and so on. Following are the string values that are properties for the location object:

hash contains the anchor name in the URL.

host contains the hostname and the port number from the URL.

hostname contains the domain name or numerical IP address from the URL. This is valid only when the document is on a remote server.

href contains the entire URL.

pathname specifies the path fragment of the URL.

port contains the port number from the URL. This is valid only when the document is on a remote server.

protocol indicates the type of protocol used from the URL, such as http, ftp, and gopher. This string contains the colon, but not the double forward slashes.

search contains the form elements compiled when a form is submitted. The form elements are placed after the path and preceded by the question mark (?).

History objects contain properties that represent the URLs the user visited previously. You can move backward in a history list using back() and move forward using forward(). You also can move around in a history list using go(*location*). The back() and forward() methods take on negative and positive numbers, depending on the direction and number of windows you want to move. For example, to move back one window, back() would take on the integer -1. go(*location*) enables you to go to the document you specify (location) within the history list. Like back() and forward(), location can be a positive or negative integer.

Note A history list is similar to an array in the C programming language.

Did you know...

You can only access one property in a history object: length. The value of length is the number of items in the history list.

document Objects

As stated earlier in this chapter, JavaScript objects mirror attributes of an HTML page's document element, such as the color of the active links, the background color of the document, and so on, as well as properties for every anchor, link, and form on a particular page.

document Object Attribute Properties

Using properties associated with the document object, you can modify or get information about attributes, such as color, in an HTML document. Because the BODY tag is where you define the main body of an HTML document, many attributes are reflected in this tag.

Did you know...

When the HTML page evaluates the BODY tag, the document object is defined; however, the object only remains in existence while the page is loaded.

Following are the document object properties you use to modify attributes when building an HTML document:

alinkColor enables you to specify the color of active links in RGB (red, blue, green) values as a string or hexadecimal triplet.

bgColor enables you to specify the color of the background of a document in RGB values.

fgColor enables you to specify the color of the foreground of a document in RGB values.

linkColor enables you to specify the color of links in RGB values as a string or hexadecimal triplet.

Did you know...

Because you cannot change the properties of a static closed document, the attribute properties are useful when building a document, but not when modifying a non-static document.

Because of several other attribute properties offered by the document object, you can get information about the title of the document, its location, and properties that were modified most recently. These properties are useful for keeping your document recent by enabling you to keep track of modification information for your document. To get modification information about your document object, use the following properties:

location is a string that contains the URL of the current document.

lastModified is a string value that contains the last date the document was modified.

title is a string that contains the title of the current document.

referrer is a string that contains the URL of the previous document whose link got you to the current document.

document Object Element Properties

The element properties of the document object enable you to get information for or modify locations and links to the HTML document, such as the number of anchors in a document or the order of hypertext links. Following are document object element properties you can use to modify or obtain information about elements in an HTML document:

anchors enables you to get or specify an array of anchor objects in the order in which they appear in the HTML document.

 To get the number of anchors in a document, you can use anchors.length in your JavaScript code. The advantage is that you find out the bounds of the anchor array. You can use the returned value as the upper limit in your *for* loop to ensure that you do not go outside the array.

images enables you to get the array that reflects all the images in a particular HTML document.

links enables you to get an array of link objects in the order the hypertext links appear in the HTML document.

 To get the number of links in a document, use links.length in your JavaScript code. The advantage is that you find out the bounds of the links array. You can use the returned value as the upper limit in your *for* loop to ensure that you do not go outside the array.

cookie is a string value that contains cookie values for the current document. For more information on cookie values, see Chapter 9, "Using Client and Server Scripts."

forms enables you to get an array of form objects in the order the forms appear in the HTML document.

Tip   To get the number of forms in a document, use forms.length in your JavaScript code. The advantage is that you find out the bounds of the forms array. You can use the returned value as the upper limit in your *for* loop to ensure that you do not go outside the array.

document Object Methods

The document object provides five methods to customize your HTML page:

◆ **clear**() method—clears the document window

◆ **close**() method—closes the current document window

◆ **open**() method—opens a stream that enables the write() and writeIn() methods to write to a document window. You also use the open() method to write MIME type text

◆ **write**() method—enables you to write HTML and text to a document you specify

◆ **writeI**() method—enables you to write HTML and text to a document you specify (the difference being that the document is followed by a newline character, which terminates the current output line)

Did you know...

MIME, which stands for Multi-purpose Internet Mail Extensions, enables you to exchange files of varying formats between computers.

document Object Event Handlers

A document object is associated with each window and has onLoad and onUnload event handlers that perform functions when a user loads or exits an HTML page. The load event onLoad occurs when a window or frames within a <FRAMESET> tag complete the load process. The load event onUnload takes place when a user exits a document. Be sure to place this tag in the <BODY> or <FRAMESET> tags.

form Objects

The form object is one you will use frequently in JavaScript. This object is an array constructed when you define a new form through HTML using the <FORM> </FORM> tag. The forms object is useful because you not only have all the information about the elements of the form, but you can modify those elements, unlike other objects discussed previously. Each time you define a form in a document, a form object also is created, so you have a form object for each form in your document. Because this object is an array, it's easy to reference all the elements of the object using the index. Following is the syntax for creating a form object:

```
<FORM
    NAME="formName"
    TARGET="windowName"
    ACTION="serverURL"
    METHOD=GET ¦ POST
    ENCTYPE="encodingType"
    [onSubmit="handlerText"]>
</FORM>
```

Did you know...

Open and close brackets ([ ]), as seen in the preceding code, indicate optional parameters. The optional parameters just used in creating a form object are [onSubmit="handlerText"].

The form object has several properties that enable you to reference and modify elements of a form. For information on these properties, continue with the following list:

action is a string that contains the value of the FORM tag's ACTION attribute. This property enables you to determine the action that was specified when the form was defined.

elements is an array that contains data for each element in the form. Elements consist of check boxes, radio buttons, drop-down lists, and so on.

encoding is a string that contains the MIME type used when the contents of the form were encoded prior to going to the server. This property provides encoding information and also enables you to set the encoding.

name is a string that contains the NAME attribute of the FORM tag; that is, this property provides to the programmer the name that was specified in the definition of the form.

target is a string that contains the name of the window into which you want the form information to load.

The form object provides one method, which is submit(); however, you also will need to take into account the methods provided by all the elements in the form object. The submit() method enables you to provide a way to imitate the action of a Submit button without actually using a Submit button in the form, as in the following example:

```
document.forms[1].submit()
```

Now that you have created a form object, you need to learn how to name a form, gain access to its information, and customize a form so it is easier to use and visually appealing.

Naming a Form

To name a form, use the NAME attribute of the FRAME tag as in the following example:

```
<FORM NAME="jillsForm" METHOD=post ACTION="http://www.newriders.com/sample">
   //Input elements like buttons, select lists, and radio-buttons go here
</FORM>
```

Code that uses named forms is easier to read than code that refers to forms by their array index values.

Gaining Access to Form Information

You have several methods available to gain access to form information. First, you can gain access to information through the index of the form array. This method is useful when you have several similar forms upon which you would want to perform the same processing. However, the downfall to this method is that it is not descriptive for someone else reading the code. To get information from several forms in a document, you can gain access to them in the order in which they appear in the document, as in the following:

```
for (i = 1; i < 5; i++) {
  alert(document.forms[i].name)
}
```

You also can gain access to information by referring to the form object name in the form tag attributes. This is advantageous in that it enables you to include descriptive names when attempting to gain access to properties or methods of forms. Look at the following example:

```
alert(document.jillsForm.name)
alert(document.billsForm.name)
```

Uploading File Elements in a Form

New in Navigator 3.0 is the upLoad object, which enables you to upload a file element on an HTML form, thus using the file you upload as input into an HTML form.

Following is the syntax:

```
fileUploadName.propertyName
```

You use the fileUploadName parameter to indicate the value of the NAME attribute of a fileUpload object.

The fileUpload object has two properties: Name and Value. Use Name to indicate the NAME attribute. Use value to indicate the current value of the element field of the file to upload, which concurs to the name of file you want to upload. Note that the value property is read-only.

Element Objects of a Form

As mentioned previously, forms contain several element objects that enable you to customize a form and make it easier to fill out. Radio buttons, check boxes, text fields, and passwords make your forms more user-friendly. The information entered by users into your forms is then passed to other programs on the server via CGI (Common Gateway Interface).

Jargon
[är-gən] CGI (Common Gateway Interface) is the interface used by servers to handle and interpret information passed on other programs on the server.

The elements of the form object discussed in the following sections contain properties and methods. JavaScript enables you to name and refer to each element of the form object in a script.

button Objects

The button element provides a trigger mechanism in your forms for doing everything from submitting a form to calling a JavaScript function. You specify a button element using the INPUT tag in which you include two properties—the name of the button and the value of the button—as in the following code:

```
<INPUT TYPE="button" NAME="myButton" VALUE="Push Me" onClick="myFunction()">
```

The preceeding example also includes an onClick event-handler, which is discussed throughout the remainder of this chapter.

The button element has a method associated with it, click(), which simulates a button being clicked. The click() method, however, does not call the onClick event, which is the event handler for the button element.

checkbox Objects

You can provide basic on/off toggle items in your forms using checkbox objects. On and off are equivalent to the Boolean True and False values. The following syntax is an example of the HTML code for the checkbox object:

```
<INPUT
    TYPE="checkbox"
    NAME="checkbox name"
    VALUE="checkbox value"
    [CHECKED]
    [onClick="JavaScript code"]>
```

The checkbox object contains several properties that enable you to better utilize this object. The checked property indicates whether the box is checked (True) or unchecked (False). The defaultChecked property enables you to specify whether the default of the check box is checked (True) or unchecked (False).

The name property indicates the name of the check box, which is equivalent to the NAME attribute in the HTML INPUT tag. The value property indicates the value and is equivalent to the VALUE attribute of the check HTML tag.

The click() method enables you to simulate the toggling of the check box to checked or unchecked. Each click toggles the box. This method, however, does not call the onClick action.

When a user clicks the check box, the onClick event handler is called and the JavaScript code is executed.

Hidden Text Objects

The hidden object is one object that the browser does not display. This element enables the programmer to hide information he or she does not want the user to see, yet does want passed on to the server, such as page access or a preference set in a previous form.

```
<INPUT TYPE="hidden" NAME="jillsHiddenInfo" VALUE="I do not want the user to
see this">
```

The hidden object contains two properties, both of which are string values: name and value. However, this object does not use any methods or event handlers.

Radio Buttons

Radio buttons usually come in a set, in which only one radio button can be activated at a time. For example, you can create a set of radio buttons in a form that enables users to specify their age groups, broken down in 18 to 29 years, 30 to 59 years, and 60 years and older. Obviously, a user will fall into only one category. You also can use radio buttons to offer several choices from which you want a user to choose only one. You can create a group of radio buttons by using a consistent name in all the INPUT tags, as in the following example:

```
<INPUT TYPE="radio" NAME="group1" VALUE="1" Checked > Ages 18 to 29<br>
<INPUT TYPE="radio" NAME="group1" VALUE="2"> Ages 38 to 59<br>
<INPUT TYPE="radio" NAME="group1" VALUE="3"> Ages 60 and over
```

You can reference each radio object or the group of radio objects by each name or as a group.

The radio object has several properties. The checked property contains a Boolean value for checked (True) or unchecked (False) buttons for each state of the property. The defaultChecked property indicates the default value of the element, which could be checked (True) or unchecked (False).

The index property indicates each button in a group and the length property indicates the number of radio buttons in a particular group.

The name property contains the name of the radio button and is the same as the name specified in the INPUT tag. The value property contains the current value of the radio object and is the same as the VALUE attribute of the INPUT HTML tag.

The click() method imitates a click in a radio button; however, it does not call the onClick event, which is the event handler for the radio button object. Using the click() method just toggles the state of the button to the opposite of what it was before the click.

Reset Buttons

In your HTML documents, use a reset button to clear all user entries and reload the form to its original state. The reset object, similar to the button object, has two properties, one method, and one event handler, as in the following code example:

```
<INPUT TYPE="reset" NAME="jillsResetButton" VALUE="Back to original settings"
onClick="MyFunction()">
```

The name property of the reset object is equal to the NAME property in the reset HTML tag. The value property is the same as the VALUE property in the reset HTML tag.

The click() method imitates a click in a reset button; however, it does not call the onClick event, which is the event handler for the reset button object.

Selection or Scrolling Lists

The select object enables you to define selections or scrolling lists that are available to the user. These lists enable users to select various options, such as items you might want to order. You can make several items available at the same time or restrict available options, enabling each option to contain its own properties and methods. Because of the versatility of this object, it is more complex. Following is the HTML code for the selector object:

```
<SELECT
    NAME="selectName"
    [SIZE="integer"]
    [MULTIPLE]
    [onBlur="handlerText"]
    [onChange="handlerText"]
    [onFocus="handlerText"]>
    <OPTION VALUE="optionValue" [SELECTED]> textToDisplay [ ... <OPTION>
textToDisplay]
</SELECT>
```

The select object has properties that enable you to customize your lists. The MULTIPLE property enables you to indicate the number of options available on a list. For example, you can specify that on a list of five options, four of those five are available to the user at the same time. The SIZE property enables you to indicate the number of items that are visible at one time.

The length property of the select object is the same as the SIZE property of the HTML tag. The name property is the same as the NAME property of the HTML tag.

The options property is an array of the available options from which a user can choose. This array actually is an array of objects that have their own properties. The defaultSelected property, which is Boolean, indicates whether an option is selected or unselected automatically when it appears. The index property specifies in the list the location of the current option. The selected property indicates whether the current object is selected. The text property contains the visible text for each option. The value property contains the data that is sent to the server when the user clicks the submit button.

The selectIndex property of the select object indicates the item selected in a list.

Did you know...

Changing the selectIndex property when the HTML MULTIPLE property is set causes all other selections to clear because the index only refers to a single option.

The select object has no available methods; however, four event handlers exist: onBlur, onChange, onFocus, and onSelect. The onBlur event handler is invoked when the specified select element loses focus, usually when the user completes the selection and clicks another element. The onChange event handler is invoked when a value of an item on a list changes states, such as from being the center of focus to receding in the background. The onFocus event handler is invoked when the user clicks a select object, thus making the list the focal point. The onSelect event handler is invoked when a user selects an option in a list.

submit Objects

The submit object is similar to the reset button; however, activating this object sends each field of the form to a URL. The URL that receives the information is the one specified in the HTML FORM tag. Following is the code for the submit object:

```
<INPUT
    TYPE="submit"
    NAME="submitName"
    VALUE="buttonText"
    [onClick="handlerText"]>
```

TYPE indicates the TYPE attribute. This attribute is dependent on the HTML element with which you are working. For this discussion, the TYPE is submit, reflecting the submit object. The name property of the submit object is equal to the NAME property in the submit HTML tag. The value property is the same as the VALUE property in the submit HTML tag.

The click() method imitates a click in a submit button; however, it does not call the onClick event, which is the event handler for the reset button object.

text Objects

The text object is one of the most used and most common entry fields in HTML forms. This object enables users to input short character sequences, such as words, sentences, or numbers that the user sees on-screen. You define a text object in an HTML document as follows:

```
<INPUT TYPE="text" NAME="textName" VALUE="" SIZE=10 onChange="myFunction">
```

The text object uses three properties and three methods. The defaultValue property contains the default value string for the text object. The name property is the same as the NAME property of the text HTML tag. The value property is the same as the VALUE property of the text HTML tag.

The focus() method moves the input focus to the text field to which the user is responding. The blur() method has the opposite effect of the focus() method and moves the focus away from the text field. The select() method highlights the text in the text field.

The text object also uses several event handlers. The onBlur event handler is invoked when the specified text element loses focus (or blurs), usually when the user completes the selection and clicks another element. The onChange event handler is invoked when the value of the text object changes, usually when a user modifies input in a text field or when the user leaves the particular field.

The onFocus event handler is invoked when the user clicks a text object, thus making the text object the focal point. The onSelect event handler is invoked when a user highlights text in a field.

textarea Objects

The textarea object is a form element that you can only define within a <FORM> tag. This object is similar to the text object in that it enables the user to enter text. The difference, however, is that textarea objects enable the user to enter longer character sequences (more than one line), such as comments and messages. You define the textarea object in the HTML document as follows:

```
<TEXTAREA
    TYPE="objectname.type"
    NAME="textareaName"
    ROWS="integer"
    COLS="integer"
    WRAP="off¦virtual¦physical"
    [onBlur="handlerText"]
    [onChange="handlerText"]
```

```
      [onFocus="handlerText"]
      [onSelect="handlerText"]>
      textToDisplay
</TEXTAREA>
```

The textarea object uses the same properties, methods, and event handlers as does the text object, enables you to specify the name of the textarea object. The default Value property contains the default value string for the textarea object. The name property is the same as the NAME property of the textarea HTML tag. The value property is the same as the VALUE property of the textarea HTML tag. You use ROWS="integer" and COLS="integer" to define the physical size, in numbers and characters, of the input field that appears on-screen. Use the textToDisplay parameter to indicate the initial value of the textarea object.

The focus() method moves the input focus to the textarea field to which the user is responding. The blur() method is the opposite of the focus() method and moves the focus away from the textarea field. The select() method highlights the text in the textarea field.

The textarea object also uses several event handlers. The onBlur event handler is invoked when the specified textarea object loses focus (or blurs), usually when the user completes the selection and clicks another element. The onChange event handler is invoked when the value of the textarea object changes, usually when a user modifies input in a textarea field or when the user leaves the particular field.

The onFocus event handler is invoked when the user clicks a textarea object, thus making the textarea object the focal point. The onSelect event handler is invoked when a user highlights text in a field.

Using JavaScript to Verify User Input in Forms

When using forms in which users input information, it is a good practice to have checks and balances that ensure that the information entered is valid before it is sent to the server. These checks and balances relieve the server of extra work it does not need to do. JavaScript enables you to insert scripts in your HTML document that do the checking for you.

In the following example, you are required to type more than two characters into the textbox. If you do not type more than two characters, an alert box, shown in figure 5.9, warns you that what you typed was incorrect.

```
<HTML>
<HEAD><TITLE>Validation Example</TITLE>
```

```
<SCRIPT LANGUAGE="JavaScript">
<!--
function ValidateInput() {
  //Checks to make sure the name is more than two characters long
  if (document.myForm.clientName.value.length < 3) {
    alert("This does not appear to be a valid name")
  }
  else {
    document.myForm.submit() //simulate a form submit
  }
}
//-->
</SCRIPT>
</HEAD>
<BODY>
<FORM NAME="myForm" >
Please enter your name below:<p>
Name:<INPUT TYPE="text" Name="clientName" VALUE="" SIZE=24><p>
<INPUT TYPE="button" NAME="Button1" VALUE="Process Name"
OnClick="ValidateInput()">
</FORM>
</BODY>
</HTML>
```

Figure 5.9

*Validating user
input.*

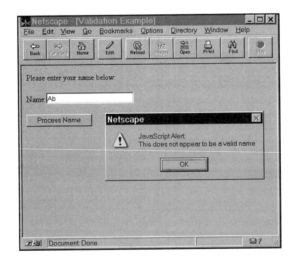

Summary

In this chapter, you have learned a great deal about how Netscape Navigator objects work and how to use them. You have learned about the object hierarchy, how to use the window and frame objects, the importance of location and history objects, and the numerous ways you can use form objects and their properties to create useful forms that are easy to use.

Chapter 6, "Netscape LiveWire Objects," takes you on a guided tour of LiveWire built-in objects on the server side, their properties, and how best to use them with JavaScript and LiveWire.

Netscape LiveWire Objects

I n Chapter 5, "Netscape Navigator Objects," you learned about built-in Netscape Navigator objects such as *document* and *window*. Those objects offer assistance in writing client-side JavaScripts. This chapter discusses the built-in objects on the server-side, which are exposed by Netscape's LiveWire or LiveWire Pro development environments. The following four objects are collectively referred to as the *LiveWire object framework*:

◆ request—Contains data specific to the current client request. When a user fills out a form and then clicks the submit button, the page that is posted contains request objects that include the data filled in by the user.

◆ client—Contains any data required by the application. This is normally user-specific data that is stored during the period of time that the person is browsing your Web site. The person's name is an example of one data item that may be saved in a client object.

◆ project—Contains global information (information available to everyone). Perhaps you want to save a counter that records how many times your Web page has been accessed. This information can be stored in a project object.

◆ server—Contains global data for the total server and makes information available among all applications running on the server. Suppose you want to store a counter that records how many times all of your Web pages have been accessed. This information also could be stored in a server object.

The Main Advantage

One of the major features of the server-side objects is that they give you an easy way on your Web server to retain important program information gathered during separate runs of the program. This retaining of information is referred to as *persistence functionality*, with which the server can take advantage of information gathered from a previous request (persistence). Without the persistence functionality, the Web server is considered *stateless*, and each request behaves the exact same way regardless of all previous circumstances.

With *persistence functionality*, the server can take advantage of information gathered from a previous request.

A *stateless server* treats each request as an independent transaction unrelated to any previous request.

Why would you want persistence? Suppose that you want to store the products a client bought from your Web site into a data object. Thanks to persistence, the client can visit your Web site, jump around to other Web sites, and then return to your site without losing the goods in her data object (or "shopping cart"). Hey, this is even better than a mall!

> **Did you know...**
>
> A data object for storing goods a consumer is ready to purchase is often referred to as a "shopping cart."

In real life, you have certain things you want to remember for a long time. Other things you want to remember for only a short time. For example, you would probably put the memory of where you last parked your car into short-term memory. You would want to store your social security number, on the other hand, in long-term memory. LiveWire objects work similarly—you want some objects to be short-lived and other objects to be long-lived.

The request object, for example, is the shortest-lived object in the framework because it contains data specific to the current client request. Each time a new client request object rolls around, the previous request object is obsolete (similar to the current spot in which your car is parked).

The client object, conversely, is longer-lived—it stores information about each client who accesses your application so that the same client object is returned each time that particular person gains access. In this example, you can see how information in the client object would be stored for a much longer period of time, just as you would store an often-used phone number in your memory.

Using LiveWire Objects

LiveWire objects are not global in scope. This means that if you have a function that needs to access a property of a LiveWire object, a simple reference to that object with statements like the following does not work:

```
function myFunction() {
 write(client.myProperty)  //does not work
}
```

Instead, you need to pass the object as a parameter to the function, as in the following code:

```
function myFunction(myClientProperty) {
 write(myClientProperty)  //does work
}
```

Suppose that you want to write a function that accepts the entries of a client's Bingo card and then evaluates whether that client's Bingo card is a winner. You most likely would store the Bingo entries in a client object. Because objects are not directly accessible by functions, each entry needs to be passed as a parameter to your function. The call to this function would look similar to the following:

```
client.winnerStatus =
isBingoCardWinner(client.row1Column1,client.row1Column2,client.row1Column3,...)
```

Furthermore, always store the properties of objects as string data types. To store logical values, for example, you need to create scripts that convert the corresponding values. In the preceding example, the isBingoCardWinner function should return a value that is the string "true" rather than the boolean data type True value.

Did you know...

A string value type contains characters, such as alphanumeric characters. A boolean data type is either True or False.

The following is correct:

```
return "true"
```

This is incorrect:

```
return true
```

The following exercises show you how to write scripts that can convert values by using the parseInt and parseFloat functions. For more information about parseInt and parseFloat functions, refer to Chapter 3, "JavaScript Language Fundamentals."

Manipulating Int and Float Values

1. Suppose that you have a JavaScript containing a client property that stores a value for the number of times a client has won Bingo (client.numWins). Now suppose that a client property in this JavaScript stores the cash value for a Bingo win (client.cashVal).

2. You need a function that returns the total Bingo winnings for this client. Recalling that a function cannot directly access an object's properties, the call to your function would look like the following:

```
totalWinningsVal = getTotalWinnings(client.numWins,client.cashVal)
```

The first parameter, client.numWins, stores the number of times the client has won. The second parameter, client.cashVal, stores the cash value received by a client for each Bingo win.

3. Remembering that both parameters store a string representation of the value of their contents, you must use the built-in parseInt and parseFloat JavaScript functions to convert the string representation into an Int and Float representation, thus making the function more suitable for numeric computations. Following is an example.

```
function getTotalWinnings(numberOfWins,cashValue) {
  var totalValue=0
  totalValue=parseInt(numberOfWins)*parseFloat(cashValue)

  return totalValue

}
```

Manipulating Boolean Values

It's easy to create a Boolean client property with the following:

```
client.winnerStatus = true
```

Which of the following methods demonstrates the correct method for checking the winnerStatus property?

Method 1:

```
if (client.winnerStatus == "true")
       write("We have a winner!")
else
       write("We do not have a winner!")
```

Method 2:

```
if (client.winnerStatus == true)
       write("We have a winner!")
else
       write("We do not have a winner!")
```

Method 1 is correct because it uses a string comparison to compare the value for client.WinnerStatus with "true." Method 2 uses a Boolean comparison, which does not work because the client.winnerStatus value is stored as a string, not a Boolean.

request Objects

The request object, the shortest-lived object in the framework, contains data specific to the current client request. The request object is only alive for the duration of the server's response to a request from the client (typically one second). Each time a new client request object rolls around, the previous request object becomes obsolete.

The following client items result in the creation of a request object:

◆ Links accessed by a user

◆ A user-requested URL (typed or bookmarked)

◆ Page navigation using the history method or the property document.location (JavaScript) set by the client

◆ Redirect function (JavaScript) performed by the server

request Object Properties

The request object has six properties. You use these properties to access information about client software, client IP addresses, HTTP methods affiliated with the particular request, and software-supported protocol:

◆ agent—enables you to get the name and version of the client software

◆ ip—enables you to get the IP address of the client. You can use this function to authorize or record access to the client

◆ method—enables you to determine the HTTP method that is associated with the request

◆ protocol—provides information about the HTTP protocol level that is supported by the software of the client

agent

The agent property provides the name and version of the client software, which you use to engage advanced features of particular browsers. A real-life example of the use of this property is to determine whether the client's browser supports Java. If it does, it displays in the browser a Java applet-enabled page. If not, it displays in the browser a default page that does not contain Java applets.

ip

The ip property enables you to access the IP address of the client. Using the ip property is a good way to keep track of client access to a site or even to authorize access to a site. Following is an example of code:

```
if (request.ip == "222.237.216.34")
  authorizationGranted()
else
  authorizationNotGranted()
```

method

The method property enables you to determine the HTTP method that is associated with the request. Applications use this information to ascertain the correct response to a request. HTTP 1.0, for example, responds with any one of its three methods: GET, POST, or HEAD.

Did you know...

GET refers to an HTTP method that retrieves whatever data is identified by the URL; so when the URL refers to a data-producing process (or a script that can be run by such a process), GET returns the data produced, not the source text of the script or process.

HEAD is an HTTP method that retrieves only HTTP headers from data identified by an URL.

POST creates a new object that the server links to the specified object. The client or server sets the message identification field of the new object; the server assigns an URL to the new object and sends the URL to the client. The new document becomes the data part of the request. This document is subordinate to the object specified in the request, just like a news article is subordinate to a newsgroup to which the article is posted.

protocol

The protocol property provides information about the HTTP protocol level that is supported by the software of the client. For example, you can use this information to check whether the client browser supports the latest high performance HTTP-NG (Next Generation) protocol.

Did you know...

Top-level variables that you declare in server JavaScript have the same lifetime as request properties, which are short-lived.

imageX

The imageX property represents the horizontal position of the mouse cursor when a client user clicks over an image map.

imageY

The imageY property represents the vertical position of the mouse cursor when a client user clicks over an image map.

Employing form Elements

All HTML forms contain form elements. Form elements enable you to create request properties; they can be anything from a check box to a radio button. Form elements enable you to specify particular actions, depending on how the user fills out the form (fills in the form elements). Each input element in an HTML form has a corresponding request object property that is made available to LiveWire applications. The name of the *request* object property is specified by the NAME attribute of the form element. Figure 6.1 shows a typical form.

Figure 6.1

A form including a text element and a submit element.

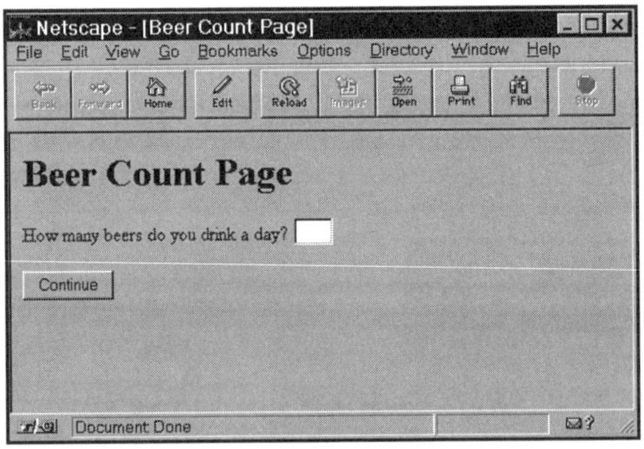

Following is the code for figure 6.1:

```
<HTML>
<Head><TITLE>Beer Count Page</TITLE></HEAD>
<H1>Beer Count Page</H1>
<BODY>
<FORM METHOD="post" ACTION="beers.html">
<P>
How many beers do you drink a day?
<INPUT TYPE="text" NAME="beerCount" SIZE="3">
<P>
<INPUT TYPE=SUBMIT VALUE="Continue">
</FORM>
</BODY>
</HTML>
```

After a user completes this form, he or she clicks on the Continue button. This action causes the client to post a query to the server requesting the "beers.html" URL. Assuming that "beers.html" is a LiveWire application, when this request is made, the text element property is created for the "beers.html" *request* object. Because the text element has a NAME attribute of beerCount, the corresponding property that is created is called request.beerCount.

 LiveWire applications do not support file upload. In other words, you cannot submit an INPUT element of TYPE="file" to a LiveWire application.

Manually Encoding Request Properties in an URL

You also can manually encode request properties into URLs by using the following syntax:

```
URL?varName=value[&varName=value...]
```

In that syntax, *URL* is the LiveWire application's URL, *varName* is a variable name, and *value* is the name of a variable. To implement this feature, first follow the LiveWire application URL with a question mark (?), and then follow the question mark with pairs of variable names and their values. Each variable pair is separated by an ampersand (&). This means that for each *varName*, a corresponding request property is created that contains the given *value*.

For example, the following code illustrates how you can use HTML to define a hyperlink to your "beers.html" page, a hyperlink that creates the request property *beerCount* and initiates its value to 3. The LiveWire application associated with "beers.html" can then reference the beerCount variable as request.beerCount.

```
<A HREF="beers.html?beerCount=3">I drink three beers a day</A>
```

The problem with this example is that the value for *beerCount* is hard-coded. There is no user interaction that enables the client to choose the number of beers he or she drinks a day. Instead of using static HTML tags, a more practical application of manually encoding request properties is to use client-side JavaScript to dynamically compose the URL address:

```
<HTML>
<HEAD>
<TITLE>Beer Count Page</TITLE>

<SCRIPT LANGUAGE="JavaScript">
<!--
function processInput(myBeerCount) {
location.href="beers.html?beerCount=" + myBeerCount
}
//-->
</SCRIPT>
</HEAD>
<H1>Beer Count Page</H1>
<BODY>
<FORM NAME="beerForm">
<P>
How many beers do you drink a day?
<INPUT TYPE="text" NAME="beerCount" SIZE="3">
<P>
<INPUT TYPE="button" VALUE="Continue"
OnClick="processInput(beerForm.beerCount.value)">
</FORM>
</BODY>
</HTML>
```

The behavior of this example should be similar to the previous example that used a submit form element. What makes client-side JavaScript powerful is its capability to validate user input.

Now add some validation that bars the user from typing in non-numeric values. Following is the previous example, along with added validation that checks for non-numeric values, as shown in figure 6.2. Please note that the bolded code in the following is bold only to demonstrate what is different from the code in the previous example.

```
<HTML>
<HEAD>
<TITLE>Beer Count Page</TITLE>

<SCRIPT LANGUAGE="JavaScript">
<!--
function processInput(myBeerCount) {
  if (((parseFloat(myBeerCount))==0)
      && (myBeerCount != "0") ) {
    alert("Please use a numeric value.")
  } else {
     location.href="beers.html?beerCount=" + myBeerCount
  }
}
//-->
</SCRIPT>
</HEAD>
<H1>Beer Count Page</H1>
<BODY>
<FORM NAME="beerForm">
<P>
How many beers do you drink a day?
<INPUT TYPE="text" NAME="beerCount" SIZE="3">
<P>
<INPUT TYPE="button" VALUE="Continue"
OnClick="processInput(beerForm.beerCount.value)">
</FORM>
</BODY>
</HTML>
```

You can use the built-in JavaScript function *parseFloat()* to verify that the user entered a numeric value. The *parseFloat* function returns 0 if the argument passed to it was not numeric, ensuring that users filling out the form do not enter 0 as the number of beers they drink a day.

Validating user input on the client-side rather than the server-side is a favorable practice because it lessens the amount of work your server has to do.

Figure 6.2

A form that validates user input.

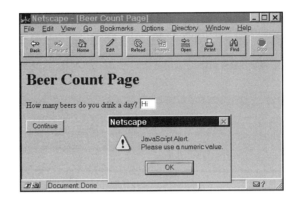

Employing Image Maps

The HTML image(<IMG>) tag comes with an ISMAP attribute indicating that the image is a server-based image map. Whenever a user clicks the mouse on a server-based image map, the horizontal and vertical positions of the pointer are returned to the server and stored in the created imageX and imageY request properties. Look at the following example:

```
<A HREF="myImage.html"> <IMG SRC="myImage.gif" ISMAP ></A>
```

The LiveWire application associated with myImage.html will have the properties request.imageX and request.imageY. These properties will contain values based on the location on the image where the user clicked.

client Objects

Imagine a thousand users connected to a Bingo Web site (yes, Bingo). Each user is looking at an HTML page that displays his or her unique Bingo card (see fig. 6.3). To provide a unique Bingo card to each user, use JavaScript's client object.

Client objects enable many clients (users) to access a single application simultaneously, and they provide a technique that enables an application to individually track multiple client actions. In the Bingo card scenario, when a client connects to the LiveWire Bingo application, a client object is created that contains this person's unique Bingo card information. Each time a new user (client) accesses the LiveWire Bingo card application, LiveWire also creates a new client object for that user, an object that contains his or her Bingo card information. The information for each person's Bingo card is kept seperate from those of other users that may be playing Bingo.

Figure 6.3

A Bingo card created using JavaScript's client object.

Each time the client returns to the application, the server provides the original client object containing Bingo card information for that client. So a user could feasibly play some Bingo, get distracted and surf to another Web site, and then come back to the Bingo Web site with his or her Bingo card information still intact. Because there is no set limit to the number of clients assigned objects, it is possible for thousands of Bingo players with their own client objects to be active simultaneously. As you can see, without client objects, tracking users is much more difficult.

client Object User-Defined Property Values

Because LiveWire uses the client object to contain any data required by the application, it has no predefined property values; however, you can use JavaScript statements to assign the client object values specific to the client object. These property values are referred to as *user-defined property values.* If a client object does not contain a property value, however, LiveWire does not save that particular client object; thus, it reduces the number of active client objects.

User-defined property values are those to which you assign property values specific to a client object.

The following example shows you how to assign an application-specific value to a client object:

```
client.bColumnRow1Value="12"
client.bColumnRow1MarkerStatus="Yes"
```

The first line stores the number 15, which can be displayed in the top left cell of this user's bingo card; to the user, it is B-12. The second line stores the status of whether the user has placed a marker on B-12 yet; in this case, the player has.

Life Expectancy of client Objects

After a client accesses an application, there is no way to gauge or guarantee that the particular client accesses the application again. To prevent a backlog of ancient or unused client objects, LiveWire has included an "expiration" mechanism that puts to pasture old, unused client objects.

Client objects in LiveWire are maintained either by the server or by the client, depending on if you are accessing the object from your machine or directly from the server. Client objects stored by client software expire and go to the great beyond when the user exits the client software. Client objects maintained by the server, however, have longer lives—they do not expire until the client object has been inactive for 10 minutes.

What happens when you want the client object to stay active longer than 10 minutes? LiveWire enables you to change the expiration of a client object by using the expiration method, as in the following example:

```
client.expiration(6000) //expires after 6000 seconds or 100 minutes
```

Use the seconds variable to indicate the amount of time you want to elapse before the client object expires.

Destroying a client Object

You also can destroy a client object, thus forcing an expiration before the previously set lifetime. The destroy() method is called by the application, and LiveWire removes the properties from the client object and destroys the client object that sent the request. Use the destroy method in the following manner:

```
client.destroy()
```

Destroying a client object is normally not necessary; however, it may be useful in circumstances when you are tuning your system and need to cut down on physical memory used by your Web application.

Maintaining client Objects

LiveWire provides several techniques that enable you to maintain a client object. You can maintain a client object either on the client side or the server side by using an addressing scheme. To maintain client property values with client-sided techniques, use either URL encoding or *cookies*. To maintain client property values with server-side techniques, use IP addresses, server cookies, or server URL encoding.

 Cookies are general mechanisms that server-side connections can use to both store and retrieve information on the client side of the connection.

Client-Side Techniques

Using cookies is best when dealing with high-volume consumer applications, enabling you to store small amounts of customer data on the client's system. For a Web site that has potentially hundreds of thousands of clients, it makes sense to store customer data on the customer's system rather than take up precious resources on the server system.

The cookie technique works only with clients that support Netscape cookie protocol. In addition, there is a limitation in the number of properties that can be stored on a client system. This limitation would make it difficult to store all the properties of a user's Bingo card in a cookie. Cookies could be used, however, for storing the Bingo player's name and personal information.

One advantage of using client-side cookies is that if the server is restarted, the cookie information will still be preserved on the client's system. So in the case of storing personal information in a client cookie, if the server is restarted, the Bingo player loses the Bingo card information; however, his or her personal information is preserved, thus saving key strokes. Encode each client object property in the cookie file in the following manner:

```
NETSCAPE_LIVEWIRE.propName=propValue;
```

The *propName* variable indicates the name of the property, and *propValue* indicates the value of the property. For a bingo Web application, you might have a statement like the following:

```
NETSCAPE_LIVEWIRE.userLastName="Farkle";
```

 A cookie file can store only 20 property files per directory and only 4,096 characters per directory entry. The cookie file then is shared by every page in a directory.

For the client URL-encoding technique, the server transfers all object information to the client as name/value pairs that are added to the URLs that reference other parts of the application. Note, however, that using this scheme demands that all URLs are generated by the server. For pages that reference multiple URLs, object information needs to be conveyed numerous times.

 Tip To generate URLs dynamically when using client URL encoding, use the writeURL function, as in the following:

```
<A HREF="<SERVER>writeURL(project.newPage)</SERVER>">
```

Did you know...

Properties of client objects are encoded into the response of the server to a client request in the HEAD of the document (client cookies) or server-generated URLs (client URL encoding); thus, you cannot change client object properties after performing a flush. LiveWire carries out an automatic flush after it generates 64 K of data.

Server-Side Techniques

Server-side techniques enable you to maintain client objects with addressing schemes. You can use IP addresses, server cookies, or server URL encoding.

The IP address technique takes advantage of a data structure on the server that is based on the IP address of the client. This is a great technique when you have internal applications that run on a single server where all clients have fixed IP addresses; however, this technique may lead you into trouble because it does not support dynamic IP access providers, multiuser systems, or users behind proxy servers.

Another server-side technique is the server cookie technique, which uses a data structure on the server that is based on a generated name. The name is generated when a client first accesses the application, and then the name is stored in the cookie file. The name is then returned upon ensuing requests. This technique, however, also offers up the same stumbling blocks as does the IP address technique—it does not support dynamic IP access providers, multiuser systems, or users behind proxy servers. For this reason, neither the server cookie nor IP address technique is suitable for wide-scale Internet applications like the Bingo example used in this chapter. Instead, these techniques hold more promise for internal intranet applications.

The server URL encoding technique offers more flexibility. It works with all browsers and contributes little to network traffic; however, it requires LiveWire to dynamically generate all URLs used in the application. This technique uses a data structure based on a generated name. The server then adds the generated name to all URLs that reference the application.

project Objects

Returning to the Bingo game, you need a way to share with all Bingo players the Bingo entries that have been called out (refer to fig. 6.3). For the game to work, the entries need to be available to all players. You can do this using the LiveWire project object.

The project object contains global information, or stored information available to everyone. This object offers a method that enables you to share information among the clients accessing the application. Each time an application is started, LiveWire creates a single new project object to which all clients have access. When the application is stopped, LiveWire automatically destroys that particular project object. Depending on the length of the Bingo game (or the necessary running time of the application), the lifetime of a project object can be days or even weeks.

Did you know...

For each Netscape HTTPD process that runs on the server, LiveWire creates a set of project objects. Suppose that you have a Bingo game running on port 80 of one server and another Bingo game running on port 142 of another server. Because there are two servers, you would have two separate Bingo project objects that are members of two separate sets of server project objects.

Each Bingo game would be one of the project objects that make up the set of project objects for a server. Other LiveWire applications also could be project objects that are part of the project object set. These other LiveWire applications could be other games, such as chess or backgammon.

---

project Object Properties

Because LiveWire uses the project object to contain data that is specific to the application and available to multiple clients, it has no predefined property values.

project Object Locking

With so many users accessing project objects, how do you ensure that clients do not simultaneously change project object properties?

Suppose that a person were to claim "Bingo." When a player claims "Bingo," a project object property is set that holds the value of that person who won. Now suppose that after the player claims "Bingo," he or she waits for a reply from the server; yet, before the reply takes place, someone else claims "Bingo" and causes that project object property to be reset to his or her name. Is that fair? Of course it's not, but by using LiveWire's locking feature, you may lock the project object, preventing other users from modifying the project object until it is unlocked.

 LiveWire does provide a built-in automatic locking method that prevents user access during the brief time the application is reading or setting the value. However, this implicit locking is extremely short-lived and is not sufficient for instances in which the application is going to read and assign a new value to a property.

Use the lock method to lock the project object, and then use the unlock method to make the object available again. To lock and unlock a project object while the application is modifying the property, use the following example:

```
project.lock()
        project.winner_id = client.user_id
project.unlock()
```

Here the project object property *winner_id* is set to the client object property *user_id*. The *user_id* property is specific to the client playing the game, and the *winner_id* is shared among all the players and needs to be protected for the reasons mentioned earlier.

 To prevent an accidental deadlock, LiveWire automatically unlocks the project object after the completion of each client request.

server Objects

Server objects are different from client and project objects—they are specific to servers and applications. A server object holds global data for the total server, makes information available among all applications running on the server, and is initialized automatically.

When the server is started, LiveWire creates a new server object that is active until the server is stopped, at which time the server object is destroyed. In addition, each application that runs on the server also shares the same server object.

In addition to the automatically initialized properties that are created with each server object, you can create properties of your own to store data to be shared among multiple applications. In the Bingo game, the variable that makes up the field in figure 6.3, which specifies the winnings "given away to date," would make a good case for being stored in a server object. Those winnings could be attributed to games outside of Bingo, such as chess or backgammon.

Did you know...

Just like with project objects, if more than one server is running on a system, more than one server object is created on the system.

server Object Properties

The server object has the following four properties:

◆ hostname—indicates the full hostname of the server, including the port number

◆ host—indicates the server name, subdomain, and domain name

◆ protocol—indicates the communications protocol used

◆ port—indicates the server port number used; the default for HTTP is 80

Use the hostname property to indicate the complete hostname of the server, including the port number, as in the following example:

```
server.hostname = "www.newrider.com:80"
```

Use the host property to indicate the name of the server, its subdomain, and the domain, as in the following:

```
server.host = "www.newriders.com"
```

The protocol property indicates the name of the communications protocol currently being used, such as HTTP. The port property indicates the port number currently being used. You can use the following; however, the default for HTTP is 80:

```
server.protocol="145"
```

Note You also can use the lock and unlock methods on server objects to prevent users or applications from changing server properties simultaneously. When a server object is locked, other applications cannot get or set server object properties until that server object is unlocked.

Summary

In this chapter, you learned about LiveWire's built-in objects on the server side: request, client, project, and server. You also learned about their properties and techniques for maintaining these objects.

Chapter 7, "Introduction to LiveWire, LiveConnect, and LivePayment," introduces you to LiveWire's Site Manager and Compiler, JavaScript and Java communication in LiveConnect, and using JavaScript and LivePayment for Internet commerce.

CHAPTER 7

Introduction to LiveWire, LiveConnect, and LivePayment

L iveWire is a technology that enables server-side JavaScript scripts to communicate with the server, with libraries written in C located on the server, and databases.

When developing desktop applications, it is a common practice to use software tools called *integrated development environments* (IDE). IDEs, such as Microsoft's Visual C++, are the "Swiss Army knives" of programming tools—they give you a standard set of development tools that are tightly integrated. Instead of using separate programs for compiling, linking, debugging, and editing code, IDEs give you a single, tightly integrated toolset that does it all. When you build Internet applications, you can use a development tool that is similar in nature to an IDE. This tool is the *LiveWire development environment*, which enables developers to create, modify, and maintain online sites and applications using a drag-and-drop and point-and-click environment.

LiveConnect is technology that enables JavaScript scripts to communicate with the Netscape client (Navigator) and plug-ins along with Java programs.

Although both are Internet technologies that enable components to communicate, LiveWire is server-side and LiveConnect is client-side.

An IDE, or *integrated development environment*, is a system for supporting the process of writing software. Such a system can include a language-sensitive editor, a project management tool, and integrated support for compiling, linking, debugging, and running the software.

Compiling is the act of converting a program from some source language (or programming language) to a destination machine language (object code) that can be interpreted by the computer. In JavaScript, this machine language is called *bytecode*. Bytecode is unique from most machine languages in that it is microprocessor-independent.

Linking is the act of gathering the object code files of one or more separately compiled program module, and binding them into a complete executable program, resolving references from one module to another.

Looking at LiveWire Basics

LiveWire is an online development environment for Web site management and client-server application development. LiveWire includes Navigator Gold, LiveWire Site Manager, and LiveWire JavaScript Compiler. LiveWire also includes the Database Connectivity Library, which enables you to get direct SQL connectivity to relational databases from Informix, Oracle, and Sybase. The Connectivity Library also provides ODBC connectivity for additional databases.

For building server-based applications, LiveWire uses JavaScript, which is an open, cross-platform object scripting language that makes it easy to develop online applications for intranets and the Internet. LiveWire compiles the HTML code into bytecodes that are platform-independent, and also parses and compiles server-side JavaScript statements. At run-time, the Netscape server translates the compiled bytecodes into HTML statements and then transmits them to the client across the network. The client Web browser then translates the client JavaScript code and renders a standard HTML page layout. By employing LiveWire, you can use server scripts to maintain data shared among applications or clients, maintain information during client access, access a database and server files, call server C libraries, and customize Java applets.

For building client-based applications, LiveWire uses JavaScript to enable you to display error or information boxes, validate user input, display confirmation boxes, process server data such as aggregate calculations, add simple programable logic to HTML, and perform functions that do not require information from the server.

LiveWire applications have functionality that is similar to CGI programs; however, LiveWire applications are better integrated with the HTML pages that host them than their CGI programs counterparts are.

When working with CGI forms, clicking on the Submit button prompts CGI to start the program and provides a command line that includes the values in the form. LiveWire not only provides the values—it can actually access the properties and modify them, thus enabling a Web programmer to add more interaction between the program and the user.

Consider a form in which you provide clothing with size information. At the beginning of the form are radio buttons in which you indicate whether you are male or female. Depending on whether you select the male button or female button, LiveWire displays sizes for men or women on the form. Because it can dynamically change the select list, depending on which radio button you click, LiveWire is considered to be event-driven; CGI can offer options but cannot dynamically adapt to the user's input.

Did you know...

CGI, or Common Gateway Interface, is a standard used for running external programs under a WWW HTTP server. External programs are referred to as gateways in that they provide an interface between an external source of information and the server.

The following three major components make up LiveWire:

◆ Site Manager and LiveWire Compiler

◆ The LiveWire server extension

◆ Netscape Navigator Gold

LiveWire Pro adds two additional development components to its development environment—a SQL database and the report generator Crystal Reports. With LiveWire, you can still access databases, but you must purchase them first. LiveWire Pro actually provides the database for you.

 SQL (pronounced "sequel"), stands for Structured Query Language. SQL is an ISO and ANSI standard language that provides a user interface to relational database management systems. It often is embedded in other programming languages.

As stated in Chapter 2, "Presenting JavaScript," LiveWire applications can be hosted only on computers that use Netscape servers.

What LiveWire Can Do

At first glance, the LiveWire development environment seems to be more oriented toward managing Web sites than developing Web applications. The look and feel of the LiveWire's Site Manager program is very similar to that of many Web site management tools, such as Microsoft Frontpage or Adobe Pagemill. In addition, the name "Site Manager" implies that this tool is a Web site manager rather than an Internet application builder. The truth is, LiveWire is both a Web site manager and an Internet application-builder that can run on Unix, Windows NT, and Macintosh systems.

Figure 7.1 shows LiveWire's Site Manager in action.

 Although a Macintosh version of LiveWire is available, a Netscape server for Mac OS does not exist; hence, you cannot run LiveWire applications on the Mac. You can, however, use the LiveWire compiler to create applications on a Mac that you can run on another platform using a Netscape server.

Figure 7.1

LiveWire's Site Manager.

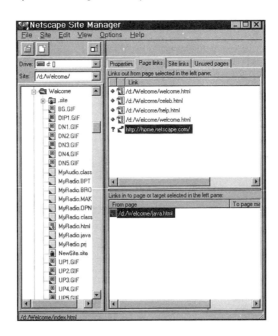

A development environment that is both a Web site management tool and an application builder might seem like an odd grouping at first. It takes a little reflection to see why this grouping makes sense. In Chapter 1, "The Internet Application Framework," you learned that since the creation of the World Wide Web, Internet applications have become centralized around documents rather than programs. Traditional desktop application programming involves creating programs that open files; Internet programming goes the other way around. When programming for the Internet, you have an HTML file that invokes a program. It would stand to reason that for an Internet development environment, instead of managing projects composed of program modules, you manage projects that are composed of HTML documents—and that is exactly what LiveWire does.

More About Site Manager

Web sites can be very complex. A single site can contain hundreds of pages, multiple images, and many links to other pages. At the drop of a hat, URLs can change or disappear, links can be broken, and information can become outdated. Because of the sheer magnitude of information you need to track, maintaining a Web site can be, at the very least, challenging. To simplify Web site maintenance, LiveWire provides Site Manager, which is a graphical, main-operator console that you, as a developer, will interface with during the course of server-side Web application development.

Site Manager comes equipped with the following features:

◆ **Wizard tools that show you how to create visually interesting, well-organized Web sites.** The wizards guide you through a set of templates, providing you with a Web site in a jiffy (see fig. 7.2). If you have programmed with IDEs before, you may recognize the parallels between this wizard tool and the wizard tools used by the IDEs.

◆ **Graphical views that display the organization of your entire Web site.** You can actually see your Web site map, which ultimately aids in the best possible organization of your Web site.

◆ **An intuitive drag-and-drop interface for managing Web sites.** See something you want to relocate? To move a page or an image, just click, drag, and drop.

◆ **Automatic hyperlink maintenance.** When you change a single link, Site Manager automatically changes all refererences to a link, page, or file within the site. No more chasing down each reference.

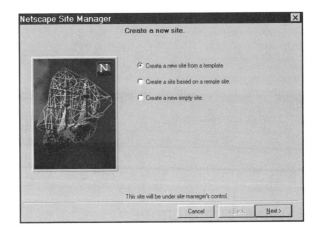

◆ **A graphical interface for compiling and linking LiveWire applications that contain server-side JavaScripts.** A compiled LiveWire application is a file with a .WEB extension.

◆ **External link checking.** Site Manager follows links from a compiled site to determine whether the links are still active and connected to live Web pages.

More About LiveWire Compiler

The LiveWire JavaScript Compiler enables you to incorporate JavaScript code into platform-independent byte codes. This helps to quickly translate the code into a format that the LiveWire engine can read. For example, when you perform a save operation in Word or another word processing application, the program takes the information you type on-screen and translates the document text into a format that the word processor engine can read. Similarly, when you compile an HTML file with embedded JavaScript, the file is compiled into a format (bytecode) that can be processed and read by the LiveWire engine.

More About LiveWire's Connectivity Library

The Connectivity Library also provides ODBC connectivity for additional databases—information formerly only available in stand-alone databases is now at your fingertips. You can actually develop applications that can access many databases, making more and more information available to clients.

LiveWire and LiveWire Pro enable you to develop client-server database applications that work with a DBMS. If you have LiveWire Pro, you already have a DBMS. LiveWire Pro is bundled with a developer version of Informix's OnLine Workgroup DBMS—the entry-level version of Informix's OnLine Dynamic Server. Should you decide in the future to upgrade to a more powerful Informix database server that supports multiprocessor systems, OnLine Workgroup databases should be fully compatible. The copy of OnLine Workgroup bundled with LiveWire Pro is licensed for a single developer on a single Web server with unlimited users.

LiveWire Pro offers two approaches toward connecting to a database. In the standard approach, the application institutes a single connection statement in the startup page, which means that all clients share the same database and user name. From there, each client automatically receives a copy of the shared connection, thus connecting all clients simultaneously. This approach is advantageous in that LiveWire manages all aspects of establishing database connections; however, all users must share the same name and access priveleges. For the standard approach, you also need a vendor license to use multiple database connections.

The other approach LiveWire offers is the serial approach, in which only one client at a time can connect to the database. With the serial approach, every page in the application that needs a database connection locks the project object (to prevent multi-user access) and then connects to the database. When the user indicates he or she is finished using the database, the connection is broken and the project object is unlocked. Note, however, that if more than one application will be connecting to one database, you must lock the server object.

Server Extension

The LiveWire server extension works as a supplement to a Netscape server (2.0 or better), giving the server the added capability to run LiveWire applications.

The following main features are provided by the LiveWire server extension:

◆ A framework that consists of objects that can be used for server-side application development.

◆ Application Manager, a program that supervises applications on the server. This executive-like program behaves similar to the way a Human Resources department is used in a corporation. It is used for adding, modifying, starting, stopping, and deleting applications on the server.

Netscape Navigator Gold 3.0

Netscape Navigator Gold is to developing Internet applications what a programmer's text editor is to writing desktop applications (see fig. 7.3). Netscape Navigator Gold is an edition of Netscape Navigator that provides a WYSIWYG (what-you-see-is-what-you-get) interface that enables you to create and edit HTML pages. With Netscape Navigator Gold, you also have the capability to edit JavaScript statements embedded in HTML.

Figure 7.3

Editing an HTML file with Netscape Navigator Gold 3.0.

 Note At the time this book is being written, Netscape Navigator Gold is a wonderful HTML editor, but its JavaScript editing leaves something to be desired. You probably will want to use your favorite text editor for editing the embedded JavaScript.

LiveWire Pro Basics

Like LiveWire, LiveWire Pro includes Navigator Gold, LiveWire Site Manager, and LiveWire JavaScript Complier. LiveWire Pro also includes the Database Connectivity Library, which enables you to get direct SQL connectivity to relational databases from Informix, Oracle, and Sybase, and provides ODBC connectivity for additional databases. LiveWire Pro also includes Informix, which is an online-workgroup, high-performance SQL database; and Crystal Software's Crystal Reports Professional Version 4.5 (Windows NT version only).

Jargon
jär-gən ODBC stands for the Open Database Connectivity standard, a standard protocol for connecting to databases.

SQL Database Server

Bundled with LiveWire Pro is a SQL database server. A developer version of Informix-OnLine Workgroup, this entry-level version of Informix's OnLine Dynamic Server is offered by LiveWire Pro to enable you to configure and maintain high-performance databases. The database server program maintains complete compatability with Informix's scaleable database architecture, which supports multiprocessor and parallel processing systems.

Crystal Reports

Crystal Reports enables you to create reports based on relationships in a database (see fig. 7.4). By drawing information from the database, you can dynamically create reports that include pie charts, bar graphs, tables, and so on. These reports are stored in your favorite open-standard document format—HTML.

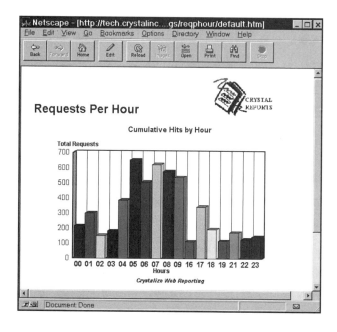

Figure 7.4

Example HTML file created by Crystal Reports.

Notes About Installing LiveWire

In order to correctly install LiveWire, you need to look at your development configuration. A LiveWire development environment consists of a development platform, a development server, and a deployment server. Use a development platform with Site Manager and Navigator Gold installed on it for authoring and compiling LiveWire applications. You also need a development server—which can be the same machine as the development platform—where you install a Netscape server and run LiveWire applications that are under development. The last server required is a deployment server where you install a Netscape server to publish finished and deployed applications on.

Development depletes resources such as ports, bandwidth, and memory. In order to avoid resource shortages, you should perform application development on a system other than your production server.

When creating database applications, you need to install the database client software on your deployment and development servers. You also must install the database server on a workstation. Although you can install the database server and Netscape server on the same machine, your development and deployment platforms need to be separate.

Looking at LiveConnect

LiveConnect enables interoperability among client Web applications. Because LiveConnect is bundled with Netscape Navigator 3.0, LiveConnect technology for end users is perceived as a Netscape browser that has more features. In other words, an end user *feels* a difference rather than *sees* a difference with LiveConnect.

From a developer's perspective, LiveConnect is a communication technology add-on to the JavaScript, Java, and plug-in technologies. With LiveConnect, you can develop a Web page whereby plug-in applications, JavaScript scripts, and Java programs can share information and control one another. For more information about LiveConnect, see Chapter 11, "Using LiveConnect with JavaScript."

JavaScript and Java Communication

LiveConnect enables you to use JavaScript to communicate with Java applets and plug-ins that are loaded on an HTML page. You also can use JavaScript to access Java variables, methods, and classes.

By accessing the Java engine directly, you can make a call to a Java method and produce the text in the Java Console, which is a Netscape Navigator window used to display Java messages much the same as if it had been produced by a Java applet.

By using LiveConnect, you easily can control Java applets—hardly any knowledge as to how the Java applet works is necessary in order to control the applet. You also can import JavaScript packages, which are structures used in JavaScript to categorize and group JavaScript classes. Packages save time and needless typing: after you reference the package to which the class belongs, you don't need to refer to the entire package each time you want to access a class. Importing a package is helpful and time-saving, especially when you need to access JavaScript methods, properties, and data structures from your Java applet. Having access to JavaScript objects and properties from an applet enables you to create smoother-working applets.

JavaScript and Plug-In Communication

JavaScript enables you to control and display plug-ins in a document as well as determine whether a particular plug-in has been installed. To check for installed plug-ins, JavaScript offers the navigator object. LiveConnect offers three plug-ins that can use JavaScript:

◆ LiveAudio

◆ LiveVideo

◆ Live3D

 Plug-ins are files that contain data used to alter, enhance, or extend the operation of a parent application program.

Live Audio

LiveAudio is a LiveConnect plug-in that supports standard sound formats such as AIFF, AU, MIDI, and WAV. With LiveAudio you can play and hear sound files that are embedded in HTML documents. LiveAudio also makes it possible to add sound to your Web page! You can play sound files without launching a separate application, and you never need to wait again to download a sound player. You also can program your applets to call LiveAudio controls to manage system volume.

LiveVideo

LiveVideo is another LiveConnect plug-in that enables you to view AVI movies that are embedded or linked to Web pages. You also can create your own AVI movies. Gone are the days when you have to wait to download a viewer or invoke a separate application in order to see a movie. Note, however, that LiveVideo currently is only available for Windows 95 and Windows NT systems.

Live3D

Live3D is a LiveWire plug-in that enables the Navigator to display VRML directly on a Web page. You now are able to experience and interact with 3D images, text, sound, and animation. Available with Netscape Navigator 3.0 for Windows 3.1, Windows 95, Windows NT, and Power Macintosh, this plug-in is multiplatform-ready.

Looking at LivePayment

Netscape's LivePayment, an extension to LiveWire, is an open cross-platform server and online payment software that enables you to perform transactions and collect payments over the Internet. LivePayment's functionality has been compared to that of an "Internet cash register," providing smooth online transaction processing capabilities that enable companies to accept credit card payments from customers.

Because of LivePayment's ease-of-use and support from major financial institutions, its functionality can be exploited by many types of merchants, including retailers, publishers, service providers, and more. LivePayment makes commerce easily accessible to small retailers because of the sheer number of consumers who have access to retail Web sites. An online store application based on LivePayment can help retailers reach a greater number of consumers at a reduced overhead. If you are an online or software publisher, LivePayment enables you to collect fees such as subscription fees, usage fees, or item access fees. LivePayment also enables you to verify a customer's credit, settle payment for goods, and deliver the product, all with the Internet. By using LivePayment, airlines, hotels, and other travel providers can provide systems that enable consumers to make their own reservations directly, thus reducing the time it takes to verify and process payments.

LivePayment enables you to develop payment processing applications in three ways: modify the Starter Application, create your own application by using LiveWire's LivePayment objects, or create your own application by using the cpcmd utility. Don't limit yourself to using just one of these options, however; you can combine these methods to create a custom application.

Security Issues with LivePayment

Security is an important issue to everyone. Every time transactions are sent, either from the consumer to the merchant or from the merchant to the acquirer and then back, that information must be protected. Because of that, Netscape's LivePayment uses a *secure transfer protocol* called *Secure Sockets Layer*, or SSL. In order to use SSL, consumers must be using a browser, such as Netscape Navigator, that supports SSL.

In addition to LivePayment's robust environment, developing online applications is made easy with LivePayment's sample applications. For example, LPAuthOnly performs an authorization and stores the information in a flat filec and LPStarterApp performs an authorization, capture/credit, and settles the batches.

At the time this is being written, LivePayment is in a restricted beta version; Netscape anticipates its release in the third quarter of 1996.

Summary

In this chapter you learned about the basics of LiveWire, including Site Manager and the LiveWire compiler. You learned about the server extension provided by LiveWire, LiveWire's use of a SQL database, and Crystal Reports. You also learned about the advantages of LiveConnect and LivePayment.

CHAPTER **8**

Getting Familiar with LiveWire's Application Manager

In Chapter 7, "Introduction to LiveWire, LiveConnect, and LivePayment," you learned about the basics of LiveWire and its development environment. This chapter talks specifically about LiveWire's Application Manager. The Application Manager enables you to add new LiveWire applications, modify attributes of an installed application, start, stop, and restart an installed application, run and debug a started application, and remove an installed application.

Typically, publishing HTML files on a Web site is a straightforward operation. The task basically is limited to the following two easy steps:

1. Create a directory place marker on the Web server to host the file.

2. Transfer to the Web server (usually via ftp) the HTML file you want to publish.

You could reasonably expect the publishing process of LiveWire applications to be similar to that of publishing HTML files—all you do is transfer the LiveWire application to a destination directory on the Web server. Figure 8.1 shows the HTML assembly line (or sequence of events) a Web administrator follows to publish a LiveWire Web application on the Netscape server. Raw HTML files with embedded JavaScript code are compiled to a Web application installed on the server, which is accessible to client users.

Figure 8.1

The process used to publish a LiveWire Web application on the Netscape server.

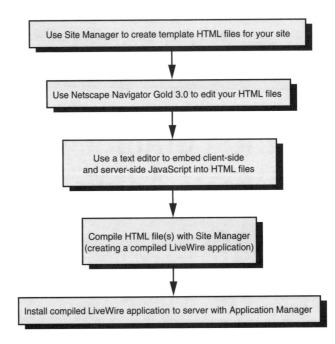

Use Site Manager to create template HTML files for your site

Use Netscape Navigator Gold 3.0 to edit your HTML files

Use a text editor to embed client-side and server-side JavaScript into HTML files

Compile HTML file(s) with Site Manager (creating a compiled LiveWire application)

Install compiled LiveWire application to server with Application Manager

Did you know...

LiveWire applications are not HTML files, but rather Web files (so called because they have a .WEB extension). Web files are HTML files, likely containing server-side JavaScript code that has been compiled.

It gets complicated when you take into account how a person with a Web browser might access this LiveWire Web application.

Suppose that you have a Web application called hello.Web that is a compiled application of the HTML file called hello.html. You want to save users the trouble of typing the entire address, such as http://www.newriders.com/hello.Web, to request this Web application. Preferably, you want to enable the user to type http://www.newriders.com/hello.html to invoke the compiled hello.Web LiveWire application. In order for this time-saver to work, the Web server requires an additional processing step during the request phase.

To process a request for a file such as http://www.newriders.com/hello.html, the Web server checks whether a LiveWire application is associated with the address http://www.newriders.com/hello.html instead of searching the hard drive for that file to serve.

If the Web server locates an association, it runs the corresponding LiveWire application, such as hello.Web, and the results are the same as if the client users accessed a standard HTML file on the server. This is how the Netscape server behaves with LiveWire.

The Application Manager, also a LiveWire application with access to special functions, directs and smoothes the configuration flow of LiveWire, in which associations are made among LiveWire Web applications and virtual HTML file locations.

> ### Did you know...
>
> The Application Manager is not a standalone application per se, but rather a LiveWire application you access through Netscape.

To get started, you need to make sure that a new application is correctly installed on your server.

Note This chapter assumes that you have correctly installed LiveWire on your system and have a Netscape 2.0 or later server.

Getting Started with Application Manager

Using Application Manager is much like programming your VCR to schedule the taping of television shows. For example, suppose that you no longer want to tape *The Price Is Right* Monday through Friday, and instead you want to begin taping *Real Stories of the Highway Patrol* (remember, this is only an example—hopefully, you won't want to try this at home). Application Manager is similar to the scheduling mechanism in your VCR in that it enables you manage applications much the same way that the VCR enables you to tape television shows at home. Before actually managing your applications, however, you must know how to start Application Manager.

Starting Application Manager

Before you can install or add a new application, you must first get your bearings set with Application Manager. To do this, follow these steps:

1. If you are using Windows 95, choose Programs from the Start menu.

2. Choose LiveWire.

3. Choose Application Manager to start the application.

4. To start Application Manager using another platform, load the following URL in Navigator:

    ```
    http://server.domain/appmgr
    ```

The Application Manager window appears, as shown in figure 8.2.

Figure 8.2

The opening screen of the Application Manager.

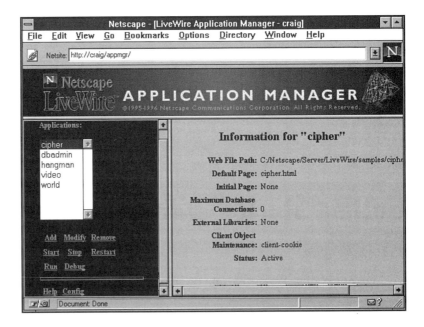

As you can see on the scrolling list on the left side of the opening screen, Application Manager displays the applications that are currently installed. To select an application, just click on the name in the scroll list, and information about the application appears in the right frame of the window.

Installing or Adding a New Application to Your Server

As mentioned previously, the purpose of Application Manager is to enable you to manage your applications, so you can install or add new applications to your server. The following exercise shows you how to install a new application to your server.

Installing a New Application

1. From the opening screen of Application Manager, click on the Add button on the left side of the screen under the Applications scroll bar. The Add Application dialog box appears (see fig. 8.3).

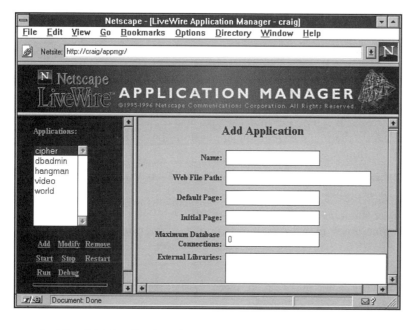

Figure 8.3

The Add Application dialog box in Application Manager.

2. The Add Application dialog box contains six fields in which you enter pertinent information about the application you want to add. Use the following list as a reference and make your choices:

    Name (required)—contains the name of the application, which defines the application URL. This parameter cannot be the same as any other application names on the server. LiveWire routes all requests that match client requests for URLs to the directory you specify for the Web file, skirting the normal document root directory of the server. The name you provide determines the URL of the application, which is the address clients use to access your LiveWire application.

When a client then requests the application URL you provide, the server produces HTML for the page the client specifies and sends that page to the client, which is what the client sees on-screen. Following is an example of LiveWire application URL:

```
http://server.domain/appName/page.html
```

Server indicates the name of the HTTP server. The *domain* parameter enables you to specify the Internet domain and includes all subdomains. Use *appName* to indicate the name of the application you provided when you went through the application installation process. The *page* parameter is the name of the page in the application.

Web File Path (required)—contains the complete file specification of the application Web file.

Default Page (optional)—contains the file LiveWire serves; it is complete only when the user does not indicate a specific page in a previously accessed application. The default page is comparable to index.html for a standard URL.

Initial Page (optional)—indicates the first file LiveWire serves when an application is first run. You usually use this field to initialize values and institute connections to databases. If you do not indicate a particular page in an application, LiveWire displays the initial page of the application. LiveWire uses the default page after your initial access to an application.

External Libraries (optional)—contains file paths of external libraries that are to be used with the application.

Client Object Maintenance (required)—enables you to indicate the mode in which you want to use to maintain the client object. You can choose from client-cookie, client-URL, server-IP, server-cookie, and server-URL.

 To reset the fields and start over, just choose Reset. The fields clear and you can begin to re-enter your information.

3. Click on Enter to install the application.

That's it! You now have completed the application installation process.

Application Manager also enables you to adjust the installation parameters of an application. In the main screen of Application Manager, in the Applications scroll box, highlight the name of the application for which you want to set installation parameters, and then click on Modify.

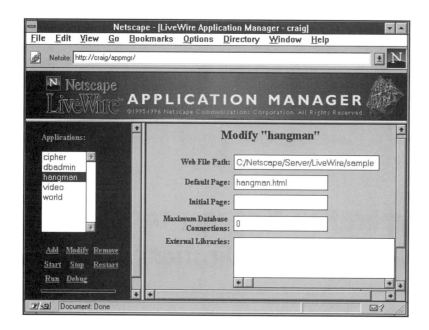

Figure 8.4

The Modify form.

Application Manager enables you to adjust all installation fields other than the Name field. For example, suppose that the location on your server for the external libraries referenced by your LiveWire application suddenly changes. To compensate for this, it is important to reflect the new location of the external libraries by modifying the External Libraries field with Application Manager. In order to change an application name, you must remove it and re-install it. For more information about removing applications, see the section "Removing Applications" later in this chapter.

 Note When changing the parameters of an active application, Application Manager automatically stops and then restarts the application for you. When changing the parameters of a stopped application, Application Manager automatically restarts the application for you after you complete the changes.

Using Application Manager to Remove Applications

As you have probably surmised by now, managing applications also means that sometimes you will want to delete applications. Application Manager enables you to easily delete applications you no longer want to be accessible to others, perhaps because you no longer need the application or you have found another application that works better for you. After you delete an application, however, it is truly gone— the only way to run the deleted application again is to re-install it.

To remove an unwanted application, follow these steps:

1. In Application Manager, choose from the Application scroll list the application you want to delete.

2. Click on the Remove button.

That's all there is to it.

 Removing an application using Application Manager prevents the application from running with LiveWire; however, removal does not delete the files from the server.

Using Application Manager to Start, Stop, and Restart Applications

Application Manager provides many features that enable you to manage your LiveWire applications. Among the features are starting, stopping, and restarting your applications.

To start an application that is not running, choose from the Applications: scroll list the application you want to start, and then click on the Start button. The application then starts up.

To restart an application that has stopped (perhaps because you stopped it, it became unstable, or you have compiled it), choose from the Applications: scroll list the application you want to restart. Click on the Restart button. The application then resumes running.

 After compiling an application, you must restart it for changes to take effect.

To stop an application, choose the application from the Applications: scroll list and then click Stop. The application then ceases to run.

 It is a popular and good practice for Webmasters to use more than one computer server. Commonly, one server is referred to as the *development server*, whereby Web applications under development are hosted, and perhaps even developed. A second server is referred to as the deployment (or production) server. The *deployment server* is used to publish finished Web applications to the end user.

In order to move the Web file of an application or update an application from a development server to a deployment server, you must stop the application. To

> resume running the application after making these changes, restart it using the
> directions mentioned previously in this section.

For the power user who would rather use a text-based interface than a graphical user
interface (GUI), Application Manager also enables you to start, stop, or restart
applications from within Netscape by using a special URL of the form. Following is
the syntax:

```
http://server.domain/appmgr/control.html?name=appName&cmd=action
```

AppName indicates the name of the application. You replace the *action* place holder
with the action you want to take place, such as start, stop, or restart.

 Although it is possible to start, stop, or restart applications from within Netscape by
using the special URL, it isn't really necessary or preferable. It is much easier to use
the Application Manager interface.

Running and Debugging Applications

Application Manager enables you to run and debug all your LiveWire applications. To
run an installed application, follow these steps:

1. In Application Manager, choose from the Applications: Scroll box the name of
   the application you want to run.

2. Click on the Run button. A new Navigator window appears that enables you to
   access the application (see fig. 8.5).

Did you know...

Starting and *running* a LiveWire application are two different acts. When you *start* a
LiveWire application, it is like starting the engine of your car, whereby your car is
started, but is in an idle, ready state. When you *run* a LiveWire application, it is like
putting your car in drive, whereby the car (or application) is no longer in a ready
state, but rather in a go state.

Figure 8.5

Running an application in Navigator by using Application Manager.

Run ———

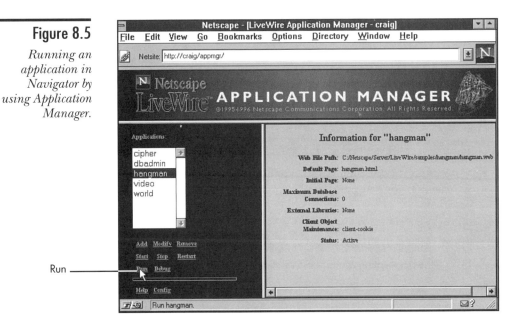

3. To load the application in Navigator, type the URL in the Location: field in Netscape Navigator (see Figure 8.6). If the application you are trying to run is stopped (inactive), Application Manager tries to start the application so that it will run.

Figure 8.6

Running an application by typing in the URL in Navigator.

Location ———

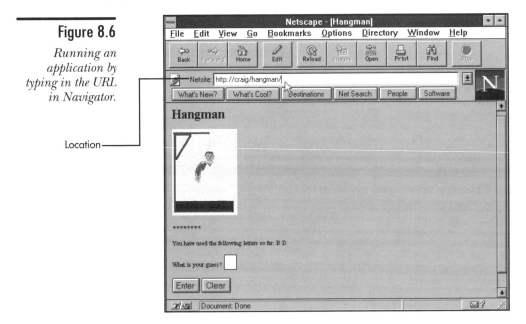

As mentioned previously, Application Manager enables you to debug your applications. To debug an application, follow these steps:

 Jargon   *Debugging* is attempting to determine the cause of the symptoms of malfunctions detected during testing or by users.

1. In Application Manager, choose from the Applications: Scroll list the application you want to debug.

2. Click on the Debug button. The application runs, and Application Manager displays the application trace in a different frame (see fig. 8.7).

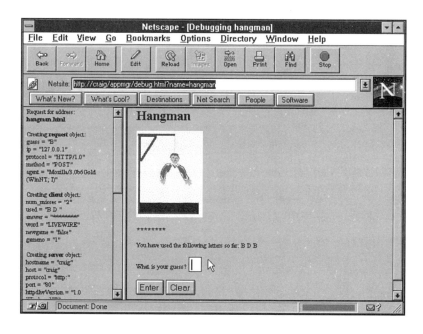

Figure 8.7

Debugging information in Application Manager.

Configuring Application Manager Default Settings

Because users' system needs vary, Application Manager provides a feature that enables you to configure its default settings. The following steps show you how to modify default settings:

1. While in Application Manager, click on the Config button at the bottom of the screen. The Default Settings dialog box appears (see fig. 8.8).

Figure 8.8

The Default Settings dialog box in Application Manager.

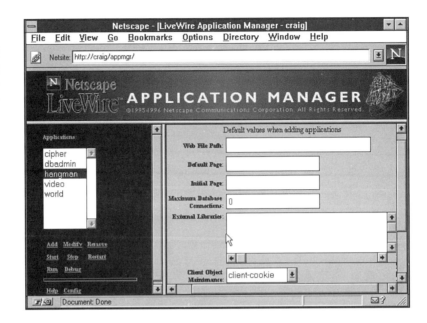

2. The Default Settings dialog box contains several fields in which you enter pertinent information about the application you want to add. Use the following list as a reference and make your choices:

   Web File Path (required)—contains the complete file specification of the application Web file.

   Default Page (optional)—contains the file LiveWire serves; it is complete only when the user does not indicate a specific page in a previously accessed application. The default page is comparable to index.html for a standard URL.

   Initial Page (optional)—indicates the first file LiveWire serves when an application is first run. You usually use this field to initialize values and institute connections to databases. If you do not indicate a particular page in an application, LiveWire displays the initial page of the application. LiveWire uses the default page after your initial access to an application.

   External Libraries (optional)—contains file paths of external libraries that are to be used with the application.

   Client Object Maintenance (required)—enables you to indicate the mode you want to use to maintain the client object. You can choose from client-cookie, client-URL, server-IP, server-cookie, and server-URL.

3. Click on the appropriate Confirm On check box to indicate whether you want to be prompted when you delete, start, stop, or restart an application.

4. For the Debug Output radio buttons, indicate whether you want the application trace to appear in the same window but different frame as the application, or in another window that is separate from the application.

5. When your settings are complete, click on the Enter button. To start over, click on the Reset button. To cancel the operation, click on the Cancel button. Now when you install a new application, the default installation parameters will be the ones you just set.

Managing Access-Rights/Security of Applications

Managing access restrictions is an important aspect of managing a Web site. On a development server, you generally want to allow developers access to all LiveWire applications, including Application Manager. On a deployment server, you definitely want to restrict access to Application Manager; however, you may not want to restrict access to other applications or put less restrictions on them. So more than likely you want to create separate configuration styles for applications other than Application Manager.

You restrict access to an application by applying a server configuration style from your Server Manager. Complete information on using Server Manager and configuration styles is available with the documentation that comes with your Netscape server.

Familiarizing Yourself with LiveWire's Sample Applications

To enable you to better learn your away around LiveWire, the following sample applications are included and installed when you install LiveWire:

◆ Hello World

◆ Hangman

◆ Cipher

◆ Video

◆ DBAdmin

These applications show you, by example, the following:

◆ How to maintain a distinct client state for multiple clients and how to maintain a persistent application state

◆ HTML code

◆ How to use JavaScript-only source code

◆ How to correct compile-time errors

◆ How to use the trace facility for run-time debugging

Learning About Hello World

Hello World is a simple application that helps you understand basic programming concepts, specifically maintaining a distinct client state for multiple clients and a persistent application state. This sample program also introduces you to reading LiveWire files, embedding JavaScript in HTML, and building and restarting an application.

The following exercise shows you the basics of those features.

Running Hello World

1. In Application Manager, from the Applications: Scroll box, choose Hello World.

 If you are in Navigator, you can start Hello World by entering the following URL in the Location field:

```
http://server.domain/world
```

2. Click on the Run button. The Hello World application appears in Netscape (see fig. 8.9).

This application shows you your IP address, displays the names of those who previously accessed this program, displays a field in which you can enter your name and indicates the number of times you have been to this application and the total number of times the page has been accessed.

If this is the first time you have accessed this page, the values for names (this time and last time) show null, and the number of times you previously accessed this page is 0. The total number of times this page has been accessed is 1, indicating that you are the first visitor.

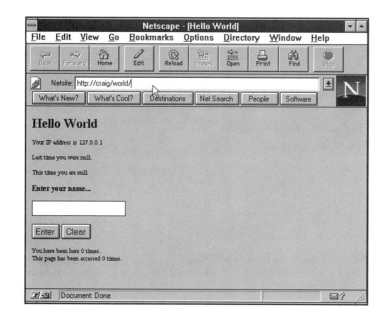

Figure 8.9

The Hello World application.

3. In the Enter Your Name field, type your name and then click on the Enter button. The page now reflects the name you just entered (after the This Time You Are line) (see fig. 8.9). The access numbers also change.

4. To further witness the incrementing this form provides, repeat step 3, entering another name in place of your own. The page now reflects the new name, and the number of accesses has increased again.

Simple, right? To really get to the nuts and bolts, you need to look at the source code used in the Hello World application.

Examining the Hello World Source Script

Using NotePad, open the SAMPLES\WORLD\HELLO.HTML file in the directory in which you installed LiveWire. You see the following HTML code:

```
1. <HMTL>
2. <HEAD>
3. <TITLE> Hello World </Title>
4. </HEAD>
5. <BODY>
6. <H1> Hello World </H1>
7. <P>Your IP address is <SERVER>write(request.ip);</SERVER>
8. <server>write("<P>Last time you were " + client.oldname + ".");</server>
9. <P>This time you are <server>write(request.newname);</server>
```

```
10. <SERVER>client.oldname=request.newname; // Get new name from form input.<
    ➥ /SERVER>
11. <h3> Enter your name... </h3>
12. <FORM METHOD="post" ACTION="hello.html">
13. <INPUT TYPE="text" NAME="newname" SIZE=20
14. <br>
15. <p><input type="submit" value="Enter">
16. <input type="reset" value="Clear">
17. </form>
18. <server>
19. if (client.number == null)  // Initialize or increment number of accesses
    ➥ by this client
20.    client.number = 0;
21.    else
22.     client.number = parseInt(client.number) + 1;
23.    project.lock();    // Initialize or increment total number of accesses.
24.    if(project.number == null)
25.     project.number = 0;
26.    else
27.     project.number = parseInt(project.number) + 1;
28.    project.unlock();
29. </server>
30. <p>You have been here <server>write(client.number);</server> times.
31. <br>This page has been accessed <server>write(project.number);</server>
    ➥ times.
32. </body>
33. </html>
```

The <SERVER> tags in line 7 indicate and enclose server JavaScript code. The IP
address of the client accessing the page is indicated in the write(request.ip) statement, which displays the IP property of the request object.

 Note   In LiveWire, you use the write function to display in HTML the values of JavaScript
expressions.

Line 10 assigns the value of the newname property of the request object to the
oldname property of the client object. Remember from the discussion in Chapter 6,
"Netscape LiveWire Objects," that request and client objects are part of the LiveWire
object framework. When a user enters a value in the form, LiveWire sets the value of
request.newname.

Line 12 indicates that hello.html, which is the current filename, is the ACTION attribute of the form; that is, Navigator reloads the current page when you (or a user) submit the form by clicking the Enter button.

> **Note** The ACTION attribute can be any page in a LiveWire application.

In line 13, newname is the NAME attribute. LiveWire assigns to a property newname of the request object the value of what is entered by you when you submit the page (which in JavaScript is request.newname).

> **Note** Request properties and form element values must always correspond.

Line 18 is a new <SERVER> tag that signifies the start of a new block of server-side JavaScript code. Lines 19 through 22 are the start of the block:

```
19. if (client.number == null)  // Initialize number of accesses by this
    ↪ client.
20.        client.number = 0
21. else
22.        client.number = parseInt(client.number) + 1
```

This code contains a conditional *if...then...else* statement that verifies that the number property of the client object has been initialized. If it has not, then it automatically sets the number property to zero. If the number property of the client object has been initialized, it increments the number property of the client object by one using the JavaScript parseInt function.

Did you know...

The parseInt function converts the string value to a number.

Remember how a unique client object is made for each user (client) that accesses the application? For this reason, the number property of the client object is distinct for each different user that accesses the application. This number tells the users how many times each has visited this Web page.

The project object, unlike the client object, is shared among all the clients accessing the application. A use for the project object is demonstrated in lines 24 through 27. Notice how the number property for the project object is being incremented for each user that visits the page. So for the project object, the number property is no longer distinct for each user as it was with the client object.

```
23.    project.lock();     // Initialize or increment total number of accesses.
24.    if(project.number == null)
25.      project.number = 0;
26.    else
27.      project.number = parseInt(project.number) + 1;
28.    project.unlock();
```

Line 23 is used to lock the project object before the block of code, and line 28 is used to unlock the project object after the block of code has executed. This ensures that each client has exclusive rights to the project object.

The final lines of the original code, 30 and 31, use the JavaScript *write* statement to display the values of client.number and project.number to the user within the body of the document.

Taking your learning experience a bit further, you can now modify the Hello World application, recompile it, and then restart it. To edit the source code, open up NotePad and proceed with the following exercise.

Having Fun Modifying Hello World

With your favorite text editor, open the hello.html source file. You should be able to find hello.html in a directory named *world* under LiveWire's *sample* directory. The following code appears on-screen:

```
1.  <HMTL>
2.  <HEAD>
3.  <TITLE> Hello World </Title>
4.  </HEAD>
5.  <BODY>
6.  <H1> Hello World </H1>
7.  <P>Your IP address is <SERVER>write(request.ip);</SERVER>
8.  <server>write("<P>Last time you were " + client.oldname + ".");</server>
9.  <P>This time you are <server>write(request.newname);</server>
10. <SERVER>client.oldname=request.newname; // Get new name from form input.</
     ➥SERVER>
11. <h3> Enter your name... </h3>
12. <FORM METHOD="post" ACTION="hello.html">
13. <INPUT TYPE="text" NAME="newname" SIZE=20
14. <br>
15. <p><input type="submit" value="Enter">
16. <input type="reset" value="Clear">
17. </form>
```

```
18. <server>
19. if (client.number == null)   // Initialize or increment number of accesses
    ➥ by this client
20.    client.number = 0;
21.   else
22.     client.number = parseInt(client.number) + 1;
23.   project.lock();     // Initialize or increment total number of accesses.
24.   if(project.number == null)
25.     project.number = 0;
26.   else
27.     project.number = parseInt(project.number) + 1;
28.   project.unlock();
29. </server>
30. <p>You have been here <server>write(client.number);</server> times.
31. <br>This page has been accessed <server>write(project.number);</server>
    ➥ times.
32. </body>
33. </html>
```

Using the "big" Method

You also can use the "big" method when modifying the Hello World example. The big method causes a string to be displayed in a big font as if it were in a BIG tag. In line 7 of the preceding code, change

```
<SERVER>write(request.ip)</SERVER>
```

to

```
<SERVER>write(request.ip.big())</SERVER>
```

Building and Compiling Modified Hello World

Now run LiveWire Site Manager by double-clicking on its icon or by selecting the LiveWire Site Manager menu item from the task bar under Windows 95. After you have invoked Site Manager, follow these steps:

1. By browsing in the left frame of Site Manager, select the WORLD directory in the LiveWire SAMPLES directory.

Note If you installed LiveWire on your C: drive, you probably can find the WORLD directory at its default location of C:\NETSCAPE\SERVER\LIVEWIRE\ SAMPLES\WORLD.

2. Should the Hello World application is not currently under site management, choose Site | Manage from the menu bar to bring the Hello World application under site management.

3. To compile your newly modified Hello World application, choose Site | Build Application. Then restart the application with Application Manager. You then can run the application again by clicking on Run in Application Manager. Notice the new behavior of the application due to your modifications. The IP address is now shown in a larger font.

Figure 8.10

The Hello World page after your modification.

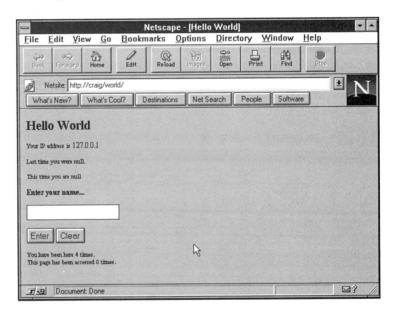

Summary

This chapter has included several hands-on examples, and more than likely you have been busy learning (as well as entering) code! In this chapter, you specifically have learned how to use Application Manager to manage your LiveWire applications, including tasks such as starting, stopping, restarting, and running applications. You also put to use one of LiveWire's sample applications, Hello World.

Chapter 9, "Using Client and Server Scripts," discusses client and server scripts, how to use LiveWire/Netscape built-in functions, and how to call external libraries.

Using Client and Server Scripts

I n Chapter 3, "JavaScript Language Fundamentals," you learned how JavaScript uses scripting techniques within HTML documents. This chapter takes that concept a bit further and explains the differences between client scripts and server scripts. Specifically, you will learn the following:

◆ When to use client or server scripts

◆ How the clients and servers communicate

◆ How to use LiveWire/Netscape built-in functions

◆ How to use files on the server

◆ How to call external libraries

Knowing When to Use Client Scripts Versus Server Scripts

As you learned in Chapter 3, you use client-side JavaScript code in HTML documents using the <SCRIPT> tag or by loading a file that contains JavaScript source code. To indicate server-side JavaScript you use the SERVER tag, as in the following example:

```
<SERVER>
write("Hello Net!")
</SERVER>
```

LiveWire compiles the HTML code into bytecodes that are platform-independent and parses and compiles server-side JavaScript statements. At run-time, the Netscape server translates the compiled bytecodes into HTML statements and then transmits them to the client across the network. The client Web browser then translates the client JavaScript code and renders a standard HTML page layout (see fig. 9.1).

Figure 9.1

JavaScript code translated into standard HTML.

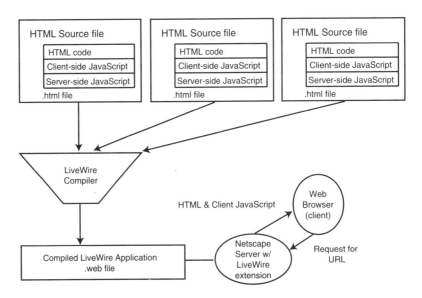

 Run-time refers to program logic that is performed during the time of execution of a certain program. In the context of the preceding paragraph, the program that is executing is the client Web browser.

You can use several methods to partition an application between server and client. Although some methods apply only to the client or the server, but not both, other methods can be used for either the client or the server. Following are the general guidelines to help you determine when to use methods for server scripts:

◆ To maintain data shared among applications or clients

◆ To maintain information during client connections

◆ To manipulate data in a database

◆ To manipulate files on a server

◆ To call server C libraries

◆ To customize Java applets

Use the following guidelines to help you determine when to use client scripts:

◆ To display error or information boxes

◆ To validate user input

◆ To display confirmation boxes

◆ To process server data, such as aggregate calculations

◆ To add simple programmable logic to HTML

◆ To perform functions that do not require information from the server

Using LiveWire/Netscape Built-In Functions

LiveWire provides the following server-side built-in JavaScript functions:

◆ **write**—This function enables LiveWire to generate HTML on the fly. The client then interprets the HTML just generated as it would interpret static HTML. The HTML generated by LiveWire is sent to the client Web browser in large 64 K blocks. Following is the syntax:

```
write(expression)
```

where *expression* is a valid JavaScript expression.

The write function is useful anytime you want to generate HTML that is dependent on a variable condition such as a date.

◆ **flush**—Clears out the buffer by sending data from previously issued write functions to the client. Suppose you had the results of a database query sent to the client via the write function. If the results contained a large amount of HTML to be generated on the fly, you likely would not want the user to have to wait for their browser to load a full 64K of data before they can first start viewing the data. It is better, instead, to use the flush function between calls of a series of write functions in order to send data in smaller chunks to the user's Web browser.

```
flush()
```

◆ **redirect**—Enables you to redirect a client browser to the URL you specify using the location parameter provided by this function. The client will load the page you specified and eliminate the current page. Following is the syntax for the redirect function:

```
redirect(location)
```

where *location* is the URL to which you are redirecting the client. This function is useful in instances where you want to programmatically change the current Web page a user is viewing. A client-side analogy to this function is the Post operation done by forms.

◆ **debug**—Enables you to display the value of an expression. You use this function when debugging code. Following is the syntax:

```
debug(expression)
```

where *expression* is any valid LiveWire expression. Note that outputs from the debug function will not be seen by the user—only by you when you are debugging the application. You might want to smatter debug statements at the beginning and ending of functions in order to track the values of variables passed to functions as well as values returned from functions.

◆ **addClient**—Enables you to maintain the property values of the client object when you are using the redirect function or are dynamically generating URLs, by appending the client property values to the URL. Following is the syntax:

```
addClient(URL)
```

where URL is the page you want to save.

If your application generates dynamic URLs, it is a good idea to always use addClient. For instance, suppose your application has a client property, beerPage, that you set to a particular beer page based on a user's selection. You could produce a hyperlink using this client property like this:

```
<A HREF='beerPage'>
```

Assuming the value of beerPage is simply a string representing the desired URL, this would work fine. However, if you are using an URL-encoding method to preserve the client object, this URL would end up not containing the client properties. To get around this, you must use addClient as follows:

```
<A HREF='addClient(beerPage)'>
```

You should also use addClient whenever you use the redirect function. For example,

```
redirect(addClient("schlitz.html"))
```

◆ **escape**—Enables you to encode in an URL values that may include special characters. Following is the syntax:

```
escape("string")
```

where string is a string in the ISO Latin-1 character set. The string parameter also can be a property of an existing object. The escape function should be used any time you generate your own name/value pairs in an URL request.

◆ **unescape**—Enables you to decode escape coded names in an URL. This function returns the ASCII string for the value you specify in the parameter. Following is the syntax:

```
unescape("string")
```

where string is the string or property of the object you are decoding. The unescape function should be used in conjunction with the escape function.

◆ **getOptionValue**—Enables you to get the values (in JavaScript) of selected options in a list. You use this function for applications that provide select lists. This function returns a string that contains the text for the selected option you specify in the parameter. Following is the syntax:

```
getOptionValue(name, index)
```

where *name* indicates the NAME attribute of the SELECT tag. Use the index parameter to indicate the zero-based ordinal index of the selected option.

♦ **getOptionValueCount**—Used with the getOptionValue function, this function enables you to process user input from SELECT form elements that provide multiple selections. This function returns (in a SELECT form element) the number of options the user has selected. You use this function to process user input you receive from SELECT form elements that provide multiple selections. Following is the syntax:

```
getOptionValueCount(name)
```

where *name* is the name specified by the NAME attribute of the SELECT tag.

With the exception of the write function, all these functions are defined for server-side JavaScript only.

Producing HTML on the Fly

LiveWire actually produces HTML on the fly. Suppose that when you went to the bookstore to buy this book, as you grabbed the book off the shelf to look at it, a robot from behind the bookshelf automatically edited some information into the book. The robot was so fast that you didn't even notice it was there. For end users using Netscape Navigator or some other Web browser, a similar occurrence happens when they browse a LiveWire Web site. What they see looks like static HTML; however, the HTML they see actually is generated on the fly by LiveWire (the "editing robot"). A function commonly used to produce the HTML on the fly is the write function.

Write Function

The write function, a top-level LiveWire function not associated with an object, outputs data to the client browser. By using the write function, you can display in HTML the values of JavaScript expressions. This makes it possible for HTML data to be dynamic enabling a user to have a customized experience at your Web site. For instance, suppose you had previous knowledge of a client user's birthday. Armed with that knowledge, you can have a Web page conditionally use write statements to display the corresponding horoscope for that user. These values are sent to the client, which in turn translates the dynamically generated HTML the same way it translates static HTML.

Did you know...

Although considered by the client to be static HTML, the HTML actually is generated dynamically by LiveWire.

LiveWire actually buffers the output of the write function and then transmits the output in large blocks to the client. Following is the syntax for the write function:

```
write(expression)
```

To use the write function in a statement, look at the following example:

```
write("<HR>Client's IP address is: " + client.ip))
```

This write statement results in LiveWire dynamically generating HTML code that includes an <HR> horizontal ruler tag and text appended with the client browser's IP address. Suppose that the IP address of the client browser is 152.213.001.123; the resulting created HTML code would look like the following:

```
<HR>Client's IP address is: 152.213.001.123
```

Figure 9.2 shows the values of JavaScript expressions in HTML.

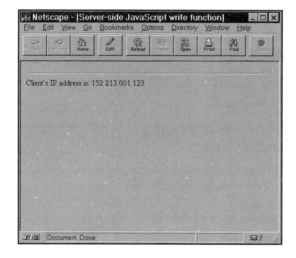

Figure 9.2

*Using the write()
statement to show
JavaScript
expressions in
HTML.*

flush Function

People want to perform tasks as efficiently as possible in order to save time. LiveWire has the same inclination. It provides the flush function, a top-level LiveWire function not associated with any object, that sends to the client data (in blocks of 64 K) from previously issued write functions. This is a complicated way of saying that the flush function breaks large blocks of code into manageable blocks, thus enabling you to move preexisting data out of the holding area (the buffer) to the client to prevent the bottlenecking of information. Instead of having to wait for the client browser to load the entire data block that is being transferred, the flush tells the browser to load the amount of data from the block that the browser has gotten so far, and then to just begin with a new data block.

Following is the syntax for the flush function:

```
flush()
```

To use the flush function in a statement, look at the following example:

```
for (i=1;i<10;i++) {
    write("Picture of beer #" + i + " <img src='beer" + i + ".gif'><p>"
    flush()
}
```

This code produces the following HTML output:

```
Picture of beer #1 <img src="beer1.gif"><p>
Picture of beer #2 <img src="beer2.gif"><p>
Picture of beer #3 <img src="beer3.gif"><p>
Picture of beer #4 <img src="beer4.gif"><p>
Picture of beer #5 <img src="beer5.gif"><p>
Picture of beer #6 <img src="beer6.gif"><p>
Picture of beer #7 <img src="beer7.gif"><p>
Picture of beer #8 <img src="beer8.gif"><p>
Picture of beer #9 <img src="beer9.gif"><p>
```

Between each of the preceding generated lines a flush occurs. Each flush allows the Web browser to display a line at a time rather than wait for all 10 lines to be sent over the Net.

Creating an HTML Detour (Client Redirection)

One of LiveWire's many features, the redirect function enables you to redirect the client browser to an URL you specify by using a location parameter. Redirection can be useful when you want to display a Web page based on a condition, such as the type of Web browser a client is using. For instance, suppose you wanted Netscape Navigator clients to see one Web page and all other clients to see a different Web page. By inspecting for the type of browser the user is viewing your page, you can automatically redirect the current page the user is viewing to the page suitable for their particular browser. The redirect function is a top-level LiveWire function that is unassociated with an object. The value of the location you specify can be absolute or relative, meaning that you can choose to (or choose not to) include the protocol, domain, and complete file path. Following is the syntax for the redirect function:redirect(*location*)

The *location* is the URL to which you want to redirect the client.

Did you know...

With relative URLs, you do not need to indicate the protocol (the section before the colon), domain, or complete path. When using absolute URLs, however, you must include the complete protocol, domain name, and file path.

When the client encounters a redirect, it loads the page you indicated in the syntax and deep-sixes prior content.

Note After the redirect function, the client browser does not execute or load any HTML or script statements that follow the redirect function call. Instead, the browser loads the URL specified by the redirect function.

To use the redirect function in a statement, look at the following example:

```
if (client.ip == "152.123.123.124") {
 redirect("http://www.netscape.com")
}
```

In this case, you check to see if the client is Fred Farkle, whose IP address is *152.123.123.124*. If it is Fred Farkle, you detour him to the Netscape home page rather than display the HTML and JavaScript codes that follow these statements.

Using the trace Facility

The trace facility is a LiveWire feature that enables you to debug functions called by an application by displaying values of object properties and arguments. Both before and after issuing HTML for a particular page, this feature displays all the property values of the request and client objects. It tells you when a particular application allocates new values to properties and when LiveWire flushes buffer content (which, as you recall from previous discussion in this chapter, is 64 K). By using Application Manager, you can specify whether you want the application trace to appear in a frame in the same window as the application you are debugging or in a separate window.

The trace facility uses the debug function, which is a top-level LiveWire function not associated with any object, to display LiveWire values used when debugging applications. Following is the syntax:

```
debug(expression)
```

The *expression* can be any LiveWire expression.

The value appears in the trace facility after the Debug message text.

Note For Web applications that are in a production environment, you should take out the debug statements, because they adversely affect the performance of your server.

Using Select List Form Elements

LiveWire provides a couple built-in functions that aid you when working with Select List form elements. A Select List element enables the user to choose one of a set of alternatives described by textual labels. Every alternative is represented by the Option element. A Select List may contain the MULTIPLE attribute, which is used to enable users to make several selections. This example uses different types of beer from which a user can choose (see fig. 9.3). Example code for a Select List in which the MULTIPLE attribute is set follows:

```
<FORM>
<SELECT NAME="Beers" MULTIPLE>
<OPTION SELECTED>Pilsner
<OPTION>Lager
<OPTION>Stout
<OPTION SELECTED>Malt Liguor
</SELECT>
<FORM>
```

Figure 9.3

A Select List with the MULTIPLE attribute set.

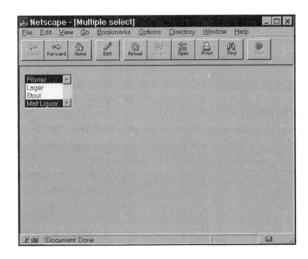

In server-side JavaScript, you use the getOptionValue function to find out which Select List option items are selected. Following is the syntax for getOptionValue:

```
getOptionValue(name, index)
```

The *name* refers to the name of the Select List in which you are interested. The name for each Select List is set by the NAME attribute of the SELECT tag. The getOptionValue parameter, *index*, refers to the particular index value of the option item in which you are interested.

Each option item is assigned a unique index value, with the first option item having a value of zero and the successive option items having values of 1, 2, 3, 4, and so on. The getOptionsValue function returns the value of the list item you specify.

Another Select List function, getOptionValueCount, returns the number of options (specified by OPTION tags) in the select list. It requires only one argument—the name of the SELECT tag, which in this case is Beers. Following is the syntax for the getOptionValue function:

```
getOptionValueCount(name)
```

Suppose you have the following form element:

```
<FORM>
<SELECT NAME="Beers" MULTIPLE>
<OPTION SELECTED>Pilsner
<OPTION>Lager
<OPTION>Stout
<OPTION SELECTED>Malt Liquor
</SELECT>
<FORM>
```

You could process the input from this select list, as follows:

```
var beerOptionsCount
var optionVal
beerOptionsCount = getOptionValueCount("Beers")
write("<HR>Below are the types of beers selected <p>"
for (i = 0; i < beerOptionsCount; i++) {
   optionVal = getOptionValue("Beers",i)
   write(optionVal + "<BR>)
}
```

If the user kept the default selections, the beer script would produce the following HTML code, which would look similar to figure 9.4.

```
<HR>Below are the types of beers selected <p>
Pilsner<BR>
Malt Liquor<BR>
```

Figure 9.4

Results from processing the values of a Select List.

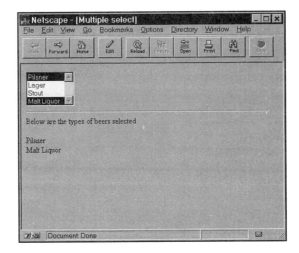

Maintaining Client Properties with URL Encoding

By automatically appending the client property values maintained by client-requested URLs to standard HTML hyperlinks, LiveWire enables you to maintain client properties by a method called *URL encoding*.

Did you know...

To maintain the client object using client URL encoding or server URL encoding, client property values are maintained in the client-requested URLs, either directly or by using a generated name.

When your application uses the redirect function or produces URLs dynamically, you need to use LiveWire's addClient function to append client property values to URLs; however, you are not required to perform any action when your application uses HTML only to link pages. Following is an example that uses the addClient function:

```
redirect(addClient("beer.html"))
```

Note   An application usually is installed initially to use a single technique to maintain a client. However, you can modify the application to use an URL encoding technique, including having the capability to generate dynamic URLs. For this reason, it is recommended that you use addClient.

Encoding Values in URLs

LiveWire enables you to encode values in URLs. There are certain instances in which you will want to encode a value in an URL that contains a special URL character, such as a blank space ( ). Suppose that the value of a variable called myBeerType was set to "Malt Liquor," as in the following value encoded URL:

```
var myURL = "http://www.newriders.com/sample.html?myBeerType=Malt Liquor"
```

Because the value "Malt Liquor" has a blank space in it, and blank spaces are special characters, it is not a valid URL.

Did you know...

Values in URLs refer to that hard-to-read text you might find at the end of an URL. The following URL contains values in which the variable FirstName is being set to the value of Fred and the variable LastName is being set to the value of Farkle.

```
http://www.newriders.com/sample.html?FirstName=Fred&LastName=Farkle
```

When using the following characters in URLs, you must encode them by using the escape and unescape functions, which LiveWire provides to enable you to encode values in an URL:

◆ & (ampersand)

◆ ( ) (blank)

◆ = (equal sign)

◆ + (plus sign)

◆ ? (question mark)

The escape function returns the ASCII value in hexadecimal format for a character or string of characters. Each ASCII value (except for one) is preceded by a percent sign (%); the blank space is encoded as a plus sign (+). For example, escape("Malt Liquor") returns the following string:

```
"%77%97%108%116+%76%105%113%117%111%114"
```

The Escape and Unescape Functions

You also need to use escape and unescape functions to ensure that all values are interpreted properly when an application needs to generate its own name/value pairs in an URL request. Following is an example that uses the escape function:

To make the following statement, set the *myURL* variable to a valid URL. You can use the *escape* function to handle the blank space in "Malt Liquor." The following is invalid because of the space between "Malt" and "Liquor":

```
var myURL = "http://www.newriders.com/sample.html?myBeerType=Malt Liquor"
```

The following is valid:

```
var myURL = "http://www.newriders.com/sample.html?myBeerType=" + escape("Malt Liquor")
```

In the preceding code, two strings are concatenated. The first is a regular string, and the second is a string created with the escape function.

The unescape function, as you might expect, performs the opposite of the escape function. The following example uses the unescape function:

```
var myBeerType = unescape("%77%97%108%116+%76%105%113%117%111%114")
```

This code is used to set myBeerType to "Malt Liquor" the hard way.

Communicating Between Client and Server Scripts

In order to learn about the way in which client and server scripts communicate, you need to understand how the roles of client scripts and server scripts differ. Servers generally are workstations that are high-powered, have copious amounts of processor speed, contain huge storage capacities, and can gather and process information from many clients and applications. Although servers are teeming with power, they still can become bogged down when continually accessed by thousands of clients. Clients, on the other hand, generally are desktop systems that have considerably less processor power and storage facilities and sometimes offer no aggregate capabilities whatsoever. Although clients offer less power and storage space than servers, they can be very useful as recipients of offload processing. In addition, if client applications can amass data, you can use them to preprocess data, thus reducing bandwidth requirements.

Bandwidth requirements refers to the amount of network traffic required by a particular system.

In addition to the client and server attributes, you need to keep a few things in mind when considering communication between clients and servers: client JavaScript is short-lived, Navigator objects only store information during the time in which the user is gaining access to the corresponding page, and objects in the LiveWire framework tend to retain information for longer periods of time (refer to Chapter 6, "Netscape LiveWire Objects," for information about object lifespans).

JavaScript enables you to communicate between clients and servers to send script information from the Navigator client to LiveWire server applications, or from LiveWire applications on the server to client JavaScript functions in Navigator.

Transmitting Values from Client to Server

When transmitting values from the client to the server in HTML, you use form elements, such as buttons, text fields, and selection lists. When an action event occurs, such as the user clicking a submit button, Navigator takes the values the user entered before clicking the submit button and sends them to the server to be processed. In the process of determining to which application to send the submitted values, HTML relies on the ACTION attribute of the FORM tag, as in the following syntax:

```
<FORM NAME="myform" ACTION="http://www.newriders.com/newPagee.html">
```

With LiveWire, processing form input is much easier. For each form element, a corresponding *request* object property is created. Should you decide to process an operation of the data on the client first (before the server gets hold of it), you must create a client-side JavaScript function. This function enables you to perform processing on the values of form elements and then assign to a hidden form element the output of the client function. Sound confusing? To help you understand, look at the following example.

Suppose that you have a client-JavaScript function named *sum* that performs summations based on the numbers that a user types into the form. You would like the results of this function to be accessible from your LiveWire application for further processing. You first need to define a hidden form element, such as the following:

```
<INPUT TYPE="hidden" NAME="sumResult" SIZE=10>
```

After that, you need to create an onClick event handler for the submit button that assigns the output of the function named *sum* to the hidden element. It would look something like the following:

```
<INPUT TYPE="submit" VALUE="Submit"
onClick="this.form.sumResult.value=sum(this.form)">
```

The value of sumResult will be submitted along with any other form element values. The sumResult value then can be easily referenced as request.sumResult in your LiveWire application.

Did you know...

A hidden form element is a text object that is suppressed from display on an HTML form.

To define a hidden object, you use the following syntax:

```
<INPUT
    TYPE="hidden"
    NAME="hiddenName"
    [VALUE="textValue"]>
```

NAME="hiddenName" specifies the name of the hidden object. You can acquire access to this value by using the name property.

VALUE="textValue" specifies the initial value of the hidden object.

Transmitting Values from Server to Client

Because LiveWire applications use HTML and client-based JavaScript to communicate with clients, you just create dynamic HTML to format the information you want to display to the user. To send values directly to client scripts, however, you can use hidden form elements, default form values, and direct substitution in event handlers or client SCRIPT statements.

 Direct substitution is a method that a server-side JavaScript can use to communicate with client-side JavaScript. Because a server-side JavaScript can dynamically create client-side JavaScript code, what the server-side JavaScript can do is directly substitute values to be passed to the client-side JavaScript as it is creating the code.

Sometimes it is desirable to display a Web page with certain parts of the form already filled out with default values. To set default values for elements in a form, use the INPUT tag to create the desired form element, and substitute a server-side JavaScript expression for the VALUE attribute. Suppose that you want to display a text element that has a default value based on the value of the server object client.favoriteBeer. You could do this with the following statement:

```
<INPUT TYPE="text" NAME="favBeerName" SIZE="25" VALUE='client.favoriteBeer'>
```

The default value for this text entry field when the page is loaded will be the value of the LiveWire variable client.favoriteBeer.

You also can set default values of hidden elements, as in the following example:

```
<INPUT TYPE="hidden" NAME="favBeerName" SIZE=25 VALUE='client.favoriteBeer'>
```

This might seem odd at first, using hidden form elements to pass variables between server-side JavaScript script and client-side JavaScript script. One way to look at it that might help: look at hidden form elements to be more like a global data type than a form object.

Using form elements to pass values between a server-side JavaScript script and a client-side JavaScript script works by setting form element values. These form element values are reflected in client-side JavaScript script as property values of Navigator objects. If the preceding element were in a form named "beerForm," these values would be reflected into the client-side JavaScript property of document.beerForm.favBeerName. It then is possible to perform client processing on these values in Navigator scripts, but only if the scripts occur after the definition of the form elements in the page.

To review, by generating the client-side JavaScript code with the server-side JavaScript script, you can use direct substitution to transfer values from the server-side to the client-side. After you perform direct substitution, the value you substituted can be used repeatedly in ensuing statements in the client-side JavaScript script. You could, for example, initialize a client-side variable named *favoriteBeer* based on the value of *client.favBeer*, as follows:

```
<SERVER>
write("<SCRIPT>var favoriteBeer = " + client.favBeer + "</SCRIPT>")
</SERVER>
```

Suppose that the value set for the server-side object client.favBeer is "Pabst Blue Ribbon." Following is the HTML code produced:

```
<SERVER>
<SCRIPT>var favoriteBeer = Pabst Blue Ribbon</SCRIPT>
</SERVER>
```

Using Cookies for Client/Server Communication

As you learned in Chapter 6, a cookie is a Netscape device in which the client retains small files between requests. Provided that an application is using client cookies to maintain the client object, you can use the cookie files to communicate between client and server scripts.

While cookies provide an unchanging implement for passing values, they also enable you to sustain persistent values on the client.

Did you know...

Persistent values are values that continue to exist and retain their values between runs of the program.

When you use a client cookie to maintain a client object, for each property, LiveWire appends the following code:

```
NETSCAPE_LIVEWIRE.propName=propValue;
```

The propName portion indicates the name of the property; propValue indicates its value.

Note You also can use JavaScript's built-in escape and unescape functions to code and decode characters. Because these functions do not recognize spaces, however, you need to manually code and decode occurrences of spaces, forward slashes, and at signs (@).

The following boilerplate code, based on code developed by Netscape, provides a good framework for writing your own custom functions for getting and setting cookie values. These functions call two helper functions, called encode and decode, that you will need to write yourself to perform the proper character encoding.

```
function getCookie(Name) {
        var search = "NETSCAPE_LIVEWIRE." + Name + "="
        var RetStr = ""
        var offset = 0
        var end    = 0
        if (document.cookie.length > 0) {
                offset = document.cookie.indexOf(search)
                if (offset != -1) {
                        offset += search.length
                        end = document.cookie.indexOf(";", offset)
                        if (end == -1)
                                end = document.cookie.length
                RetStr = decode(document.cookie.substring(offset, end))
                }
        }
        return (RetStr)
}
```

```
function setCookie(Name, Value, Expire) {
        document.cookie = "NETSCAPE_LIVEWIRE." + Name + "="
        + encode(Value)
        + ((Expire == null) ? "" : ("; expires=" + Expire.toGMTString()))
}
```

The *getCookie* and *setCookie* functions could be called in your client JavaScript to get and set values of the client object, as in the following example:

```
var tempValue
var expireDate
expireDate = new Date()
expireDate.setDate(expireDate.getDate() + 9)  //Set the expiration date to 9
➥days past the current date
tempValue = getCookie("myFavBeer")
if (tempValue != "")
        document.write("My favorite beer is ", value)
else
        setCookie("myFavBeer", "Blatz", expireDate)
```

This block of code checks whether there is an entry called *myFavBeer* in the user's cookie file. If there is such an entry, the block displays its value. Otherwise, it goes ahead and creates an entry with a value set to "Blatz."

Using Files on the Server

Using files and storing them on the server rather than in a LiveWire object enables you to protect your information from server instabilities. The folks at Netscape anticipated this and have created the LiveWire file object that enables applications to write directly to the server's file system. Using the file object also is advantageous in that you can generate persistent HTML files and store information without using a database server. The following methods are available with the file object:

byteToString

clearError

close

eof

error

exists

flush

getLength

getPosition

open

read

readByte

readln

setPosition

stringToByte

write

writeByte

writeln

Note   Due to security precautions, Netscape does not enable you to gain access to the file systems of client machines.

The following two exercises show you how to create and use a file object.

Creating file Objects

When creating a file object, use the JavaScript syntax for creating objects:

1. In your favorite text editor, create a file that contains the following text:

```
Credo Quia Absurdum
I believe what is absurd
Moose Moose Moose
Moose
and Squirrel
```

2. Name this file absurd.txt and save it to your favorite directory.

3. To create a file object, use the following standard JavaScript syntax for object creation:

```
fileObjectName = new File("path")
```

The fileObjectName portion is the JavaScript object name by which you refer to the file, and path is the complete file path.

 The path should be in the format of the server's file system, not an URL path.

To experiment with creating a file object, create an HTML file that includes the following text (replacing *c:\temp\absurd.txt* with the location in which you stored your text file):

```
<HTML>
<HEAD><TITLE>Creating a File object</TITLE></HEAD>
<BODY>
<SERVER>
myAbsurdFile = new File("c:\temp\absurd.txt")
write(myAbsurdFile)
</SERVER>
</BODY>
</HTML>
```

Notice that you are creating a file object called *myAbsurdFile.* On the next line, you display the name of the file by using the write statement. When a file object is passed to a write statement, the statement produces a filename.

Tip There are times when it is good to know the physical location of a file. Suppose that a text file needs updating, and you need a way to get access to it immediately. To display the name and path of a physical file, just call the write function and pass to it the name of the file object you want.

4. In the left frame of Site Manager, select the directory in which you recently created HTML file is located.

5. Choose Site | Manage to bring the application under site management.

6. Choose Site | Build Application to compile the application.

7. Start the application with Application Manager.

8. Run the application by clicking Run in Application Manager. You will see the name of the file, absurd.txt, generated by your Web application.

The following exercise shows you how to open and close files using the file object.

Opening and Closing Files

To open a file object after you create it, use the open method, which enables you to read from or write to the file object.

1. If you did the previous exercise, you have already created a file that contains the following text named *absurd.txt*. Otherwise, go ahead and create this file with your favorite text editor.

```
Credo Quia Absurdum
I believe what is absurd
Moose Moose Moose
Moose
and Squirrel
```

2. After you create a file object, you must open the file with the open method to read from it or write to it. Following is the syntax for the open method:

```
result = fileObjectName.open("mode")
```

The *mode* parameter is a string that specifies the mode in which to open the file. This method will return True if the operation is a success and False otherwise. If the file is already open, the operation will fail, and the original file will remain open. Table 9.1 shows how the file is opened for each mode.

TABLE 9.1
Mode Keys

Mode Key	Description of open Statement
r	Opens the file. If the file exists as a text file for reading, it returns True. If the file does not exist, it returns False.
w	Opens the file as a text file for writing. Creates a new blank text file whether or not the file exists.
a	Opens the file as a text file for appending. If the file does not already exist, the file is created.
r+	Opens the file as a text file for reading and writing. Reading and writing originates at the beginning of the file. If the file exists, it returns True. If the file does not exist, it returns False.

Mode Key	Description of open Statement
w+	Opens the file as a text file for reading and writing. Creates a new blank file whether or not the file already exists.
a+	Opens the file as a text file for reading and writing. Reading and writing originates at the end of the file. If the file does not exist, it creates it.
b	You can append this mode to any of the other modes to open the file as a binary file rather than a text file. This mode is only applicable on Windows operating systems.

Note
When the physical file you specify in the path already exists, LiveWire references it when you call methods for that object. In the event that the file does not exist, you can create it by calling the open method.

3. To experiment with opening and closing a file object, create an HTML file that includes the following text (replacing *c:\temp\absurd.txt* with the location that you stored your text file):

```
<HTML>
<HEAD><TITLE>Opening and Closing a File object</TITLE></HEAD>
<BODY>
<SERVER>
var result
myAbsurdFile = new File("c:\temp\absurd.txt")
result = myAbsurdFile.open("r")    //open for read
write(myAbsurdFile.readln()+ "<BR>")
write(myAbsurdFile.readln()+ "<BR>"))
write(myAbsurdFile.readln()+ "<BR>"))
write(myAbsurdFile.readln()+ "<BR>"))
write(myAbsurdFile.readln()+ "<BR>"))
result = myAbsurdFile.close()
</SERVER>
</BODY>
</HTML>
```

This LiveWire application will create a file object, open the file object, read five lines from the file object, and then close the file object.

4. In the left frame of Site Manager, select the directory in which your recently created HTML file is located.

5. Choose Site | Manage to bring the application under site management.

6. Choose Site | Build Application to compile the application.

7. Start the application with Application Manager.

8. Run the application by clicking Run in Application Manager. You will see the following text generated by your Web application:

```
Credo Quia Absurdum
I believe what is absurd
Moose Moose Moose
Moose
and Squirrel
```

Locking Files

In the early days of computing, networks didn't exist. Later came the introduction of local area networks and wide area networks in which multiple users could gain access to a single file—one at a time, not simultaneously. In today's age of computing, thousands of users can gain access to a single file at the same time. Gaining access to a file and modifying a file are not the same, however. Allowing multiple users to gain access to and modify a file is not such a good practice—errors can be introduced. You can remedy this situation by *locking* applications.

LiveWire provides a locking facility you can use with the project object and server object. To prevent more than one user from gaining access to a file when it is in use, use the lock method of the project object, as in the following example:

```
project.lock()
```

In cases where more than one application can gain access to the same file, use the lock method of the server object, as in the following example:

```
project.lock()
        myAbsurdFile.open("r")
        // Edit the file until done
        myAbsurdFile.close()
project.unlock()
```

Now that you have created, opened, and locked file objects, you are ready to learn how to work them.

Positioning Within a File

To position within a file, you can use the setPosition, getPosition, and eof methods. Each file object has a file pointer that indicates the current position within the relevant file. When you first open a file, the pointer is located at the beginning or end of the file, depending on the mode you used to open it.

 A *file pointer* indicates the current position in a file.

Did you know...

In an empty file, the beginning of the file and the end of the file are the same.

To specify the position in the file in which you want the pointer to be, use the setPosition method, as in the following example:

```
fileObj.setPosition(position [,reference])
```

Use fileObj to indicate the file object. Use *position*, which is an integer, to indicate where you want to position the pointer. Use *reference* to indicate the reference point for the position. The value of 0 is relative to the beginning of the file; 1 is relative to the current position; and 2 is relative to the end of the file. You also can use other (which indicates unspecified), which is relative to the beginning of the file.

When you successfully position the pointer, the setPosition method returns True. If the positioning of the pointer is unsuccessful, the method returns False.

At times you will want to determine the exact position of the pointer. LiveWire enables you to do that with its getPosition method, as in the following example:

```
fileObj.getPosition()
```

This method returns the current position in the file in which the first byte in the file is 0. If an error is encountered, this method returns –1.

The eof method (end of file) enables you to determine whether the pointer is positioned at the end of the file, as in the following:

```
fileObj.eof()
```

This method returns True when the pointer is positioned at the end of the file and False when it is not.

The eof method of the file object returns True after the first read operation that tries to read past the end of the file.

Reading from a File

To read from a file, LiveWire provides the read, readln, and readByte methods of the file object. Following is the syntax for the read method:

```
fileObj.read(count)
```

This method reads the number of bytes in a file and then returns a string. You use FileObj to specify the file object you want to read. You use an integer for count to indicate the number of bytes you want to read. If you specify more bytes than the file contains, this method will read to the end of the file.

To read the next line from the file and get the next line from the file as a string, you use the readln method, as in the following:

```
fileObj.readln()
```

To read the next byte from the file, starting from the current position of the pointer, and get the numeric value of the following byte, you use the readByte method of the file object, which moves the pointer one byte, as in the following:

```
fileObj.readByte()
```

This method returns –1 when the pointer is at the end of the file.

Writing to a File

To write to a file, you can use the write, writeln, or writeByte methods; all of these file methods are buffered internally. To write the buffer to the file on disk, use the flush method of the file object, as in the following:

```
fileObj.flush()
```

This method returns True when the flush is successful and False when it is not.

To write a string to a binary file, use the write method, as in the following:

```
fileObj.write(string)
```

Use fileObj to indicate the name of the file object to which you want to write. Use string to indicate the JavaScript string. This method returns True if the write is successful and False if the write is not.

To write a string followed by carriage return (\n or \r\n for text mode on Windows) to a file, use the writeln method, as in the following:

```
fileObj.writeln(string)
```

If the write is successful, the writeln method returns True. If the write is unsuccessful, the method returns False.

To write a byte of data to a binary file on the server, use the writeByte method of the file object, as in the following:

```
fileObj.writeByte(number)
```

The *fileObj* portion indicates the file object to which you want to write. The *number* portion indicates a number that specifies a byte of data.

When the write is successful, the writeByte method returns True. When the write is unsuccessful, this method returns False.

Converting Data Between ASCII and Binary Text

The file object uses two methods to convert data between ASCII and binary text. To convert a number into a one-character string, use the byteToString method, as in the following:

```
File.byteToString(number)
```

Because this method is static, it requires no object. An empty string is returned when the argument is not a number.

To convert the first character of an argument (a string) into a number, use the stringToByte method, as follows:

```
File.stringToByte(string)
```

Because this method is static, it requires no object. This method returns a numeric value of the first character (0).

Retrieving File Information

The file object provides methods that enable you to get information about file objects, such as file length, and offers methods that enable you to work with error status.

The exists method enables you to determine whether a file even exists by returning True (it does indeed exist) or False (no such file). Following is the syntax:

```
fileObj.exists()
```

The getLength method enables you to get the number of bytes or characters in a file you specify. This method also returns –1 when there is an error. Following is the syntax:

```
fileObj.getLength()
```

To determine whether a file is unopened or cannot be opened, use the error method, which returns the error status or –1 for opened or inaccessible files. The error method uses the following syntax:

```
fileObj.error()
```

This method returns a nonzero when an error has occured or zero when no error has occurred.

To clear the error status, that is, the value of the error, and the value of eof, you can use the clearError method, as in the following:

```
fileObj.clearError()
```

The following exercise shows you how to retrieve information.

Retrieving Information

1. If you did one of the previous exercises, you have already created a file that contains the following text named *absurd.txt*. Otherwise, go ahead and create this file with your favorite text editor.

   ```
   Credo Quia Absurdum
   I believe what is absurd
   Moose Moose Moose
   Moose
   and Squirrel
   ```

2. Attempting to open a file without first checking to see whether the file exists is a poor programming practice. Add some validation code to the HTML code in the previous exercise so that it looks like the following:

   ```
   <HTML>
   <HEAD><TITLE>Opening and Closing a File object</TITLE></HEAD>
   <BODY>
   <SERVER>
   var result
   myAbsurdFile = new File("c:\temp\absurd.txt")
   ```

```
if (myAbsurdFile.exists()) {
   result = myAbsurdFile.open("r")   //open for read
   write(myAbsurdFile.readln() + "<BR>")
   write(myAbsurdFile.readln()+ "<BR>")
   write(myAbsurdFile.readln()+ "<BR>")
   write(myAbsurdFile.readln()+ "<BR>")
   write(myAbsurdFile.readln()+ "<BR>")
   result = myAbsurdFile.close()
} else {
   write("File does not exist")
}
</SERVER>
</BODY>
</HTML>
```

3. Another area of this script that needs improvement is the need to be able to work with files that happen to be either more than five lines of text or fewer than five lines of text. The previous code can be changed to use the eof function so that you can tell whether you are at the end of a file before a read.

```
<HTML>
<HEAD><TITLE>Opening and Closing a File object</TITLE></HEAD>
<BODY>
<SERVER>
var result
myAbsurdFile = new File("c:\temp\absurd.txt")
if (myAbsurdFile.exists()) {
   result = myAbsurdFile.open("r")   //open for read
   while (!myAbsurdFile.eof()) {
      write(myAbsurdFile.readln() + "<BR>")
   }
   result = myAbsurdFile.close()
} else {
   write("File does not exist")
}
</SERVER>
</BODY>
</HTML>
```

4. In the left frame of Site Manager, select the directory in which your recently created HTML file is located.

5. Choose Site I Manage to bring the application under site management.

6. Choose Site | Build Application to compile the application.

7. Start the application with Application Manager.

8. Run the application by clicking Run in Application Manager. You will see the following text generated by your Web application:

```
Credo Quia Absurdum
I believe what is absurd
Moose Moose Moose
Moose
and Squirrel
```

Calling External Libraries

External libraries are resources written in other programming languages and are compiled into libraries that are stored on the server. LiveWire applications are capable of calling functions, referred to as external functions, written in other programming languages, such as C, C++, and Pascal.

 External functions are those that are written in other programming languages, such as C or C++, are compiled into libraries, and are available to you from the server.

Using external functions can be advantageous when your application already contains other code written in the same programming language as the external functions you want to use, or when the application requires programming for a task JavaScript cannot handle.

> **Did you know...**
>
> The Windows operating system refers to external libraries as DLLs or dynamic link libraries; Unix systems refer to external libraries as SOs, or shared objects.

Identifying Library Files

To determine external libraries before running them, use Application Manager when installing the application or modifying the installation parameters of the application (refer to Chapter 8, "Getting Familiar with LiveWire's Application Manager"). After entering the library file paths in Application Manager, restart the server, and compile and restart the application so that the changes can take effect.

 Note When using Application Manager to determine external libraries, the applications on the server can call functions in those libraries using the registerCFunction and callC functions.

Registering External Functions

To use external functions with LiveWire applications, you must register them using the registerCFunction function, as in the following:

```
registerCFunction(JSFunctionName, libraryPath, CFunctionName)
```

JSFunctionName indicates the name by which the function will be referred in JavaScript with the callC function. Use libraryPath to indicate the complete file path of the library (using your operating system conventions).

Note JavaScript's callC function returns only string values.

Use the CFunctionName parameter to indicate the name of the C function as it is defined in the library.

Note Remember that JavaScript uses a backslash (\) as a special character. To separate Windows directories and file names, you must use the double backslash characters.

The registerCFunction function returns True when the function registers successfully and False when it does not. Situations in which the function would not register might be when LiveWire is unable to locate the library at the position you specified or cannot find the function you specified within the library.

Note Before an application can call a function using callC, it must register the function with registerCFunction. After the function registration, the application can call the function repeatedly.

External Functions in JavaScript

After your application uses registerCFunction to register specific functions, it can call the registered functions using the JavaScript callC function, which returns a string value that was returned by the external function, as in the following:

```
callC(JSFunctionName, arguments)
```

The JSFunctionName parameter indicates the name of the function as it was determined with the RegisterCFunction function. The arguments parameter is a comma-delimited list of arguments to the external function. The arguments parameter can be any JavaScript values. Note, however, that the number of arguments you use must correspond with the number of arguments the external function requires.

The following exercise shows you how to use an external library in a LiveWire application. Note, however, that for this example, you need a C compiler.

Using an External Library

1. In Windows 95 or Windows NT, go to the MS-DOS prompt and change the current directory to the directory called lwccall. This directory is in the LiveWire samples directory and includes the C source code file lwccall.c. This file defines a C function named mystuff_EchoCCallArguments. This function accepts any number of arguments and returns a string that contains the arguments in an HTML listing.

2. If you have the Microsoft Visual C++ 4.0 compiler, type in the following command line.

   ```
   cl -LD lwccall.c /link /EXPORT:mystuff_EchoCCallArguments
   ```

   If you use another manufacturer's compiler, consult the documentation found in lwccall.c for compiling procedures.

3. After you compile the C program using your favorite text editor, create the following HTML file. The following JavaScript statements register the C function echoCCallArguments, call the function with some arguments, and then generate HTML based on the value returned by the C library.

   ```
   <HTML>
   <HEAD><TITLE>Calling External Functions</TITLE></HEAD>
   <BODY>
   <SERVER>
   var isRegistered = registerCFunction("echoCCallArguments",
           "c:livewiresamplesccallappmystuff.dll",
           "mystuff_EchoCCallArguments")
   ```

```
if (isRegistered == true) {
      var cFunctionReturnValue = callC("echoCCallArguments",
            "Spies tell lies",
            32,
            false,
            "Rain dog")
      write(cFunctionReturnValue)
}
</BODY>
</HTML>
```

4. In the left frame of Site Manager, select the directory in which your recently created HTML file is located.

5. Choose Site | Manage to bring the application under site management.

6. Choose Site | Build Application to compile the application.

7. Start the application with Application Manager.

8. Run the application by clicking Run in Application Manager. You will see the following text generated by your Web application:

```
argc = 4<BR>
argv[0].tag: string; value = Spies tell lies<BR>
argv[1].tag: double; value = 32<BR>
argv[2].tag: boolean; value = false<BR>
argv[3].tag: string; value = Rain dog<BR>
```

Summary

This chapter discussed client and server scripts, including when to use them, communication between client and server scripts, using files on the server, and calling external libraries.

Chapter 10, "Creating Database Applications Using LiveWire Pro," teaches you how you can use LiveWire Pro to create database applications. It includes how to install database components, how to gain access to databases, and more about database types.

Creating Database Applications Using LiveWire Pro

A large percentage of real-world business applications makes use of a database management system (DBMS). To manage large, structured sets of persistent data, offering ad hoc query facilities to many users, you can use a DBMS as a standalone program or as a utility program used by standalone applications.

A DBMS, or database management system, is a database system that enables you to control the organization, storage, and retrieval of data in fields, records, and files.

A DBMS controls the organization, storage, and retrieval of data (fields, records, and files) in a database. It also controls the security and integrity of the database. The DBMS accepts requests for data from the application program and instructs the operating system to transfer the appropriate data.

By using a DBMS, you can easily modify your application as its information requirements change. You can add new categories of data to the database without disruption to your existing application.

LiveWire and LiveWire Pro enable you to develop client-server database applications that work with a DBMS. If you have LiveWire Pro, you already have a DBMS. LiveWire Pro is bundled with a developer version of Informix's OnLine Workgroup DBMS— the entry-level version of Informix's OnLine Dynamic Server. Should you decide in the future to upgrade to a more powerful Informix database server that supports multiprocessor systems, OnLine Workgroups databases should be fully compatible. The copy of OnLine Workgroup bundled with LiveWire Pro is licensed for a single developer on a single Web server with unlimited users.

In addition to a DBMS, LiveWire Pro comes with the Crystal Reports 4.5 database report writer. Crystal Reports adds versatile reporting to your LiveWire database applications via a simple graphical user interface. With this reporting tool, you can design reports that include cross-tabs and sophisticated graphs.

Did you know...

Cross-tabs, or cross tabulations, perform statistical analysis of tabular data. They commonly are used in reports to quickly compare and identify trends.

Because standard LiveWire does not come with a DBMS, in order to develop database applications with it, you need to have an existing DBMS on your system. This database system must be from Informix, Oracle, or Sybase, or support a database connectivity standard called the Open DataBase Connectivity (ODBC) standard. Microsoft SQL Server, Borland's Paradox, and Microsoft Access are examples of ODBC-compliant database systems.

The LiveWire Architecture

LiveWire is based on a client-server architecture called a *three-tier architecture*. Figure 10.1 shows the relationship between the three tiers that make up this architecture.

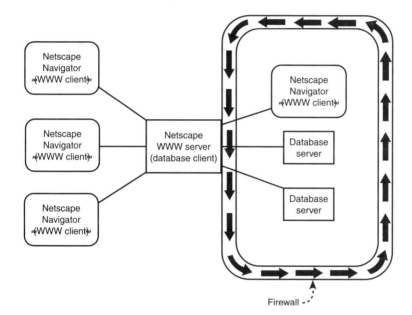

Figure 10.1

LiveWire's three-tier architecture.

Before three-tier client-server systems, there were two-tier client-server systems. With the classic two-tier system, the client always handled data presentation, and the server managed the database system. The primary problem of the two-tier system is that the application logic could be implemented only on either the server or the client system, but not both at the same time.

If application logic was implemented on the server, you encountered problems with the server becoming overloaded; the server handled not only database inquiries, but also provided the computational resources to run the application. If the application logic was implemented on the client, then typically the client software became monolithic and platform-dependent.

The three-tier client-server architecture provides an additional separation of the application logic from the database and the actual presentation. A three-tier architecture offers a flexible way of organizing client-server systems.

In a three-tier architecture, an intermediate connecting layer is introduced. Each of the client programs and servers communicates with the intermediate layer rather than directly with each other. This provides a clear separation of the client programs from the data sources, enabling you to maintain them more easily. Because of these inherent advantages, the three-tier client-server architecture is replacing the classic two-tier architecture of the past.

Following are the three tiers that make up the LiveWire architecture:

Web browser tier: Web browsers such as Netscape Navigator provide an end user interface to LiveWire applications. This tier often provides application functionality in the form of JavaScript. Functionality usually is limited to small tasks, such as validating user input. You can find Web browsers either inside or outside a corporation's firewall.

Did you know...

A firewall is a collection of components placed between two networks that acts as a door through which all traffic must pass (incoming and outgoing). Only authorized traffic is allowed. Programs and data inside the firewall are immune to penetration.

Netscape server tier: A Netscape server is in charge of providing a large amount of application functionality, in addition to managing security and access control. The Netscape server tier acts as a server to clients (Web browsers) from both inside and outside the corporate firewall. In addition, the Netscape server acts as a client to the database server.

Database server tier: The database server is a SQL DBMS that consists of data, metadata, and referential integrity rules used by the LiveWire application. Typically, this tier exists inside the corporate firewall.

Did you know...

SQL (pronounced "sequel"), or Structured Query Language, provides a user interface to database management systems. Developed by IBM in the 1970s, SQL has become the de facto standard.

Metadata is data that describes aspects of other data, such as name, format, and so on.

Referential integrity is a collection of properties possessed by data in a database. In a database of family members, for example, if you enter Kathleen Brennan as a spouse of Tom Waits, Tom Waits automatically is entered as a spouse of Kathleen Brennan. Similarly, if you remove one end of the relationship, the other also will be removed.

Installing Database Components

Running a LiveWire database application requires you to install on your machine all the components the application will use, including LiveWire on your development machine. The following list describes the components needed to run a LiveWire database application:

◆ On your database server machine, relational database server software

◆ On your WWW server machine, Netscape Web server

◆ On your server machine, client and networking software for your database

◆ On client machines, Netscape Navigator (or another Web client)

If you are using a separate machine for your database server and Web server, you must take extra precautions when installing the Web server. The installation program may examine your machine and, after noticing a database system absent, will leave out the installation of the Web server's database client software. If this should happen, simply run the installation program a second time, forcing the program to install the database client software.

 Note If you are under a tight budget, you might want to install the Web server and the database server on the same machine, saving you from having to purchase a database server machine.

To install the server, follow the steps in the ensuing exercise.

Installing the Server

1. After you insert the CD in the drive, choose File|Run from the main menu.

2. In the dialog box that appears, enter **D:\SETUP**, where D: is the drive letter for your CD-ROM drive.

3. Read the information about technical support and click Continue.

4. A dialog box appears, prompting you to enter the directory in which you want to install the server. The default is C:\NETSCAPE. You can enter another drive and directory if you want. This is the server root directory in which you install all servers (if you plan to have more than one server installed on your machine). Click Continue.

Warning | The directory name must be eight characters or fewer—you can't use long directory names as you can in Windows 95.

Because the server uses the directory name for log and error files and for the document root, do not rename the directory after installation.

5. A dialog box appears, asking you to confirm whether your machine has a DNS entry in a DNS server. If you choose DNS Configured, the installation process assumes you want to use host names (you still can use IP addresses if you want). If you choose No DNS Entry, the installation process uses only IP addresses.

Note | If your machine doesn't have access to a DNS server that can perform DNS lookups, or if your machine doesn't have an entry in the DNS map of a DNS server, you must click No DNS Entry and use IP addresses throughout installation.

Also, if your machine has an entry in the DNS server but isn't configured to perform DNS lookups on the DNS server, you should click No DNS Entry. If you select No DNS Entry, clients can acquire access to your server using your host name, but the server will use IP addresses rather than DNS host names. For example, it might use IP addresses for user authorizations.

6. The installation program goes to your computer's Registry and determines your host name or IP address. Confirm the entry or change it in the dialog box. Click Continue.

7. The installation program copies all the files to your hard disk and starts a service called Netscape Install. This service runs on a random port and is destroyed automatically after the installation process.

When the message about configuring the server using the Server Manager forms appears, click OK. The remainder of the configuration process is done through forms you use with Netscape Navigator.

8. When Netscape Navigator appears displaying a form, click Install New Server.

9. You'll see three buttons. The Server Config button takes you through a series of forms that configure the server. The Document Config button displays a form for configuring the document root directory and the types of documents your server can send to clients. The Admin Config button displays a form for configuring the administration server. You can specify which users have permission to use the administration forms to configure all your installed servers.

Gaining Access to a Database

To gain access to a database from LiveWire Pro, use the connect method of the database object, as in the following:

```
database.connect("type", "server", "user", "password", "database")
```

Note the double quotation marks that enclose each parameter. Use the type parameter to indicate the type of the database you want to access. You can use INFORMIX, ORACLE, SYBASE, ILLUSTRA, or ODBC.

Use the server parameter to indicate the name of the server on which the database resides, which is usually the place in which you installed the database.

The user parameter indicates the name you use to log into the database.

The password parameter indicates the password needed to log into the database. For instances in which the database you want to gain access to does not require a password, you can use an empty string ("").

Use the database parameter to specify a particular database in instances where your database server supports more than one database on a single server. If only one database is on the server, you can use an empty string ("") for this parameter.

Establishing a Database Connection

After you attain access to the database, you need to establish a connection. LiveWire Pro offers two approaches. In the standard approach, the application institutes a single connection statement in the initial startup page, which enables all clients to share the same database and user name. Each client automatically receives a copy of the shared connection, thus connecting all clients simultaneously. This approach is advantageous in that LiveWire manages all aspects of establishing database connections; however, all users must share the same name and access priveleges. To use the standard approach, you also need a vendor license to use multiple database connections.

The other approach LiveWire offers is the serial approach, in which only one client at a time can connect to the database. With this approach, every page in the application that needs a database connection locks the project object (to prevent multi-user access) and then connects to the database. When the user indicates he or she is finished using the database, the connection is broken, and the project object is unlocked. Note, however, that if more than one application will be connecting to one database, you must lock the server object.

Database Object's Connect Method

There are many ways to connect to a database; however, LiveWire has made it easy with the connect method of the database object. The database object enables an application to interact with a relational database. The method, connect, is what gets you there and enables you to create database objects. To connect to a database, use the following code:

```
database.connect("type", "server", "user", " password", " database")
```

Use the type parameter to specify the type of the database to which you want to connect. You can use INFORMIX, ORACLE, SYBASE, or ODBC.

Use the server parameter to indicate the name of the database server, which usually is established when you install the database.

The user parameter is where you specify the user name you use to log onto the database. In some cases, this must be the same as your OS login name; however, some systems provide valid user names you can choose from.

Use the password parameter to specify the password you use when logging onto the database. If the database you want to access does not require a password, you can use an empty string ("") for this parameter.

The database parameter is where you specify the name of the database you want to get access to, provided that your database server supports multiple databases. Use an empty string ("") here if your server does not support multiple databases.

Displaying Queries in HTML with SQLTable

Database queries provide different ways for you to view, change, and analyze data. You can combine data from different places and sort it in a particular order, perform calcuations on groups of records, and calculate data and group the results.

 A query is a way in which you can view, modify, and analyze data. Queries also are referred to as cursors or answer sets.

LiveWire enables you to display query results in HTML documents by using the SQLTable method of the database object. The SQLTable method takes a SQL SELECT statement as its argument and returns an HTML table. Each row and column in the query is displayed as a row and column of the table. This is the easiest way to display query results in HTML.

Note | SQLTable does not enable you to format your query results. For more information about formatting output, see "Using Cursors" later in this chapter.

Did you know...

The SQL select statement is probably the most used SQL statement. As its name implies, it is used to select information from tables. The full syntax for the select statement is:

```
select [all¦distinct] <select-list>
[into <target>]
[from <source>[holdlock][,...]]
[where <search-conditions>]
[group by [all] <aggregate-free-expression> [,...]
having <search-conditions>]]
[order by {<column-name>[,...] ¦ <column-number>[,...] ¦ <expression>}
➡ [asc¦desc]]
[compute <row-aggregate>(<column-name>)[,...]
[by <column-name>[,...]]
[for browse]
```

Shown here with all of its options, the select statement appears to be quite complicated. Fortunately, the typical use of the statement is much simpler.

The following example shows you how to display queries in HTML using SQLTable.

Displaying Queries in HTML

1. Suppose you have a database on your computer that you use to store information about your personal belongings. You name this database "MyDatabase." In that database is a table called "MyMusic." The "MyMusic" table has three categories— "Recording Artist," "Title," and "Music Format." In that table you have two entries (pretty lame music collection). Table 10.1 looks like the following:

TABLE 10.1
Table Entries Stored in a Database

Recording Artist	Title	Music Format
Tom Waits	Blue Valentine	CD-ROM
Screamin' Jay Hawkins	Cow Fingers and Mosquito Pie	Cassette

2. You would like your Web page to display your music collection for all your friends to see, but you don't want to have to update your Web page every time you add or remove an entry to your "MyMusic" table. You can accomplish this with only three lines of server-side JavaScript code. Suppose that you start out with the following HTML file to which you want to add your record collection table.

```
<HTML>
<HEAD><TITLE>My Music Collection</TITLE></HEAD>
<BODY>
<H1>My Music Collection</H1>
<HR>
Below is my music collection:<br>
</BODY>
</HTML>
```

3. Now you can add some server-side JavaScript to connect to the database. By performing a simple SELECT statement with the SQLTable method on your database table—an HTML listing of your music collection is dynamically generated.

```
 1. <HTML>
 2. <HEAD><TITLE>My Music Collection</TITLE></HEAD>
 3. <BODY>
 4. <H1>My Music Collection</H1>
 5. <HR>
 6. Below is my music collection:<br>
 7. <SERVER>
 8. database.connect("ORACLE","MyServerName","FredFarkle","phantom309",
    MyDatabase")
 9. database.SQLTable("select * from MyMusic")
10. database.disconnect()
```

```
11. </SERVER>
12. </BODY>
13. </HTML>
```

Line 8 establishes a connection to your database. In this example, your database is of the "ORACLE" type, your server is named "MyServerName," your database user name is "FredFarkle," your password is "phantom309," and as mentioned previously, your database is called "MyDatabase." In line 9, you use the SQLTable method to perform the SELECT on your "MyMusic" table. This SELECT uses a wildcard(*) to select everything from the "MyMusic" table. In Line 10, you disconnect from the database after completing your database operations.

4. When the client views the LiveWire application with the preceding compilation of HTML and JavaScript code, the following HTML content is sent to the client Web Browser, and the user sees the table shown in figure 10.2.

```
 1. <HTML>
 2. <HEAD><TITLE>My Music Collection</TITLE></HEAD>
 3. <BODY>
 4. <H1>My Music Collection</H1>
 5. <HR>
 6. Below is my music collection:<br>
 7. <TABLE BORDER>
 8. <TR>
 9. <TH>Recording Artist</TH>
10. <TH>Title</TH>
11. <TH>Music Format</TH>
12. </TR>
13. <TR>
14. <TD>Tom Waits</TD>
15. <TD>Blue Valentine</TD>
16. <TD>CD-ROM</TD>
17. </TR>
18. <TR>
19. <TD>Screamin' Jay Hawkins</TD>
20. <TD>Cow Fingers and Mosquito Pie</TD>
21. <TD>Cassette</TD>
22. </TR>
23. </TABLE>
24. </BODY>
25. </HTML>
```

Figure 10.2

A dynamically generated HTML table from database table.

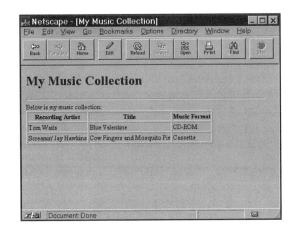

Disconnecting from a Database

To close a database connection, LiveWire provides the disconnect method of the database object. Use the following syntax:

```
database.disconnect()
```

After you disconnect from the database using the disconnect method, your application cannot create cursors or use any other database methods. To reconnect to the database, you must use the connect method of the database object.

To use the disconnect method, simply type the statement *database.disconnect()* in your SERVER script at a location in your script in which you are certain all database operations are complete.

Utilizing Passthrough SQL Statements

Rather than using the available LiveWire database object methods, LiveWire enables your application to pass directly to the server SQL statements that do not return a cursor (or answer set). This is referred to as *passthrough*. Passthrough is useful when you want to perform a SQL database operation that does not need any feedback from the database system. You might use passthrough to add or remove a database record, for example. You would not use passthrough to perform a query, however, because queries involve feedback.

Did you know...

An answer set also is referred to as a query or cursor. Back to the record example, suppose that you wanted to create a printout of your CD-ROM entries sorted in alphabetic order. Rather than sort all your music, you probably would sort an answer set that is an answer to the question, "Which music of mine is of the CD-ROM format?"

You accomplish the addition or removal of a database record using the execute method of the database object. To perform passthrough SQL statements, you need to provide the SQL statement as the argument, as in the following:

```
database.execute("delete from MyMusic r where r.recordingArtist = " +
➥client.MusicSold)
```

Here, client.MusicSold matches the name of a recording artist that you sold and need to remove from your database. This statement can be executed anywhere inside a SERVER script as long as it follows the execution of a database.connect() statement.

To indicate whether the method was successful in completion, the execute method returns a status code that is based on the database server message. The method returns 0 when successful and a non-zero integer that indicates the reason for failure.

Note | Unless you begin a transactoin with the beginTransaction method of the database object, the SQL statement that is passed as a parameter to the execute method is carried out automatically.

Note | To execute SQL statements that return answer sets, use the cursor or SQLTable methods. For more information about cursor methods, see "Using Cursors" later in this chapter.

You can use the execute statement for any statement that is supported by the database server and does not return a cursor. These statements include the INSERT, UPDATE, and DELETE statements, as well as the CREATE, ALTER, and DROP data definition language (DDL) statements. Also included are any other control statements supported by the server. To make your application more database-platform independent, use cursors rather than passthrough statements whenever possible. Being database-platform independent means that should you ever wish to switch to a new database system offered by a different vendor, there will be little or no modifications necessary for your program.

Handling Transactions

Transactions are groups of database actions that are carried out conjointly. The way transactions work is much the same as a team: all the actions either succeed together or fail together.

LiveWire provides an unvaried interface that enables you to manage your transactions. You can count on an unvaried interface—it's not going to change even when database servers accomplish transactions differently. Part of managing your transactions is transaction control, which refers to the actions you take to modify a database (such as SQL INSERT, UPDATE, and DELETE).

Committing a transaction refers to attempting to perform all the actions at one time. To cancel the actions, you perform a rollback, which refers to a transaction that you have not committed.

Default Transactions Performed by LiveWire

LiveWire views each database update as a separate transaction. If you don't control specific transactions, LiveWire does it for you by beginning an implicit transaction before each statement and then attempting to commit the transaction after each statement. So, suppose you are adding an entry to a table. LiveWire makes it impossible for this statement to get only half way complete, before some other user's database operation takes place. You can override this feature, however, by explicitly handling your transactions yourself. Explicitly handling transactions yourself enables you to perform several database statements within a transaction block, which enables you to commit the transaction only after the entire set of database statements have performed.

Handling Transactions Yourself

Although LiveWire has transactions that it controls, the database object provides several different methods you can use to manage transactions. In order to use these methods, however, your application must be connected to the database.

To start a new transaction, use the beginTransaction method. The actions you use to modify the database are grouped in this transaction and are referred to as the current transaction.

To commit the current transaction, use the commitTransaction method, which attempts to commit all actions subsequent to the most recent call to beginTransaction.

To roll back (or cancel) the current transaction, use the rollbackTransaction method. Using this method reverses all updates subsequent to the last call to beginTransaction.

To begin a transaction, for example, use the following syntax:

```
database.beginTransaction()
```

To commit a transaction, use the following code:

```
database.commitTransaction()
```

Note The extent of a transaction is restricted to the current HTML page in an application. In other words, you cannot perform transactions on HTML pages other than the corresponding page. For example, if your application leaves the HTML page before you issue a commitTransaction or rollbackTransaction statement, the transaction will be performed regardless of your ensuing actions. Conversely, if no current transaction action exists, LiveWire ignores any commitTransaction and rollbackTransaction statements.

Using Cursors

A cursor is a pointer that you advance through a set of rows retrieved with a SELECT statement. Database queries (or tables) also are referred to as cursors. After connecting to a database, you can create a cursor. To do this, use the cursor method of the database object, giving database object a SELECT statement as its argument, as in the following syntax:

```
cursorName = database.cursor("SELECT statement", updatable)
```

Use the cursorName parameter to indicate the name you give the cursor object. SELECT statement is a SQL SELECT statement supported by the database server. To ensure database independence, use SQL 89/92-compliant syntax. The updatable parameter, which is optional, is a Boolean parameter that enables you to indicate whether you want to request an updatable cursor.

Properties and Methods of Cursors

Cursors have a range of available properties and methods you can use to perform different actions, such as getting the number of columns in a row, adding a row, and deleting a row. The following list outlines and describes these methods and properties:

columns	This method enables you to find out the number of columns in a cursor. It has no parameters.
ColumnName	This method returns the names of the columns in the cursor. The parameter is a zero-based ordinal number in the query.
close	This method closes a query. It has no parameters.
deleteRow	This method deletes the current row in the table you specify. You must include the string that specifies the name of the row you want to delete.
insertRow	This method inserts a new row in the table you specify. The new row is inserted after the current row. You must include the string that specifies the name of the table into which you want to insert the row.
next	This method enables you to move the current row to the next row in the cursor. If the current row is the last row in the cursor, this method returns False. Otherwise, it returns True.
updateRow	This method updates records in the current row of the table you specify in the cursor. You must include the string that specifies the name of the table you want to update.
colName	This cursor object property enables you to refer to a cursor column by the column's name in the database. For example, to refer to the "Recording Artist" column, given the database name for this column is recordingArtist, you would refer to it as musicCursor.recordingArtist. Likewise, if a database name for the "Music Format" column is musicFormat, you would refer to it as musicCursor.musicFormat, where musicCursor is the name for this cursor object, and musicFormat is the colName property name.

Accessing Record Values

For each cursor you create, the SELECT statement creates a property with a name that matches the database column name for each column in the answer set. It is by this property that you specify the value (or column) you want to access.

Consider this example. Knowing ahead of time that the name for the "Music Format" column in the database is "musicFormat," you can create a cursor named cursorName with the following code:

```
musicCursor=database.cursor("SELECT * FROM MyMusic WHERE musicFormat = CD-ROM")
```

This answer set consists of all your music entries that are in CD-ROM format. To display the first entry in your answer set, you could use the following code:

```
<SERVER>musicCursor.next()</SERVER>
Recording Artist is <SERVER>write(musicCursor.recordingArtist)</SERVER><BR>
Music Title is <SERVER>write(musicCursor.title)</SERVER><BR>
Music Format is <SERVER>write(musicCursor.musicFormat)</SERVER><P>
```

In case you are wondering why to perform the *next* method, it is to compensate for the fact that, by default, the current row is positioned before the first row in the cursor. To get to the first row, you need to execute a *next* first.

Accessing the Number of Columns in a Cursor

To display the number of columns in a cursor, use the columns method of the cursor method, as in the following example:

```
The number of columns in musicCursor is <SERVER>write(musicCursor.columns
➥())<SERVER>
```

Accessing Column Names

To get the name of each column in a result set, use the columnName method, as in the following:

```
The name of the first  column is <SERVER>write(musicCursor.columnName
➥(0))<SERVER><BR>
The name of the second column is <SERVER>write(musicCursor.columnName
➥(1))</SERVER><BR>
The name of the third  column is <SERVER>write(musicCursor.columnName
➥(2))</SERVER><P>
```

The parameter is an integer, starting with 0, in which you specify the ordinal number of the column for which you want the name. The first column in the result set is zero, the second is one, and so on.

Analyzing Data with Cursors

LiveWire enables you to retrieve from a database values other than columns, such as SQL expressions and aggregate values. You use SELECT statements to do this. You also can display SQL expressions and aggregate values using the array index property of the cursor method, referring to the expression as the following:

```
cursor[n]
```

The variable *n* is the ordinal position (starting at zero) of the expression in the SELECT list.

Suppose that you had a cursor named beerData that was created like the following:

```
beerData = database.cursor("SELECT MIN(ALCOHOL), AVG(ALCOHOL), MAX(ALCOHOL)
➥from BEERS")
```

To display the result obtained by the aggregate function MAX, you could do the following:

```
Strongest beer is <SERVER>write(beerData[2])</SERVER>
```

Navigating Tables with Cursors

When you first create a table, the current row (or pointer) for a cursor is located immediately before the first row. Use the next method to move the pointer through the records in the table. The next method advances the pointer to the subsequent row and returns True when another row in the table is present. This method returns False when it has reached the final row in the table. The following example shows you how to use the next method:

```
<SERVER>
write("<TABLE BORDER>")
while (musicCursor.next()) {
    write("<TR>")
    write("<TD>" + musicCursor.recordingArtist + "</TD>")
    write("<TD>" + musicCursor.title + "</TD>")
    write("<TD>" + musicCursor.musicFormat + "</TD>")
    write("</TR>")
}
write("</TABLE>")
</SERVER>
```

Closing a Cursor

Closing a cursor is simply a matter of using the close method. Closing a cursor frees memory. The following code shows you how to use the close method:

```
musicCursor.close()
```

At the end of every client request, LiveWire automatically closes all cursors, so there is no need to worry about using the close method.

Updating a Cursor

LiveWire provides a way you can update cursors; that is, you can modify a table based on the current row of the cursor. Typically, the current row is set to the row you want to update, and then the update is performed on the current row. Having the capability to update a cursor is useful in situations where you would like to update the database via your Web pages rather than through a database utility.

To create a cursor that is enabled for updating, simply add a parameter of *true* when creating the cursor, as in the following example:

```
musicCursor=database.cursor("SELECT * FROM MyMusic WHERE musicFormat =
➥CD-ROM",true)
```

 LiveWire enables you to create an updatable cursor for single-table queries; however, the capability to create updatable cursors for multiple-table queries or queries that contain joins does not exist.

In order to use an updatable cursor, you must follow these steps:

1. Assign values to columns in the cursor, such as in the following:

   ```
   musicCursor.recordingArtist="Buster Poindexter"
   musicCursor.title="Buster's Happy Hour"
   musicCursor.musicFormat="LP"
   ```

2. Establish the *current row* value for the cursor through the use of the *next* method.

 In order to avoid receiving null for unassigned values when inserting rows into a table, you must perform the next method. Also note that, when inserting values into a table, insertRow returns null when columns in the table are not in the cursor.

3. Use the *insertRow, updateRow,* or *deleteRow* to substitute the current row values (set in second step) with new column values (set in first step).

 You do not need to assign values to columns when using deleteRow—it deletes the entire row.

The following exercise walks you through the process of creating and using a cursor.

Creating and Using a Cursor

The LiveWire development comes bundled with several sample applications. One of them is a sample database application called Video. This sample is useful for reviewing what you have learned so far. Before you can run this sample, you must create the Video database first. Following are the required files and procedures for creating your Video database, depending on which database server you are using.

◆ **Informix (LiveWire Pro)**

1. Find the SQL files for creating the video database with Informix in the NETSCAPE\SERVER\LIVEWIRE\SAMPLES\VIDEO\IFX directory.

2. Using Windows NT's Program Manager, open the program group named Informix On-line Dynamic Server. Inside this program group, double-click on the Command Line Utilities icon. A DOS window opens, and you can enter the following command:

```
cd netscape\server\LiveWire\samples\video\ifx
```

3. Enter **dbaccess** in the DOS window. This runs a DOS utility. Navigate in this utility by selecting a highlighted choice with the Enter key and moving the highlight with the arrow keys. After this program is running, make the following selections:

```
Query Language
sysmaster@servername
Choose
rwtut
Run - This will create the sample video database called "livewire".
Exit - To exit the command line utilities
```

You have now created an Informix sample video database.

◆ **Oracle**

1. Find the SQL files for creating the video database with Oracle in the NETSCAPE\SERVER\LIVEWIRE\SAMPLES\VIDEO\ORA directory.

2. Start Oracle's SQL Plus program. When prompted with the SQL>, enter the following command, which is a SQL script that creates the oracle tables necessary to run the video application:

```
START C:\NETSCAPE\SERVER\LIVEWIRE\SAMPLES\VIDEO\ORA\ORATABLE
```

3. From the DOS prompt that appears, run the batch file, video.bat.

This batch program loads the video tables with data.

◆ **Sybase**

1. Find the SQL files for creating the video database with Sybase in the NETSCAPE\SERVER\LIVEWIRE\SAMPLES\VIDEO\SYB directory.

2. Open a DOS window. From the prompt run create_syb userid password, as in the following:

```
C:\NETSCAPE\SERVER\LIVEWIRE\SAMPLES\VIDEO\CREATE_SYB SA
```

This batch file creates and loads the Sybase tables necessary to run the video application.

◆ **Microsoft SQL Server**

1. Find the SQL files for creating the video database on MS SQL in the NETSCAPE\SERVER\LIVEWIRE\SAMPLES\VIDEO\MSS directory.

2. Open a DOS window. From the DOS prompt, run create_mss userid password, as in the following:

```
C:\NETSCAPE\SERVER\LIVEWIRE\SAMPLES\VIDEO\CREATE_MSS SA
```

This batch file creates and loads the MS SQL Server tables necessary to run the video application.

3. Now that the database is configured correctly, you need to edit the connect statement in the sample Video file, which establishes connection with your database. In your favorite text editor, open the sample HTML file NETSCAPE\SERVER\LIVEWIRE\SAMPLES\VIDEO\START.HTM. Edit the database.connect statement, depending on which database server you are using.

◆ **Informix (LiveWire Pro)**

1. Leave the first argument of the database.connect statement as it is.

2. Change the second argument of the database.connect statement to reflect your server name.

3. If you've since changed the Informix default username/password, change the third and fourth arguments to reflect the current user/password. If you kept the default, leave them as "informix," "informix."

4. Change the fifth and final argument (database name) of database.connect to "livewire."

◆ **Oracle**

1. Change the first argument to "ORACLE."

2. Change the second argument of the database.connect statement to specify your server name, such as "T:\SERVERNAME\:ORCL."

3. If you've since changed the Oracle default username/password, change the third and fourth arguments to reflect the current user/password. If you kept the default, leave them as "SYSTEM," "MANAGER."

4. Change the fifth and final argument (database name) of database.connect to blank ("").

◆ **Sybase**

1. Change the first argument to "SYBASE."

2. Change the second argument of the database.connect statement to specify your server name.

   If you changed the Sybase default username/password, change the third and fourth arguments to reflect the current username/password. If you kept the default, leave them as "sa," blank ("").

3. Change the last argument (database name) of database.connect to blank, ("").

4. When you finish editing the connect statement, save the START.HTML file to disk.

5. Compile the application using Site Manager or the supplied batch file, build.bat.

   To compile the application in Site Manager, access LiveWire Site Manager from program Manager. In the left frame of Site Manager, select the directory NETSCAPE\SERVER\LIVEWIRE\SAMPLES\VIDEO\. Choose Site|Manage to invoke the VIDEO application under site management, if it is not under site management already. Choose Site|Build Application to compile the application.

6. Start the application with Application Manager. Run the application by clicking Run in Application Manager. Using your favorite client Web browser, play around with the Video application. Notice that you can use

the Video application as either a customer or an administrator. As a customer, you can rent a movie or look at the movies you currently have rented. As an administrator, you can see who has rented which movies, and return a video for a customer. In addition, as an administrator, you can add or delete a customer.

7. Take a look at the RENTALS.HTML file. This file is used to display a list of all rented videos and is an excellent example of how to create cursors and display items contained in them. Look at how the file ADD.HTML is used to add customers to the database. This file is a good example of using a passthrough statement. Also, take a look at RETURN.HTML, which performs the logic of returning the video. This file serves as a good demonstration of creating a cursor, updating a row, performing a transaction, and closing a cursor.

Database Datatypes

Databases have a profusion of datatypes that enable you create all kinds of databases, such as those for currency, graphic images, and so on. Regardless of the datatype, LiveWire converts these datatypes to JavaScript values (which either are strings or numbers), thus enabling you to work with all of them. For example, numeric data types are converted to numbers, character datatypes are converted to strings, and so on. LiveWire even converts null values to JavaScript null.

 LiveWire does not, however, support packed decimal notation. Because of this, some conversions may not be as accurate when reading and writing packed decimal datatypes.

To avoid problems, be sure to check your results before you re-insert your values into the database.

The date Datatype

LiveWire enables you to work with date datatypes by converting database date values to JavaScript's built-in Date objects. To insert a date value into a database, for example, use the following JavaScript code:

```
cursorName.dateColumn = dateObj

musicCursor.dateColumn = dateObj
```

You use the cursorName parameter to indicate a cursor. The dateColumn parameter indicates a column that corresponds to a date, and dateObj indicates a JavaScript Date object. To create a Date object, use the new operator and the Date constructor, as in the following example:

```
dateObj = new Date(dateString)
```

The dateObj parameter indicates a JavaScript Date object, and the dateString parameter indicates a string that represents a date. If the date string is empty, LiveWire creates a Date object for the current date.

Depending on which database system you are using, the datatype conversion would be handled as in tables 10.2 through 10.5.

TABLE 10.2
Informix Datatype Conversion

LiveWire Datatype	Informix Datatype
string	char or nchar, text, varchar, or nvarchar
number	decimal(p,s), double precision, float, integer, money(p,s), serial, smallfloat, smallint
date	date, datetime
BLOb	byte
Not supported	interval

TABLE 10.3
Oracle Datatype Conversion

LiveWire Datatype	Oracle Datatype
string	long, char or varchar2(n), rowid, mislabel
number	number(p,s), number(p,0), float(p)
date	date
BLOb	raw(255), long raw

TABLE 10.4
Sybase Datatype Conversion

LiveWire Datatype	Sybase Datatype
string	char(n), varchar(n), nchar(n), nvarchar(n), text
number	bit, tinyint, smallint, int, float(p), double precision, real, decimal(p,s), numeric(p,s), money, smallmoney
date	datetime, smalldatetime
BLOb	binary(n), varbinary(n), image

TABLE 10.5
ODBC Datatype Conversion

LiveWire Datatype	ODBC Datatype
string	SQL_LONGVARCHAR, SQL_VARCHAR, SQL_CHAR
number	SQL_SMALLINT, SQL_INTEGER, SQL_DOUBLE, SQL_FLOAT, SQL_REAL, SQL_BIGINT, SQL_NUMERIC, SQL_DECIMAL
date	SQL_DATE, SQL_TIME, SQL_TIMESTAMP
BLOb	SQL_BINARY, SQL_VARBINARY, SQL_LONGBINARY

The BLOb Datatype

BLObs are binary large objects that store binary data for multimedia content, such as sounds or images. You can use BLObs to store your binary data in LiveWire applications and then access this data using the BLObs methods LiveWire provides.

You also can store BLOb data elsewhere (outside of the database) while storing just the file names in the database, and then access the file names using standard HTML tags. To display an image of a music title, you could use code similar the following:

```
<SERVER>
write("<IMG SRC='" + musicCursor.imageFileName + "'>")
</SERVER>
```

For those of you who need to store the actual binary data in the database, LiveWire features methods that enable you to display and insert BLOb data. Look at table 10.6.

TABLE 10.6
Methods for Inserting BLOb Data

Method	Description
blobImage	Displays BLOb data stored in a database. Returns an HTML IMG tag for the specified image type (GIF, JPEG, and so on). You must include a string that specifyies an image type, such as GIF, JPEG, and so on.
blobLink	Displays a link that references BLOb data with a hyperlink. This method creates an HTML hyperlink to the BLOb. You must include a string that specifies the MIME (Multipurpose Internet Multimedia Extensions) type of BLOb data.
BLOb	Assigns BLOb data to a column in a cursor. Use this method to insert or update a row that contains a BLOb in an updatable cursor. Note that this is a top-level function, not a cursor method.

blobImage

LiveWire's blobImage method enables you to retrieve from your database a BLOb, which is stored in a temporary file of the format you specify, and then is referred to by an HTML image tag. The temporary file remains in effect until the HTML page is generated and sent to the client. Storing image data in a database system is theoretically the best method to use because database systems are a more robust technology than file systems. From a practical standpoint, however, storing image data on a file system can give your server better performance than on a database. Deciding whether to use blobLink and blobImage versus storing images on a file system is a trade-off decision that you will have to make based on your needs.

During the time LiveWire is creating the page, the binary data blobImage retrieves from the database is stored in active memory. Thus, it is possible for requests that retrieve large amounts of data to exceed the dynamic memory available on the server. For this reason, you should limit the number of rows you want to retrieve at one time by using blobImage to remain within the limits of the server's dynamic memory.

You also can use the blobImage method to create HTML image tags for standard-format graphic images such as .GIF or .JPEG, as in the following example:

```
<SERVER>
write(musicCursor.musicTitleImage.blobImage('gif'))
</SERVER
```

All blobImage parameters, with the exception of ismap, are JavaScript string expressions.

blobLink

You use LiveWire's blobLink method to create temporary files that have reduced bandwidth requirements or provide a link to multimedia content that is not viewable to the user. Using the blobLink method enables you to retrieve BLOb data from the database. LiveWire then creates a temporary file in memory and produces a link to that temp file. After the user clicks on the link (or 60 seconds after the link is processed), LiveWire removes the temporary file that blobLink created, thus freeing that memory space. The binary data stored in the database does not disappear; however, LiveWire retains the retrieved data in active memory (RAM). This is important to know because requests for large amounts of data can surpass the dynamic memory available on the server, resulting in an unproductive server.

To stay within the server's dynamic memory limits when using blobLink, you should limit the number of rows you want to retrieve at one time.

Use blobLink if you do not want to display graphics (so that you reduce bandwidth requirements). You also should use blobLink to provide a link to an audio clip or other multimedia content not viewable online. To retrieve data without displaying the graphics, use the following syntax:

```
cursorName.colName.blobLink(mimeType, linkText)
```

You use colName to indicate the name of a column in the cursor that contains BLOb data. You use the mimeType parameter to specify the MIME type of binary data, such as image/gif. Specify in the linkText parameter the text you want to display in the link, which can be any JavaScript string expression.

blob

To insert or update a row in an updatable cursor that contains a BLOb column, use the BLOb function, which is a top-level LiveWire function not associated with any object. By stipulating the name and path of the file that contains the BLOb, the blob function assigns BLOb data to that particular column. Following is the syntax:

```
cursorName.cursorColumn=blob(blobFileName)
```

You use cursorName to indicate the name of a cursor object and cursorColumn to indicate the name of the column in the cursor that contains the BLOb data. You use the blobFileName parameter to specify the full path and name of the file that contains the BLOb data.

Handling Database Errors

Because statements can fail for many reasons, you need a way to get error information. You can't fix it if you don't know what's broken. The LiveWire development team is aware of this and has provided two ways for you to obtain error information. You can get error information from status codes that are returned by database methods, such as insertRow and beginTransaction. You also can obtain error information from special database properties, such as majorErrorMessage and majorErrorCode, that contain error messages and code.

Status Codes

Status codes, which are integers between 0 and 27, are abbreviations for error messages. Zero indicates that an execution is successful, and subsequent numbers indicate an error. When you get an error message, take that number and refer to a status code table or library to determine where your application failed. Status codes can be useful in that they are abbreviated versions of error messages; however, if you don't have access to the error library or don't use it very often, these codes can be perplexing and frustrating.

If you need to use status codes, you can use methods with which you already are familiar. All the following methods return a status code:

◆ execute

◆ deleteRow

◆ insertRow

◆ updateRow

◆ beginTransaction

◆ updateTransaction

◆ rollbackTransaction

Table 10.7 shows the code and explanation for LiveWire status codes.

TABLE 10.7
LiveWire Database Status Codes

Status Code	Explanation
0	No error
1	Out of memory
2	Object never initialized
3	Type conversion error
4	Database not registered
5	Error reported by server
6	Message from server
7	Error from vendor's library
8	Lost connection
9	End of fetch
10	Invalid use of object
11	Column does not exist
12	Invalid positioning within object (bounds error)
13	Unsupported feature
14	Null reference parameter

continues

TABLE 10.7, CONTINUED
LiveWire Database Status Codes

Status Code	Explanation
15	Database object not found
16	Required information is missing
17	Object cannot support multiple readers
18	Object cannot support deletions
19	Object cannot support insertions
20, 21	Object cannot support updates
22	Object cannot support indices
23	Object cannot be dropped
24	Incorrect connection supplied
25	Object cannot support privileges
26	Object cannot support cursors
27	Unable to open

Error Methods

When some database methods, such as execute, insertRow, updateRow, deleteRow, beginTransaction, commitTransaction, and rollbackTransaction, fail, status codes sometimes are not enough to help you determine the exact reason for failure. The database object provides error methods that return additional information that can tell you more about why the database method failed. When the status code is 5 for server error or 7 for vendor library error, for example, the majorErrorCode method returns the major error code (supplementary information) that was reported by the database server.

Table 10.8 shows the four error methods the database object offers.

TABLE 10.8
Database Error Methods

Method	Description
majorErrorCode	Indicates the major error code returned by the database server or ODBC. For server errors, this usually corresponds to the SQLCODE of the servers.
MajorErrorMessage	Indicates the major error message returned by database server or ODBC.
minorErrorCode	Indicates the secondary error code returned by database vendor library.
minorErrorMessage	Indicates the secondary message returned by database vendor library.

The results returned by the methods in Table 10.8 are determined by the current database server and the database status code. Tables 10.9 through 10.12 provide database-specific information about error methods and status codes.

TABLE 10.9
Informix Database Error Methods with Status Code 7 (Vendor Library Error)

Method	Description
majorErrorMessage	Indicates Vendor Library Error: *string*. String is the error text provided by Informix.
minorErrorMessage	Indicates ISAM Error: *string*. String is the text of the ISAM error code from Informix. If no ISAM error exists, this method returns an empty string.
majorErrorCode	Indicates Informix error code.
minorErrorCode	Indicates ISAM error code. When no ISAM error code exists, this method returns 0.

Did you know...

ISAM, or Indexed Sequential Access Method, is a database methodology for supporting both sequential and indexed data access.

TABLE 10.10
Database Error Methods for Oracle with Status Code 5 (Server Error)

Method	Description
majorErrorMessage	Indicates Server Error: *string*. String is the translation of returned code provided by Oracle.
minorErrorMessage	Indicates Oracle server name.
majorErrorCode	Indicates return code as reported by Oracle OCI (Oracle Call-level Interface).
minorErrorCode	Indicates an operating system error code as reported by OCI.

TABLE 10.11
Database Error Methods for Sybase with Status Code 7 (Vendor Library Error)

Method	Description
majorErrorMessage	Indicates Vendor Library Error: *string*. The string indicates error text from DB-Library.
minorErrorMessage	Indicates operating system error text as reported by DB-Library.
majorErrorCode	Indicates DB-Library error number.
minorErrorCode	Indicates the severity level as reported by DB-Library.

TABLE 10.12
Database Error Methods for Sybase with Status Code 5 (Server Error)

Method	Description
majorErrorMessage	Indicates Server Error: *string*. The string indicates text from SQL Server. Message text only is displayed unless the severity and message numbers are both 0.
minorErrorMessage	Indicates the name of the SQL Server.
majorErrorCode	Indicates SQL Server message number.
minorErrorCode	Indicates the security level reported by SQL Server.

Summary

This has been a long chapter and you have learned many new things, including how to install database components using LiveWire Pro, how to access a database, how to use cursors, about database types, and how to handle database errors.

In Chapter 11, "Using LiveConnect with JavaScript," you will learn about LiveConnect and how it works with JavaScript. You also will learn about JavaScript and plug-in communication, including LiveAudio, LiveVideo, and Live3D.

CHAPTER 11

Using LiveConnect with JavaScript

LiveConnect is a new Internet technology developed by Netscape to allow interoperability between client Web applications. Because LiveConnect is bundled with Netscape Navigator 3.0, LiveConnect technology for end users is perceived as a Netscape browser that has more features. In other words, an end user *feels* a difference rather than sees a difference.

From a developer's perspective, LiveConnect is an add-on communication technology to the JavaScript, Java, and plug-in technologies. With LiveConnect, you can develop a Web page whereby plug-in applications, JavaScript scripts, and Java programs can share information and control one another.

In this chapter, you will learn about the different ways JavaScript and Java communicate. You also will learn about JavaScript and plug-in communication with LiveAudio, LiveVideo, and Live3D.

> **Note** If you have Netscape Navigator 3.0 Beta 4 or later, you have a browser that supports LiveConnect. To ensure that your Navigator browser is configured correctly, choose Network Preferences from the Options menu, and then choose the Language tab: both Enable Java and Enable JavaScript should be checked.

JavaScript and Java Communication

Because LiveConnect is a programming extension to both JavaScript and Java, a developer wanting to establish communication between JavaScript and Java can add the communication logic either on the JavaScript side or the Java side. This section describes communication with Java using JavaScript, including how to access Java directly and how to control Java applets with JavaScript. It also contains information on HTML communication using Java.

Communication via JavaScript

With LiveConnect, you can use JavaScript to communicate with Java applets and plug-ins that are loaded on a page. You also can use JavaScript to access Java variables, methods, and classes. Currently, JavaScript scripts can communicate with Java in the following two ways:

♦ Accessing the Java interpreter directly from within a JavaScript

♦ Communicating with Java applets

Accessing the Java Engine Directly

With a LiveConnect-enabled Netscape Navigator browser, a JavaScript script has the capability to use statements that make direct calls to Netscape's Java interpreter, producing results that act as if they had come from a Java program itself. This enables you to make a call to a Java method, such as System.out.println ("Hello Net!"), and produce the "Hello Net!" text in the Java Console the same as if it had been produced by a Java applet.

> **Did you know...**
>
> The Java Console is a Netscape Navigator window used to display Java messages. A typical use for the Java Console is to log information regarding a Java applet's execution. In a similar manner, you can use the Java Console to log information regarding a JavaScript script's execution.

The following is a simple Java program that prints "Hello Net!" to the Java Console window:

```
class HelloNet extends java.applet.Applet {
    public void init() {
      System.out.println("Hello Net!");
    }
}
```

The following code is the related HTML document that embeds the preceding Java program. Figure 11.1 shows what is displayed in both the main window as well as the Java Console when this document is loaded.

```
<HTML>
<HEAD>
<TITLE>Hello Net with Java</TITLE>
</HEAD>
<BODY>
<H1>Hello Net with Java</H1>
<APPLET CODE="HelloNet.class"></APPLET>
</BODY>
</HTML>
```

Figure 11.1

A simple Java program that writes to the Java Console.

Likewise, by using the following code, you also can write a script in JavaScript that prints "Hello Net!" to the Java console. Figure 11.2 shows the results.

```
<HTML>
<HEAD>
<TITLE>Hello Net with JavaScript</TITLE>
</HEAD>
<BODY>
<H1>Hello Net with JavaScript</H1>
<SCRIPT Language="JavaScript">
<!--
java.lang.System.out.println("Hello Net!")
//-->
</SCRIPT>
</BODY>
</HTML>
```

Figure 11.2

A JavaScript script that writes to the Java Console.

Warning It is easy to make the assumption that by having accessibility to Java objects with JavaScript, you can do everything with JavaScript that you can do with Java. This assumption falls flat on its face, however, when you take into account that JavaScript does *not* support inheritance, meaning that you cannot create JavaScript objects that extend Java or JavaScript objects. This limits you, for example, from extending (or subclassing) the Java *applet* object in your JavaScript script.

All Java packages and classes are represented as a property of the JavaScript *Packages* object. To reference Java objects, use the same syntax as you do in Java, but prepend the name of the *Packages* object, as in the following syntax:

```
Packages.packageName.className.methodName
```

 Packages are structures used in Java to categorize and group Java classes.

To reference the System.out.println() method, the syntax for calling this method in JavaScript looks like the following:

```
Packages.java.lang.System.out.println()
```

 The preceding JavaScript example referred to the System.out.println("Hello Net!") method without prepending *Packages* to the package reference. It is not a requirement to prepend *Packages* when referring to either the *sun*, the *java*, or the *netscape* package. This is intended to save time when a programmer is typing.

Although it is impossible to inherit a JavaScript class from a Java class, it is possible to use a Java class constructor in JavaScript, as in the following example:

```
var myRandomNumber = new java.util.Random()
```

Controlling Java Applets with JavaScript

Arguably, the single most powerful feature of LiveConnect (and JavaScript, for that matter) is the capability to control Java applets. Controlling Java applets is easy because hardly any knowledge as to how the Java applet works is necessary in order to control the applet.

You can design a Java applet with certain variables, methods, and properties defined as *public*. Variables, methods, and properties defined as public in an applet automatically become accessible to JavaScript scripts. You make variables, methods, and properties public by simply using the *public* keyword when you define them, as in the following definition:

```
public void setAlarm() {
...
...
}
```

In addition to the applet's public variables, all public parent classes and packages are accessible as well. The static methods declared in a Java applet are referred to by

JavaScript as *methods* of the applet object. Similarly, the properties declared in a Java applet are referred to by JavaScript as *properties* of the applet object. You can get and set applet property values that are strings, numbers, or Boolean values. Likewise, you can call applet methods that return strings, numbers, or Boolean values.

In JavaScript, you can refer to an applet in a document by *document.appletName*, where *appletName* is the value set by the NAME attribute of the APPLET tag. The following is the HTML markup for a Java applet called *Tumbling Duke*:

```
<applet code="TumbleItem.class" NAME="TumblingDukeApplet" width=600 height=95 >
<param name=maxwidth value="120">
<param name=nimgs value="16">
<param name=offset value="-57">
<param name=img value="images/tumble">
</applet>
```

You can reference this applet in JavaScript in either of the following ways:

```
document.TumblingDukeApplet
document.applets["TumblingDukeApplet"]
```

In addition, you can reference the Tumbling Duke applet with the *applets* array. Assuming that Tumbling Duke is the only Java applet on an HTML page, you can reference it as the following:

```
document.applets[0]
```

You can access the number of applets located on a Web page with the *length* property of the *applets* array, such as in the following syntax:

```
document.applet.length.
```

One of the very first sample Java applets that a beginning Java programmer runs across is the Tumbling Duke applet. Tumbling Duke is a basic animation applet that consists of the Java mascot, Duke, tumbling from right to left on the screen. Without looking at the source code to Tumbling Duke, suppose that you were given the information that Tumbling Duke has a public stop() method and a public start() method. The stop() method is used to halt the animation, and the start() method is used to restart the animation. Armed with this simple knowledge, you now have enough information to do some basic controlling of the Tumbling Duke applet from within JavaScript, as the following code demonstrates:

```
1. <HTML>
2. <HEAD>
3. <title>Tumbling Duke</title>
4. </HEAD>
```

```
 5. <BODY>
 6. <hr>
 7. <applet code="TumbleItem.class" NAME="TumblingDukeApplet" width=600
    ➥height=95 >
 8. <param name=maxwidth value="120">
 9. <param name=nimgs value="16">
10. <param name=offset value="-57">
11. <param name=img value="images/tumble">
12. </applet>
13. <hr>
14. <FORM>
15. <INPUT TYPE="button" VALUE="Stop Duke"
    ➥OnClick="document.TumblingDukeApplet.stop()">
16. <INPUT TYPE="button" VALUE="Restart Duke"
    ➥OnClick="document.TumblingDukeApplet.start()">
17. </FORM>
18. </BODY>
19. </HTML>
```

In line 7, the Tumbling Duke applet is given the name *TumblingDukeApplet* so that you can reference it easily in JavaScript. In lines 15 and 16, the JavaScript event handler, *onClick*, is used to call the applet methods stop() and start(), respectively. Figure 11.3 shows, with the added JavaScript control, the Tumbling Duke applet in action.

Figure 11.3

The Tumbling Duke applet with added JavaScript control.

Suppose that you have an "Alarm Clock" applet that has a public method used to set the alarm. Following is the definition for this method:

```
setAlarm(int myHour,int myMinute, int mySecond)
```

The way this applet normally works is that you set the alarm parameters inside the APPLET tag, and the Alarm Clock applet calls the *setAlarm* method itself by using the APPLET tag parameters you gave it, as in the following:

```
<APPLET CODE="AlarmClock.class" NAME="AlarmClockApplet" HEIGHT=75 WIDTH=400>
  <PARAM NAME="Hour" Value="6">
  <PARAM NAME="Minute" Value="30">
  <PARAM NAME="Second" Value="0">
  <PARAM NAME="AudioFile" Value="wakeUp.au">
</APPLET>
```

Editing the HTML file every time you want to set the alarm is impractical. You could change the Java code to allow user input, but doing that would be time-consuming. An easy solution is to add an HTML form and some JavaScript logic that calls the Java method *setAlarm* with the form that the user filled out. The following code does exactly this:

```
<HTML>
<HEAD>
<TITLE>Java Alarm Clock</TITLE>
<SCRIPT Language="JavaScript">
<!--
function processInput(myHour,myMinute,mySecond) {
  //Convert from string to integer
  myHour = parseInt(myHour)
  myMinute = parseInt(myMinute)
  mySecond = parseInt(mySecond)
  //Validate user input
  if ( (myHour > 23 ) || (myHour < 0) || (myMinute > 59) || (myMinute < 0) ||
    ↪(mySecond > 59) || (mySecond < 0) ) {
      //Invalid input
      alert("Invalid values used to set alarm clock.\n\n Please try again")
  } else {
      //Set the alarm
      document.AlarmClockApplet.setAlarm(myHour,myMinute,mySecond)
  }
}
//-->
</SCRIPT>
</HEAD>
```

```
<BODY>
<APPLET CODE="AlarmClock.class" NAME="AlarmClockApplet" HEIGHT=75 WIDTH=400>
  <PARAM NAME="Hour" Value="6">
  <PARAM NAME="Minute" Value="30">
  <PARAM NAME="Second" Value="0">
  <PARAM NAME="AudioFile" Value="wakeUp.au">
</APPLET>

<H1>Java Alarm Clock</H1>
<FORM NAME="AlarmForm">
Please enter alarm values below:<br>
Hour<INPUT TYPE="text" NAME="formHour" SIZE="2">
Minute<INPUT TYPE="text" NAME="formMinute" SIZE="2">
Second<INPUT TYPE="text" NAME="formSecond" SIZE="2">
<INPUT TYPE="button" VALUE="Change Alarm"
OnClick="processInput(AlarmForm.formHour.value,AlarmForm.formMinute.value,
  ➥AlarmForm.formSecond.value)">
</FORM>
</BODY>
</HTML>
```

Figure 11.4 shows how the parameters are entered.

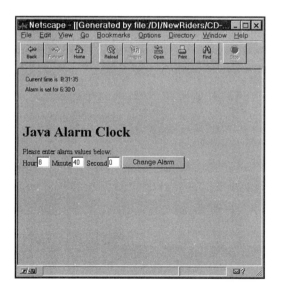

Figure 11.4

An Alarm Clock controlled with JavaScript.

For information on how to create Java applets that take advantage of JavaScript control, refer to Appendix B, "JavaScript to Java Communication."

Note The Microsoft Internet Explorer 3.0 Web browser (like the Netscape Navigator 3.0 Web browser) supports this type of communication in which JavaScript scripts can call methods in Java applets.

Communication via Java

Just as JavaScript scripts can access Java variables, methods, and properties, Java applet programs can likewise control JavaScript methods, properties, and variables.

Note This section is intended for those who have experience programming with Java.

Importing the JavaScript Package

As mentioned earlier in this chapter, packages are structures used in Java to categorize and group Java classes. The concept of packaging classes is much like the way movies are categorized in a store, where a class would be the movie and the package would be the section. If you were interested in renting Alfred Hitchcock movies, for example, you might need to ask where they are located in the movie store. Although the clerk might tell you that Hitchcock movies are in the Mystery section under Classics, you wouldn't think to yourself "Mystery.Classics.Hitchcock" each time you returned for another Hitchcock movie. Packages are created to work in a similar way. After you create a reference to the package with the use of the Java import statement, you no longer need to refer to the entire package each time you want to access a class inside the package. You may now access the class directly, without having to specify the package it is in.

The concept of importing a package is helpful and time-saving, especially when you need to access JavaScript methods, properties, and data structures from your Java applet.

To import the netscape.javascript package into Java, you use the following code:

```
import netscape.javascript.*
```

With the Java import statement, instead of referring to a JavaScript method in a verbose manner as in the following,

```
netscape.javascript.JSObject.getWindow(this);
```

you can now access it in the following abbreviated form:

```
import netscape.javascript.* ;
JSObject.getWindow(this) ;
```

Note The netscape.javascript package includes the JSObject class and the JSException exception class. These classes enable you to access JavaScript objects and properties.

Permitting Applets to Access Your JavaScript Program

For security reasons, you must give permission for the applet to access JavaScript by specifying the MAYSCRIPT attribute of the APPLET tag. This action prevents an applet from accessing JavaScript on a page without the knowledge of the creator of the page. The following code shows you how to do this:

```
<APPLET CODE="friendly.class" NAME="friendlyApplet" HEIGHT=75 WIDTH=400
    ➡MAYSCRIPT></APPLET>
```

Referencing the JavaScript Window

In order to be able to access JavaScript through Java, you need to acquire a handle or pointer for the Navigator window. This handle provides a communication link between your Java applet and your JavaScript objects. To get a window handle, you can use the getWindow method in the JSObject class, as in the following example:

```
public void init() {
  JSObject hWindow;
  hWindow = JSObject.getWindow(this);
}
```

Using JavaScript Objects and Properties

Access to JavaScript objects and properties from an applet enables you to create applets that are no longer isolated from the rest of the Web page. This access is useful should you want functionality in a Java applet that is available to JavaScript programs but not to Java applets. After you call getWindow to get a handle for the JavaScript window, you can use the getMember method of the JSObject class in the netscape.javascript package to access JavaScript objects and properties, as in the following example:

```
1. public void init() {
2.    JSObject hWindow = JSObject.getWindow(this);
3.    JSObject hDocument = (JSObject) hWindow.getMember("document");
4.    JSObject hForm = (JSObject) hDocument.getMember("beerForm");
5.    JSObject hText = (JSObject) hForm.getMember("beerText");
6. }
```

In line 2, a window handle variable, hWindow, is set with a handle (pointer) to the current window of the browser that the Java applet is contained in. Equipped with the window handle, it is possible in line 3 to set the variable, hDocument, with a handle to the document that is loaded inside the window. After a handle to the document is obtained, it is possible in line 4 to set the variable, hForm, to the handle of the form named "beerForm" located inside the document. Then with the handle to the form, it is possible in line 5 to get a handle to the text element named "beerText" which is located inside the form named "beerForm." Now, armed with the handle to the text object, it is easy within the Java applet to read and modify the value found inside the text element name "beerText."

Calling JavaScript Methods Via Java

In addition to having access to JavaScript objects and properties, you can call JavaScript methods. To do this, you use the call and eval methods of the JSObject class in the netscape.javascript package. After you get a handle for the JavaScript window, you can use either of the following two lines of syntax to call JavaScript methods:

```
JSObject.getWindow().call("methodname", arguments)
```

```
JSOjbect.getWindow().eval("expression")
```

The first syntax is a more programmatic method of calling a JavaScript method. The second syntax merely uses the eval method to send a JavaScript line of code to the JavaScript interpreter.

In the first line of code, you use the methodname parameter to specify the method you want to call; you use the arguments parameter to specify the array of arguments you want to pass to the JavaScript method.

In the second line of code, you use expression to specify the JavaScript expression you want to evaluate the JavaScript method.

The following example shows you how to use the call method:

```
JSObject hWindow;
String argStr[] = new String[1];

public void init() {
  hWindow = JSObject.getWindow(this);
  JSObject hDocument = JSObject.getMember("document");
}
```

```
public void stop() {
  argStr[0]="-3";
  hDocument.call("history",argStr);
}
```

The following example shows you how to use the eval method:

```
JSObject hWindow;
public void init() {
  hWindow = JSObject.getWindow(this);
  JSObject hDocument = JSObject.getMember("document");
}
public void stop() {
  hDocument.eval("history(\"-3\");");
}
```

The previous two examples both use the JavaScript history function to cause the current window to be loaded with the third document back in the history list.

> **Note**   Because the "JSObject" object that Netscape Navigator 3.0 implements is not implemented in the initial release of Microsoft Internet Explorer 3.0, it is not possible to develop a Java applet that can call JavaScript methods while viewed by an Internet Explorer 3.0 browser.

JavaScript and Plug-In Communication

JavaScript enables you to control plug-ins in a document as well as determine whether a particular plug-in has been installed. After you have this information, you can conditionally display the embedded plug-in data, should the plug-in be installed, or display some alternative, such as an image, if the plug-in is not installed. Using JavaScript, you also can determine whether a client can handle certain MIMEs. You can check for installed plug-ins using the navigator object, which contains two properties that enable you to do this.

> **Did you know...**
>
> Multipurpose Internet Mail Extensions, or MIME, is a standard for multipart, multimedia electronic mail messages and World Wide Web hypertext documents on the Internet. MIME provides the ability to transfer non-textual data, such as graphics, audio, and fax.

The mimeTypes object actually is an array that contains all MIME types the client supports. Each element of the array is considered a mimeTypes object. Each of these subsequent mimeTypes objects contains properties for a description, the object type, file extensions, and plug-ins.

A demonstration of the mimeType object can be found by simply choosing the About plug-ins menu item in your Netscape Help menu. When you select this menu item, the following HTML file is displayed (see fig. 11.5).

```
<HTML>
<HEAD>
<TITLE>About plug-ins</TITLE>
</HEAD>
<BODY>
<SCRIPT language="javascript">

<!-- JavaScript to enumerate and display all installed plug-ins

numPlugins = navigator.plugins.length;

if (numPlugins > 0)
        document.writeln("<b><font size=+3>Installed plug-ins</font></b><br>");
else
        document.writeln("<b><font size=+2>No plug-ins are installed.</font></
        ➡b><br>");


for (i = 0; i < numPlugins; i++)
{
        plugin = navigator.plugins[i];

        document.write("<center><font size=+1><b>");
        document.write(plugin.name);
        document.writeln("</b></font></center><br>");

        document.writeln("<dl>");
        document.writeln("<dd>File name:");
        document.write(plugin.filename);
        document.write("<dd><br>");
        document.write(plugin.description);
        document.writeln("</dl>");
        document.writeln("<p>");

        document.writeln("<table width=100% border=2 cellpadding=5>");
        document.writeln("<tr>");
```

```
document.writeln("<th width=20%><font size=-1>Mime Type</font></th>");
document.writeln("<th width=50%><font size=-1>Description</font></
th>");
document.writeln("<th width=20%><font size=-1>Suffixes</font></th>");
document.writeln("<th><font size=-1>Enabled</th>");
document.writeln("</tr>");
numTypes = plugin.length;
for (j = 0; j < numTypes; j++)
{
        mimeType = plugin[j];

        if (mimeType)
        {
                enabled = "No";
                enabledPlugin = mimeType.enabledPlugin;
                if (enabledPlugin && (enabledPlugin.name ==
                plugin.name))
                        enabled = "Yes";

                document.writeln("<tr align=center>");
                document.writeln("<td>");
                document.write(mimeType.type);
                document.writeln("</td>");
                document.writeln("<td>");
                document.write(mimeType.description);
                document.writeln("</td>");
                document.writeln("<td>");
                document.write(mimeType.suffixes);
                document.writeln("</td>");
                document.writeln("<td>");
                document.writeln(enabled);
                document.writeln("</td>");
                document.writeln("</tr>");
        }
}

document.write("</table>");
document.write("<p><hr><p>");
}
//-->
</SCRIPT>
</BODY>
</HTML>
```

The previous HTML code gives a tabular listing of the plug-ins currently installed on the client's Web browser.

To demonstrate the mimeTypes feature, use the following script to check whether the Shockwave plug-in is installed and displays an embedded Shockwave movie:

```
var myPlugin = navigator.plugins["Shockwave"];
if (myPlugin)
    document.write("<EMBED SRC='beerMovie.dir' HEIGHT=200 WIDTH=200>")
else
    document.write("<IMG src='beerImage.gif' HEIGHT=200 WIDTH=200 >")
</SCRIPT>
```

As seen in the preceding example, the other property the navigator object provides to help you with JavaScript and plug-in communication is the plug-ins object. The plug-ins object is an array of all the plug-ins installed on the client. As with the mimeTypes object, each element of the array also is considered a plug-ins object that contains properties for its name and description. This object also contains an array of mimeTypes objects for the MIME types that the plug-in supports.

JavaScript considers each plug-in in a document to be an element in the embeds array. HTML code defines the first plug-in in a document. To access the first plug-in in a document, you can use the following code:

```
document.embeds[0]
```

The embeds array contains a length property that enables you to get the number of plug-ins embedded in your document. To check whether the Shockwave plug-in is installed, you can use the following code:

```
<HTML>
<HEAD><TITLE>Martian Popping Thing</TITLE></HEAD>
<BODY>
<H1>Martian Popping Thing</H1>
<SCRIPT LANGUAGE="JavaScript">
<!--
if (navigator.plugins["Director"]) {
   document.write("<EMBED SRC='Martian.dir' HEIGHT=200 WIDTH=320>")
} else {
   document.write("<TABLE><TR><TD><IMG SRC='Martian.gif' HEIGHT=200
   ➥WIDTH=320></TD>")
   document.write("<TD>This site is best viewed with the Shockwave plug-in. ")
   document.write("The Shockwave plugin can be obtained at <A HREF='http://
www.macromedia.com'>Macromedia's Web site.</A></TD></TR></TABLE>")
}
//-->
</SCRIPT>
</BODY>

</HTML>
```

In the preceding code, the client browser is inspected for the Shockwave plug-in (named "Director"). If Shockwave is installed, an embedded Shockwave movie appears. Otherwise, a plain graphic is displayed with some text that informs the user about the Shockwave plug-in (see fig. 11.6).

Figure 11.6

Testing for existence of a Shockwave plug-in.

LiveAudio

LiveAudio is a LiveConnect plug-in that supports standard sound formats, such as AIFF, AU, MIDI, and WAV. Using LiveAudio, you can play and hear sound files that are embedded in HTML documents. This innovative concept is changing the way people create and view Web pages. Rather than driving to a music store, for example, you now can shop for CDs from the comfort of your computer command post by visiting Web sites that offer CDs and tapes. When you see a title that interests you, just click, and voilà! Sound bites roll through your speakers. Listen to and buy what you want, all without leaving home.

LiveAudio also makes it possible to add sound to your own Web page! Add your favorite music, voice your points of view, and talk a visitor through your Web page. You can play sound files without launching a separate application, and you never need to wait again to download a sound player. You can also program your applets to call LiveAudio controls to control system volume.

You have many tools at your disposal with which you can create LiveAudio audio files. Depending on the way the file is called in the HTML document or JavaScript, you can use views once or repeatedly in your Web page. You control the size the audio controls appear by specifying the WIDTH and HEIGHT parameters in the EMBED tag. You also can create an audio console using the following console views provided by LiveAudio:

Console	Contains Play, Pause, and Stop buttons, as well as a volume control lever.
SmallConsole	Contains Play and Stop buttons that are smaller than the standard Console buttons. This console also provides a volume control lever. If you invoke this view of the applet class, by default, a sound will start automatically.
PlayButton	Contains a Play button that starts the play of a sound with just a click.
PauseButton	Contains a Pause button that pauses a sound when in play. This button merely suspends the sound, without unloading it from memory.
StopButton	Contains a Stop button that causes the sound to stop playing and to unload from memory.
VolumeLever	Contains a lever that enables you to adjust volume level for playback of the sound. This lever also adjusts the volume level of the system.

Following is the HTML syntax for LiveAudio:

```
<EMBED SRC=[URL] AUTOSTART=[TRUE¦FALSE] LOOP=[TRUE¦FALSE¦INTEGER]
STARTTIME=[MINUTES:SECONDS] ENDTIME=[MINUTES¦SECONDS] VOLUME=[0-100] WIDTH=[#
➡PIXELS]
HEIGHT=[# PIXELS] ALIGN=[TOP¦BOTTOM¦CENTER¦BASELINE¦LEFT¦RIGHT
¦TEXTTOP¦MIDDLE¦ABSMIDDLE¦ABSBOTTOM] CONTROLS=[CONSOLE¦SMALL
CONSOLE¦PLAYBUTTON¦PAUSEBUTTON¦STOPBUTTON¦VOLUMELEVER] HIDDEN=[TRUE]
➡MASTERSOUND
NAME=[UNIQUE NAME TO GROUP CONTROLS TOGETHER SO THAT THEY CONTROL ONE
➡SOUND]...>
```

SRC=[URL] indicates the URL of the source sound file. You use
AUTOSTART=[TRUE|FALSE] to set the value to TRUE, which enables the sound,
music, or voice to begin to play automatically when the Web page loads (the default is
FALSE).

You use LOOP=[TRUE|FALSE|INTEGER] to set the value to TRUE, which enables
the sound to play continuously until the user clicks the stop button on the console or
goes to another page. When you use an INTEGER value, the sound repeats the
number of times you specify.

You use STARTTIME=[MINUTES:SECONDS] to designate the place in the sound file
you want playback to begin. For example, 15 seconds would be reflected as 00:15.
Note that you can only implement this parameter if you are on a Windows 95,
Windows NT, or Macintosh machine.

You use ENDTIME=[MINUTES:SECONDS] to designate the place you want the
playback of the sound file to end. To stop the sound at 1 minute, for example, set the
value at 1:00. Note that you can only implement this parameter if you are on a
Windows 95, Windows NT, or Macintosh machine.

Suppose you have a two-minute program, in which the STARTTIME is at the 15
second mark, and the ENDTIME is at the 1 minute mark. The audio will start at the
15 second mark and play for a total duration of 45 seconds.

You use VOLUME=[0-100] to set the volume for the sound playing. The value you use
must be a number from 0 to 100 (representing 0 to 100 percent). Note that, unless
you use MASTERVOLUME, the value sets the sound for the entire system. The
current system volume is the default volume level.

You use WIDTH=[# PIXELS] to display the width of the console or console element.
The default for the CONSOLE and SMALLCONSOLE is WIDTH=144. The default
for VOLUMELEVER is WIDTH=74. The default for a button is WIDTH=37.

The HEIGHT=[# PIXELS] attribute enables you to specify the display height of the console. The default for CONSOLE is HEIGHT=60. The default for SMALLCONSOLE is HEIGHT=15. The default for VOLUMELEVER is HEIGHT=20. The default for a button is HEIGHT=22.

The ALIGN=[TOP|BOTTOM|CENTER|BASELINE|LEFT|RIGHT|TEXTTOP|MIDDLE| ➥ABSMIDDLE|ABSBOTTOM] attribute enables you to specify the way you want text to align as it flows around the consoles. This parameter acts in a way similar to the IMG tag.

You use the CONTROLS=[CONSOLE|SMALLCONSOLE|PLAYBUTTON|PAUSEBUTTON| ➥STOPBUTTON|VOLUMELEVER] attribute to define which control console you want to use. The default value is CONSOLE.

You use the HIDDEN=[TRUE] value to indicate whether to include it in the EMBED tag. If you specify TRUE, LiveAudio will not load any controls, and the sound will behave as a background sound.

You must use the MASTERSOUND value when you group controls together in a NAME group. Although this attribute requires no value, it must be present in the EMBED tag. It informs LiveAudio which file is a genuine sound file and allows LiveAudio to ignore any stub files. Stub files, which normally do not contain any practical audio data are necessary in order to activate LiveAudio. Stub files must have some audio data, but they can be as small as you like. An example using the MASTERSOUND value will be demonstrated later in this section. The NAME=[UNIQUE NAME TO GROUP CONTROLS TOGETHER SO THAT THEY CONTROL ONE SOUND] attribute enables you to set a unique ID for a group of CONTROLS elements. This is done so that the elements all act on the same sound as it plays. To have one sound controlled by two EMBEDed objects (a PLAYBUTTON and a STOPBUTTON), for example, you must use this attribute to group the CON-TROLS. In this case, to flag LiveAudio and specify which of the two EMBED tags actually contains the sound file you want to control, the MASTERSOUND tag is necessary. Note that LiveAudio ignores EMBEDs with no MASTERSOUND tag.

 To specify that one VOLUMELEVER control multiple NAMEs (or the system volume), you need to create an EMBED using the VOLUMELEVER CONTROL. Then set NAME to MASTERVOLUME.

The following are JavaScript functions you can use to control embedded LiveAudio instances. All these functions return a Boolean value of True, upon successful completion of the operation.

play('TRUE/FALSE or int')	Starts playing the source file from the current position. If you pass an argument of TRUE, the audio source is played in a continuous loop. If you pass an argument of FALSE, the audio is played only one time. If you pass an integer value, the audio will be played the number of times of the integer value.
stop()	Stops the currently playing audio. When stop() is invoked, the audio rewinds automatically.
pause()	Stops the currently playing audio; however, unlike the stop function, the audio is not rewound.
start_time(seconds)	Specifies the number of seconds into the audio source that play should begin. Note that *seconds* is an integer.
end_time(seconds)	Specifies the number of seconds into the audio source that play should end. Note that *seconds* is an integer.
setvol(percent)	Specifies the percentage of volume at which the audio should play. The maximum is 100, the minimum is 0.
fade_to(to_percent)	Fades the volume to a specific volume level, where *to_percent* is the desired percentage level to fade to.
fade_from_to(from_percent,to_percent)	Causes the volume to fade from a specific volume percentage to a new volume percentage. Acceptable values for from_percent and to_percent are 0–100.
start_at_beginning()	Causes the audio to be played from the beginning of the audio source when it is played, regardless of previous settings made with the start_time function. Note that start_at_beginning does not cause the audio to be played. It just configures the audio to be played from the beginning.

stop_at_end()	Causes the audio to be played all the way to the end of the audio source when it is played, regardless of previous settings made with the end_time function. Note that stop_at_end does not cause the audio to be played. It just configures the audio to be played all the way to the end.

The following are JavaScript functions you can use to get current state information on embedded LiveAudio instances.

IsReady()	Determines whether an audio source can be played. IsReady returns False if the audio source file has not been loaded yet or if the audio source is currently playing.
IsPlaying()	Determines whether an audio instance is curretly playing. IsPlaying returns True when the audio is playing.
IsPaused()	Determines whether an audio instance is currently paused. IsPaused returns True when the audio is paused.
GetVolume()	Determines the volume to which the current audio instance is set. GetVolume returns an integer value ranging from 0 to 100, which specifies the volume percent.

With LiveAudio, the use of the HIDDEN attribute gives you the capability to play a background sound in a Web page, as in the following:

```
<EMBED SRC="Minuet.mid" HIDDEN=TRUE>
```

 Note   Background sounds are compatible with Microsoft Internet Explorer 3.0.

LiveAudio has a feature that enables you to postpone the loading of an audio file until the user clicks on the Play button. This reduces the worry of embedded audio files causing a Web page to take a long time to load. To implement this feature, you insert code similar to the following inside your HTML file:

```
<SCRIPT LANGUAGE=SoundScript>
  OnPlay("Chicken.wav");
</SCRIPT>
```

There may be times when you want your button controls for an audio source to be scattered across a Web page rather than all together as one control (see fig. 11.7). The following code demonstrates how to have several CONTROLS control one audio file:

```
<HTML>
<HEAD><TITLE>Seperated Controls</TITLE></HEAD>
<BODY>
<CENTER>
<H1>Seperated Controls</H1>
<TABLE BORDER=5>
  <TR>
  <TD>
  Play<EMBED SRC="Chicken.wav" HEIGHT=22 WIDTH=37 CONTROLS=PLAYBUTTON
  ➡NAME="ChickenControl" MASTERSOUND>
  </TD>
  <TD>
  Pause<EMBED SRC="nothing1.wav" HEIGHT=22 WIDTH=37 CONTROLS=PAUSEBUTTON
  ➡NAME="ChickenControl">
  </TD>
  <TD>
  Stop<EMBED SRC="nothing2.wav" HEIGHT=22 WIDTH=37 CONTROLS=STOPBUTTON
  ➡NAME="ChickenControl">
  </TD>
  <TD>
  Volume<EMBED SRC="nothing3.wav" HEIGHT=20 WIDTH=74 CONTROLS=VOLUMELEVER
  ➡NAME="ChickenControl">
  <TD>
  </TR>
</TABLE>
</CENTER>
</BODY>
</HTML>
```

In the preceding example, all the CONTROLS are tied to the same audio file by using the common name of "ChickenControl." The audio file that these CONTROLS control is the "Chicken.wav" file that is referenced in the first EMBED tag. The reason that the "Chicken.wav" audio file is chosen rather than the audio files referenced in the other EMBED tags is due to the added MASTERSOUND attribute in the first EMBED tag. You may notice that the other EMBED tags reference the"nothing1.wav," "nothing2.wav," and "nothing3.wav" files. These files are actual audio files, but they serve no purpose other than to act as a place holder, keeping LiveAudio "happy." If instead, you chose to use "chicken.wav" as one of your stub files, you would get the same results.

Figure 11.7

Separated audio control elements.

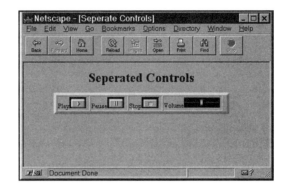

By using JavaScript's controlling functions and state functions, you can easily add audio interaction to your Web pages. The following sample code shows you different methods of using JavaScript to let the user experience several audio clips (see fig 11.8):

```
1.  <HTML>
2.  <HEAD>
3.  <TITLE>Chicken and a Rooster</TITLE>
4.  <SCRIPT LANGUAGE="JavaScript">
5.  <!--
6.  function playChicken() {
7.    if (document.ChickenSnd.IsReady()) {
8.       document.ChickenSnd.play(false)
9.    }
10. }
11. function playRooster() {
12.   if (document.RoosterSnd.IsReady()) {
13.      document.RoosterSnd.play(false)
14.   }
15. }
16. //-->
17. </SCRIPT>
18. </HEAD>
19. <BODY BGCOLOR=#FFFFFF TEXT=#000000>
20. <EMBED SRC="Minuet.mid" HIDDEN=TRUE>
21. <CENTER>
22. <MAP NAME="myMap1">
23. <AREA SHAPE="RECT" COORDS="1,2,50,37" HREF="#noWhere"
     ↪onMouseOver="playChicken()" >
24. </MAP>
```

```
25. <MAP NAME="myMap2">
26. <AREA SHAPE="RECT" COORDS="1,2,50,37" HREF="#noWhere"
    ➥onMouseOver="playRooster()" >
27. </MAP>
28. <IMG  WIDTH=161 HEIGHT=80 SRC="audio.gif"><BR>
29. <TABLE>
30. <TR>
31. <TD align=center><IMG SRC="Chicken.gif" USEMAP="#myMap1"></TD>
32. <TD align=center><IMG SRC="Rooster.gif" USEMAP="#myMap2"></TD></TR>
33. <TR>
34. <TD>
35. <EMBED SRC="chicken.wav" AUTOSTART=false VOLUME=60
36.        WIDTH=144 HEIGHT=60 NAME="ChickenSnd" MASTERSOUND></TD>
37. <TD>
38. <EMBED SRC="rooster.wav" AUTOSTART=false VOLUME=60
39.        WIDTH=144 HEIGHT=60 NAME="RoosterSnd" MASTERSOUND></TD>
40. </TR>
41. <TR>
42. <TD align=center><B>Chicken</B></TD><TD ALIGN=center><B>Rooster</B></TD>
43. </TR>
44. </TABLE>
45. <FORM>
46.   <INPUT Type="Button" Value="Chicken"
47.         OnClick="document.ChickenSnd.play(false)">
48.   <INPUT Type="Button" Value="Rooster"
49.         OnClick="document.RoosterSnd.play(false)">
50. </FORM>
51. <A HREF="http://www.newriders.com/"
52.         OnClick ="document.ChickenSnd.play(false)">Click for Chicken</A>
53. <A HREF="http://www.newriders.com/"
54.         OnClick ="document.RoosterSnd.play(false)">Click for Rooster</A>
55. </CENTER>
56. </BODY>
57. </HTML>
```

In the previous code, lines 35–36 are used to embed the audio for the chicken into the Web page; lines 38–39 are used to embed the audio for the rooster.

In line 20, a MIDI file to be played in the background is added to the document. Lines 45–50 define a form with two buttons that, when pushed, prompt the play operation for the chicken or rooster audio instance.

In lines 51–54, two hyperlinks are defined that cause the associated audio to be played when you click the link.

Lines 31–32 define the chicken and rooster images. These images have hotspot image-maps that are defined in lines 22–27. Within the image-map definitions are event handlers that handle the onMouseOver event. Each event handler calls an associated handler function defined in lines 6–15. Before attempting a play operation, each handler function in lines 6–15 uses the IsReady function call to ensure that the audio is not playing.

Figure 11.8

A LiveAudio enabled Web page.

LiveVideo

LiveVideo is another LiveConnect plug-in that enables you to view AVI movies that are embedded or linked to Web pages. You also can create your own AVI movies. Gone are the days you had to wait to download a viewer or invoke a separate application in order to see a movie.

Did you know...

AVI, or Audio Video Interlaced, is a compressed video format developed by Microsoft.

Note LiveVideo currently is only available for Windows 95 and Windows NT systems.

You use the EMBED tag to place AVI movies in your Web documents in order to control the onscreen size of your AVI movie. You even can control the way in which your text flows around the movie.

Following is the HTML syntax for LiveVideo:

```
<EMBED SRC=[URL] AUTOSTART=[TRUE¦FALSE] LOOP=[TRUE¦FALSE] WIDTH=[# PIXELS]
➥HEIGHT=[# PIXELS]
ALIGN=[TOP¦BOTTOM¦CENTER¦BASELINE¦LEFT¦RIGHT¦TEXTTOP¦MIDDLE¦ABSMIDDLE¦ABSBOTTOM]...>
```

The EMBED tag enables you to place AVI movies into your Web documents. You use SRC=[URL] to indicate the URL of the source AVI file.

You use the AUTOSTART=[TRUE|FALSE] value to specify whether the AVI movie is to begin playing when the Web page is loaded. True indicates to begin playing; the default for this value is FALSE. You use the LOOP=[TRUE|FALSE] value to indicate whether you want the AVI movie to play continuously until the user either clicks on the movie to stop playing or moves to another page. FALSE is the default for this value.

The WIDTH=[# PIXELS] attribute enables you to specify the width, in pixels, of the on-screen display of the AVI movie. The HEIGHT=[# PIXELS] attribute enables you to specify the on-screen height, in pixels, of the AVI movie. Standard sizes for movies are 90×120, 120×160, 180×240, and 240×320 (all size references are HEIGHT x WIDTH). These are all standard sizes using the 3:4 aspect ratio.

The ALIGN=[TOP|BOTTOM|CENTER|BASELINE|LEFT|RIGHT|TEXTTOP|MIDDLE| ➥ABSMIDDLE|ABSBOTTOM] attribute enables you to specify the way in which you want text to align as it flows around the AVI movie. This parameter acts in a way similar to the IMG tag.

Following are the Java and JavaScript functions you can use with LiveVideo:

play()	Starts playing the source file from the current location.
stop()	Stops the currently playing video. When stop() is invoked, the video rewinds automatically.
rewind()	Sets the current position of the video file to the beginning.
seek(frame-number)	Enables you to set the video to the given frame number.

The following example shows you how to control a LiveVideo AVI movie using JavaScript. Figure 11.9 shows the results.

```
1. <HTML>
2. <HEAD>
3. <Title>NASA's Top Secret Video</Title>
4. <SCRIPT LANGUAGE="JavaScript">
```

```
 5. <!--
 6. function validate() {
 7.    if ((parseInt(document.myForm.frameNumber.value) > 31) ¦¦
(parseInt(document.myForm.frameNumber.value) < 1)) {
 8.       alert("Invalid frame number entry. Please try again.")
 9.       document.myForm.frameNumber.value = "1"
10.       document.myForm.frameNumber.focus()
11.    }
12. }
13. //-->
14. </SCRIPT>
15. </HEAD>
16. <BODY BGCOLOR=#FFFFFF TEXT=#000000>
17. <CENTER>
18. <H1>NASA's Top Secret Video</H1>
19. <TABLE>
20. <TR>
21. <TD>
22. <EMBED NAME="MartianAvi" SRC="Martian.avi" WIDTH=320 HEIGHT=200
      ➡AUTOSTART=TRUE LOOP=TRUE>
23. <CENTER>
24. <FORM NAME="myForm">
25. <INPUT Type="Button" Value="Play" OnClick="document.embeds[0].play()">
26. <INPUT Type="Button" Value="Stop" OnClick="document.embeds[0].stop()">
27. <INPUT Type="Button" Value="Rewind"
      ➡OnClick="document.embeds[0].rewind()"><P>
28. <INPUT Type="Button" Value="Seek to frame #..."
29. OnClick="document.embeds[0].seek(parseInt(document.myForm.frameNumber.
      ➡value))">
30. <INPUT TYPE="TEXT" NAME="frameNumber" VALUE="1" SIZE=2
      ➡onChange="validate()">
31. </FORM>
32. </CENTER>
33. </TD><TD VALIGN=top>
34. <FONT COLOR="BLUE">Note: As of the writing of this book, Navigator 3.0
      ➡Beta 6
35. does not support LiveConnect with LiveVideo.<P> Hopefully, Netscape will
      ➡resolve this
36. issue by the time of the release of Navigator 3.0.</FONT>
37. </TD>
38. </TABLE>
39. </CENTER>
40. </BODY>
41. </HTML>
```

Figure 11.9

A LiveVideo-enabled Web page.

In line 22, the AVI file is embedded inside the Web page. The form that contains the buttons and input box in figure 11.9 are defined in lines 24–31. Each of the buttons has an OnClick event handler that is used to call the associated LiveVideo function. The TEXT input element in line 30 validates user input to ensure that the frame chosen is within the acceptable range for this video file. The validate function that is called by the TEXT input element is located in lines 6–12. The validate function checks to make sure the input is between 1 and 31. If the input is outside that range, an alert is given to the user, the value for the input box is reset, and focus is set to the TEXT box.

Note   At the time of this writing, Navigator 3.0 does not support LiveVideo's seek method. Hopefully, Netscape will resolve this issue in future releases of Navigator.

Live3D

Live3D is a LiveWire plug-in that enables the Navigator to display VRML directly on a Web page. What this means to you is that you now are able to experience and interact with 3D images, text, sound, and animation. Available with Netscape Navigator 3.0 for Windows 3.1, Windows 95, Windows NT, and Power Macintosh, Live3D is multiplatform-ready.

  VRML stands for Virtual Reality Modeling Language, a language that you use to display three-dimensional models.

Live3D enables you to access distributed 3D spaces at pinnacle speeds. You can fill your Web pages with lifelike renditions of your family, favorite animals, and so on. You can even navigate your way through the sky or a virtual forest.

Live3D also offers the capability of running 3D applications that include games, geographical information, and interactive advertisements.

Following is the HTML syntax for Live3D:

```
<EMBED SRC=[URL] ...>
```

Live3D consists of the following four classes that are accessible from within JavaScript:

♦ **L3DObserver**—The L3DObserver class is an interface class designed to provide callbacks from Live3D to the JavaScript script. In order to use any of the callbacks outlined in this class, you must take advantage of the advise method described in the L3DScene class.

 A *callback* is a scheme used in event-driven programs where the program registers a callback handler for a certain event. The program does not call the handler directly, but when the event occurs, the handler is called, possibly with arguments describing the event.

♦ **L3DMath**—The L3DMath class provides a basic set of general math and vector math functions that are particularly suited for writing programs that work with 3D. The L3DMath functions are intended to complement the Math class provided with JavaScript.

 Use of the L3DMath class, as well as the other Live3D classes, requires that a Live3D plug-in be active at the time—you would not be able to use these functions with JavaScript scripts unless a 3D scene is currently active.

♦ **L3DObject**—The L3DObject class is the main toolkit class of the Live3D JavaScript API. This class is used to manipulate shape nodes and group nodes, which are defined by the VRML 1.0 specification as follows:

Shape Nodes:

Cylinder, Cube, AsciiTextCone, IndexedFaceSet, IndexedLineSet, PointSet, Sphere

Group Nodes:

WWWAnchor, Group, Separator, Switch, TransformSeparator

In order for these nodes to be accessible by Live3D functions, they must be defined (DEF'd) inside the VRML file.

◆ **L3DScene**—The L3DScene class is used to access methods that impact the entire scene, identify the scene itself, identify nodes within the scene, and access the camera (viewpoint). It is through this class that the plug-in itself is made accessible to JavaScript. Therefore, in order to use any of the functions defined in the other classes, you must use the L3DScene class first.

Following are the JavaScript callback functions currently available in Netscape 3.0 that can be accessed from objects created with the Live3D L3DObserver class:

onMouseMove(objectOver)	Notifies a mouse move event within a Live3D VRML object. It accepts objectOver as a parameter, which is a NULL L3DObject used to hold the return value from the call to this method.
onMouseClick(objectClicked)	Signals a mouse click event within a VRML scene. It accepts as a parameter objectClicked, a NULL L3DObject used to hold the return value from the call to this method.
onCameraMove(matrix[])	Notifies a camera move (viewpoint change) event within a Live3D VRML scene. It accepts as a parameter matrix, a Null 16 element float array used to hold the return value from the call to this method.
onAnchorClick(objectClicked, strAnchor)	Signals an anchor click event within a VRML scene. It accepts as parameters objectClicked, a NULL L3DObject used to hold the return value of the object clicked; as well as the parameter strAnchor, a NULL string that holds the text string representing the anchor return value from this method.
onObjectAdded(object)	Notifies that a particular object within a Live3D VRML scene has finished loading. It accepts as a parameter the NULL L3DObject object, which is used to hold the return value from the call to this method.

The L3DMath class contains more than 30 mathematical toolkit methods that can assist a program in low-level 3D operations. Unless you are an expert 3D programmer, you more than likely will not be confronted with these mathematical toolkit methods. For detailed information on the L3DMath methods, please refer to the Live3D SDK (Software Developers Kit) that is available from Netscape.

Following are the JavaScript methods currently available in Netscape 3.0 that can be accessed from objects created with the Live3D L3DObject class:

hide()   Hides an L3DObject.

show()   Shows an L3DObject.

rotate(fPitch,fYaw,fRoll,nMode, nLocal)

Rotates an L3DObject. The parameter, fPitch, is the X rotation value in radians. The parameter, fYaw, is the Y rotation value in radians. The parameter, fRoll, is the Z rotation value in radians. The nMode parameter specifies the mode value; Pre-concatenate=0, Post-concatenate=1, and Replace=2. The nLocal parameter contains an integer value that specifies the local mode; 0=false, and 1=true.

scale(fScaleX,fScaleY,fScaleZ,nMode,nLocal)

Scales an L3DObject. The parameters fScaleX, fScaley, and fScaleZ are of the float data type and are used to specify the X, Y, and Z scale values. The nMode parameter specifies the mode value; Pre-concatenate=0, Post-concatenate=1, and Replace=2. The nLocal parameter contains an integer value that specifies the local mode; 0=false, and 1=true.

translate(fTranslateX, fTranslateY, fTranslateZ, nMode, nLocal)

Translates an L3DObject. The parameters fTranslateX, fTranslateY, and fTranslateZ are of the float data type and are used to specify the X, Y, and Z translation values. The nMode parameter specifies the mode value; Pre-concatenate=0, Post-concatenate=1, and Replace=2. The nLocal parameter contains an integer value that specifies the local mode; 0=false, and 1=true.

Did you know...

Translate means to change the location of an object's center.

Rotate means to change the orientation of an object's axes.

Scale means to change the dimensions of an object.

A transform is a superset of the above object conversion functions.

transform(fMatrix[], nMode)	Transforms an L3DObject. The transform method accepts the parameter fMatrix, a floating point array of 16 values for the transform matrix. The nMode parameter specifies the mode value; Pre-concatenate=0, Post-concatenate=1, and Replace=2.
getTransform(fMatrix[])	Accesses the transform values of an L3DObject. The getTransform method accepts the parameter fMatrix, a floating point array of 16 values for the transform matrix.
setTransparency(fTransparency)	Sets the transparency of an L3DObject. The setTransparency method accepts the parameter fTransparency, a floating point value ranging from 0.0 to 1.0, where 1.0 is transparent.
setColor(fRed,fGreen,fBlue)	Sets the color of an L3DObject through the use of RGB values. The parameters fRed, fGreen, and fBlue are floating point values ranging from 0.0 to 1.0; the values specify the intensity for each primary color.
setColorHLS(fHue,fLightness,fSaturation)	Sets the color of an L3DObject through the use of HLS values. The parameters fHue, fLightness, and fSaturation are floating point values ranging from 0 to 1; the values specify the intensity for hue, lightness, and saturation.

Following are the JavaScript methods currently available in Netscape 3.0 that can be accessed from objects created with the Live3D L3DScene class:

advise(observer,object,szEvent)   Obtains access to the callbacks discussed for the L3DObserve class. The parameters observer and object are L3DObserver objects. The parameter szEvent is a string that specifies the event to access.

Note   In order to use any of the callbacks outlined in the L3DObserve class, you must take advantage of the advise method just described.

setBackgroundColor(fRed,fGreen,fBlue)

Sets the color behind the objects to a specific color. The color is specified with the parameters fRed, fGreen, and fBlue, which are floating point values ranging from 0.0 to 1.0; the values specify the intensity for each primary color.

setBackdropImage(strURL)   Sets the background behind the objects to a specific image. The method setBackdropImage accepts the parameter strURL, which specifies the URL and the name of the background image.

render()   Forces a scene to render. Manipulations of the VRML scene and the VRML objects through the use of the Live3D methods only become evident to the user after execution of the render method.

Did you know...

Rendering is the generation of a graphical image from a mathematical model of a three-dimensional object or scene.

Note   Manipulations of the VRML scene and the VRML objects through the use of the Live3D methods only become evident to the user after execution of one of the render methods.

requestRender()   Places the scene render request in a queue.

loadSceneURL(strURL)	Replaces the current VRML scene with the identified scene specified in strURL, the full URL and name of the replacement VRML scene.
getSceneURL(strURL)	Obtains the current VRML scene; strURL is set to the full URL and name of the VRML scene.

setCollisionDetectionMode(nCollisionDetectionMode)

	Makes it so that you cannot virtually walk through VRML objects in the scene. Set the parameter nCollisionDetectionMode to 1 to enable collision detection, and set it to 0 to disable collision detection.
getCollisionDetectionMode()	Obtains the current collision detection settings for the scene. If getCollisionDetectionMode returns 1, collision detection is turned on. If a value of 0 is returned, collision detection is turned off.
setBankingMode(nBankingMode)	Banks like an airplane when navigating in a flying mode. To turn banking on, use the setBankingMode method, passing it an argument equal to 1. To turn banking off, pass an argument equal to 0 to the setBankingMode method.
getBankingMode()	Gets the current state of the scene's banking mode. The getBankingMode method returns 1 when banking is turned on, and it returns 0 when banking is turned off.

setStayOnGroundMode(nStayOnGroundMode)

	Forces you to stay on the ground when navigating in walk mode. To turn the mode on, use the setStayOnGroundMode method, passing it an argument equal to 1. To turn stay on ground mode off, pass an argument equal to 0 to the setStayOnGroundMode method.

getStayOnGroundMode()	Gets the current state of the scene's stay on ground mode. The getStayOnGroundMode method returns 1 when stay on ground mode is turned on, and it returns 0 when stay on ground mode is turned off.
setHeadlightState(nHeadlightState)	Provides you with the means of turning on a headlight (head lamp) that shines a light at the top of your objects. To turn on this headlight mode, use the setHeadlightState method, passing it an argument with the value of 1. To turn off headlight mode, pass an argument with the value of 0.
getHeadlightState()	Gets the current headlight state for the scene. If the result is 1, the headlight is turned on. If the result is 0, the headlight state is turned off.
increaseLightIntensity()	Increases the light intensity of the scene by one point.
increaseLightIntensity()	Decreases the light intensity of the scene by one point.
setLightIntensity(fIntensity)	Sets the light intensity for the scene to a precise value. The parameter to this method is fIntensity, which ranges in value from 0.0 to 1.0.
getLightIntensity()	Retrieves the current light intensity for the scene. This method returns a value ranging from 0.0 to 1.0.
setFastrenderMode(nMode)	Controls fast rendering for the scene. To turn fast rendering on, pass a value of 1 as the nMode argument. To turn fast rendering off, pass a value of 0 as the nMode argument.
getFastrenderMode()	Allows you to obtain current rendering state information. If this method returns a value of 1, fast rendering is enabled. If getFastrender-Mode returns a value of 0, fast render mode is turned off.

setMotionBlurMode(nMode)	Sets the motion blur state for the scene. If nMode is set to 1, motion blur is turned on. If nMode is set to 0, motion blur is turned off.
getMotionBlurMode()	Retrieves the current motion blur state for the scene. If getMotionBlurMode returns a value of 1, motion blur is turned on. If getMotionBlurMode returns a value of 0, motion blur is turned off.
setAnimationMode(nMode)	Sets the animation mode state for the scene. If animation is turned on, when a user clicks on an object, the view is animated to the location of that object. If nMode is set to 1, animation mode is turned on. If nMode is set to 0, animation mode is turned off.
getAnimationMode()	Retrieves the current Animation setting for the scene. If getAnimationMode returns a value of 1, animation mode is turned on. If getAnimationMode returns a value of 0, animation mode is turned off.
setSceneTextureLightingMode(nMode)	Sets the scene texture lighting mode. If nMode is set to 1, texture lighting is turned on. If nMode is set to 0, texture lighting is turned off.
getSceneTextureLightingMode()	Retrieves the current texture lighting setting for the scene. If getSceneTextureLightingMode returns a value of 1, texture lighting is turned on. If getSceneTextureLightingMode returns a value of 0, texture lighting is turned off.
setGravityMode(nMode)	Controls the gravity property for the scene. If nmode is set to a value of 1, gravity is turned on. If nmode is set to a value of 0, gravity is turned off.
getGravityMode()	Retrieves the current gravity property for the scene. If getGravityMode returns a value of 1, gravity is turned on. If this method returns a value of 0, gravity is turned off.

setWireframeMode(nMode)	Sets the method of rendering to the faster wireframe method (rather than solid). If nmode is set to a value of 1, wireframe rendering is turned on. If nmode is set to a value of 0, wireframe rendering is turned off.
getWireframeMode()	Retrieves the current wireframe rendering mode for the scene. If getWireframeMode returns a value of 1, wireframe rendering is turned on. If this method returns a value of 0, wireframe rendering is turned off.

addURL(strURL,strObject,fXPos,fYPos,fZPos,fPitch,fYaw,fRoll)

Adds an URL hyperlink to a scene. When the user places the mouse pointer over the added URL, a link is displayed; when a user clicks on that link, the URL is loaded. The parameter strURL specifies the URL. The parameter strObject specifies the name of the VRML object. The fXPos, fYPos, fZPos, fPitch, fYaw, and fRoll parameters specify the object's X, Y, and Z translation and X, Y, and Z rotation. This method returns the L3DObject of the acquired object.

addVRML(strVRML,strObject,fXPos,fYPos,fZPos,fPitch,fYaw,fRoll)

Adds a VRML object to the current scene. The parameter strVRML specifies the URL and name of the .wrl file. The parameter strObject specifies the name of the VRML object within the source file. The parameters fXPos, fYPos, fZPos, fPitch, fYaw, and fRoll specify the X, Y, and Z object translation and the X, Y, and Z object rotation. This method returns the L3DObject of the acquired object.

getObject(strObject)	Useful for retrieving an L3DObject from a scene. This method accepts the argument strObject, which specifies the name of the object to declare.

Note | getObject is useful in JavaScript for getting a particular L3DObject from a scene. This allows you to make use of the methods in the L3DObject class, which let you manipulate an individual object. Following is a typical implementation of this method:

```
MartianObject=document.embeds[0].getObject("ObjectNamedMartian")
```

getRoot()

Retrieves the top-level object. This method returns an L3DObject of the acquired top-level object.

deleteObject(object)

Deletes an object. The parameter object specifies an L3DObject to delete.

addCone(fHeight,fRadius,nSides)

Adds a cone object to the scene. The parameters fHeight, fRadius, and nSides specify the height, radius, and number of sides of the cone. This method returns the L3DObject object created.

gotoViewpoint(strViewPoint,nAnimationSteps)

Automatically animates an object to a particular location in the scene. The parameter strViewPoint specifies the name of the viewpoint. The parameter nAnimationSteps specifies the number of frames to be rendered during the move.

setCameraPosition(fXPos,fYPos,fZPos)

Useful for changing the position of the camera (point of view) of the scene. The parameters fXPos, fYPos, and fZPos are the new X, Y, and Z position of the camera.

setCameraOrientation(fPitch,fYaw,fRoll)

Rotates the camera and changes its orientation (perspective). The parameters fPitch, fYaw, and fRoll are the new X, Y, and Z rotational values for the camera.

getCameraPosition(fPosition[])

Retrieves the position of the camera. The parameter fPosition is a Null 3 item array to hold returned position info. The getCameraPosition method returns a 3-item array (fPosition) containing camera X, Y, and Z position coordinates.

getCameraOrientation(fOrientation[])

> Retrieves the rotational aspects of the camera. The parameter fOrientation is a Null 3 item array to hold returned position info. The getCameraOrientation method returns a 3-item array (fOrientation) containing camera X, Y, and Z rotation coordinates.

setCameraView(fXPos,fYPos,fZPos,fXLookAt,fYLookAt,fZLookAt,fXLookUp,
➥fYLookUp,fZLookUp)

> Can be used to automatically set the camera view. The parameters fXPos, fYPos, and fZPos refer to the camera's X, Y, and Z position. The parameters fXLookAt, fYLookAt, and fZLookAt refer to the vector X, Y, and Z LookAt compo nent. The parameters fXLookUp, fYLookUp, and fZLookUp refer to the vector X, Y, and Z LookUp components.

setCameraNearClipping(fNearClipping)

> Sets the camera's near clipping value when you call the setCameraNearClipping method using the fNearClipping argu- ment, which specifies a float value to set for near clipping.

getCameraNearClipping()

> Retrieves the current value of the scene's near clipping when you use the getCameraNearClipping method. The method returns a float value that specifies the setting for near clipping.

setCameraFarClipping(fFarClipping)

> Sets the camera's far clipping value when you call the setCameraFarClipping method using the fFarClipping argument, which specifies a float value to set for far clipping.

getCameraFarClipping()

> Retrieves the current value of the scene's far clipping when you use the getCameraFarrClipping method. The method returns a float value that specifies the setting for near clipping.

setCameraTransform(fMatrix[])

> Applies a matrix transform to camera. The parameter fMatrix specifies a 16-item array holding a new camera matrix.

getCameraTransform(fMatrix[])	Retrieves the matrix transform for the camera. The parameter fMatrix is a Null 16-item array for holding the camera matrix. The method returns the 16 items in the fMatrix array, items that hold the camera transform matrix.
panCamera(fAngle)	Pans the camera a specified number of degrees. The parameter fAngle is a float value that contains the number of degrees to pan the camera.
tiltCamera(fAngle)	Tilts the camera a specified number of degrees. The parameter fAngle is a float value that specifies the number of degrees to tilt the camera.
revolveCamera(fAngle)	Revolves the camera a specified number of degrees. The parameter fAngle is a float value that contains the number of degrees to revolve the camera.
moveCamera(fX,fY,fZ)	Moves the camera to a new position. The parameters fX, fY, and fZ specify the new X, Y, and Z location to move the camera to.

The following example shows you how to control a Live3D VRML scene using JavaScript. The result is shown in figure 11.10.

```
1.  <html>
2.  <head>
3.  <title>VRML JavaScript Test Case!</title>
4.  <script language = "JavaScript">
5.  <!--
6.  var collisionMode=false
7.  function initializeScene() {
8.     document.vrmlMartian.setLightIntensity(0.5)
9.     document.vrmlMartian.setCameraPosition(0,0,200)
10.    document.vrmlMartian.setBackgroundColor(0,0,.2)
11. }
12. function leaving() {
13.    var MartianObject=document.vrmlMartian.getRoot()
14.    MartianObject.setTransparency(.85)
15.    document.vrmlMartian.render()
16.    for (var i = 1; i < 16; i++) {
17.      MartianObject.setTransparency(.85 +(i / 100.0))
```

```
18.        document.vrmlMartian.render()
19.    }
20. }
21. function tiltCamera() {
22.   for (var i = 0; i < 72; i++) {
23.     document.vrmlMartian.tiltCamera(5.0);
24.     document.vrmlMartian.render();
25.   }
26. }
27. function collisionToggle() {
28.    if (collisionMode == false) {
29.      document.vrmlMartian.setCollisionDetectionMode(1)
30.      collisionMode = true
31.      alert("Collision mode is turned on. You will now bump into the
             ➥Martian")
32.    }else {
33.      document.vrmlMartian.setCollisionDetectionMode(0)
34.      collisionMode = false
35.      alert("Collision mode is turned off. You can now walk through the
             ➥Martian")
36.    }
37. }
38. function panCamera() {
39.    for (var i = 0; i < 72; i++) {
40.      document.vrmlMartian.panCamera(5.0);
41.      document.vrmlMartian.render();
42.    }
43. }
44. function revolveCamera() {
45.    for (var i = 0; i < 72; i++) {
46.      document.vrmlMartian.revolveCamera(5.0);
47.      document.vrmlMartian.render();
48.    }
49. }
50. function playWithLights() {
51.    for (var i = 0; i < 5; i++) {
52.      document.vrmlMartian.increaseLightIntensity();
53.      document.vrmlMartian.render();
54.    }
55.    for (var i = 0; i < 10; i++) {
56.      document.vrmlMartian.decreaseLightIntensity();
57.      document.vrmlMartian.render();
58.    }
59.    for (var i = 0; i < 5; i++) {
```

```
60.      document.vrmlMartian.increaseLightIntensity();
61.      document.vrmlMartian.render();
62.    }
63. }
64. //—>
65. </script>
66. </head>
67. <body background="back.jpg" TEXT="#FFFFFF" onLoad="initializeScene()"
    ➥onUnload="leaving()">
68. <center>
69. <h1>Controlling VRML using JavaScript</h1>
70. <embed name="vrmlMartian" SRC="martian.wrl" WIDTH=275 HEIGHT=300><BR>
71. <form>
72. <input type=button
73.          onclick="document.vrmlMartian.setBackgroundColor(Math.random(),
             ➥Math.random(), Math.random())"
74.          value="Change Background Color">
75. <input type=button
76.          onclick="panCamera()"
77.          value="Pan Camera">
78. <input type=button
79.          onclick="revolveCamera()"
80.          value="Revolve Camera">
81. <input type=button
82.          onclick="tiltCamera()"
83.          value="Tilt Camera">
84. <input type=button
85.          onclick="collisionToggle()"
86.          value="Toggle collision mode">
87. <input type=button
88.          onclick="playWithLights()"
89.          value="Play with lights">
90. </form>
91. </center>
92. </body>
93. </html>
```

The previous example uses methods of the L3DScene class to manipulate the view of the VRML Martian Popping Thing. Elements of the view that are controlled include the lighting, the camera position, the collision properties, and the background color.

Line 70 contains the EMBED tag that defines the initial display of the Martian VRML file by the Live3D plug-in. In line 67 is the BODY tag, which contains both an onLoad and onUnload event handler. The onLoad event handler causes the initializeScene function in lines 7–11 to be called. In the initializeScene function, some presentation work is done to ensure that the user initially sees the Martian model in a suitable lighting, position, and pretty dark blue background color. The BODY tag's onUnload handler causes the leaving function in lines 12–20 to be called when the user leaves this Web page. In the leaving function, an L3DObject object for the Martian VRML object is created through the use of the getRoot method. After the object is created, the object is faded out through the use of the setTransparency method of the L3DObject class.

Figure 11.10

Controlling a Live3D scene with JavaScript.

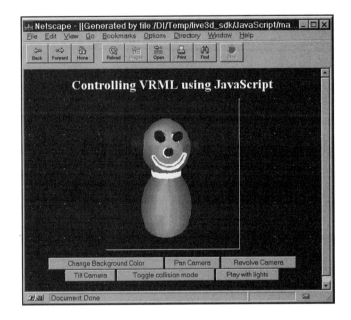

In lines 71–90, the buttons below the Martian are constructed. Notice that each of these buttons has corresponding event handlers. For the Change Background Color button in lines 72–74, the Live3D setBackGroundColor method is called. The setBackGroundColor method accepts three parameters—red, blue, and green. The accepted range for these values is 0 to 1.0. Through the use of JavaScript's built-in Math object, it is easy to simply give random values for the background color each time the "Change Background Color" button is clicked.

In lines 21–25 is the tiltCamera function that is called by the Tilt Camera button's event handler. This function simply tilts the camera 5 degrees for 72 intervals (a total of 360 degrees). Notice that in line 15, after each instance the camera is tilted, the scene is rendered. If this render did not occur, the user would not see the change—although the camera position has changed, a refresh of the model has not changed. The event handler functions for the Pan Camera button and the revolveCamera button work in a similar fashion.

In lines 27–37 is the event handler function for the Toggle collision mode button. This function toggles the collision detection mode back and forth by using the previous state of the collisionMode flag. If you want to experiment with this feature, try moving the view into the Martian by using your up-arrow key. When the collision detection is set, you will not be able to seemingly walk right through the Martian.

In lines 50–61 is the programming logic for the event handler function for the Play With Lights button. The playWithLights function simply increases the lighting intensity by five units, then decreases it by ten units, and then brings it back up to its original state.

Summary

You've been able to have fun with this chapter, tumbling with Duke and playing with a virtual Martian Popping Thing. You've learned about the way you can use JavaScript and Java to communicate with plug-ins. You've also learned about LiveConnect's plug-ins that work with JavaScript, plug-ins such as LiveAudio, LiveVideo, and Live3D.

In Chapter 12, "Internet Commerce (LivePayment) with JavaScript," you will learn how you can use LivePayment, a new open, cross-platform server software, to receive (or woefully pay) payments for online credit card processing.

CHAPTER 12

Internet Commerce (LivePayment) with JavaScript

O pportunities for small businesses today are much greater than in years past. It used to be that the cost of advertising, merchandising, overhead, and reaching consumers made it almost impossible for small businesses to succeed without major financial backing. The Internet has made it possible for all businesses to feature their wares to consumers all over the world. Commerce over the Internet is changing the way people shop. No longer will you need to get in your car, drive to your favorite store, and hurry up your shopping just to wait in line at the cash register. Netscape's LivePayment is going to change the way we make purchases.

LivePayment is a collection of objects that extend LiveWire. Live-Payment is an open cross-platform server and online payment software that enable you to perform transactions and collect payments over the Internet. LivePayment's functionality has been compared to that of an Internet cash register, providing smooth online transaction processing capabilities that enable companies to accept credit card payments from customers. Although LivePayment is in a restricted beta release at the time this is being written, Netscape is anticipating its final product release in the third quarter of 1996. In this chapter, you will learn about the following:

- Requirements for installing and running LivePayment

- Who can use LivePayment

- Roles in LivePayment

- LivePayment features

- Developing applications with LivePayment

- LivePayment security features

- Examples of LivePayment in action

- Creating an application by using the LivePayment utility commands

LivePayment Requirements

In order to run LivePayment successfully, you will need to have the following:

- An Intel Pentium-based workstation or Unix workstation/server.

- Windows NT 3.51 operating system with Service Pack 4 or Unix system that Netscape supports with Netscape Enterprise Server 2.0. Note that when running under Windows NT 3.51 you must apply all recommended patches to the operating system.

- A minimum of 32 MB of RAM.

- Netscape Enterprise Server Version 2.0, Netscape Navigator Version 2.02 or later, or LiveWire Version 1.0.

- 20 MB hard disk space for the installation staging area and a minimum of 50 MB hard disk space for the installed software.

- CD-ROM drive for installation and a 4 mm DDS (DAT) tape drive for backup and maintenance.

◆ Superuser privileges and experience for the system administrator.

◆ A secure server.

◆ A banking relationship established between merchant and bank.

Netscape Merchant System, Netscape Publishing System, and Netscape Community System are complete applications that use the same payment processing technology as the LivePayment standalone product, enabling LivePayment to coexist with these products.

To conduct credit card business, you must have the following:

◆ Approval for credit worthiness through a bank card acquirer

◆ Mail Order/Telephone Order (MOTO) approval through a Netscape-supported bank card acquirer

◆ Business agreement with a bank card acquirer that encompasses the arrangement for settlement of credit card purchases between the merchant bank and the consumer's bank card issuer.

A *bank card acquirer* is a financial institution that acts as a gateway between Internet merchants and the customer's bank card issuer.

To configure the LivePayment credit card processor, you must obtain the following from your bank card acquirer:

◆ Merchant source ID

◆ Merchant ID

◆ Credit card gateway host name

◆ Credit card gateway host port number

◆ Terminal ID

◆ List of Certificate authorities

Who Can Use LivePayment?

Because of LivePayment's ease of use and support from major financial institutions, its functionality can be used by many types of merchants, including retailers, publishers, service providers, and more.

Small Merchants

LivePayment makes commerce easily accessible to small retailers because of the sheer number of consumers who have access to retail Web sites. An online store application based on LivePayment can help retailers reach a greater number of consumers at a reduced overhead. If you have or are thinking about starting a small retail business, the Web is the place to begin. You can display goods on your Web site, accept orders, and process them, all without renting retail space, spending income on overhead, or training sales staff. You even can make available online catalogs from which consumers can order products such as CDs, books, and software. You can use the Web to display your retail goods and LivePayment to process consumer payments for a fraction of the cost of setting up a traditional mail order system or a physical shop.

Did you know...

In addition to payment processing features, LivePayment also includes templates that can help you set up payment-ready applications, thus easily turning your Web site into an Internet store.

Online and Software Publishing

If you are an online publisher or software publisher, LivePayment enables you to collect fees, such as subscription fees, usage fees, or item access fees. LivePayment also enables you to verify a customer's credit, settle payment for goods, and deliver your product, all over the Internet. Gone are the days when offline verification and processing ruled the retail world. As another benefit of performing transactions over the Internet, your customers can receive their goods immediately without wading through the "red tape" of traditional transactions.

Other Services

By using LivePayment, airlines, hotels, and other travel representatives can provide systems that enable consumers to make their own reservations directly, thus reducing the time it takes to verify and process payments. This brings significant cost savings to the customer—the savings the service provider experiences using this type of system can be passed on to the customer in the form of lower prices for goods.

Roles in LivePayment

An integral part of using LivePayment successfully is understanding the parties involved in making purchases over the Internet. The following list shows the parties involved, both directly and indirectly:

◆ Consumer (directly)

◆ Merchant (directly)

◆ Acquirer (directly)

◆ Issuer

◆ Merchant bank

Consumer

The consumer, who is the credit card holder, uses a Web browser to interact with the merchant's Web site. To make credit card purchases, the consumer must have a credit card and be able to provide bank card information when he or she is ready to make a purchase.

Merchant

The merchant is the person or company selling products or services. The merchant develops the LivePayment application that makes products or services available and also establishes a relationship with a merchant bank and acquirer.

Acquirer

The acquirer is the financial institution that acts as a gateway. Acting on behalf of merchant banks, the acquirer processes Internet transactions from merchants. Note that the acquirer can be an institution the same as or different from the merchant bank.

Issuer

The issuer is the financial institution that issues the consumer's credit card. Credit cards valid for use with LivePayment include Visa, MasterCard, American Express, Discover, JCB, Diner's Club, and Carte-Blanche.

Merchant Bank

The merchant bank is where the merchant's account is established. Merchant banks also can act as the acquirer or can designate another financial institution to function as an acquirer on its behalf.

LivePayment Features

LivePayment features include many benefits to merchants and consumers. In addition to being able to shop from their computer command posts, consumers benefit from reduced costs merchants experience in running a business online—the cost savings are passed on to the consumer.

Merchants benefit from using LivePayment in the following ways:

◆ The cost of setting up an Internet business is low.

◆ Developing online applications is made easy with LivePayment's sample applications, such as LPAuthOnly, which performs an authorization and stores the information in a flat file; and LPStarterApp, which performs an authorization, capture/credit, and settles the batches.

◆ Using JavaScript and LiveWire to customize payment processing applications.

◆ Support for standard client interfaces enables applications to be available to many merchants while not limiting the choice of browsers used by consumers.

◆ Instant payment for goods or services sold. Applications you create using LivePayment can verify customer credit and transmit charges to the bank when the product is delivered or the service is performed.

◆ Communication with credit card and banking institutions is done over the Internet using a secure transfer protocol.

◆ Using the additional set of LiveWire objects specifically for handling online payments from Web pages makes application development easy.

Payment Processor

The payment processor holds the logic, functionality, and algorithms for programming payment operations. You can access payment processing through the LiveWire development environment's LivePayment objects or the LivePayment utility commands, which will be discussed in the following sections.

LivePayment Objects

To accept and process credit card transactions on Web sites, LivePayment provides an additional set of predefined JavaScript object types (LivePayment objects) to use on the server, including Batch, Merchant, Processor, PayEvent, Slip, and Terminal. You can find a detailed discussion of each of these objects in the section entitled "LiveWire's LivePayment Objects," later in this chapter.

LivePayment Utility Commands

LivePayment provides a cpcmd utility that authorizes, captures, credits, and creates electronic credit card slips and provides a command line interface to the card processor (ccpd), whereby all JavaScript and LiveWire functionality is bypassed. This set of utilities also settles information from credit card batches. You can find more information about the cpcmd and other utilities in the section entitled "Creating an Application Using the LivePayment Utility Commands" later in this chapter.

 "cpcmd" (Card Processor Commands) provides a command line interface to the card processor (ccpd). All JavaScript and LiveWire functionality is bypassed. This utility provides a developer an interface to the card processing functions that use a command line, thus enabling users to integrate the utility into an existing CGI Perl script.

Administrative Interface

The administrative interface provided by LivePayment enables system administrators to set up and administer the LivePayment environment, including configuring and administrating merchants, terminals, card processor parameters, and administration of the LiveWire applications running on the server. For detailed information about how to use the administrative interface, see "Using the Starter Application" later in this chapter.

Developing Applications with LivePayment

LivePayment enables you to develop payment processing applications in three ways. You can modify the Starter Application, create your own application using LiveWire's LivePayment objects, or create your own application using the cpcmd utility. Don't limit yourself to using just one of these options, however. You can combine these methods to create a custom application. Before you jump into LivePayment application development, however, take a few minutes to read some basic information about how credit card transactions are processed.

Credit Card Processing Basics

Just as understanding the participants in the transaction process is integral to using LivePayment successfully, so is understanding the credit card process. This section takes you through the process of handling a transaction with LivePayment. Figure 12.1 is an overview of the transaction process.

Figure 12.1

An overview of the credit card transaction process using LivePayment.

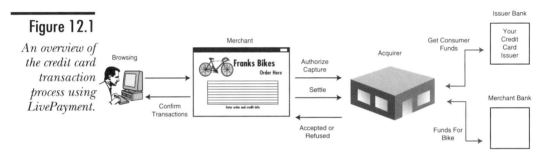

Suppose that you are browsing the Web in search of a site that offers bicycles. You find a site that offers the type of bicycle and components you are looking for, and you decide to make your purchase from this bicycle merchant. After you go through the merchant's process to indicate your purchase, the LivePayment Web application prompts you to enter your credit card information. This prompt usually includes fields for your credit card number, expiration date, and type of credit card. The prompt also contains prompts for your billing address, shipping address, and the maximum amount the merchant can charge you for the bike.

You enter your payment information into an SSL-secured form or a SET-compliant application. If the merchant is using the secured form, your payment is protected and sent to the merchant via SSL. The merchant then creates a slip from the secured form. If the merchant is using the SET protocol, the information is enclosed in an encrypted electronic credit card slip.

SSL (Secure Sockets Layer) is a protocol that uses channel encryption technology to protect information transferred over the Web from consumer to merchant.

SET (Secure Electronic Transaction) is a protocol used to secure credit card transactions over open networks.

When the merchant receives the secured form or slip, he or she sends it to the credit card acquirer, via the LivePayment card processor (ccpd utility), to have the information authorized. When the acquirer receives the slip, he or she replies with an authorization for the amount of money specified in the slip or issues a rejection of the transaction. An authorization does not take the money from your credit card account but rather acts as a reserve or hold on your account for the amount of the purchase. The authorization includes the amount of the purchase, the type of currency, and the slip information.

Congratulations, your transaction is approved!

The merchant then takes the information from the authorization and charges the authorized amount to your credit card. This is referred to as a *capture*.

 Performing a *capture* entails taking information from an authorized transaction and charging the authorized amount to the consumer's credit card.

 You may experience a lag time between the authorization and the capture if the merchant does not perform a capture until the goods you ordered can be shipped.

After the capture has taken place, the step of settling the transactions between the merchant and acquirer takes place. For reasons of efficiency, captured transactions usually are settled in batches. *Settling* reconciles the transactions between the merchant and the acquirer. The *batch* settlement operation requests that the acquirer transfer the money from the customer's account to the merchant's account.

 A *batch* is a group of transactions that are settled, or reconciled, as a group rather than individually and is retrieved from the acquirer.

Settling reconciles the transactions between the merchant and the acquirer. The *batch* settlement operation requests that the acquirer transfer the money from the customer's account to the merchant's account.

During settlement, the batch continues to collect capture and credit data until the batch is settled. For checks and balances, during this time the merchant checks the total number and amount in sales (and credits), and then compares those amounts to the numbers in the recorded batch. If any discrepancies are found, the merchant must contact the acquirer to solve them.

After the current batch is settled, a new batch starts up automatically. Note that in order to capture a credit or an amount, the merchant needs to know the batch number, which is supplied by the acquirer. During settlement, the acquirer starts the transfer of money from your account to the merchant's account at the merchant bank.

That's it! You now have your new bike, and the bank has drawn against your account for the amount of the purchase. Figure 12.2 shows an example of an electronic credit card slip.

Figure 12.2

An example of an electronic credit card slip.

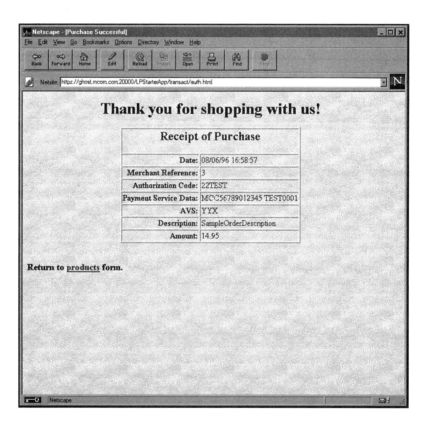

If for some reason you choose to cancel your order or return your new bike, the merchant performs a credit or refund. Credits also are processed as settlement in batch form.

Setting Up a Commerce System

Setting up a commerce system doesn't have to be complicated; however, you need to do several things in order to get a LivePayment system up and running successfully. The first items on your to-do list should be to establish a relationship with an acquirer and establish a security identity.

Establishing a Relationship with an Acquirer

In order to use LivePayment to process transactions, you first need to establish a relationship with a bank card acquirer that includes arranging for credit card purchase settlements between your bank and the consumer's bank card issuer. As mentioned earlier, the bank card acquirer is the financial institution authorized to accept credit card transactions in the interest of the merchant.

When setting up a working relationship, the acquirer you choose needs to provide the following information:

◆ Merchant number

◆ Terminal number

◆ Merchant source ID

◆ Host name of the bank card gateway

◆ Port numbers of the bank card gateway—one for the test gateway and one for the production gateway

Note The following information is from Netscape:

"Netscape Communications can refer you to available acquirers set up to handle credit card business, but cannot guarantee your business approval. Owning and using Netscape software does not guarantee you the privilege to conduct credit card business over the Internet. Your capability to handle credit card transactions is subject to the acquirer's approval only."

Establishing a Security Identity

LivePayment provides two ways for you to configure security: the same key pair file and certificates used by the server, or separate key pair and certificates for LivePayment. Note, however, that using separate certificates offers higher level security. In order to use the server's key pair file and certificate, you need to copy them from the server's configuration directory to LivePayment's configuration directory. To learn how to do this, go through the steps in the following exercise.

Configuring the Server's Key Pair File and Certificate

1. Locate the server key pair file, as in the following example code:

```
serverDirectory/https- ID/config/ServerKey.db
serverDirectory/https- ID/config/ServerCert.db
serverDirectory/https- ID/config/ServerCert.nm
```

   Use serverDirectory to specify the directory in which the server is installed. ID indicates the server identifier of your HTTP server.

2. Copy the files to the LivePayment administration directory, as in the following example:

```
serverDirectory\livepayment -ID\config\ServerKey.db
serverDirectory\livepayment -ID\config\ServerCert.db
serverDirectory\livepayment -ID\config\ServerCert.nm
```

   Use server_dir to specify the server directory and ID to indicate the server identifier.

3. To update the card processor parameters using file names, display the Configure Card Processor Parameters form (see fig. 12.3). On the Netscape LivePayment page, click on the Configure Card Processor Parameters link: the Configure Card Processor Parameters form appears.

4. Update the file names to the following, making sure to enter the certificate file name (ServerCert) without an extension:

```
serverDirectory\livepayment -ID\config\ServerKey.db
serverDirectory\livepayment -ID\config\ServerCert
```

5. To generate a key pair file that contains public and private keys for LivePayment's card processor, access the Generate a Key Pair File page.

6. On the Netscape LivePayment page, click the Generate a Key File link: the Generate a Key Pair File form appears (see fig. 12.4). Note that the help window that contains steps for generating a key pair file opens automatically.

7. Open a new browser window next to the browser window.

8. Log on as the LivePayment installing user. This is usually "siteadm."

9. Change your directory to the server root.

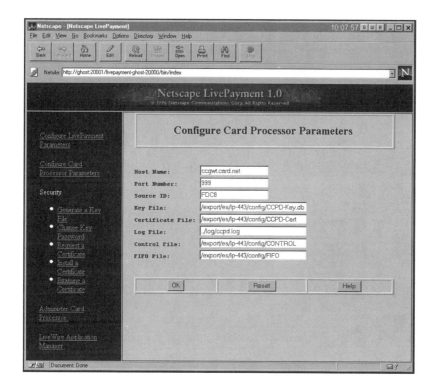

Figure 12.3

The Configure Card Processor Parameters form.

10. To run the key file generation program, which is in the bin directory of your LivePayment directory, enter the following:

```
bin\livepayment\admin\bin\sec-key
```

11. Enter the location in which you want to store the new key pair file. Note that the key pair file is usually stored in the server root in the livepayment-ID/config and with the CCPD-Key.db as the file name. ID indicates the name of the server identifier.

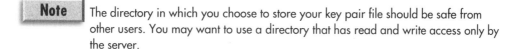

Note The directory in which you choose to store your key pair file should be safe from other users. You may want to use a directory that has read and write access only by the server.

12. Generate the key pair. During the generation process, a screen that contains a progress meter appears. Depending on your operating system, randomly move the mouse or press random keys and different speeds until the progress meter is full. Random movement creates a unique key pair file.

Figure 12.4

*The Generate a
Key Pair File
form.*

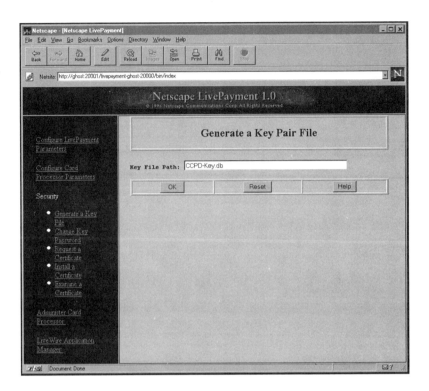

13. When the generation process is complete, type the password you want to use for your key pair. In order to decrypt the key file and extract the public and private keys, you will need to enter your password each time you restart the card processor. The password you choose must consist of eight characters, including one non-alphabetical character (such as a number or punctuation character) within characters two through six (Zep;pelin, for example).

Note   Be sure to memorize your password.

14. Confirm your password by retyping it, and then click on OK.

15. Click on the browser window that shows the Generate a Key Pair File page.

16. In the Key File Path field, enter the path and file name of your key file. Note that other users should not be able to access this directory.

17. Click on OK to save your changes. LivePayment generates the key pair file and stores it in the directory you specified.

Requesting a Certificate

As you will recall from previous discussions in this chapter, you need a certificate to prove your identity to the acquirer before you can begin a secure transaction. You do this through third-party companies, called Certificate Authorities (CAs). CAs are trusted companies that approve (or deny) requests for signed digital certificates—not everyone who applies is granted a digital certificate. The LivePayment package includes a list of CAs and the necessary screens you use to apply and install a certificate.

 Note Receipt of your certificate can take anywhere from a day to two or more months.

In order to request a certificate, you need to choose and contact a CA. The CA you contact will ask you to prove your identity before issuing you a certificate. Most likely you will need to furnish the name of your company, names of those authorized to administer LivePayment, and whether you have the legal right to use the information you provide.

Tip Because you are responsible for providing all the necessary information, be sure to ask about the Certificate Authority's list of prerequisites.

The following exercise shows you how to request a security certificate.

Requesting a Security Certificate

1. From the LivePayment page, click on the Request a Certificate link to display the Request a Card Processor Certificate form.

2. The Request a Card Processor Certificate form contains the following fields in which you need to provide information.

   Certificate Authority: Enter the e-mail address of the CA you have chosen.

   New Certificate or Certificate Renewal: Indicate whether you are applying for a new certificate or a renewal. Many certificates expire after a specific period of time, such as six months, 12 months, and so on; alternately, some CAs renew your certificate automatically.

   Key File Location: Indicate the location of your previously generated key pair file. The server uses this information to encrypt a message to the CA and send the public key.

Common Name: Indicate the fully qualified host name used in DNS lookups (such as www.newriders.com). If you are unsure whether this is the type of information this field requires, be sure to contact the CA.

Email Address: Specify your business e-mail address, which is used for correspondence between you and the CA.

Organization: Enter the official, legal name of your company, educational institution, or partnership. Most CAs require you to provide legal documents, such as a copy of your business license, to verify this information.

Organizational Unit: Enter an organization within your company. You also can use this field to note a less formal company name (such as MCP rather than Macmillan Computer Publishing). Filling out this field is optional.

Locality: Enter the city, principality, or country for your organization. Filling out this field is optional.

State or Province: This usually is a required field; however, some CAs might not require this information. Note that you cannot use abbreviations.

Country: This is a required two-character abbreviation of your country name (in ISO format). The country code for the United States, for example, is US.

Telephone Number: Indicate your phone number, including your area code and any international codes, as applicable. The CA uses this number to contact you regarding your request for a certificate.

3. After you complete the fields in the Request a Card Processor Certificate form, click on OK to send the request to the CA. The server sends your information to the CA via e-mail. This e-mail contains a digital signature LivePayment created with your private key. The CA uses this digital signature to ensure that the information was not tampered with en route from your server to the CA. If the e-mail was altered, the CA will contact you directly by phone.

 Note Until your request for a certificate is approved and you receive confirmation by e-mail, you cannot continue your security configuration.

The certificate you receive via e-mail from the CA is encrypted with your public key—only you, through your server, can decrypt the certificate when you install it. Figure 12.5 shows a sample certificate.

You can save the e-mail so that it is accessible to the server; or you can copy the text of the e-mail and paste the text into the Install a Card Processor Certificate form. The following exercise shows you how to install your certificate.

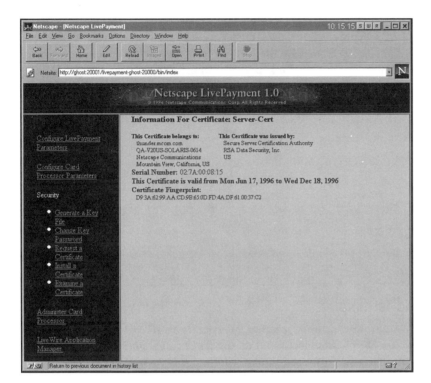

Figure 12.5

An example of a certificate.

Installing Your Certificate

1. To display the Install a Card Processor Certificate form that you use to begin the installation process, click on the Install a Certificate link on the Netscape LivePayment page.

2. In the "Message is in this file:" text box, specify the file in which you saved the entire certificate authorization message. You also can paste the actual message text into the "Message text (with headers)" text box.

3. In the Certificate database text box, specify a destination directory for your certificate. Do not specify your document root directory or any directory that is available for general use.

4. Click on OK. Your server will extract the certificate from the e-mail and save it to the directory you specify.

That's it! You now have chosen a CA and requested and obtained your security certificate.

LiveWire's LivePayment Objects

LivePayment provides objects that you use with the LiveWire development environment to create server-based applications that are comparable to CGI programs. You also can use JavaScript to develop your client and server Internet applications. This section discusses the following LivePayment objects:

◆ Merchant

◆ Terminal

◆ Processor

◆ Slip

◆ Batch

◆ PayEvent

Merchant and Terminal

To process credit card transactions, you first must create Merchant and Terminal objects. You use the Merchant object to set up the part of the application representing the merchant that is performing commerce on the Internet. In this object you store the information that identifies the merchant to the acquirer, such as your company name and certificate. The Terminal object contains information about the terminal on which the credit card processing takes place. Note that your application can have more than one terminal, and each terminal is assigned a number by the acquirer. In order to create either object, you must have the merchant number and terminal number provided by the bank card acquirer.

The Merchant object has the following properties:

merchantNumber	Required string that contains the merchant number, which you get from the acquirer.
name	Required string in which you specify the name of your company (merchant company).

The Terminal object has the following property:

terminal	Number Required string in which you specify the terminal number provided by the acquirer.

When creating objects, you use the new operator, which is a standard JavaScript operator.

To create an instance of a merchant object, use the steps in the following exercise.

Creating an Instant of the Merchant and Terminal Objects

1. After receiving the merchant number and terminal number from your acquirer, use the following syntax to create instances of the Merchant and Terminal objects.

```
1. // create a Merchant and Terminal object
2. mer = new Merchant("00000405999", "FFarkle");
3. term = new Terminal("00001205999");
```

2. Use your merchant number and company name in line 2 and your terminal number in line 3.

You now have created a merchant object and terminal object.

Processor

Developers can use the processor object to set up the part of the application that represents the bank card acquirer that handles payment transactions. The processor object offers two syntax options that enable you to create a new processor object. The first syntax option requires you to provide strings for the name and the encryptPasswordFile properties, as in the following:

```
processorObject = new Processor( "name", "encryptPasswordFile");
```

The second syntax option requires you to provide the string for the name property—the default password file is retrieved from the default configuration, as in the following:

```
processorObject = new Processor( "name");
```

You use the processorObject parameter to specify the new processor object. You use the name and encryptPasswordFile parameters to indicate the processor name and the password file used to encrypt the slip.

 A slip is an electronic, rather than paper, credit card slip.

The processor object uses the following five methods:

authorize	Checks whether the transaction can be executed
capture	Applies charges to the consumer's card
credit	Enables a merchant to generate a credit or refund

	when a customer cancels an order or returns goods
GetCurrentBatch	Enables the financial provider to start the next batch of transactions
SettleBatch	Enables the LivePayment user to compare the totals you enter with the totals contained within the batch

To use the first syntax option that requires you to provide strings for the name and the encryptPasswordFile properties, look at the following example:

```
processor = new Processor("FRED", "Password.txt");
```

In the preceding example code, "FRED" is the name of the processor object, and Password.txt is the name of the file that contains the encryption password.

The following example illustrates the syntax that uses the password from the default configuration:

```
processor = new Processor("FRED");
```

The following exercise shows you how to create a new Processor object.

Creating an Instance of a Processor Object

1. Have ready the name of your acquirer and the file name that contains the password for your slip encryption key.

2. Using the acquirer name and password, apply the following syntax:

```
// create a Processor object
processor = new Processor("LINCOLN", "Password.txt");
```

LINCOLN is the name of the acquirer in this example, and Password.txt is the password of the slip encryption key.

3. To create a Processor object by using the password default in the LivePayment configuration, use the following syntax:

```
// create a Processor object
processor = new Processor("LINCOLN");
```

LINCOLN in this case is the name of the acquirer.

Slip

The Slip object, which is analogous to an electronic credit card slip, contains the consumer's credit card information as well as billing and shipping addresses for the customer. Because this type of information is personal, for security reasons this object encodes the credit card information. The encoded information in this object is then decoded by the acquirer in order to approve and settle the payment for the merchant.

The Slip object uses the following methods:

appendMerchantOrder-Desc   Updates the merchant's description of the order. This order must match the customer's description of the order. You can append the order numerous times, with the sequence matching the sequence of the customer's order; however, you must complete the append processing before you authorize the transaction.

AppendOrderDesc   Updates the customer's order description—do not use this method after you encode the description

Encode   You use this method to encode the Slip object into an encrypted DER code string

getDER   Enables you to get the printable ASCII-encoded information from the DER slip.

InitMerchantOrderDesc   Enables you to initialize the merchant's order description, including the slip amount and currency. You must use this method before you use the appendMerchantOrderDesc method.

DER stands for Distinguished Encoding Rules.

In addition to the preceding methods, the Slip object has the following properties:

amount   Required string in which you indicate the amount of the purchase, using the exact amount without the decimal point. This unit is based on the currency in which you are dealing. The unit for the U.S. dollar, for example, is a cent.

BillingStreet   Optional string in which you specify the billing address of the credit card holder. This string must be fewer than 40 characters. Any additional characters are truncated.

BillingZip	Optional string in which you specify the billing ZIP code of the credit card holder.
CardExpirationDate	Required string in which you specify the expiration date of the credit card. You use the yyyymm format; for example 199804 (April, 1998).
CardNumber	Required string in which you specify the card holder's credit card number used in the transaction.
CardType	Required string in which you specify the type of credit card the card holder is using for the purchase. LivePayment accepts Visa, MasterCard, American Express, Discover, JCB, Diner's Club, and Carte-Blanche.
currency	Required string in which you indicate the type of currency with which you are dealing. This string uses the three-character ISO 4217 currency code. The currency code for the U.S. dollar, for example, is USD.
merchantReference	Optional alphanumeric string in which you specify your merchant reference information, such as an invoice. Note that this string must be fewer than 16 characters.
PurchaseRequest-Time	String that is set automatically by Slip object. This string contains the time the slip was generated. Note that this string is read-only.

The following exercise illustrates how to create a Slip object at the merchant site.

Creating a Slip Object at the Merchant Site

1. Create the Slip object using JavaScript's new operator. In the following code used to create a Slip object, you need to have the card number, expiration date, amount of money, and currency information ready before you begin this process. You use this information to define the properties of the Slip object.

```
// Create and generate a slip for max amount of 100.00
cardNumber = "5200000000001234"; cardExpiration = "199804";
currency = "USD";
maxAmount = "50000";
slip = new Slip(cardNumber, cardExpiration, maxAmount, currency);
```

2. After you create your Slip object, you can set other fields in the object. The following code adds a card type field, an invoice number reference, the billing street, and the ZIP code of the customer. It also appends an order description. Note that the example uses a Slip object called "slip."

```
// set other fields before generating the encrypted slip
slip.cardType = "MasterCard";
slip.merchantReference = "invoice 1205";
slip.billingStreet = "1122 Boogie Woogie Ave";
slip.billingZip = "47203";

slip.appendOrderDesc("Inside JavaScript and LiveWire Pro");
slip.appendOrderDesc("satisfaction guaranteed");
```

3. You can append multiple lines of text to the order description. You can append as many times as you need to; however, you cannot append any more information after you encode your slip.

Batch

As mentioned earlier in this chapter, captured transactions are settled in batches. The Batch object, identified by a batch ID, is an accumulation of transactions that need to be settled and contains information about each of those unsettled transactions. You can create an instance of the Batch object in two ways. To return the current batch from the acquirer, use getCurrentBatch. You also can use the new operator. Unless you have stored the batch number, however, you first must use getCurrentBatch to get the batch number. The Batch object contains the following properties:

batchNumber	A required string that gets the batch number returned from the getCurrentBatch method. This number comes from the acquirer.
CreditCount	A number argument, required for the settleBatch method, that totals the number of credits in a batch.
Currency	A string, required for the settleBatch method, that consists of the three-character ISO 4217 currency code. USD, for example, stands for U.S. dollars.
MerchantReference	A string, required for the settleBatch method, that references information provided by the merchant for tracking purposes. Note that for FDC, the merchant reference cannot be more than ten alphanumeric characters.
SalesCount	A number, required for settleBatch, that represents the total number of sales in a batch.

| TotalSalesAmount | A string, required for the settleBatch method, that represents the total sales amount of all credit card transactions in the batch. |
| TotalCreditAmount | A string, required for the settleBatch method, that represents the total credit amount of all credit card transactions in a batch. |

Creating a Batch Object

To create a Batch object using the getCurrentBatch method, and then check the batch and store the batch number, use the following code (you get the current batch number with the Processor, Terminal, and Merchant objects created as "processor," "term," and "mer"):

```
// get the most current batch
myBatch = processor.getCurrentBatch(term, mer);


// check the errors
if (processor.bad())
{
    write("getCurrentBatch operation failed");
    write("Processor status code is ", processor.getStatusCode());
    write("Processor status message is ",processor.getStatusMessage());
    processor.clearStatus();
}
// remember the batchNumber or store in a database
batchNumber = myBatch.batchNumber;
```

The code also checks for errors and sends messages if the batch was not opened successfully. If the batch was opened successfully, the getCurrentBatch method returns a Batch object with the batchNumber property assigned by the acquirer.

Creating a Batch Object Using the new Operator

To create a Batch object using the new operator, you only need to set the batchNumber property; the other properties are required for settling the batch. Assuming that you have run the getCurrentBatch method, use the following code:

```
// Create the Batch object using the
// batch number of the batch which was defined earlier
myBatchObject = new Batch(batchNumber);
```

The Batch object created is called myBatchObject.

Note In order to get the current batch from your acquirer, you first need to create the Terminal and Merchant objects, discussed earlier in this section.

PayEvent

You use PayEvent objects to store records of complete financial transactions that may consist of a credit card authorization, capture, and settlement.

The PayEvent object has the following properties:

amount	Required string for authorized, capture, and credit properties. Specify the amount of money, using the exact amount (must be greater than zero). This unit is based on currency. The unit for the U.S. dollar is a cent.
authCode	Required string for capture. Specify the authorization code that you receive from the acquirer when the authorization is approved.
avsResp	Required string for capture. Specify the address verification system response that you receive from the acquirer when the authorization is approved.
eventID	Required string for capture and credit. Specify the unique ID for a transaction within a batch, which you use for capturing and crediting. The merchant sets the eventID, which must be unique for the event. Note that for FDC, your ID cannot contain more than five alphanumeric characters.
eventTime	A string set automatically after authorize, capture, and credit. It indicates the time the payEvent occurs and is provided by the acquirer when the capture or credit is approved. Note that this property is read-only.
merchantReference	Required string in which you specify the information the merchant assigns to the payEvent, such as an invoice number. Note that for FDC, you cannot use more than ten numeric characters.
PaySvcData	Required string for capture. Specify the payment service data or interchange compliant code that is provided by the acquirer when the authorization is approved. Note that payment service data is used only for Visa and MasterCard.

Each time you use a payEvent object, you need to define the merchant reference. You set all other PayEvent properties when the object is passed to the methods of the processor object.

The following exercise shows you how to create and use a PayEvent object.

Creating and Using a PayEvent Object

1. To create a PayEvent object, use JavaScript's new operator, as in the following:

```
// create a PayEvent object
MerchantReference = "0087";
pay = new PayEvent(MerchantReference);
```

Indicate your own merchant reference rather than using 0087.

2. You also can assign the merchant reference value when you create the PayEvent object, as in the following:

```
ßPayEvent("0087");
```

Using the Starter Application

LivePayment's Starter Application shows you how to process credit card payments by using a simple processing application. If you are new to the concept of LivePayment, using the Starter Application can help you understand how to implement your own LivePayment application.

Starter Application Requirements

In order to successfully run the Starter Application, you must have the following:

◆ A running Enterprise Server

◆ An installed and running Informix database

◆ An installed and running LiveWire environment

◆ An installed and running LivePayment environment

You also need to configure the Starter Application for your environment, beginning with the line in the start.html file that calls the database.connect method, which connects the Starter Application to your database. Look at the following call syntax:

```
database.connect ("server","serverName","userName","password","databaseName")
```

When using an Informix database, specify INFORMIX for server, the name of your server for serverName, and LIVEPAYMENT for databaseName. For userName and password, use those provided with the Informix database.

To learn how to start the Starter Application and make a mock purchase, go through the steps in the following exercise.

Making a Mock Purchase with Starter Application

1. From the LiveWire Application Manager, choose LPStarterApp, as shown in figure 12.6 (for more information about Application Manager, see Chapter 8, "Getting Familiar with LiveWire's Application Manager"). The Starter Application opening screen appears (see fig. 12.7).

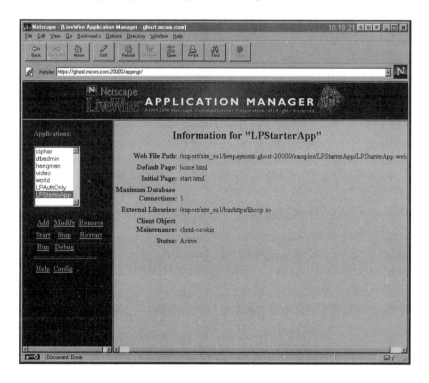

Figure 12.6

Choosing LPStarterApp from LiveWire Manager.

Figure 12.7

The opening screen for LivePayment's Starter Application.

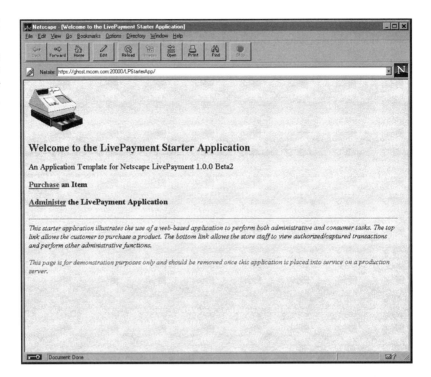

2. From the initial screen, you can choose from two modes of operation: the store, which enables you to make purchases; or administration, which enables you to supervise transaction records and collect payments. For this exercise, choose the Purchase link to start the purchasing process.

3. From the Purchase Information screen, you can choose one of three items you want to purchase: a T-shirt, mouse pad, or ceramic pig (for this exercise, it doesn't matter which item you choose). Click the radio button of the item you want to purchase.

4. The resulting screen contains fields in which you enter your billing and shipping information. Be sure to include your full name, credit card type, credit card number, and expiration date (see fig. 12.8).

 **Tip**   To clear the fields and start over, click the Reset Form button.

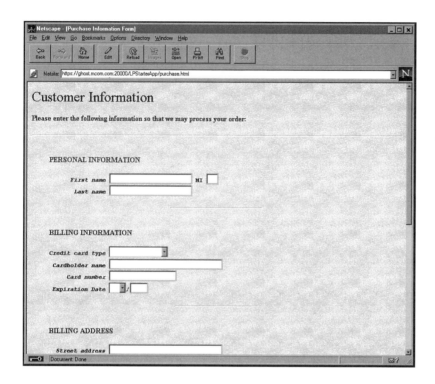

Figure 12.8

Enter the correct billing and shipping information in the fields provided.

5. After you complete the shipping and billing form, click the Complete the Purchase button. Starter Application checks the information you entered in the shipping and billing fields, creates a payment slip, and attempts authorization. If the purchase is successful, Starter Application displays an on-screen receipt that verifies that your purchase was authorized. If the authorization is unsuccessful, Starter Application displays an error message, in which case you need to re-enter your billing and shipping information.

6. Choose the Return Home link, which returns you to the Starter Application home screen.

Now that you have made a purchase, you will want to see how the system has recorded your transaction. The following exercise shows you how to use the administration interface to view the purchasing process, starting from the Home screen.

Using the Administration Interface

1. On the Home screen, choose the Administer link (refer to fig. 12.7). The Administration screen appears.

2. The Administration screen displays links to other pages that enable you to view transaction information and perform collections. Following is the first series of available links:

   View Transactions: Current, Previous, Failed, and Query

   Following is the second series of links:

   Perform Tasks: Capture, Cancel, Credit, and Settle

   For this exercise, click on the Current link in the View Transactions area. The Current Batch screen appears (see fig. 12.9).

Figure 12.9

The Current Batch screen.

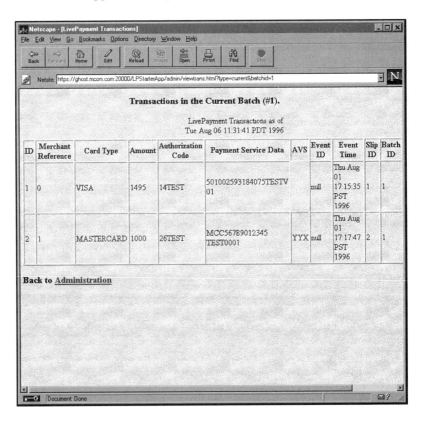

3. Choose the Back to Administration link. To view an uncaptured authorization, click the Capture button. The resulting screen displays a table that shows the information the system recorded in order to identify your authorized purchase (see fig. 12.10). The table includes the purchase you made in the preceding exercise, the merchant, type of credit card, authorization code, payment service, AVS data, event ID, event time, slip ID, batch ID, and status.

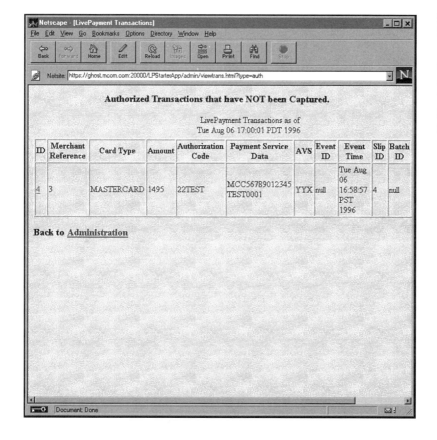

Figure 12.10

You can see the information you entered when you made your purchase in the preceding exercise.

Within the figure:

Authorized Transactions that have NOT been Captured.

LivePayment Transactions as of
Tue Aug 06 17:00:01 PDT 1996

ID	Merchant Reference	Card Type	Amount	Authorization Code	Payment Service Data	AVS	Event ID	Event Time	Slip ID	Batch ID
4	3	MASTERCARD	1495	22TEST	MCC56789012345 TEST0001	YYX	null	Tue Aug 06 16:58:57 PST 1996	4	null

Back to **Administration**

4. Choose the Back to Administration Page link. Click on the transaction ID. A transaction summary screen appears.

5. Choose the Back to Administration Page link. Click on Capture Transaction. The resulting screen shows that your transaction was captured.

Note LivePayment performs capturing in batches of transactions. To capture a single transaction (for example, to capture a transaction in which goods have been provided), however, you use the Capture Transaction screen.

6. If the transaction you want has not been captured, you can cancel it. Choose the Back to Administration Page link. To cancel a transaction, just click on the Cancel Transaction button. A message appears, confirming that the transaction is canceled.

7. In some cases, such as when goods are returned or you need to cancel a captured transaction, you must credit a customer's credit card. To credit a transaction, on the Administration page, click on the Credit button. A list of batches in the database appears.

8. To display the list of transactions in the batch you want, choose the batch ID of your transaction.

9. To display a summary page that contains information about your transaction, click on the transaction ID of your transaction (see fig. 12.11). Return to the Administration page.

Figure 12.11

A summary page that contains transaction information.

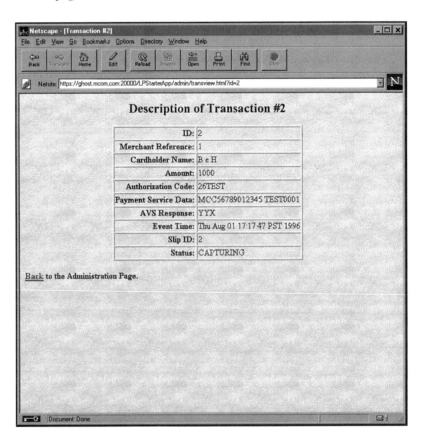

10. To credit your transaction and display a confirmation message, click on the Credit Transactions button. A list of batches from which you can choose a single transaction to credit appears. Click on the ID of the transaction you want to credit. Return to the Administration Page.

11. To settle a current batch of transactions (this includes all transactions that are captured or capturing, credited or crediting), click on the Settle button. Note that the current batch does not include authorized transactions. Alternately, to capture outstanding authorizations and settle the current batch of transactions, click on the Autocapture button. The transactions are now settled.

This concludes the Starter Application training. Now you are ready to set up your own commerce system.

LivePayment Security Features

Credit card information that is sent over the Internet is protected in several ways. Every time transactions are sent, either from the consumer to the merchant or from the merchant to the acquirer and then back, that information must be protected. Currently, information is protected by a *secure transfer protocol* called *Secure Sockets Layer*, or SSL. In order to use SSL, consumers must be using a browser that supports SSL, such as Netscape Navigator. Also, the merchant must be running a secure server. This section walks you through the credit card process and explains security measures that are taken to protect credit card information.

After you send your credit card information to the merchant, he or she encodes it using Distinguished Encoding Rules, after which most of the slip information is unreadable by the merchant. Encrypted slips then are stored in a database to ensure a record of the transaction.

Encrypted information leaves the merchant and, protected by SSL, travels to the acquirer. In addition to the secure transfer protocol, LivePayment uses a system of mutual verification by which the identities of the merchant and acquirer are encrypted but are recognized by both the acquirer and merchant. In order to prove identity, the merchant and acquirer use security certificates issued by a known Certificate Authority, which verifies the identities of both by using *public/private key cryptography*.

Public/private key cryptography uses a key for encrypting and a key for decrypting. The public key encrypts information and then is publicized as much as possible; all those who receive messages from owners of a particular public key can ascertain the sender. The private key information, however, remains unavailable. Merchants encrypt information using the acquirer's public key and then send the information to the acquirer.

The information the acquirer receives is protected by SSL, DER encryption, public/ private key encryption, and authentication. The acquirer then decrypts the information by using the private key, to which only they have access. When returning information to the merchant, the acquirer encrypts the message by using the merchant's public key so that only the merchant can decrypt it. Subsequent replies from the merchant to the customer also are protected by SSL.

LivePayment Examples

This section contains exercises for generating and encoding a slip and instructions for authorizing a transaction. You will use the Slip object and the PayEvent object, as well as methods and properties associated with each object.

Generating and Encoding a Slip Object

LivePayment first creates a Slip object. In that Slip object you can include properties, such as the billing street address, ZIP code, description of the order, and so on. When you generate a slip, LivePayment encodes the information in a format that you can send to the acquirer for purchase authorization. The following exercise illustrates how to generate and encode a Slip object.

Generating Your Slip Object

1. To create the Slip object you want to generate and encode, use the GenerateSlip function found in the JavaScript authorize.js file. The GenerateSlip function encodes the slip, and then recreates it, thus protecting the credit card information. Look at the following:

   ```
   slip = new Slip(request.CCardNumber, request.CCardExpDate, amount, cur-
   rency);
   ```

   In the code you requested the credit card number (CCardNumber), the expiration date of the credit card (CCardExpDate), the amount of the purchase, and then the currency used in the transaction.

2. After you create the Slip object, you can add values from the original transaction. The following code requests from the order the street address and ZIP code for the billing statement, the type of credit card the customer is using, and an order description.

   ```
   slip.billingAddress = request.Address;
   ```

```
slip.billingZipcode = request.Zipcode;
slip.cardType = request.CCType;

slip.appendOrderDesc(orderDesc);
```

3. Now that you have generated the slip and appended order information, you can encode it for issuance to the acquirer. To encode a slip, LivePayment inserts the slip information into a DER encoded string—the application can re-create the slip from the string; however, it can't access the card number after the slip is encoded. To encode the Slip object and then instruct the application to extract the resulting DER string, use the following syntax:

```
var encodeStatus
encodeRetStatus = slip.encode(processor)
if (!encodeRetStatus)
{
    PrintFmtError("Error occurred encoding slip with message, ",
        slip.getStatusMessage());
}
DERstring = slip.getDER();
```

4. Provided that you are using a database in which to place customer order information, you can use the following code to store the transaction. For this example, the name of the table in the database is crSlip. To create a cursor object in which to save the DER string, use the following syntax:

```
var nextSlipID = GetNextSlipID();
if ((error == database.beginTransaction()))
    PrintError("Could not start transaction in authorize() block.",
        "An error code of " + error + " was returned.",
    "Please contact your system administrator for further assistance.");

cursor = database.cursor("select * from crSlip", true);
cursor.ID = nextSlipID;
cursor.slipDER = DERstring;
if ((error == cursor.insertRow("crSlip")))
{
    cursor.close();

    database.rollbackTransaction();
    PrintError("Failed to insert slip into database, error ", error);
}
cursor.close();

database.commitTransaction();
```

5. Now that you have saved the encoded slip, you use GenerateSlip to recreate the slip from the one you just encoded. The new slip, slip2, contains information in encoded form, as in the following:

```
mySlip = new Slip(DERstring);
if (mySlip.bad())
{
    PrintFmtError("Failed to construct slip object from DER.",
        mySlip.getStatusMessage());
}
mySlip.initMerchantOrderDesc(amount, currency);
mySlip.appendMerchantOrderDesc(orderDescription);
slipID = nextSlipID;// set Global var slipID
return (mySlip);
}
```

Credit Card Authorization

Now that you have generated and encoded a slip, the next step is to authorize your transaction. An authorization does not take the money from your credit card account—it acts as a reserve or hold on the customer's account for the amount of the purchase. The authorization includes the amount of the purchase, the type of currency, and the slip information.

The following exercise shows you how to authorize a transaction.

Authorizing a Transaction

To authorize a transaction, LivePayment creates a PayEvent object. It then makes a call to the authorize method of LivePayment's process object, as in the following syntax:

```
1. if ((authResult == processor.authorize(terminal, merchant, payevent,
     ➥slip)))
2.     {
3.     avsFail = CheckAVS(payevent);
4.     // Save transaction info to the database
5.     SavePayevent(payevent, slip, avsFail, authResult,
        ➥request.cardHolderName);
6.     if (avsFail)
7.     {
8.         PrintAVSError(avsFail);
9.     }
```

```
10.    else
11.    {
12.         returnval = true; // else, no errors so return TRUE
13.    }
14. }
15. else
16. {
17.     // Save transaction info to the database
18.     SavePayevent(payevent, slip, false, authResult,
        ➥request.cardHolderName);
19.     PrintFmtError("Uh OH, Credit Card Authorization Failed.",
20.     processor.getStatusMessage());
21. }
```

In line 3, CheckAVS calls the Address Verification Service code to ensure that the address the customer provided when making the purchase matches the address of cardholder.

Creating an Application by Using the LivePayment Utility Commands

LivePayment provides a cpcmd utility that authorizes, captures, credits, and creates electronic credit card slips and provides a command line interface to the card processor (ccpd), whereby all JavaScript and LiveWire functionality is bypassed (see fig. 12.12).

This set of utilities also settles information from credit card batches. The cpcmd utility uses the following six commands to process credit card transactions:

◆ Authorize

◆ Capture

◆ CreateSlip

◆ Credit

◆ GetCurrentBatch

◆ SettleBatch

Figure 12.12

*The Administer
Card Processor
screen.*

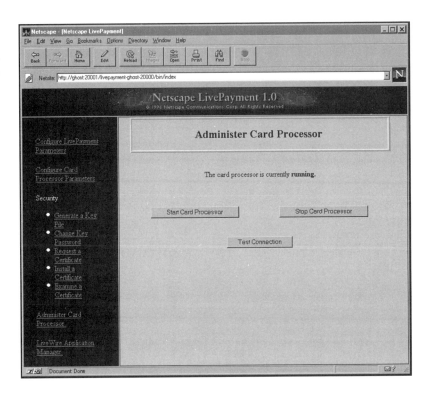

> **Note** LivePayment requires a space between the argument and its value. Also note that arguments and command names are not case sensitive; however, the values of arguments are case sensitive. An authorization code of B123456, for example, is not the same as an authorization code of b123456.

Authorize

The Authorize command approves credit for an amount you specify. It puts a hold on the account for the amount authorized; however, it does not make a charge against the credit card account. Following is the syntax:

```
cpcmd -Command Authorize -MerNum merchant_number -TermNum terminal_
➥number -Currency currency
➥-SlipAmount slip_ amount -Amount amount [-SlipFile slip_file] [-MerchantRef
merchant_reference]
➥-OrdDescFile order_description_file [-PswdFile password_file]
```

When authorization is successful, the authorize command outputs a message indicating the payment was authorized. It also outputs the Authorization Code, the Payment Service Data, and the Address Verification Code. The Capture command requires these values, which are stored for use during capture (for more information on the Capture command, see the following section).

-Amount is a required integer in which you specify the amount of money. The unit is based on the currency code; the unit for the US dollar is a cent. -Currency is a required alpha argument that indicates a three-character ISO 4217 currency code. USD, for example, indicates US dollar, CAD indicates Canadian dollar, and so on.

 For the complete list of currency codes, refer to the Web page named "currency.html" that is found on the accompanying CD-ROM.

-MerchantRef is an optional alphanumeric argument in which you reference information (for tracking) that is provided by the merchant. If you do not specify this argument, this command defaults to MerchantRef from the slip. If you are using LivePayment objects, this command is analogous to the merchantReference method of the PayEvent object. -MerNum is a required alphanumeric argument in which you indicate the merchant number, which is provided by the acquirer.

-OrdDescFile is a required string argument in which you specify the file that contains the order description (price, type of goods ordered, and so on).

-PswdFile is an optional string argument in which you indicate the file name of the password file that contains the password used to encode or decode the slip. If you do not specify this string, the authorize command defaults to /CONFIG/LP-DEFAULT-PSWDFILE.

-SlipAmount is a required integer argument in which you indicate the amount from the slip. -SlipFile is an optional string in which you indicate the file name of the slip. If you do not specify this string, the authorize command defaults to cpslip.slp. Lastly, -TermNum is a required alphanumeric in which you specify the terminal number, which is provided by the acquirer.

The following shows an example of the Authorize command:

```
cpcmd -command authorize -termnum 0000428812345 -mernum 00002031684 -slipamount
1995 -amount 1995 -orddescfile ord.dsc -currency USD
```

The preceding code produces the following output:

```
Payment Authorized for USD1995
Authz code: 50TEST
Payment Svc data:MCC56789012345
AVS result: YYX
```

The preceding example authorizes the amount of $19.95 (in U.S. dollars). It uses the credit card information encoded in the file cpslip.slp, references the order description file ord.desc and defaults to the slip's merchant reference. The code then outputs the authorized amount, the Authorization Code, Payment Service Data, and the Address Verification result. Note that depending on the card type, the Payment Serve Data may display all blanks.

In order to authorize transactions, you must adhere to the following rules:

◆ Authorizations must be at least for the amount that you capture. When authorizing an amount that is less than the captured amount, you must carry out another authorization. For example, some applications are programmed to perform an initial authorization of a small amount in order to ensure the credit card is valid. When the product is ready to ship, the application is authorized for the entire amount.

◆ You must notify your acquirer when authorizing an amount larger than the capture; however, the same authorization code can still be used.

◆ After you authorize payment, the acquirer returns to you the results from the address verification service (AVS), which verifies the billing address provided by the customer against the billing address of the card holder.

 Address verification service (AVS) is a security precaution that verifies that the person using the credit card actually is the card holder. Merchants should not accept the transaction if one or more parts of the transaction do not match the verification.

◆ After a payment is authorized, the authorization remains current for the amount of time determined by the issuing bank. If the purchase amount is not captured during this period of time, you must re-authorize the payment.

Capture

Use the Capture command to charge a customer for the amount authorized. When the transaction between the merchant and customer is complete, the Capture command sends information back to the acquirer that authorized the transaction.

 Arguments themselves are not case sensitive; however, their values can be case sensitive.

In the following code, arguments are in mixed upper- and lowercase to make them easy to read:

```
cpcmd -Command Capture -MerNum merchant_number
-TermNum terminal_number -Amount amount
-AuthzCode authorization_code -PaySvcData "payment_service_data "
-AVS address_verification_code [-SlipFile slip_file]
[-MerchantRef merchant_reference] -BatchNumber batch_number
[-PswdFile password_file] -TranxId transaction_ID
```

When this command is successful, it outputs the currency code and the amount captured.

-Amount is a required integer that indicates the amount of money. The unit is based on the currency code; the unit for the U.S. dollar is a cent. -AuthzCode is a required alphanumeric integer that indicates the authorization code, which is returned from the Authorize command.

-AVS is a required alpha argument that indicates the address verification service result, which is returned from the Authorize command. -BatchNumber is a required integer that indicates the batch number that is generated by the getCurrentBatch command.

-MerchantRef is an optional alphanumeric argument in which you reference information (for tracking) that is provided by the merchant. If you do not specify this argument, this command defaults to MerchantRef from the slip. If you are using LivePayment objects, this command is analogous to the merchantReference method of the PayEvent object. MerNum is a required alphanumeric argument that indicates the merchant number, which is provided by the acquirer.

-PaySvcData is a required alphanumeric argument that indicates the payment service data or interchange-compliant code, which is returned from the Authorize command. Note that payment service data is only used for Visa and MasterCard.

-PswdFile is an optional string argument that indicates the file name of the password file that contains the password used to encode or decode the slip. If you do not specify this argument, the Capture command defaults to /CONFIG/LP-DEFAULT-PSWDFILE.

-SlipFile is an string argument that indicates the file name of the slip. If you do not specify this argument, the Capture command defaults to cpslip.slp. -TermNum is a required alphanumeric argument that indicates the terminal number that is provided by the acquirer. Lastly, -TranxId is a required integer argument that indicates the transaction ID. When within a batch, this argument must be unique.

The following shows an example of the Capture command:

```
cpcmd -command capture -termnum 0000428812345 -mernum 00002031684 -amount
1995 -authzcode 50TEST -paysvcdata "MCC56789012345 TEST0001" -AVS YYX
-batchnumber 00010 -tranxid 99912
```

The preceding code produces the following output:

```
captured USD1995
```

The example captures $19.95 in U.S. dollars. It uses the authorization code, payment service data, and AVS response returned by the authorization. It also uses the default values for the password file and the slip file and the merchant reference from the slip.

In order to capture transactions, you must adhere to the following rules:

◆ Do not capture transactions until the goods are shipped; however, you can authorize a transaction when the customer places the order.

◆ You must get the current batch number from the acquirer.

◆ Your eventID or transactionID must be unique within the batch when your acquirer is FDC. Failure to use a unique ID may result in the inability to settle the batch.

CreateSlip

The CreateSlip command creates the electronic equivalent of a paper credit card slip. For security reasons, the information in this file is encrypted.

Note Arguments are not case sensitive; however, their values can be case sensitive.

In the following code, arguments are in mixed upper- and lowercase to make them easy to read:

```
cpcmd -Command CreateSlip -Currency currency
-SlipAmount slip_amount [-ClientRef client_reference]
[-MerchantRef merchant_reference] [-SlipFile slip_file]
[-SlipExpDate slip_expiration_date] -CardType card_type
-PAN personal_account_number -PANExpDate PAN_expiration_date
[-OrdDescFile order_description_file] [-BillStreet billing_street]
[-BillZip billing_zip_code] [-PswdFile password_file]
```

When the slip is created successfully, the CreateSlip command outputs a "slip created" message.

-BillStreet is an optional string argument that indicates the billing street address of the credit card holder. Note that you must enclose in quotes the value for this argument. -BillZip is an optional string argument that indicates the billing zip code of the credit card holder. Note that you must enclose in quotes the value for this argument.

-CardType is a required alphanumeric argument that indicates the credit card types, which are not case-sensitive. You can use Visa, MasterCard, American Express, Discover, JCB, Diner's Club, and Carte-Blanche. -ClientRef is an optional string argument that enables you to reference information the customer provides. You can use this information for tracking purposes.

-Currency is a required alpha argument that indicates a three-character ISO 4217 currency code. USD, for example, indicates U.S. dollar, CAD indicates Canadian dollar, and so on.

-MerchantRef is an optional alphanumeric argument in which you reference information (for tracking) that is provided by the merchant. If you do not specify this argument, this command defaults to MerchantRef from the slip.

-OrdDescFile is an optional string argument that enables you to specify the name of the file that contains a description of the order, including the price, goods ordered, and so on. If you do not specify this string argument, CreateSlip defaults to cporddsc.slp.

-PAN is a required integer argument that enables you to specify the personal account number or credit card number of the customer. -PANExpDate is a required string that enables you to specify the expiration date of the credit card. The format you need to use is yyyymm; for example, 199604 specifies April, 1996.

-PswdFile is an optional string argument in which you indicate the file name of the password file that contains the password used to encode or decode the slip. If you do not specify this string, the authorize command defaults to /CONFIG/LP-DEFAULT-PSWDFILE.

-SlipAmount is a required integer argument in which you indicate the amount from the slip. Note that this unit is based on the currency code; the unit for the U.S. dollar is a cent. -SlipExpDate is an optional string argument that enables you to indicate the slip expiration date by using the mmyy format. Lastly, -SlipFile is an optional string argument that enables you to indicate the name of the slip. If you do not specify this argument, CreateSlip defaults to cpslip.slp.

The following shows an example of the CreateSlip command:

```
cpcmd -command createslip -currency USD -amount 1995 -merchantref 1234
-cardtype Visa -pan 4200000000000005 -panexpdate 199812
-orddescfile ord.dsc -billstreet "412 First Street" -billzip "47203"
```

The preceding code produces the following output:

```
Slip created.
```

This example creates a slip for an amount of $19.95 in U.S. dollars for a Visa card with a card number 4200000000000005 that expires on 12/98. Because no slip file was specified, the slip is in the default file cpslip.slp. Order description information is in the file ord.dsc. The billing street address and ZIP code are 412 First Street, 47203.

Credit

Use the Credit command to send a credit order to the acquirer for all or part of the amount originally captured.

Note   Arguments are not case sensitive; however, their values can be case sensitive.

In the following code, arguments are in mixed upper- and lowercase to make them easy to read:

```
cpcmd  -Command Credit  -MerNum merchant_number
-TermNum terminal_number  -Amount amount  -TranxId transaction_id
[-SlipFile slip_file] [-MerchantRef merchant_reference]  -BatchNumber
batch_number [-PswdFile password_file]
```

When this command is successful, it outputs the amount credited.

-Amount is a required integer that indicates the amount of money. The unit is based on the currency code; the unit for the U.S. dollar is a cent. -BatchNumber is a required integer argument that indicates the batch number that was generated by the GetCurrentBatch command (for more information on the GetCurrentBatch command, see the following section).

-MerchantRef is an optional alphanumeric argument in which you reference information (for tracking) that is provided by the merchant. If you do not specify this argument, this command defaults to MerchantRef from the slip. If you are using LivePayment objects, this command is analogous to the merchantReference method of the PayEvent object. MerNum is a required alphanumeric argument that indicates the merchant number, which is provided by the acquirer.

-PswdFile is an optional string argument in which you indicate the file name of the password file that contains the password used to encode or decode the slip. If you do not specify this string, the authorize command defaults to /CONFIG/LP-DEFAULT-PSWDFILE.

-SlipFile is an optional string in which you indicate the file name of the slip. If you do not specify this string, the authorize command defaults to cpslip.slp.

-TermNum is a required alphanumeric argument that enables you to indicate the terminal number, which is provided by the acquirer. -TranxId is a required integer argument in which you specify the transaction ID. If within a batch, this argument must be unique.

The following shows an example of the Credit command:

```
cpcmd -command credit -termnum 0000428812345 -mernum 00002031684 -amount 1995 -
tranxid 99913 -batchnumber 00010
```

The preceding code produces the following output:

```
credited USD1995
```

The example credits $19.95 in U.S. dollars. It uses the default slip file and password file and the merchant reference from the slip.

In order to credit transactions, you must adhere to the following rules:

◆ The card to which you are issuing the credit must be valid; however, you are not required to run an authorization before you credit the account.

◆ You must get the current batch number from the acquirer.

◆ Your eventID or transactionID must be unique within the batch when your acquirer is FDC—do not use the ID of the capture. Failure to use a unique ID results in your transaction not being recognized.

GetCurrentBatch

GetCurrentBatch provides the number of the current batch for credit card transaction information. An open batch collects payment information to forward, in batch mode, through the gateway.

> **Note** Arguments are not case sensitive; however, their values can be case sensitive.

In the following code, arguments are in mixed upper- and lowercase to make them easy to read:

```
cpcmd -Command GetCurrentBatch -MerNum merchant_number
-TermNum terminal_number
```

The preceding code outputs the current batch number.

-MerNum is a required alphanumeric argument which indicates the merchant number, which is provided by the acquirer. -TermNum is a required alphanumeric in which you specify the terminal number, which is provided by the acquirer.

The following shows an example of the GetCurrentBatch command:

```
cpcmd -command getcurrentbatch -termnum 0000428812345 -mernum 00002031684
```

The preceding code produces the following output:

```
Batch Number: 00375
```

The preceding example opens a batch for a merchant with a merchant number of 00002031684 and a terminal number of 00003277999. It returns the batch number 00375.

SettleBatch

SettleBatch settles in batch mode a batch of credit card transaction information. Note that some SettleBatch arguments are sales totals and amounts you have kept track of. This command compares your record totals with the batch totals.

 Note Arguments are not case sensitive; however, their values can be case sensitive.

In the following code, arguments are in mixed upper- and lowercase to make them easy to read:

```
cpcmd -Command SettleBatch -MerNum merchant_number
-TermNum terminal_number -Currency currency
-MerchantRef merchant_reference -BatchNumber batch_number
[-TSalesAmt total_sales_amount] [-TCreditAmt total_credit_amount]
[-TSalesCount total_sales_count] [-TCreditCount total_credit_count]
```

When the SettleBatch command is successful, it produces a message that tells you the batch has been closed.

-BatchNumber is a required integer argument that enables you to specify the batch number generated by the GetCurrentBatch command.

-Currency is a required alpha argument that indicates a three-character ISO 4217 currency code. USD, for example, indicates U.S. dollar, CAD indicates Canadian dollar, and so on.

-MerchantRef is an optional alphanumeric argument in which you reference information (for tracking) that is provided by the merchant. If you do not specify this argument, this command defaults to MerchantRef from the slip. If you are using LivePayment objects, this command is analogous to the merchantReference method of the PayEvent object. MerNum is a required alphanumeric argument that indicates the merchant number, which is provided by the acquirer.

-TCreditAmt is an optional integer argument in which you can specify the total credit amount. If you do not specify this argument, it defaults to 0. -TCreditCount is an optional integer argument in which you can specify the total number of credits. If you do not specify this argument, it defaults to 0.

-TermNum is a required alphanumeric argument in which you specify the terminal number, which is provided by the acquirer. -TSalesAmt is an optional integer argument in which you can specify the total sales amount. If you do not specify this argument, it defaults to 0. -TSalesCount is an optional integer argument in which you can specify the total number of sales. If you do not specify this argument, it defaults to 0.

The following shows an example of the SettleBatch command:

```
cpcmd -command settlebatch -mernum 00002031684 -termnum 0000428812345
-currency USD -merchantref 1234 -batchnumber 0062 -tsalesamt 412.62
-tsalescount 10
```

The preceding code produces the following output:

```
batch 0062 closed
```

The example shows a command that settles the batch numbered 0062, where the merchant reference information is 1234. The total sales of the batch, in U.S. dollars, is $412.62, in which ten sales make up the batch. The -TCreditAmt and -TCreditCount arguments default to zero because they are not specified.

In order to settle transactions, you must adhere to the following rules:

◆ After settlement of any batch, all new transactions fall into the next batch.

◆ You cannot capture transactions while settling a batch.

◆ In order to settle, totals for credits and captures must match those provided by your bank card acquirer. You must contact your acquirer and resolve unmatched captures and credits.

Summary

This has been a long chapter, and you have learned a great deal.

This chapter has presented material on Netscape's LivePayment software. It has discussed hardware and software requirements, those who can use LivePayment and their roles in the transaction process, and LivePayment features. It also has covered developing applications with LivePayment, security features, and the LivePayment utility commands.

Chapter 13, "Intranet Solutions with JavaScript," features an overview of an Intranet system and compares protocol and uses to the Internet. It also includes a real life example of an employee directory that you can put to use in your organization.

Intranet Solutions with JavaScript

An intranet is a Web-based network system that is used within organizations and corporations. Proprietary systems, such as Novell Network and Lotus Notes, use standards and protocols that can only be used by those companies that purchase the particular proprietary product, thus forcing companies to purchase upgrades and software from that single manufacturer. An intranet system, on the other hand, is not proprietary: it uses non-proprietary protocols and standards and replaces client browsers with products, such as Netscape Navigator, thus providing companies with more freedom than being bound to one server and tied to one manufacturer's client/server product. An intranet system uses the same protocols and standards found on the Internet, such as HTML and JavaScript, MIME, TCP/IP, and ftp. Just as the Internet enables public connectivity, intranet systems enable connectivity within an organization by using Web servers and browsers.

Although an intranet system uses the same protocol as the Internet, its functional purpose is different. The Internet makes information available to the public. An intranet system uses the same means of making information available, such as HTML, but access to an intranet Web remains within your organization. Those within the intranet can look outside the Web organization, but those outside the organization cannot look in.

Additionally, the intranet is more than an information distributor. You can develop your intranet system so that you can perform searches and queries, update your databases, and increase user interaction. This added integration is where JavaScript fits in. JavaScript ties together content with client- or server-side applications.

In this chapter you will learn about the following:

◆ Advantages of developing for the intranet

◆ Intranet protocol versus proprietary standards and protocols

◆ Firewalls

◆ The thin client

◆ Specific ways you can take advantage of an intranet system

◆ A scenario that takes advantage of an intranet system

◆ A real-life application you can use on your intranet

Advantages of Developing for the Intranet

Developing for an intranet system rather than a system that uses proprietary standards and protocols can open up communication among employees as well as make your company more efficient and cheaper to run. In addition to monetary benefits, developing for an intranet system enables you to take advantage of the following:

◆ **One-to-many communication.** Because of easy access to the internal Web, information in an intranet can be more accurate and reliable because of one-to-many communication. How many times have you experienced the "telephone syndrome," where information you have sent or received has been distorted due to other interpretations? By using an intranet system, you can deliver accurate and reliable information from one point, distributing it to all those employees who need to learn about it.

◆ **Quick access to information within your organization.** Because an intranet system is Web-based, you can use powerful search engines that provide quick ways for you to get the information you need. You can perform a single query to produce an organized list of all the matches found in an Internet-like interface that provides links to pertinent data.

◆ **No need to replicate databases.** With proprietary networks, you need to replicate current databases to cross the firewall and make database material available to the public. By using an intranet system from the beginning, you don't need to rewrite code—the code you have is reusable.

◆ **Access to databases.** With an intranet in place, employees can quickly and easily access databases that contain information they need, all with a single interface. You can access a product database, for example, that contains information such as product names and numbers, prices, items in stock, and so on. Having this information online makes accurate and up-to-date product lists available. You can create new applications by using JavaScript, and then you can use them in any desktop and server operating environments.

◆ **Information can easily be disseminated and updated.** Because of an intranet's one-to-many communication, you can use it to easily distribute information to particular people or to the entire company. As changes occur within the company, you can easily update information. This attribute provides a cost-saving way to keep employees informed without facing the expenditures of paper and distribution. You can index and organize documents as they are created, managing them from the desktop within the appropriate department and in one location.

◆ **Security.** In an intranet you can choose to whom you make information available, just as you would on a non-intranet system. You can issue and manage security and passwords that enable employees to perform company business securely across the intranet.

◆ **The ease of making product information available to the public.** Although intranet systems do not allow those outside the network to access information, you can cross the firewall and choose to make product information available to the public via the Internet technology used.

◆ **Reduced distribution costs.** The distribution of information can be expensive, especially when you factor in the cost of paper, printing, and postage. Intranet systems enable you to disperse information easily and cost-effectively because the information stays on the Web until you remove it. All those who have access to the intranet Web can have access to information you want to distribute.

◆ **Integration and personalization of interactive online content.**
Taking advantage of Internet tools, you can use hyperlinks and embedded objects to create interesting, efficient, and easy-to-use online contents on your intranet.

◆ **E-mail.** With an intranet system, employees can use standard e-mail addresses within the organization. Employees also can gain access to outside your company Web by using the same interface and e-mail address.

Using Intranet Protocol Versus Proprietary Standards and Protocols

Historically, network systems within an organization consisted of proprietary standards and protocols; you purchased a server and server software from a company and then installed that particular software on your client terminals. Proprietary systems were created without open- or cross-platform capabilities in mind. The system used in one company most likely would not be the same system found in the company in the next office building. The disadvantage of using proprietary systems is that after you spend all that money on the network system, it is extremely expensive, not to mention time-consuming, to change to another system. Upgrades must come from the vendor from which you purchased the original network system. Proprietary networks also limit communications with other systems: you can only connect to companies that use the same proprietary system as your company.

Did you know...

Non-proprietary systems, or those with open protocol, are not owned by any one manufacturer. Open protocol results in better-developed products; many companies compete fairly in the development of tools that conform to these open protocols, resulting in a level playing field, competitive products, and fair competition. The incentive is developing better products rather than being the only company to offer a product.

An intranet system, however, uses the standard protocols implemented by the Internet that are not set by vendors. Standard protocol makes interconnectivity easier, more cost effective than proprietary systems, and easier to update and upgrade.

Crossing the Firewall

A firewall is a collection of components placed between two networks that acts as a door through which all traffic must pass (incoming and outgoing). Only authorized traffic is allowed. Programs and data inside the firewall are immune to penetration.

Having a firewall between the Internet and your intranet system is a common setup. Those inside the firewall have outside access to the Internet, but those outside the company do not have access to the system within the organization. The advantage to using an intranet system versus a proprietary system is simple: because of its open standards, if you choose, you can easily cross the firewall, gaining access to the Web.

Intra- and Internet Architecture (Thin Client)

Internet client/servers used by the intranet are based on a thin client. A *thin client* (also called a *smart terminal*) is a terminal that has only what the users need to perform their jobs—therefore, it does not need to be extremely powerful. Client terminals only need to be able to support a Web browser, word processor, spreadsheet, and so on. This type of architecture reduces the cost of a network system. Because the databases, tools, and other software can be stored on the server, the expense of client terminals is greatly reduced.

Uses for the Intranet

So far, this chapter has discussed what the intranet is and the advantages of developing for an intranet system rather than a proprietary system. This section looks at the different ways you can use an intranet system to better serve your company's needs. The following list discusses ways you can use an intranet system:

◆ **Online technical documentation.** Storing online technical documentation on your server enables employees to easily access the information; users can put away the handbooks and just go to the client browser to find what they are looking for. Storing technical documentation online also makes it easy and cost-effective to update content as technology changes and grows, thus making the information available to all without ever facing the cost of printing, paper, and distribution.

◆ **Company information.** Empower your new employees to access information on company procedures, your organization, and company benefits.

◆ **Presentation and training material.** You can archive presentation and training materials on your Web, making them accessible to new hires or those who were unable to attend a function. Archiving on your company Web also reduces the cost of distributing numerous copies of slides and presentation material.

◆ **Product databases.** Keep your product database current and accurate, thus reducing the error margin for quoting incorrect information. Using a product database with an intranet network enables employees to easily find out product progress, price changes, and product availability.

◆ **Interoffice memos.** Reduce the cost of printing and distributing interoffice memos by sending them via the intranet Web. Memos can be stored on the server and accessed as needed.

◆ **Office procedures.** Store your office procedures online, thus enabling employees to access accurate and up-to-date information. This ensures consistency among procedures, reducing the margin for error.

◆ **Calendar of events.** Keep your employees updated on the upcoming conferences, seminars, and training schedules. By using the intranet, you can even determine the number of people who will be in attendance.

◆ **Employee directories.** Using online employee directories enables employees to get to know each other and easily contact those in other departments. You can create a directory, for example, that lists employees by name, department, and location, and can include each employee's phone number, e-mail address, office location, department and title, and special interests.

◆ **Job lines.** Use the intranet to post job listings within your company. Using this type of protocol makes it easy to cross the firewall and make job listings available to those on the Internet.

◆ **Information gathering for projects.** Enable project team members to communicate and share information across time zones and regions so that they can work together more efficiently. Using the intranet for projects also provides co-workers ways to collaborate, such as discussion groups or forums.

◆ **Mailings.** Reduce the cost of sending mailings by taking advantage of an intranet system. Sending mailings with an intranet also makes it easy to cross the firewall and make mailings available to the public, thus reducing the cost of paper, printing, and postage.

An Intranet Scenario

To help you understand how you can use an intranet system in your organization, this section takes you through a typical scenario of intranet use, before an intranet system is in place and after an intranet system is implemented. The hypothetical company used in this example is Farkle's Boomerangs, Inc., which manufactures all types and sizes of boomerangs. In fact, you can even order a custom-made boomerang through Farkle.

Our story begins with Farkle's Boomerangs, Inc., which has a toll-free number that customers can call to place orders. Orders are taken verbally, over the phone, by folks who work in the sales department. The following steps outline the current process, before crossing the firewall.

1. Customers call Farkle's toll-free number to custom-order their boomerangs.

2. The two people in the order/sales department answer the customer order line. Each time a new customer places an order, the clerk enters the consumer information onto an order Web page. Information included on this page is the customer's billing information, shipping information, the date the order is placed, and specifics about the boomerang, such as model number, size, and color.

3. When the form is complete, the clerk clicks on the Submit button, and the form is sent to the database on the Web server.

4. Customer orders are stored and tracked in the customer database. Forms are then passed on to the manufacturing department. Employees in the manufacturing department see only the pertinent information, such as customer name and boomerang specifics. For the purposes of building a boomerang, employees in the manufacturing department do not need to know the customer's billing information.

5. As progress is made on the customer's boomerang, the manufacturing department enters updated information into the Web order form.

6. The updated information goes to the database so that the order clerks can check on delivery dates of the boomerangs ordered. Customers can call the order clerk to check on the progress of their boomerangs.

7. Because the growing number of orders for boomerangs has become unmanageable, Fred, owner of Farkle's Boomerangs, Inc., decides to offer consumers the option of placing their own orders via the World Wide Web, thus crossing the firewall.

8. Information available to the order taker, such as completion dates for individual orders, now is also available to the consumer. Although Fred still has the toll-free number available to those consumers not on the World Wide Web, he has opened up his business to a wider audience and saved money by not increasing his overhead with additional sales/order employees.

This concludes the intranet scenario. The remainder of this chapter is devoted to showing you how you can use an employee time-tracking system and an employee directory, which is included on the CD, to make your company run more efficiently.

For a complete, in-depth discussion on intranet architecture and implementation, see *Intranet Web Development* (New Riders, 1996) by John Desborough.

Putting JavaScript to Work in an Intranet System

When developing any intranet system, user interaction is key, and to provide user interaction, it becomes necessary to either create plug-ins or Java programs, or use a simple scripting language like JavaScript. What makes JavaScript scripting so appealing is that it is easy to code in, and is compatible with the two most popular Web browsers (Netscape 3.0 and Internet Explorer 3.0). JavaScript also provides the glue often times necessary to integrate HTML, plug-ins, database queries, and Java applets with each other. The following intranet examples will be presented:

◆ Time-Clock example

◆ Employee Directory example

In the Time-Clock example, client-side JavaScript will be used exclusively to demonstrate how JavaScript can be used to dynamically calculate live data as it is typed in by a user (employee). In the Employee Directory example, a combination of both server-side and client-side JavaScript is used to demonstrate the process of building an intranet system that takes advantage of a corporate database. If you do not have a Netscape server with LiveWire installed on your system, you should probably focus on the Time-Clock example, since it does not contain any server-side JavaScript which requires LiveWire.

Time-Clock Example

Almost every company has some sort of procedure for keeping track of employees' time on the job. Many companies opt for off-the-shelf programs that run on their specific local area network. Although these programs may be adequate at first, problems eventually arise as operating systems and networks are updated, and suddenly, the time-tracking software does not work with their system. Then they need to buy either a different time-tracking system or a newer version of the software. Another problem involved with most of these packages is that, although they work well on desktop computers on a local area network, it is usually cumbersome to get them to work from a remote site, such as when an employee has been traveling all week long and needs to turn in a summary of the hours he or she worked.

A solution to this scenario is to develop a time-tracking program for the intranet, and by doing so, ensure that you are not only developing for a platform that will continue to function with future operating systems, but also developing an application enabled for remote access (via the Internet) from the beginning.

Intranet Prototyping

Assuming that you have decided to build your own time tracking-system, a likely first step would be to develop a prototype. When programming desktop applications, it is common to use a commercial-grade prototyping tool to build your prototype. With the intranet, however, you use standard HTML for prototyping that leaves you with a basic text editor and a Web browser as your prototyping tool. To prototype the time tracking system, experiment in HTML using text, graphics, and forms to create an appearance you believe the customer would be happy with, as in figure 13.1, a result of the following HTML code:

```
<HTML>
<HEAD><TITLE>Timecard Form</TITLE>
</HEAD>
<BODY>
<FORM NAME="TimeCardForm">
<TABLE BORDER BGCOLOR="#A080AF">
<TH>Project</TH><TH>Mon</TH><TH>Tue</TH><TH>Wed</TH><TH>Thu</TH>
<TH>Fri</TH><TH>Sat</TH><TH>Sun</TH><TH>Total</TH>
<TR>
<TD BGCOLOR="blue"><SELECT NAME="ProjectList1" SIZE="1">
<OPTION SELECTED>Windows 2001
<OPTION>Doomsday Machine
<OPTION>Genesis Project
<OPTION>Hiding
<OPTION>Coffee Machine
<OPTION>Shirking
</SELECT></TD>
<TD BGCOLOR="blue"><INPUT TYPE="text" NAME="Mon1" VALUE="0" SIZE=4 ></TD>
<TD BGCOLOR="blue"><INPUT TYPE="text" NAME="Tue1" VALUE="0" SIZE=4 ></TD>
<TD BGCOLOR="blue"><INPUT TYPE="text" NAME="Wed1" VALUE="0" SIZE=4 ></TD>
<TD BGCOLOR="blue"><INPUT TYPE="text" NAME="Thu1" VALUE="0" SIZE=4 ></TD>
<TD BGCOLOR="blue"><INPUT TYPE="text" NAME="Fri1" VALUE="0" SIZE=4 ></TD>
<TD BGCOLOR="blue"><INPUT TYPE="text" NAME="Sat1" VALUE="0" SIZE=4 ></TD>
<TD BGCOLOR="blue"><INPUT TYPE="text" NAME="Sun1" VALUE="0" SIZE=4 ></TD>
<TD BGCOLOR="blue"><INPUT TYPE="text" NAME="Tot1" VALUE="0" SIZE=5></TD>
</TR>
<TR>
```

```
<TD BGCOLOR="black"><SELECT NAME="ProjectList2" SIZE="1">
<OPTION>Windows 2001
<OPTION SELECTED>Doomsday Machine
<OPTION>Genesis Project
<OPTION>Hiding
<OPTION>Coffee Machine
<OPTION>Shirking
</SELECT></TD>
<TD BGCOLOR="black"><INPUT TYPE="text" NAME="Mon2" VALUE="0" SIZE=4 ></TD>
<TD BGCOLOR="black"><INPUT TYPE="text" NAME="Tue2" VALUE="0" SIZE=4 ></TD>
<TD BGCOLOR="black"><INPUT TYPE="text" NAME="Wed2" VALUE="0" SIZE=4 ></TD>
<TD BGCOLOR="black"><INPUT TYPE="text" NAME="Thu2" VALUE="0" SIZE=4 ></TD>
<TD BGCOLOR="black"><INPUT TYPE="text" NAME="Fri2" VALUE="0" SIZE=4 ></TD>
<TD BGCOLOR="black"><INPUT TYPE="text" NAME="Sat2" VALUE="0" SIZE=4 ></TD>
<TD BGCOLOR="black"><INPUT TYPE="text" NAME="Sun2" VALUE="0" SIZE=4 ></TD>
<TD BGCOLOR="black"><INPUT TYPE="text" NAME="Tot2" VALUE="0" SIZE=5></TD>
</TR>
<TR>
<TD BGCOLOR="blue"><SELECT NAME="ProjectList3" SIZE="1">
<OPTION>Windows 2001
<OPTION>Doomsday Machine
<OPTION SELECTED>Genesis Project
<OPTION>Hiding
<OPTION>Coffee Machine
<OPTION>Shirking
</SELECT></TD>
<TD BGCOLOR="blue"><INPUT TYPE="text" NAME="Mon3" VALUE="0" SIZE=4 ></TD>
<TD BGCOLOR="blue"><INPUT TYPE="text" NAME="Tue3" VALUE="0" SIZE=4 ></TD>
<TD BGCOLOR="blue"><INPUT TYPE="text" NAME="Wed3" VALUE="0" SIZE=4 ></TD>
<TD BGCOLOR="blue"><INPUT TYPE="text" NAME="Thu3" VALUE="0" SIZE=4 ></TD>
<TD BGCOLOR="blue"><INPUT TYPE="text" NAME="Fri3" VALUE="0" SIZE=4 ></TD>
<TD BGCOLOR="blue"><INPUT TYPE="text" NAME="Sat3" VALUE="0" SIZE=4 ></TD>
<TD BGCOLOR="blue"><INPUT TYPE="text" NAME="Sun3" VALUE="0" SIZE=4 ></TD>
<TD BGCOLOR="blue"><INPUT TYPE="text" NAME="Tot3" VALUE="0" SIZE=5></TD>
</TR>
<TR>
<TD BGCOLOR="black"><SELECT NAME="ProjectList4" SIZE="1">
<OPTION>Windows 2001
<OPTION>Doomsday Machine
<OPTION>Genesis Project
<OPTION SELECTED>Hiding
<OPTION>Coffee Machine
```

```
<OPTION>Shirking
</SELECT></TD>
<TD BGCOLOR="black"><INPUT TYPE="text" NAME="Mon4" VALUE="0" SIZE=4 ></TD>
<TD BGCOLOR="black"><INPUT TYPE="text" NAME="Tue4" VALUE="0" SIZE=4 ></TD>
<TD BGCOLOR="black"><INPUT TYPE="text" NAME="Wed4" VALUE="0" SIZE=4 ></TD>
<TD BGCOLOR="black"><INPUT TYPE="text" NAME="Thu4" VALUE="0" SIZE=4 ></TD>
<TD BGCOLOR="black"><INPUT TYPE="text" NAME="Fri4" VALUE="0" SIZE=4 ></TD>
<TD BGCOLOR="black"><INPUT TYPE="text" NAME="Sat4" VALUE="0" SIZE=4 ></TD>
<TD BGCOLOR="black"><INPUT TYPE="text" NAME="Sun4" VALUE="0" SIZE=4 ></TD>
<TD BGCOLOR="black"><INPUT TYPE="text" NAME="Tot4" VALUE="0" SIZE=5></TD>
</TR>
<TR>
<TD BGCOLOR="blue"><SELECT NAME="ProjectList5" SIZE="1">
<OPTION>Windows 2001
<OPTION>Doomsday Machine
<OPTION>Genesis Project
<OPTION>Hiding
<OPTION SELECTED>Coffee Machine
<OPTION>Shirking
</SELECT></TD>
<TD BGCOLOR="blue"><INPUT TYPE="text" NAME="Mon5" VALUE="0" SIZE=4 ></TD>
<TD BGCOLOR="blue"><INPUT TYPE="text" NAME="Tue5" VALUE="0" SIZE=4 ></TD>
<TD BGCOLOR="blue"><INPUT TYPE="text" NAME="Wed5" VALUE="0" SIZE=4 ></TD>
<TD BGCOLOR="blue"><INPUT TYPE="text" NAME="Thu5" VALUE="0" SIZE=4 ></TD>
<TD BGCOLOR="blue"><INPUT TYPE="text" NAME="Fri5" VALUE="0" SIZE=4 ></TD>
<TD BGCOLOR="blue"><INPUT TYPE="text" NAME="Sat5" VALUE="0" SIZE=4 ></TD>
<TD BGCOLOR="blue"><INPUT TYPE="text" NAME="Sun5" VALUE="0" SIZE=4 ></TD>
<TD BGCOLOR="blue"><INPUT TYPE="text" NAME="Tot5" VALUE="0" SIZE=5></TD>
</TR>
<TR>
<TD BGCOLOR="black">
<SELECT NAME="ProjectList6" SIZE="1">
<OPTION>Windows 2001
<OPTION>Doomsday Machine
<OPTION>Genesis Project
<OPTION>Hiding
<OPTION>Coffee Machine
<OPTION SELECTED>Shirking
</SELECT></TD>
<TD BGCOLOR="black"><INPUT TYPE="text" NAME="Mon6" VALUE="0" SIZE=4 ></TD>
<TD BGCOLOR="black"><INPUT TYPE="text" NAME="Tue6" VALUE="0" SIZE=4 ></TD>
<TD BGCOLOR="black"><INPUT TYPE="text" NAME="Wed6" VALUE="0" SIZE=4 ></TD>
```

```
<TD BGCOLOR="black"><INPUT TYPE="text" NAME="Thu6" VALUE="0" SIZE=4 ></TD>
<TD BGCOLOR="black"><INPUT TYPE="text" NAME="Fri6" VALUE="0" SIZE=4 ></TD>
<TD BGCOLOR="black"><INPUT TYPE="text" NAME="Sat6" VALUE="0" SIZE=4 ></TD>
<TD BGCOLOR="black"><INPUT TYPE="text" NAME="Sun6" VALUE="0" SIZE=4 ></TD>
<TD BGCOLOR="black"><INPUT TYPE="text" NAME="Tot6" VALUE="0" SIZE=5></TD>
</TR>
<TR>
<TD COLSPAN=8><CENTER><INPUT TYPE="button" NAME="submitCard" VALUE="Submit
timecard"></CENTER></TD>
<TD BGCOLOR="red"><INPUT TYPE="text" NAME="timeTotals" VALUE="0" SIZE=5></TD>
</TR>
</TABLE>
</FORM>
</BODY>
</HTML>
```

Figure 13.1

A nonfunctioning time-tracking system prototype.

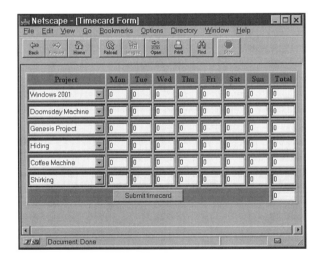

Adding Functionality to Your Prototype

After you build the prototype, it is time to add the programming logic to the Web page. The first step is to add event handlers and function stubs, as in the following:

```
<INPUT TYPE="text" NAME="Sun6" VALUE="0" SIZE=4 OnChange="calculateTotals()">
function calculateTotals() {


}
```

Then you add code to each function stub you make, turning what was once just a Web page into a Web application, as in the following:

```
function calculateTotals()
{
  var rowTot = new Array(6)
  document.TimeCardForm.Tot1.value="0"

  document.TimeCardForm.Tot2.value="0"
  document.TimeCardForm.Tot3.value="0"
  document.TimeCardForm.Tot4.value="0"
  document.TimeCardForm.Tot5.value="0"
  document.TimeCardForm.Tot6.value="0"
  for (i= 1; i < 8; i++) {
     document.forms[0].Tot1.value =
parseFloat(document.forms[0].elements[i].value) +
parseFloat(document.forms[0].Tot1.value)
     rowTot[0]=document.forms[0].Tot1.value
  }
  for (i= 10; i < 17; i++) {
     document.forms[0].Tot2.value =
parseFloat(document.forms[0].elements[i].value) +
parseFloat(document.forms[0].Tot2.value)
     rowTot[1]=document.forms[0].Tot2.value
  }
  for (i= 19; i < 26; i++) {
     document.forms[0].Tot3.value =
parseFloat(document.forms[0].elements[i].value) +
parseFloat(document.forms[0].Tot3.value)
     rowTot[2]=document.forms[0].Tot3.value
  }
  for (i= 28; i < 35; i++) {
     document.forms[0].Tot4.value =
parseFloat(document.forms[0].elements[i].value) +
parseFloat(document.forms[0].Tot4.value)
     rowTot[3]=document.forms[0].Tot4.value
  }
  for (i= 37; i < 44; i++) {
     document.forms[0].Tot5.value =
parseFloat(document.forms[0].elements[i].value) +
parseFloat(document.forms[0].Tot5.value)
     rowTot[4]=document.forms[0].Tot5.value
  }
```

```
    for (i= 46; i < 53; i++) {
        document.forms[0].Tot6.value =
parseFloat(document.forms[0].elements[i].value) +
parseFloat(document.forms[0].Tot6.value)
        rowTot[5]=document.forms[0].Tot6.value
    }
    document.forms[0].timeTotals.value = "0"
    for (var i =0; i<6 ;i++) {
        rowVal = rowTot[i]
        document.forms[0].timeTotals.value = (parseFloat(rowVal) +
parseFloat(document.forms[0].timeTotals.value))
    }
}
```

The preceding code takes advantage of the JavaScript feature whereby form elements
can be accessed as items in an elements array. This code adds up each element of a
row and saves the total to the rowTot array; after every row has been evaluated, each
rowTot array element is accumulated, and that value is saved in the form element
document.forms[0].timeTotals.value.

Following is working code that supports the calculation aspects of the time-tracking
system:

```
<HTML>
<HEAD><TITLE>Timecard Form</TITLE>
<SCRIPT Language="JavaScript">
<!--
function calculateTotals() {
  var rowTot = new Array(6)
  document.TimeCardForm.Tot1.value="0"

  document.TimeCardForm.Tot2.value="0"
  document.TimeCardForm.Tot3.value="0"
  document.TimeCardForm.Tot4.value="0"
  document.TimeCardForm.Tot5.value="0"
  document.TimeCardForm.Tot6.value="0"
  for (i= 1; i < 8; i++) {
      document.forms[0].Tot1.value =
parseFloat(document.forms[0].elements[i].value) +
parseFloat(document.forms[0].Tot1.value)
      rowTot[0]=document.forms[0].Tot1.value
  }
  for (i= 10; i < 17; i++) {
      document.forms[0].Tot2.value =
parseFloat(document.forms[0].elements[i].value) +
```

```
parseFloat(document.forms[0].Tot2.value)
    rowTot[1]=document.forms[0].Tot2.value
 }
 for (i= 19; i < 26; i++) {
    document.forms[0].Tot3.value =
parseFloat(document.forms[0].elements[i].value) +
parseFloat(document.forms[0].Tot3.value)
    rowTot[2]=document.forms[0].Tot3.value
 }
 for (i= 28; i < 35; i++) {
    document.forms[0].Tot4.value =
parseFloat(document.forms[0].elements[i].value) +
parseFloat(document.forms[0].Tot4.value)
    rowTot[3]=document.forms[0].Tot4.value
 }
 for (i= 37; i < 44; i++) {
    document.forms[0].Tot5.value =
parseFloat(document.forms[0].elements[i].value) +
parseFloat(document.forms[0].Tot5.value)
    rowTot[4]=document.forms[0].Tot5.value
 }
 for (i= 46; i < 53; i++) {
    document.forms[0].Tot6.value =
parseFloat(document.forms[0].elements[i].value) +
parseFloat(document.forms[0].Tot6.value)
    rowTot[5]=document.forms[0].Tot6.value
 }
 document.forms[0].timeTotals.value = "0"
 for (var i =0; i<6 ;i++) {
    rowVal = rowTot[i]
    document.forms[0].timeTotals.value = (parseFloat(rowVal) +
parseFloat(document.forms[0].timeTotals.value))
 }
}
function submitProcedure(){
 //Put your code here to handle timecard submittal
 alert("Your timecard was submitted. Have a nice day.")
}
//-->
</SCRIPT>
</HEAD>
<BODY>
```

```
<FORM NAME="TimeCardForm">
<TABLE BORDER BGCOLOR="#A080AF">
<TH>Project</TH><TH>Mon</TH><TH>Tue</TH><TH>Wed</TH><TH>Thu</TH><TH>Fri</
TH><TH>Sat</TH><TH>Sun</TH><TH>Total</TH>
<TR>
<TD BGCOLOR="blue"><SELECT NAME="ProjectList1" SIZE="1">
<OPTION SELECTED>Windows 2001
<OPTION>Doomsday Machine
<OPTION>Genesis Project
<OPTION>Hiding
<OPTION>Coffee Machine
<OPTION>Shirking
</SELECT></TD>
<TD BGCOLOR="blue"><INPUT TYPE="text" NAME="Mon1" VALUE="0" SIZE=4
OnChange="calculateTotals()"></TD>
<TD BGCOLOR="blue"><INPUT TYPE="text" NAME="Tue1" VALUE="0" SIZE=4
OnChange="calculateTotals()"></TD>
<TD BGCOLOR="blue"><INPUT TYPE="text" NAME="Wed1" VALUE="0" SIZE=4
OnChange="calculateTotals()"></TD>
<TD BGCOLOR="blue"><INPUT TYPE="text" NAME="Thu1" VALUE="0" SIZE=4
OnChange="calculateTotals()"></TD>
<TD BGCOLOR="blue"><INPUT TYPE="text" NAME="Fri1" VALUE="0" SIZE=4
OnChange="calculateTotals()"></TD>
<TD BGCOLOR="blue"><INPUT TYPE="text" NAME="Sat1" VALUE="0" SIZE=4
OnChange="calculateTotals()"></TD>
<TD BGCOLOR="blue"><INPUT TYPE="text" NAME="Sun1" VALUE="0" SIZE=4
OnChange="calculateTotals()"></TD>
<TD BGCOLOR="blue"><INPUT TYPE="text" NAME="Tot1" VALUE="0" SIZE=5></TD>
</TR>
<TR>
<TD BGCOLOR="black"><SELECT NAME="ProjectList2" SIZE="1">
<OPTION>Windows 2001
<OPTION SELECTED>Doomsday Machine
<OPTION>Genesis Project
<OPTION>Hiding
<OPTION>Coffee Machine
<OPTION>Shirking
</SELECT></TD>
<TD BGCOLOR="black"><INPUT TYPE="text" NAME="Mon2" VALUE="0" SIZE=4
OnChange="calculateTotals()"></TD>
<TD BGCOLOR="black"><INPUT TYPE="text" NAME="Tue2" VALUE="0" SIZE=4
OnChange="calculateTotals()"></TD>
<TD BGCOLOR="black"><INPUT TYPE="text" NAME="Wed2" VALUE="0" SIZE=4
```

```
OnChange="calculateTotals()"></TD>
<TD BGCOLOR="black"><INPUT TYPE="text" NAME="Thu2" VALUE="0" SIZE=4
OnChange="calculateTotals()"></TD>
<TD BGCOLOR="black"><INPUT TYPE="text" NAME="Fri2" VALUE="0" SIZE=4
OnChange="calculateTotals()"></TD>
<TD BGCOLOR="black"><INPUT TYPE="text" NAME="Sat2" VALUE="0" SIZE=4
OnChange="calculateTotals()"></TD>
<TD BGCOLOR="black"><INPUT TYPE="text" NAME="Sun2" VALUE="0" SIZE=4
OnChange="calculateTotals()"></TD>
<TD BGCOLOR="black"><INPUT TYPE="text" NAME="Tot2" VALUE="0" SIZE=5></TD>
</TR>
<TR>
<TD BGCOLOR="blue"><SELECT NAME="ProjectList3" SIZE="1">
<OPTION>Windows 2001
<OPTION>Doomsday Machine
<OPTION SELECTED>Genesis Project
<OPTION>Hiding
<OPTION>Coffee Machine
<OPTION>Shirking
</SELECT></TD>
<TD BGCOLOR="blue"><INPUT TYPE="text" NAME="Mon3" VALUE="0" SIZE=4
OnChange="calculateTotals()"></TD>
<TD BGCOLOR="blue"><INPUT TYPE="text" NAME="Tue3" VALUE="0" SIZE=4
OnChange="calculateTotals()"></TD>
<TD BGCOLOR="blue"><INPUT TYPE="text" NAME="Wed3" VALUE="0" SIZE=4
OnChange="calculateTotals()"></TD>
<TD BGCOLOR="blue"><INPUT TYPE="text" NAME="Thu3" VALUE="0" SIZE=4
OnChange="calculateTotals()"></TD>
<TD BGCOLOR="blue"><INPUT TYPE="text" NAME="Fri3" VALUE="0" SIZE=4
OnChange="calculateTotals()"></TD>
<TD BGCOLOR="blue"><INPUT TYPE="text" NAME="Sat3" VALUE="0" SIZE=4
OnChange="calculateTotals()"></TD>
<TD BGCOLOR="blue"><INPUT TYPE="text" NAME="Sun3" VALUE="0" SIZE=4
OnChange="calculateTotals()"></TD>
<TD BGCOLOR="blue"><INPUT TYPE="text" NAME="Tot3" VALUE="0" SIZE=5></TD>
</TR>
<TR>
<TD BGCOLOR="black"><SELECT NAME="ProjectList4" SIZE="1">
<OPTION>Windows 2001
<OPTION>Doomsday Machine
<OPTION>Genesis Project
<OPTION SELECTED>Hiding
<OPTION>Coffee Machine
```

```
<OPTION>Shirking
</SELECT></TD>
<TD BGCOLOR="black"><INPUT TYPE="text" NAME="Mon4" VALUE="0" SIZE=4
OnChange="calculateTotals()"></TD>
<TD BGCOLOR="black"><INPUT TYPE="text" NAME="Tue4" VALUE="0" SIZE=4
OnChange="calculateTotals()"></TD>
<TD BGCOLOR="black"><INPUT TYPE="text" NAME="Wed4" VALUE="0" SIZE=4
OnChange="calculateTotals()"></TD>
<TD BGCOLOR="black"><INPUT TYPE="text" NAME="Thu4" VALUE="0" SIZE=4
OnChange="calculateTotals()"></TD>
<TD BGCOLOR="black"><INPUT TYPE="text" NAME="Fri4" VALUE="0" SIZE=4
OnChange="calculateTotals()"></TD>
<TD BGCOLOR="black"><INPUT TYPE="text" NAME="Sat4" VALUE="0" SIZE=4
OnChange="calculateTotals()"></TD>
<TD BGCOLOR="black"><INPUT TYPE="text" NAME="Sun4" VALUE="0" SIZE=4
OnChange="calculateTotals()"></TD>
<TD BGCOLOR="black"><INPUT TYPE="text" NAME="Tot4" VALUE="0" SIZE=5></TD>
</TR>
<TR>
<TD BGCOLOR="blue"><SELECT NAME="ProjectList5" SIZE="1">
<OPTION>Windows 2001
<OPTION>Doomsday Machine
<OPTION>Genesis Project
<OPTION>Hiding
<OPTION SELECTED>Coffee Machine
<OPTION>Shirking
</SELECT></TD>
<TD BGCOLOR="blue"><INPUT TYPE="text" NAME="Mon5" VALUE="0" SIZE=4
OnChange="calculateTotals()"></TD>
<TD BGCOLOR="blue"><INPUT TYPE="text" NAME="Tue5" VALUE="0" SIZE=4
OnChange="calculateTotals()"></TD>
<TD BGCOLOR="blue"><INPUT TYPE="text" NAME="Wed5" VALUE="0" SIZE=4
OnChange="calculateTotals()"></TD>
<TD BGCOLOR="blue"><INPUT TYPE="text" NAME="Thu5" VALUE="0" SIZE=4
OnChange="calculateTotals()"></TD>
<TD BGCOLOR="blue"><INPUT TYPE="text" NAME="Fri5" VALUE="0" SIZE=4
OnChange="calculateTotals()"></TD>
<TD BGCOLOR="blue"><INPUT TYPE="text" NAME="Sat5" VALUE="0" SIZE=4
OnChange="calculateTotals()"></TD>
<TD BGCOLOR="blue"><INPUT TYPE="text" NAME="Sun5" VALUE="0" SIZE=4
OnChange="calculateTotals()"></TD>
<TD BGCOLOR="blue"><INPUT TYPE="text" NAME="Tot5" VALUE="0" SIZE=5
OnChange="calculateTotals()"></TD>
```

```
</TR>
<TR>
<TD BGCOLOR="black">
<SELECT NAME="ProjectList6" SIZE="1">
<OPTION>Windows 2001
<OPTION>Doomsday Machine
<OPTION>Genesis Project
<OPTION>Hiding
<OPTION>Coffee Machine
<OPTION SELECTED>Shirking
</SELECT></TD>
<TD BGCOLOR="black"><INPUT TYPE="text" NAME="Mon6" VALUE="0" SIZE=4
OnChange="calculateTotals()"></TD>
<TD BGCOLOR="black"><INPUT TYPE="text" NAME="Tue6" VALUE="0" SIZE=4
OnChange="calculateTotals()"></TD>
<TD BGCOLOR="black"><INPUT TYPE="text" NAME="Wed6" VALUE="0" SIZE=4
OnChange="calculateTotals()"></TD>
<TD BGCOLOR="black"><INPUT TYPE="text" NAME="Thu6" VALUE="0" SIZE=4
OnChange="calculateTotals()"></TD>
<TD BGCOLOR="black"><INPUT TYPE="text" NAME="Fri6" VALUE="0" SIZE=4
OnChange="calculateTotals()"></TD>
<TD BGCOLOR="black"><INPUT TYPE="text" NAME="Sat6" VALUE="0" SIZE=4
OnChange="calculateTotals()"></TD>
<TD BGCOLOR="black"><INPUT TYPE="text" NAME="Sun6" VALUE="0" SIZE=4
OnChange="calculateTotals()"></TD>
<TD BGCOLOR="black"><INPUT TYPE="text" NAME="Tot6" VALUE="0" SIZE=5></TD>
</TR>
<TR>
<TD COLSPAN=8><CENTER><INPUT TYPE="button" NAME="submitCard" VALUE="Submit
timecard" OnClick="submitProcedure()"></CENTER></TD>
<TD BGCOLOR="red"><INPUT TYPE="text" NAME="timeTotals" VALUE="0" SIZE=5></TD>
</TR>
</TABLE>
</FORM>
</BODY>
</HTML>
```

Where to Go From Here

You may note, however, that when a user clicks the Submit Timecard button, nothing happens. The implementation for this aspect has not been coded yet. But this is a necessary feature for any time-tracking system, and this program would be useless without some manner of informing someone of the values for a timecard.

One approach you could take to remedy this problem is through the use of an external CGI mailer program. With the use of CGI and a mailer program, anytime someone submits a timecard, an e-mail message is constructed and sent to the appropriate location. Several CGI mailer utilities are available. They include NTMail, sendMail, and ToMail.

Another approach is to use server-side scripting with LiveWire Pro in which you store the timecard information in a database. After you've done that, you write a separate Web application for the folks in the administrative department, enabling them to access the time-tracking database from their end.

The time-tracking application, even as basic as it seems, provides a good stepping stone to eventually building more complex intranet applications that take on a higher skill set. One such application would be an employee directory.

Employee Directory Example

An employee directory, as discussed earlier, enables employees to get to know one another and easily contact those in other departments. Before you actually start building an employee directory, a good first step is to investigate what type of employee information would be relevant for your site. A good way to visualize the needed data is by making a prototype of the screen seen by the end user (see fig. 13.2).

Figure 13.2

Prototype of an employee directory Web page.

The end user's screen can give a good clue as to how to organize the database system. For this example, the database structure consists of a database named employeeDir, which is composed of the following three tables and their associated fields.

TABLE NAME: employees

Table's Fields and meaning:

- **lastName**—Employee's last name

- **firstName**—Employee's first name

- **department**—Employee's department

- **title**—Employee's title

- **phone**—Employee's office phone number

- **idNumber**—Employee's ID number

- **fax**—Employee's fax number

- **pager**—Employee's pager or cellular phone number

- **email**—Employee's e-mail address

- **homePhone**—Employee's home phone number

- **building**—Employee's building name

- **office**—Employee's office number

- **interests**—Employee's interests

- **pictureURL**—an URL address to the employee's picture

- **webPage**—an URL address to the employee's Web page

TABLE NAME: buildings

Table's Fields and meaning:

- **name**—Name of building

TABLE NAME: departments

Table's Fields and meaning:

- **name**—Name of department

Tip In order to run the employee directory example on the CD-ROM disc that accompanies this book, you need to first create a database named employeeDir that contains the previous three completed tables. It is highly recommended that you enter a few entries for each table. This ensures success when running the program for the first time.

The next step in the design of an intranet program is to define the applications control flow. A flow diagram for the employee directory is shown in figure 13.3.

Figure 13.3

Employee directory flow diagram.

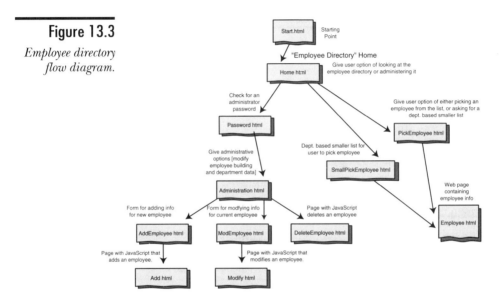

Typically, a user will begin at the Starting Point Web page (Start.html). The Starting Point Web page is responsible for establishing a connection with the database server. After connecting to the database server, the user is instantly transported (by means of the redirect function) to the Employee Directory Home page (Home.html). The Employee Directory Home page acts as the main menu for this application. The home page offers the user two choices—either the "Employee Access" area or the "Administrator Access" area. The home page is shown in figure 13.4.

If the user chooses the Employee Access button, the Web page (PickEmployee.html) shown in figure 13.5 appears. This Web page enables the user to choose the employee for which he or she wants information. If the user chooses an employee, and then clicks on the pick button, the employee Web page that was shown in figure 13.2 appears.

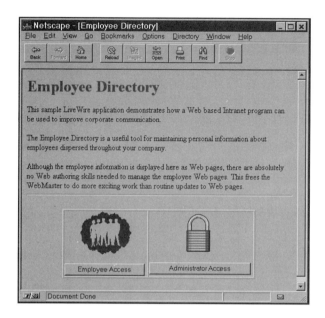

Figure 13.4

*Employee
Directory
Home page
(Home.html).*

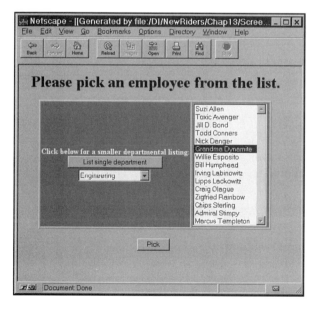

Figure 13.5

*Choosing an
employee from
the company
(PickEmployee
.html).*

If the user chooses the List Single Department button shown in figure 13.5, the page (SmallPickEmployee.html) that only shows employees found in the specified department appears (see figure 13.6).

Figure 13.6

Choosing an employee from a department (SmallPick-Employee.html).

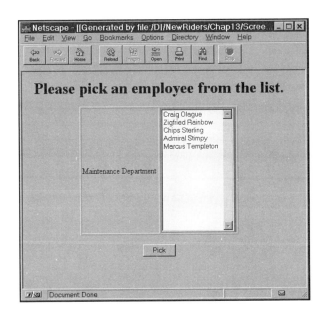

Remember that the Home page (refer to fig. 13.4) offers a button choice for administrators too. If you were to click on the Administrator Access button on the home page, you would be directed to the password Web page (Password.html). The password Web page, shown in figure 13.7, is used to keep out everyone except the administrator. Because this is a demo, however, this functionality is disabled. To re-enable password protection, remove the following comments from the file administration.html:

```
<SERVER>
// The below code may be uncommented when you desire password validation
// if (request.passWord != "BrewHaHA") {
//    redirect("password.html")
// }
cursor = database.cursor("select * from employees order by lastName");
</SERVER>
```

Should the user's password be accepted (or password checking be disabled), the user would be taken to the Web page for administrators (Administration.html), as shown in figure 13.8.

Figure 13.7

Password protection (password.html).

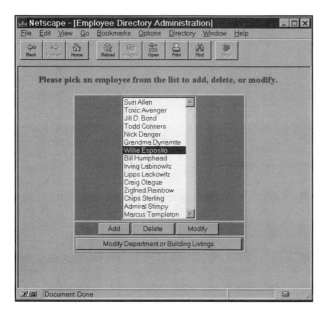

Figure 13.8

Administrator's main page (administration.html).

The Administrator's page gives you the choices of adding, modifying, or deleting an employee entry. In addition, you can add or remove buildings and departments to and from your database. By adding or removing a building or department, you affect the way the select list appears when employee data is entered (refer to figure 13.8). If you choose the Add or Modify buttons from the Administrator page, you are given a form to fill out (see fig. 13.9). If you click on Add, you are taken to the AddEmployee.html page. If you click on Modify, you are taken to the ModEmployee.html location. Note that the AddEmployee.html and the ModEmployee.html files are very similar files. They both have the same form elements, only their functionality is different.

Figure 13.9

*Employee
Information
Form (ModEm-
ployee.html).*

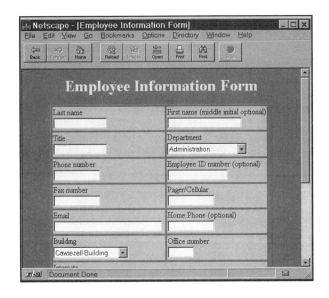

If you want to modify the building and departments data from the Administrators
page, you are taken to a page that enables you to add or remove buildings and
departments (see fig. 13.10).

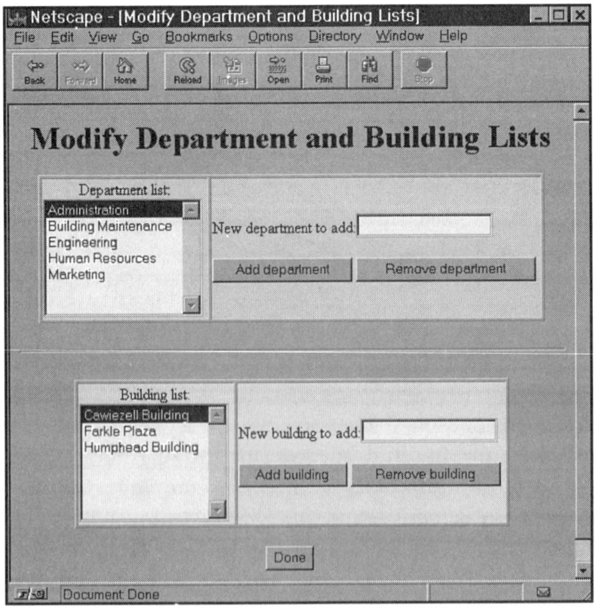

Figure 13.10

*Modifying
buildings and
departments
(deptbldg.html).*

Several other Web pages that also make up the employee directory application have not been mentioned yet. These files are add.html, modify.html, deleteEmployee.html, addBldg.html, removeBldg.html, addDept.html, and removeDept.html. Although none of these pages interface with the user, they are important in that they perform database operations.

The following exercise shows you how to run the sample employee directory application.

Running the Sample Employee Directory Application

1. Ensure that you have either LiveWire Pro or standard LiveWire with a compatible database installed on your system.

2. Ensure that you have a Netscape server on your system.

3. If you have LiveWire Pro, make sure that the Informix server is properly installed on your system.

4. Create the employeeDir database with the three tables specified in the previous section.

5. Copy the entire directory for the Employee Directory application to a writable directory on your hard drive.

6. Edit the connect.database line in the file Start.html in the following way:

```
database.connect("INFORMIX","netscape","informix","informix","employeeDir")
```

That code is in the following format:

```
database.connect("type", "server", "user", "password", "database")
```

Here is a description of each element:

◆ type—a database type of either INFORMIX, ORACLE, SYBASE, ILLUSTRA, or ODBC.

◆ server—a database server name. The server name is typically established when the database is installed.

◆ user—the user name to log in to the database.

◆ password—the password you use to log onto the database. If the database does not require a password, use an empty string ("").

◆ database—the name of the database, provided that your database server supports the notion of multiple databases on a single server. If it does not, use an empty string ("").

7. Access the LiveWire Site Manager and select the site directory that contains your source files. (For information on how to access the LiveWire Site Manager, refer to Chapter 10, "Creating Database Applications Using LiveWire Pro.")

8. Click on the Properties tab and type a Web file name for the site.

9. Choose Site | Build application. A compile progress box appears. The source files are compiled into a .web file (LiveWire application) and can be installed with Application Manager. (For more information about Application Manager, refer to Chapter 8, "Getting Familiar with LiveWire's Application Manager.")

Now that you are aware of what the employee directory sample application does, try taking it for a test drive, and check out the source code for this application while you are at it.

Start.html

Start.html, the first page to be accessed, connects to the database and, if successful, sends the user to the Home.html Home page. Following is the code for that page.

```
<HTML>
<HEAD>
<TITLE> Start Employee Directory </TITLE>
</HEAD>
<BODY>
<SERVER>
if (!database.connected()) {
  //Customize the code below to suit your database system
  database.connect("INFORMIX","netscape","informix","informix","employeeDir")
}
if (!database.connected()) {
  write("Error: Unable to connect to database. Check start.html file")
} else {
  redirect("home.html")
}
</SERVER>
</BODY>
</HTML>
```

Home.HTML

The home page is requested by the Start.html page. This is the first page that users see for this application:

```
<HTML>
<HEAD>
<TITLE> Employee Directory </TITLE>
</HEAD>
<BODY>
<SERVER>
if (!database.connected()) {
  redirect("start.html")
}
</SERVER>
<H1><FONT COLOR="blue">Employee Directory</FONT></H1>
<p>This sample LiveWire application demonstrates how a Web based
Intranet program can be used to improve corporate communication.
<p>The Employee Directory is a useful tool for maintaining personal
information about employees dispersed throughout your company.
<p>Although the employee information is displayed here as Web pages, there are
absolutely no Web authoring skills needed to manage the employee Web
pages. This frees the WebMaster to do more exciting work than
routine updates to Web pages.<HR>
<FORM>
<CENTER>
<TABLE BORDER>
<TR>
<TD>
<CENTER><IMG SRC="people.gif"></CENTER><BR>
<INPUT TYPE="button" Value="Employee Access"
OnClick="window.location.href='pickEmployee.html'">
</TD>
<TD >
<CENTER><IMG SRC="lock.GIF"></CENTER><BR>
<INPUT TYPE="button" Value="  Administrator Access  "
OnClick="window.location.href='password.html'">
</TD>
</TABLE>
</CENTER>
</FORM>
</BODY>
</HTML>
```

PickEmployee.html

The Pick Employee Web page is requested by the Home.html page. This page gives
the user the choice of either picking an employee to get information about or
accessing a new page that has only a departmental list that is easier to browse.

```
<HTML>
<HEAD><TITLE>Pick Employee</TITLE>
<SCRIPT Language="JavaScript">
function smallListing() {
 document.pickForm.action="smallPickEmployee.html?departmentLoc="+document.pickForm.
 ➥Departments.selectIndex
  document.pickForm.submit()
}
function pickPerson() {
  document.pickForm.action="employee.html?employeeLoc="+document.pickForm.
  ➥pickList.selectIndex
  document.pickForm.submit()
}
</SCRIPT>
</HEAD>
<BODY>
<CENTER>
<H1>Please pick an employee from the list.</H1>
<FORM METHOD=POST NAME="pickForm" ACTION="smallPickList.html">
<TABLE BORDER>
<TR>
<TD BGColor="#0080FF">
<FONT COLOR="white"><B>
<CENTER>
Click below for a smaller departmental listing:</B></FONT><BR>
<INPUT TYPE="button" Name="smallListingBtn" onClick="smallListing()"
        Value="List single department"><BR>
<SELECT NAME="Departments" SIZE=1>
<SERVER>
deptCursor = database.cursor("select * from departments order by name")
firstFlag="first"
while(deptCursor.next()) {
  if (firstFlag == "first") {
    write("<OPTION SELECTED>"+ deptCursor.name)
    firstFlag = "notFirst"
  }else {
    write("<OPTION>"+ deptCursor.name)
  }
}
deptCursor.close()
</SERVER>
</SELECT>
</CENTER>
</TD>
```

```
<TD BGColor="#0080FF">
<SELECT NAME="pickList" SIZE="15">
<SERVER>


cursor = database.cursor("select * from employees order by lastName")
firstFlag = "first"
while(cursor.next()) {
  if (firstFlag == "first") {
      write("<OPTION SELECTED>" + cursor.firstName + " " + cursor.lastName)
      firstFlag = "notFirst"
  }else {
      write("<OPTION>" + cursor.firstName + " " + cursor.lastName)
  }
}
cursor.close()
</SERVER>
</SELECT>
</TD>
</TR>
</TABLE><P>
<CENTER>
<INPUT TYPE="button" Name="OKButton" Value="   Pick   " OnClick="pickPerson()">
</CENTER>
</FORM>
</CENTER>
</BODY>
</HTML>
```

Password.html

Password.html is requested by home.html. It takes user input and posts it to Administration.html. It actually is Administration.html that checks the password.

```
<HTML>
<HEAD>
<TITLE> Administrator Password </TITLE>
</HEAD>
<BODY>
<H1> Please Enter Your Admin. Password </H1>
<FORM METHOD="post" action="administration.html">
<P>Password
<INPUT TYPE="text" NAME="passWord" SIZE="12">
<INPUT TYPE="submit" VALUE=" OK ">
```

```
</FORM>
<HR>
<FONT size=-1><B>NOTE: </B>For now, you can enter anything in the text field
and click the OK button, and you will be granted access. As an administrator,
you should implement password protection in the future. </FONT>
</BODY>
</HTML>
```

Administration.html

Administration.html is requested by password.html. This page posts requests to Web pages, which perform the database tasks of adding an employee, deleting an employee, and modifying an employee.

```
<HTML>
<HEAD><TITLE>Employee Directory Administration</TITLE>
<SCRIPT Language="JavaScript">
function modifyDeptBldg() {
  window.location.href = "deptbldg.html"
}
function modifyEmployee() {
  window.location.href =
"modEmployee.html?employeeLoc="+document.pickForm.pickList.selectIndex
}
function deleteEmployee() {
  window.location.href =
"deleteEmployee.html?employeeLoc="+document.pickForm.pickList.selectIndex
}
function addEmployee() {
  window.location.href = "addEmployee.html"
}
</SCRIPT>
</HEAD>
<BODY>
<SERVER>
// The below code may be uncommented when you desire password validation
// if (request.passWord != "BrewHaHA") {
//   redirect("password.html")
// }
cursor = database.cursor("select * from employees order by lastName")
</SERVER>
<CENTER>
<FONT SIZE=+1 COLOR= "Blue">
<B>Please pick an employee from the list to add, delete, or modify.</B>
```

```
</FONT>
<FORM NAME="pickForm">
<TABLE BORDER>
<TR ALIGN=CENTER>
<TD BGColor="#0080FF">
<SELECT NAME="pickList" SIZE="15">
<SERVER>
firstFlag="first"
while(cursor.next()) {
  if (firstFlag == "first") {
     write("<OPTION SELECTED>" +cursor.firstName + " " + cursor.lastName)
     firstFlag = "notFirst"
  }else {
     write("<OPTION>" +cursor.firstName + " " + cursor.lastName)
  }
}
cursor.close()
</SERVER>
</SELECT>
</TD>
</TR>
<TR ALIGN=CENTER><TD BGColor="#0080FF">
<INPUT TYPE="button" Name="AddButton" Value="   Add   "
➥OnCLick="addEmployee()">
<INPUT TYPE="button" Name="DeleteButton" Value="  Delete   "
➥OnClick="deleteEmployee()">
<INPUT TYPE="button" Name="ModifyButton" Value="   Modify   "
➥OnClick="modifyEmployee()">
<TR ALIGN=CENTER><TD BGColor="magenta">
<INPUT TYPE="button" Name="ModDeptBldg" Value="Modify Department or Building
Listings"  " OnClick="modifyDeptBldg()">
</TR></TD>
</TABLE><P>
</FORM>
</CENTER>
</BODY>
</HTML>
```

SmallPickEmployee.HTML

This page is requested by PickEmployee.html whenever a user wants to choose from just the employees in a specific department. This page requests employee.html, which is a Web page with the specified employee's information.

```
<HTML>
<HEAD><TITLE> Small Pick Employee</TITLE>
<SCRIPT Language="JavaScript">
function pickPerson() {
  document.smallPickForm.action="employee.html?employeeLoc="
          +document.smallPickForm.pickList.selectIndex
  document.smallPickForm.submit()
}
</SCRIPT>
</HEAD>
<BODY>
<CENTER>
<H1>Please pick an employee from the list.</H1>
<FORM METHOD=POST NAME="smallPickForm" ACTION="employee.html">
<TABLE BORDER>
<TR>
<TD>
<SERVER>
if (request.departmentLoc != null) {
  deptCursor = database.cursor("select * from departments order by name",true)
  deptCursor.next()
  for (i =0; i < parseInt(request.departmentLoc); i++) {
    deptCursor.next()
  }
  write(deptCursor.name)
  client.departmentName=deptCursor.name
  deptCursor.close
}
</SERVER>
</TD>
<TD BGColor="#0080FF">
<SELECT NAME="pickList" SIZE=15>
<SERVER>
cursor=database.cursor("select * from employees where department = " +
client.departmentName,true)
firstFlag="first"
while(cursor.next()) {
  if (firstFlag == "First") {
    write("<OPTION SELECTED>"+ cursor.firstName + " " + cursor.lastName)
    firstFlag = "notFirst"
  } else {
    write("<OPTION>"+ cursor.firstName + " " + cursor.lastName)
```

```
    }
  }
</SERVER>
</SELECT>
</TD>
</TR>
</TABLE><P>
<CENTER><INPUT TYPE="button" Name="OKButton"
                Value="  Pick  " OnClick="pickPerson()"></CENTER>
</FORM>
</CENTER>
</BODY>
</HTML>
```

Employee.html

Employee.html is used to display to the user the information for the specified employee. Employee.html is requested by both SmallPickEmployee.html and PickEmployee.html.

```
<HTML>
<HEAD><TITLE>Bill Humphead</TITLE></HEAD>
<BODY>
<SERVER>
if (request.employeeLoc != null) {
  cursor = database.cursor("select * from employees order by lastName",true)
  cursor.next()
  for (i =0; i < parseInt(request.employeeLoc); i++) {
    cursor.next()
  }
}
</SERVER>
<CENTER>
<TABLE>
<TR>
<TD>
<IMG SRC="<SERVER>write(cursor.pictureURL)</SERVER>">
</TD>
<TD>
<H1><I><SERVER>write(cursor.firstName + " " + cursor.lastName)</SERVER>
➥</I></H1>
</TD>
</TR>
```

```
</TABLE>
<TABLE>
<TR>
<TD>
<B>Title:</B>
</TD>
<TD BGCOLOR="#FFFFFF">
<SERVER>write(cursor.title)</SERVER>
</TD>
</TR>
<TR>
<TD>
<B>Email:</B>
</TD>
<TD BGCOLOR="#FFFFFF">
<A HREF="<SERVER>write(cursor.email)</SERVER>"><SERVER>write(cursor.email)</
➡SERVER></a>
</TD>
</TR>
<TR>
<TD>
<B>Department</B>
</TD>
<TD BGCOLOR="#FFFFFF">
<SERVER>write(cursor.department)</SERVER>
</TD>
</TR>
<TR>
<TD>
<B>Employee ID:</B>
</TD>
<TD BGCOLOR="#FFFFFF">
<SERVER>write(cursor.idNumber)</SERVER>
</TD>
</TR>
<TR>
<TD>
<B>Fax Number: </B>
</TD>
<TD BGCOLOR="#FFFFFF">
<SERVER>write(cursor.fax)</SERVER>
</TD>
```

```
</TR>
<TR>
<TD>
<B>Pager/Cellular Number: </B>
</TD>
<TD BGCOLOR="#FFFFFF">
<SERVER>write(cursor.pager)</SERVER>
</TD>
</TR>
<TR>
<TD>
<B>Home Phone: </B>
</TD>
<TD BGCOLOR="#FFFFFF">
<SERVER>write(cursor.phone)</SERVER>
</TD>
</TR>
<TR>
<TD>
<B>Building: </B>
</TD>
<TD BGCOLOR="#FFFFFF">
<SERVER>write(cursor.building)</SERVER>
</TD>
</TR>
<TR>
<TD>
<B>Office Number: </B>
</TD>
<TD BGCOLOR="#FFFFFF">
<SERVER>write(cursor.office)</SERVER>
</TD>
</TR>
<TR>
<TD>
<B>Interests: </B>
</TD>
<TD BGCOLOR="#FFFFFF">
<SERVER>write(cursor.interests)</SERVER>
</TD >
</TR>
<TR>
```

```
<TD>
<B>Personal Web page: </B>
</TD>
<TD BGCOLOR="#FFFFFF">
<A HREF="<SERVER>write(cursor.webPage)</
➥SERVER>"><SERVER>write(cursor.webPage)</SERVER></a>
</TD>
</TR>
</TABLE>
<FORM>
<INPUT TYPE="button" Value="Back to previous page" OnClick="window.history.
➥go(-1)">
</FORM>
</CENTER>
</BODY>
</HTML>
```

AddEmployee.html

AddEmployee.html displays a form for the user to fill out, including information on a new employee he or she wants to add. AddEmployee.html is requested by Administration.html and requests, in turn, Add.html to do the actual addition of a record to the "employees" table.

```
<HTML>
<HEAD><TITLE>Employee Information Form</TITLE></HEAD>
<BODY BGCOLOR="gray">
<SERVER>
if (request.employeeLoc != null) {
  cursor = database.cursor("select * from employees order by lastName",true)
  cursor.next()
  for (i =0; i < parseInt(request.employeeLoc); i++) {
    cursor.next()
  }
}
</SERVER>
<CENTER>
<FONT COLOR="yellow"><H1>Employee Information Form</H1></FONT>
<FORM METHOD="post" NAME="EmployeeForm" action="add.html">
<TABLE BORDER=2  BGCOLOR="#CfCfCf">
<TR>
<TD>
Last name<BR>
```

```
<INPUT TYPE="text" Name="LastName" VALUE="" SIZE=14>
</TD>
<TD>
First name (middle initial optional)<BR>
<INPUT TYPE="text" Name="FirstName" VALUE="" SIZE=20>
</TD>
</TR>
<TR>
<TD>
Title<BR>
<INPUT TYPE="text" Name="Title" VALUE="" SIZE=14>
</TD>
<TD>
Department<BR>
<SELECT NAME="departmentList" SIZE="1">
<SERVER>
deptCursor = database.cursor("select * from departments",true)
firstTime="first"
while (deptCursor.next()) {
  if (firstTime == "first") {
    firstTime="notFirst"
    write("<OPTION SELECTED>"+deptCursor.name)
  }else{
    write("<OPTION>"+deptCursor.name)
  }
}
deptCursor.close()
</SERVER>
</SELECT>
</TD>
</TR>
<TR>
<TD>
Phone number<BR>
<INPUT TYPE="text" Name="Phone" VALUE="" SIZE=12>
</TD>
<TD>
Employee ID number (optional)<BR>
<INPUT TYPE="text" Name="IDNumber" VALUE="" SIZE=16>
</TD>
<TD>
</TR>
```

```
<TR>
<TD>
Fax number<BR>
<INPUT TYPE="text" Name="Fax" VALUE="" SIZE=12>
</TD>
<TD>
Pager/Cellular<BR>
<INPUT TYPE="text" Name="Pager" VALUE="" SIZE=12>
</TD>
</TR>
<TR>
<TD>
Email<BR>
<INPUT TYPE="text" Name="Email" VALUE="" SIZE=30>
</TD>
<TD>
Home Phone (optional)<BR>
<INPUT TYPE="text" Name="HomePhone" VALUE="" SIZE=12>
</TD>
</TR>
<TR>
<TD>
Building<BR>
<SELECT NAME="BuildingList" SIZE="1">
<SERVER>
bldgCursor = database.cursor("select * from buildings",true)
while (bldgCursor.next()) {
  if (firstTime == "first") {
    write("<OPTION SELECTED>"+bldgCursor.name)
    firstTime = "notFirst"
  }else{
    write("<OPTION>"+bldgCursor.name)
  }
}
bldgCursor.close()
</SERVER></SELECT>
</TD>
<TD>
Office number<BR>
<INPUT TYPE="text" Name="Office" VALUE="" SIZE=6>
</TD>
</TR>
```

```
<TR>
<TD NOWRAP COLSPAN=2>
Interests<BR>
<TEXTAREA NAME="Interests" ROWS=3 COLS=50></TEXTAREA>
</TD>
</TR>
<TR>
<TD NOWRAP COLSPAN=2>
URL for employee's picture<BR>
<INPUT TYPE="text" Name="Picture" VALUE="file://" SIZE=55>
</TD>
</TR>
<TR>
<TD NOWRAP COLSPAN=2>
Employee's personal Web page (URL)<BR>
<INPUT TYPE="text" Name="WebPage" VALUE="http://" SIZE=55>
</TD>
</TR>
</TABLE><P>
<INPUT TYPE="submit" Name="Addbutton" Value="  Add User  ">
<INPUT TYPE="reset" Name="resetbutton" Value="Reset">
</FORM>
</CENTER>
</BODY>
</HTML>
```

ModEmployee.html

ModEmployee.html displays a form for the administrator to fill out, including information on an employee he or she wants to modify. ModEmployee.html is requested by Administration.html and requests, in turn, Modify.html to do the actual modification of a record in the "employees" table.

```
<HTML>
<HEAD><TITLE>Employee Information Form</TITLE></HEAD>
<BODY BGCOLOR="gray">
<SERVER>
if (request.employeeLoc != null) {
  cursor = database.cursor("select * from employees order by lastName",true)
  cursor.next()
  for (i =0; i < parseInt(request.employeeLoc); i++) {
    cursor.next()
  }
```

```
      }
      </SERVER>
      <CENTER>
      <FONT COLOR="yellow"><H1>Employee Information Form</H1></FONT>

      <FORM METHOD=POST NAME="EmployeeForm"
            action="modify.html<SERVER>write("?locEmployee="+request.employeeLoc></
      SERVER>>
      <TABLE BORDER=2  BGCOLOR="#CfCfCf">
      <TR>
      <TD>
      Last name<BR>
      <INPUT TYPE="text" Name="LastName" VALUE="<SERVER>write(cursor.lastName)</
      ➥SERVER>" SIZE=14>
      </TD>
      <TD>
      First name (middle initial optional)<BR>
      <INPUT TYPE="text" Name="FirstName"
      ➥VALUE="<SERVER>write(cursor.firstName)</SERVER>" SIZE=20>
      </TD>
      </TR>
      <TR>
      <TD>
      Title<BR>
      <INPUT TYPE="text" Name="Title"
      ➥VALUE="<SERVER>write(cursor.title)</SERVER>" SIZE=14>
      </TD>
      <TD>
      Department<BR>
      <SELECT NAME="departmentList" SIZE="1">
      <SERVER>
      deptCursor = database.cursor("select * from departments",true)
      while (deptCursor.next()) {
        if (deptCursor.name == cursor.department) {
          write("<OPTION SELECTED>"+deptCursor.name)
        }else {
            write("<OPTION>"+deptCursor.name)
        }
      }
      deptCursor.close()
      </SERVER>
      </SELECT>
```

```
</TD>
</TR>
<TR>
<TD>
Phone number<BR>
<INPUT TYPE="text" Name="Phone" VALUE="<SERVER>write(cursor.phone)</SERVER>"
➥SIZE=12>
</TD>
<TD>
Employee ID number (optional)<BR>
<INPUT TYPE="text" Name="IDNumber" VALUE="<SERVER>write(cursor.idNumber)</
➥SERVER>" SIZE=16>
</TD>
<TD>
</TR>
<TR>
<TD>
Fax number<BR>
<INPUT TYPE="text" Name="Fax" VALUE="<SERVER>write(cursor.fax)</SERVER>"
➥SIZE=12>
</TD>
<TD>
Pager/Cellular<BR>
<INPUT TYPE="text" Name="Pager" VALUE="<SERVER>write(cursor.pager)</SERVER>"
➥SIZE=12>
</TD>
</TR>
<TR>
<TD>
Email<BR>
<INPUT TYPE="text" Name="Email" VALUE="<SERVER>write(cursor.email)</SERVER>"
➥SIZE=30>
</TD>
<TD>
Home Phone (optional)<BR>
<INPUT TYPE="text" Name="HomePhone" VALUE="<SERVER>write(cursor.homePhone)</
➥SERVER>" SIZE=12>
</TD>
</TR>
<TR>
<TD>
Building<BR>
```

```
<SELECT NAME="BuildingList" SIZE="1">
<SERVER>
bldgCursor = database.cursor("select * from buildings",true)
while (bldgCursor.next()) {
  if (bldgCursor.name == cursor.building) {
    write("<OPTION SELECTED>"+bldgCursor.name)
  }else {
    write("<OPTION>"+bldgCursor.name)
  }
}
bldgCursor.close()
</SERVER>
</SELECT>
</TD>
<TD>
Office number<BR>
<INPUT TYPE="text" Name="Office" VALUE="<SERVER>write(cursor.office)</SERVER>"
➥SIZE=6>
</TD>
</TR>
<TR>
<TD NOWRAP COLSPAN=2>
Interests<BR>
<TEXTAREA NAME="Interests" ROWS=3
➥COLS=50><SERVER>write(cursor.interests)</SERVER></TEXTAREA>
</TD>
</TR>
<TR>
<TD NOWRAP COLSPAN=2>
URL for employee's picture<BR>
<INPUT TYPE="text" Name="Picture"
➥VALUE="<SERVER>write(cursor.pictureURL)</SERVER>" SIZE=55>
</TD>
</TR>
<TR>
<TD NOWRAP COLSPAN=2>
Employee's personal Web page (URL)<BR>
<INPUT TYPE="text" Name="WebPage" VALUE="<SERVER>write(cursor.webPage)</
➥SERVER>" SIZE=55>
</TD>
</TR>
</TABLE><P>
```

```
<INPUT TYPE="submit" Name="Submitbutton" Value="  Enter   ">
<INPUT TYPE="reset" Name="resetbutton" Value="Reset">
</FORM>
</CENTER>
</BODY>
</HTML>
```

DeleteEmployee.html

DeleteEmployee.html carries out the deletion of an employee record from the
database. This Web page is requested by Administration.html.

```
<HEAD>
<TITLE> Remove Employee </TITLE>
</HEAD>
<BODY>
<SERVER>
if (request.employeeLoc != null) {
  cursor = database.cursor("select * from employees order by lastName",true)
  cursor.next()
  for (i =0; i < parseInt(request.employeeLoc); i++) {
    cursor.next()
  }
  database.execute("delete from employees where lastName = " + cursor.
➥lastName + "AND firstName = " + cursor.firstName)
}
cursor.close()
redirect("administration.html")
</SERVER>
</BODY>
</HTML>
```

DeptBldg.html

DeptBldg.html handles user input for adding or removing departments or buildings
to or from the database. DeptBldg.html is requested by Administration.html, and
DeptBldg.html requests, in turn, AddBldg.html, RemoveBldg.html, AddDept.html,
and RemoveDept.html to actually carry out the add and remove operations on the
database.

```
<HTML>
<HEAD><TITLE>Modify Department and Building Lists</TITLE>
<SCRIPT Language="JavaScript">
function addBuilding() {
```

```
    document.BldgForm.action="addBldg.html"
    document.BldgForm.submit()
  }
  function removeBuilding() {
    document.DeptForm.action="removeBldg.html"
    document.DeptForm.submit()
  }
  function addDept() {
    document.DeptForm.action="addDept.html"
    document.DeptForm.submit()
  }
  function removeDept() {
    document.DeptForm.action="removeDept.html"
    document.DeptForm.submit()
  }
  </SCRIPT>
  </HEAD>
  <BODY>
  <SERVER>
  bldgCursor = database.cursor("select * from buildings order by name",true)
  deptCursor = database.cursor("select * from departments order by name",true)
  </SERVER>
  <CENTER>
  <H1>Modify Department and Building Lists</H1>
  <FORM METHOD=POST NAME="DeptForm" ACTION="addBldg.html">
  <TABLE BORDER>
  <TR>
  <TD BGCOLOR="cyan">
  <CENTER>Department list:<BR>
  <SELECT NAME="DepartList" SIZE="7">
  <SERVER>
  firstFlag = "first"
  while (deptCursor.next()) {
    if (firstFlag == "first") {
      write("<OPTION SELECTED>"+deptCursor.name)
      firstFlag = "notfirst"
    }else{
      write("<OPTION>"+deptCursor.name)
    }
  }
  </SERVER>
  </SELECT>
```

```
</CENTER>
</TD>
<TD BGCOLOR="cyan">
New department to add:
<INPUT TYPE="text" NAME="newDepartment" Value="" SIZE=18"><P>
<INPUT TYPE="button" NAME="addDepartment" VALUE="Add department" OnClick=
"addDept()">
<INPUT TYPE="button" NAME="removeDepartment" VALUE="Remove department" OnClick=
"removeDept()">
</TD>
</TR>
</TABLE>
<P>
</FORM>
<HR>
<FORM METHOD=POST Name="BldgForm" action="addDept.html">
<TABLE BORDER>
<TR>
<TD BGCOLOR="yellow">
<CENTER>Building list:<BR>
<SELECT NAME="BuildingList" SIZE="7">
<SERVER>
firstFlag = "first"
while (bldgCursor.next()) {
  if (firstFlag == "first") {
    write("<OPTION SELECTED>"+bldgCursor.name)
    firstFlag = "notfirst"
  }else {
    write("<OPTION>"+bldgCursor.name)
  }
}
</SERVER>
</SELECT>
</CENTER>
</TD>
<TD BGCOLOR="yellow">
New building to add:
<INPUT TYPE="text" NAME="newBuilding" Value="" SIZE=18 ><P>
<INPUT TYPE="button" NAME="addBuilding" VALUE="Add building" OnClick=
"addBuilding()">
<INPUT TYPE="button" NAME="removeBuilding" VALUE="Remove building" OnClick=
"removeBuilding()">
```

```
</TD>
</TR>
</TABLE>
<P>
</FORM>
</CENTER>
</BODY>
```

Modify.html

Modify.html is requested by ModEmployee.html to carry out modifications to a database of an employee record.

```
<HTML>
<HEAD><TITLE>Modify Information Form</TITLE></HEAD>
<BODY>
<SERVER>
if (request.locEmployee != null) {
  cursor = database.cursor("select * from employees order by lastName",true)
  cursor.next()
  for (i =0; i < parseInt(request.locEmployee); i++) {
    cursor.next()
  }
  cursor.lastName=request.LastName
  cursor.firstName=request.FirstName
  cursor.department=request.departmentList
  cursor.title=request.Title
  cursor.phone=request.Phone
  cursor.idNumber=request.IDNumber
  cursor.fax=request.Fax
  cursor.pager=request.Pager
  cursor.email=request.Email
  cursor.homePhone=request.HomePhone
  cursor.building=request.BuildingList
  cursor.office=request.Office
  cursor.interests=request.Interests
  cursor.pictureURL=request.Picture
  cursor.webPage=request.WebPage
  cursor.updateRow("employees")
  cursor.close()
  redirect("administration.html")
}
</SERVER>
```

```
</BODY>
</HTML>
```

Add.html

Add.html is requested by AddEmployee.html to carry out additions to a database of an employee record.

```
<HTML>
<HEAD><TITLE>Add to Information Form</TITLE></HEAD>
<BODY>
<SERVER>
cursor = database.cursor("select * from employees",true)
cursor.next()
cursor.lastName=request.LastName
cursor.firstName=request.FirstName
cursor.department=request.departmentList
cursor.title=request.Title
cursor.phone=request.Phone
cursor.idNumber=request.IDNumber
cursor.fax=request.Fax
cursor.pager=request.Pager
cursor.email=request.Email
cursor.homePhone=request.HomePhone
cursor.building=request.BuildingList
cursor.office=request.Office
cursor.interests=request.Interests
cursor.pictureURL=request.Picture
cursor.webPage=request.WebPage
cursor.insertRow("employees")
cursor.close()
redirect("administration.html")
</SERVER>
</BODY>
</HTML>
```

AddDept.html

AddDept.html is requested by DeptBldg.html. AddDept.html is responsible for the addition new departments to the database.

```
<HTML>
<HEAD><TITLE>Add a Department</TITLE></HEAD>
<BODY>
```

```
<SERVER>
cursor = database.cursor("select * from departments",true)
cursor.next()
cursor.name=request.DepartList
cursor.insertRow("departments")
cursor.close()
redirect("administration.html")
</SERVER>
</BODY>
</HTML>
```

RemoveDept.html

RemoveDept.html is requested by DeptBldg.html. RemoveDept.html is responsible for removing departments from the database.

```
<HTML>
<HEAD><TITLE>Remove a Department</TITLE></HEAD>
<BODY>
<SERVER>
  database.execute("delete from departments where name = " +
➥request.DepartList)
</SERVER>
</BODY>
</HTML>
```

AddBldg.html

AddBldg.html is requested by DeptBldg.html. AddBldg.html is responsible for adding new buildings to the database.

```
<HTML>
<HEAD><TITLE>Add a Building</TITLE></HEAD>
<BODY>
<SERVER>
cursor = database.cursor("select * from buildings",true)
cursor.next()
cursor.name=request.newBuilding
cursor.insertRow("buildings")
cursor.close()
redirect("administration.html")
</SERVER>
</BODY>
</HTML>
```

RemoveBldg.html

RemoveBldg.html is requested by DeptBldg.html. RemoveBldg.html is responsible for removing buildings from the database.

```
<HTML>
<HEAD><TITLE>Remove a Building</TITLE></HEAD>
<BODY>
<SERVER>
  database.execute("delete from buildings where name = " +
➥request.BuildingList)
</SERVER>
</BODY>
</HTML>
```

Summary

In this chapter, you have learned more about the intranet and how you can use JavaScript with an intranet system in your organization to reduce costs and boost business. Specifically, you have learned about the advantages of developing for the intranet, intranet protocol versus proprietary standards and protocols, and the many ways in which you can use the intranet in your business. You also have learned how to use the employee directory, which is included on the CD that accompanies this book.

This concludes the last chapter of *Inside JavaScript*. Be sure to check out the appendices for information on terms used in this book, additional WWW resources, and technical insight into developing plug-ins and Java applets with JavaScript in mind.

APPENDIX A

The JavaScript Programming Reference

by Kevin Ready, Paul Vachier, and Benoit Marsot, authors of
Plug-n-Play JavaScript (New Riders 1996).

This appendix defines all of the JavaScript programming elements available in browser versions up to and including Navigator 3.0. If you are looking for a description of event handlers, objects, properties, methods, operators, and other syntactical elements, they are all contained here.

Event Handlers

Events are user-triggered actions such as button clicking, image loading, mouseover, or other user-initiated actions that can invoke a JavaScript. An event handler, thus, is a JavaScript command that triggers a script when an event occurs as illustrated below:

```
<A HREF="http://www.malicepalace.com" onClick="alert('This could be
dangerous')">Click me/A>
```

For the HTML programmer, event handlers appear as attributes in tag definitions. That is to say that they are included within existing HTML tags, such as <A> (as shown above), in the same way that attributes are included in a tag definition. Event handlers were chosen as the element around which to write this book.

By directing your attention to event handlers, your existing knowledge of HTML and Web page design is leveraged by using familiar actions (like entering or exiting a text box) to sensibly design JavaScripts. In other words, when you design a JavaScript, you want it to begin in response to a certain event—button click, text entry, page loading, or other event. This book leads you through the event handlers available in JavaScript with relevant examples provided for each of them. The event handlers are described in detail in the following sections.

onAbort

onAbort is a new event handler that is designed to work with the image object from Navigator 3.0 and later. The event handler initiates a script when you abort loading an image. You can abort loading an image by selecting another URL, clicking the Stop button, and by other means. In the following example, the *alert()* method displays an alert box when the loading of the image named *"image.gif"* is aborted.

```
<IMG SRC="image.gif" onAbort="alert('Are you really too busy to wait?')">
```

If your image contained information that was really critical for the viewer to see, you can alert them using this event handler if they abort loading the image.

onBlur

The *onBlur* event handler is used with the <SELECT>, <TEXTAREA>, and the text TYPE <INPUT> tags. With Navigator 3.0, this handler is also available for the <BODY> and <FRAMESET> tags. With these tags, the event handler is activated when the window or frame loses the focus of the mouse or cursor. With form elements, the *onBlur* event handler initiates a script when a form field is exited. In the following example, the form element is a text box that contains the *onBlur* event handler. The event handler calls a function named *functionx* when the text box is exited.

```
<FORM>
<INPUT NAME=FIRSTBOX SIZE=20 TYPE=TEXT onBlur="functionx()">
</FORM>
```

onChange

The *onChange* event handler is used with the <SELECT>, <TEXTAREA>, and the text TYPE <INPUT> tag. This event handler initiates a script when the contents of the form field are changed, again valuable for initiating a script when a user modifies an input field. In the following example, the form element is a select list that uses the *onChange* event handler. Once you select an option, the event handler calls a function named *functionA* when the selection has been changed.

```
<FORM>
<SELECT NAME=select onChange="functionA()">
<OPTION VALUE="LA">Los Angeles
<OPTION VALUE="NY">New York
<OPTION VALUE="CH">Chicago
</SELECT>
</FORM>
```

onClick

The *onClick* event handler can be used with submit, reset, button, checkbox, and radio <INPUT> tag types and the <A> tag. In response to a mouse click, the script specified by this event handler will be executed. In the following example, the anchor contains the *onClick* event handler. Clicking on the anchored image calls the function named *functionB*. In JavaScript, the <A> tag is referred to as a link object when it contains the *HREF* attribute. The anchor object itself does not use the event handler. It is the link object that responds to the *onClick* event handler.

```
<A HREF=#TopofDocument onClick="functionB()">
<IMG SRC="picture.gif">
</A>
```

onError

The *onError* event handler is new to Navigator 3.0. It is used with the <IMG> tag, or image object, and is activated when an image tag's attributes produce an error, such as trying to access an image file that doesn't exist. In the following example, the event handler is used for a clothing catalog that looks for a certain color and feature combination in its inventory. When no clothing fitting the *"Red44OS.gif"* source file is found, the event handler generates an alert box saying that the store is out of stock of that item. The HTML document will likely be generated, at least in part, in conjunction with a database backend that could use the presence or absence of specific image files on the server to generate appropriate messages.

```
<IMG SRC="Red44OS.gif" onError="alert('We have no more red 44 from OceanSail in
stock. Please select another')">
```

In this example, you can have someone fill in the size and color information. After they fill in the information, all of the calculations can be done in the browser.

onFocus

The *onFocus* event handler is used with the <SELECT>, <TEXTAREA>, and text TYPE <INPUT> tags. As with the *onBlur* event handler, *onFocus* is also being made available for the <BODY> and <FRAMESET> tags; however, it was still under development at the time of this writing. The *onFocus* event handler is the opposite of *onBlur* and activates a script when the form field is entered. In the following example, the event handler calls the *functionZ* function when the text area is entered with either a mouse click or through tabbing.

```
<FORM>
<TEXTAREA ROWS=10 COLS=50 onFocus="functionZ()">
</FORM>
```

onLoad

The *onLoad* event handler is used with the <BODY>, <FRAMESET>, and <IMG> tags. There are two distinct uses of the *onLoad* event handler. The first (which has been enabled since Navigator 2) executes a script once the window or all frames are loaded. In the following example, the *functionY* function is called by the event handler. This means that when the page is opened the first time, the script will be executed.

```
<BODY onLoad="functionY()">
```

The second use of the *onLoad* event handler is associated with images. Specifically, when an image has finished loading, the event handler is activated. This does not work with looping animated GIF files. This usage has only been enabled since Navigator 3.0 and later versions.

```
<IMG SRC="some.gif" onLoad="function999()">
```

In this example, *function999* is initiated by the *onLoad* event handler after the picture has loaded.

onMouseOut

The *onMouseOut* event handler is activated when the mouse passes outside of text or images contained within <A> anchor tags. This works the opposite of *onMouseOver*. One use of the tag could be for children's sites, where you want to have different functions occur based on the mouse's screen position. This event handler is available for Navigator 3.0 and later versions. In the following example, *functionR* is initiated once the mouse leaves the text "Function R."

```
<A HREF="http://www.3pdesign.com" onMouseOut="functionR()">Function R</A>
```

onMouseOver

The *onMouseOver* event handler is used with the <A> tag and is activated when the mouse passes over an anchored reference. A popular implementation of this works in conjunction with a window status function to make specified text appear in the status bar. In the following example, the *functionK* function is called by the event handler when the mouse is dragged over the text "Function K."

```
<A HREF="http://www.3pdesign.com" onMouseOver="functionK()">Function K</A>
```

onReset

The *onReset* event handler is activated when the <INPUT TYPE="reset"> tag is selected within a form. The event handler itself is contained within the <FORM> tag. This handler is available for Navigator 3.0 and later versions. In the following example, an alert box displays when the Reset button is selected.

```
<FORM onReset="alert('The form has been reset.')">
<INPUT NAME=FIRSTBOX SIZE=20 TYPE=TEXT>
<INPUT NAME=Resat TYPE=RESET>
</FORM>
```

onSelect

The *onSelect* event handler is used with the <TEXTAREA> and the text TYPE <INPUT> tag. This event handler initiates a script when the text is selected within a text box. In the following example, the event handler initiates the *functionQ* function when any text is selected within the text box. It is easy to confuse this event handler with the *onFocus* event handler. In the case of *onFocus*, the script is executed when the element is first entered, or selected in the traditional sense (for example, being clicked with a mouse or entered using the tab key). In the case of *onSelect*, it is activated when text within a form element is selected by highlighting the characters using the mouse or the shift and arrow keys.

```
<FORM>
<INPUT NAME=FIRSTBOX SIZE=20 TYPE=TEXT onSelect="functionQ()">
</FORM>
```

onSubmit

The *onSubmit* event handler executes a script upon form submission and is used with the <FORM> tag. It can be used to provide functionality without relying on traditional CGI programming. In the following example, the *functionXYZ* function is initiated when the *onSubmit* event handler is called by clicking the submit button. Notice the **return** statement prior to *functionXYZ*. This directs the JavaScript to pass the information on to the server after *functionXYZ* has been executed. You must return true in the event handler for the form to be submitted; return false prevents the form from being submitted. You do not have to use a CGI script in conjunction with the JavaScript.

```
<FORM METHOD=POST ACTION="anyscript.cgi"
      onSubmit="return functionXYZ()">
<INPUT NAME=FIRSTBOX SIZE=20 TYPE=TEXT>
<INPUT TYPE=SUBMIT>
</FORM>
```

onUnload

The *onUnload* event handler executes a script when the document is exited and is used within the <BODY> or <FRAMESET> tags. In the following example, the *functionABC* function is initiated when the visitor leaves the HTML page. You may want to include a sound or an alert message for your visitors when they leave your page.

```
<BODY onUnload="functionABC()">
```

The next part of JavaScript's mystery will be solved by the introduction of objects and statements.

♦ Objects: The elements that you use JavaScript to affect or interpret.

♦ Statements: The elements that direct the flow of the JavaScript.

◆ Functions: Special types of statements that contain other statements to perform one or more actions.

◆ Methods: Special types of functions that require an object to perform.

Before getting lost in programming soup, you should become familiar with JavaScript objects. Understanding the JavaScript Object Hierarchy will help give order to what may otherwise seem like one more bowl of gobbledygook.

Objects

Objects are entities that can be interpreted or affected by using JavaScript. For you to be able to affect or read anything on the HTML page, there must exist a corresponding object in JavaScript. You cannnot, for example, reference Bookmarks, because there is no bookmark object in JavaScript. On the other hand, you can go forward or backward using the History object. The primary objects in Navigator are the Window, Document, History, Location, and Navigator objects.

Some of these objects, such as History, can be interpreted by JavaScript. Others have properties that can be interpreted or affected through scripting. The BGCOLOR property of the Document object, for instance, can be interpreted, affected, or changed by JavaScript. Before introducing the objects, their hierarchy and related properties, methods, and event handlers will be presented.

The JavaScript Object Model

When using the JavaScript object model, you are able to refer to distinct programming elements by defining them through parent-child relationships. This means that you can use the object model to refer to an object much like the way you would use a full directory path to designate a particular file. You can also refer to individual elements by using their name, as given using the NAME attribute. In the following example, a form named *FormName* is created with an element named "*SampleText*." The two statements that follow both refer to the same *Text* element (*SampleText*):

```
<FORM NAME=FormName>
    <INPUT TYPE="Text" NAME="SampleText" SIZE=20>
</FORM>
```

```
document.forms[0].SampleText;
document.FormName.SampleText;
```

In the example, the *document.forms[0].SampleText* property belongs to the *forms* array property of the *document* object. The *SampleText* property belongs to the *form* object named *FormName*. *FormName* is a property of the document object.

The object model extends individual objects through controlling properties of their properties. This can seem rather strange at first. Many properties are themselves objects with their own properties. There are also array properties, such as the *forms* property of the document object in the example above. The index number in the brackets following the array determines which object is selected. The first object is numbered zero [0]. If there were two or more forms, you can use the array property to define which form your JavaScript concerns. Using the hierarchical model, you will be able to control objects succinctly and directly. Once you become familiar with the model, the JavaScript examples in the book will be much less intimidating.

In Table A.1 on the next few pages, all of the JavaScript objects available in Navigator 2 and Navigator 3.0, along with their associated properties, methods, and event handlers will be presented. Remember, you can only affect or interpret objects that exist in JavaScript. The built-in objects are listed separately following the table, while all others are presented in their hierarchical position. When an object functions as a property of another object, it is indented.

The way that objects are referred to in JavaScript is *object1.object2.property2*, in which *object1* is the highest level object, *object2* is a property of *object1*, and *property2* is a property of *object2*. An example is *navigator.plugins.name*, in which the *name* of the *plugins* object, which is itself a property of the *navigator* object, is referenced. The sections on properties and methods following will give you the tools you need to begin working with statements and functions.

TABLE 1
JavaScript Object Hierarchy

Object	Properties	Methods	Event Handlers
Window	defaultStatus	alert	onLoad
	frames	blur	onUnload
	opener	close	onBlur
	parent	confirm	onFocus
	scroll	focus	

Object	Properties	Methods	Event Handlers
	self	open	
	status	prompt	
	top	clearTimeout	
	window	setTimeout	
Frame	defaultStatus	alert	none (the onLoad and onUnload event handlers belong to the window object)
	frames	blur	
	opener	close	
	parent	confirm	
	scroll	focus	
	self	open	
	status	prompt	
	top	clearTimeout	
	window	setTimeout	
Location	hash	reload	none
	host	replace	
	hostname		
	href		
	pathname		
	port		

continues

3

TABLE 1, CONTINUED
JavaScript Object Hierarchy

Object	Properties	Methods	Event Handlers
	protocol		
	search		
History	length	back	none
	forward		
	go		
Navigator	appCodeName	javaEnabled	none
	appName		
	appVersion		
	mimeTypes		
	plugins		
	userAgent		
mimeTypes	description	none	none
	enabledPlugin		
	type		
	suffixes		
plugins	description	refresh	none
	filename		
	length		
	name		
document	alinkColor	clear	None (the onLoad and onUnload event handlers belong to the window object)

Object	Properties	Methods	Event Handlers
	anchors	close	
	applets	open	
	area	write	
	bgColor	writeln	
	cookie		
	fgColor		
	forms		
	images		
	lastModified		
	linkColor		
	links		
	location		
	referrer		
	title		
	vlinkColor		
applet	dependent on applet	dependent on applet	none
image	border	none	none
	complete		
	height		

continues

TABLE 1, CONTINUED
JavaScript Object Hierarchy

Object	Properties	Methods	Event Handlers
	hspace		
	lowsrc		
	name		
	src		
	vspace		
	width		
form	action	submit	onSubmit
	elements	reset	onReset
	encoding		
	FileUpload		
	method		
	name		
	target		
button	name	click	onClick
	type		
	value		
checkbox	checked	click	onClick
	defaultChecked		
	name		

Object	Properties	Methods	Event Handlers
	type		
	value		
FileUpload	name	none	none
	value		
hidden	defaultValue	none	none
	name		
	type		
	value		
password	defaultValue	blur	onBlur
	name	focus	onChange
	type	select	onFocus
	value		onSelect
radio	checked	click	onClick
	defaultChecked		
	name		
	type		
	value		
reset	name	click	onClick
	type		

continues

TABLE 1, CONTINUED
JavaScript Object Hierarchy

Object	Properties	Methods	Event Handlers
	value		
select	length	none	onBlur
	name		onChange
	options		onSelect
	selectedIndex		
	type		
options	defaultSelected	none	none
	index		
	length		
	name		
	selected		
	text		
	value		
submit	name	click	onClick
	type		
	value		
text	defaultValue	focus	onBlur
	name	blur	onChange
	type	select	onFocus

Object	Properties	Methods	Event Handlers
	value		onSelect
textarea	defaultValue	focus	onBlur
	name	blur	onChange
	type	select	onFocus
	value		onSelect
ink	hash	none	onClick
	host		onMouseOut
	hostname		onMouseOver
	href		
	pathname		
	port		
	protocol		
	search		
	target		
area	hash	none	onClick
	host		onMouseOut
	hostname		onMouseOver
	href		
	pathname		

continues

TABLE 1, CONTINUED
JavaScript Object Hierarchy

Object	Properties	Methods	Event Handlers
	port		
	protocol		
	search		
	target		
anchor	none	none	none

Built-in Objects

In addition to the objects that are extensible from the object hierarchy, JavaScript contains several built-in objects that exist independently of the hierarchy. These objects enable you to work with object types that are not otherwise defined. The *Date* object, for example, gives you the ability to work with date-type data that is not possible with the value types that JavaScript supports (which are *numbers, logical, strings*). To make a new object that is based on the Array, Date, or String objects, use the following syntax:

```
var MyDate = New Date();
```

Object	Properties	Methods	Event Handlers
Array	length	join	none
		reverse	
		sort	
Date	none	getDate	none
		getDay	
		getHours	
		getMinutes	

Object	Properties	Methods	Event Handlers
		getMonth	
		getSeconds	
		getTime	
		getTimeZoneoffset	
		getYear	
		parse	
		prototype	
		setDate	
		setHours	
		setMinutes	
		setMonth	
		setSeconds	
		setTime	
		setYear	
		toGMTString	
		toLocaleString	
		UTC	
Math	E	abs	none
	LN10	acos	
	LN2	asin	

continues

Object	Properties	Methods	Event Handlers
	PI	atan	
	SQRT1_2	atan2	
	SQRT2	ceil	
		cos	
		exp	
		floor	
		log	
		max	
		min	
		pow	
		random	
		round	
		sin	
		sqrt	
		tan	
		toString	
String	length	anchor	none
	prototype	big	
		blink	
		bold	

Object	Properties	Methods	Event Handlers
		charAt	
		fixed	
		fontColor	
		fontSize	
		indexOf	
		italics	
		lastIndexOf	
		link	
		small	
		split	
		strike	
		sub	
		substring	
		sup	
		toLowerCase	
		toUpperCase	

User-Defined Objects

In addition to the objects available to you in JavaScript, you are also able to create your own objects with properties and methods. To do this, you need to write a function that has the name of the object you want to create. Functions, discussed later in this appendix, are necessary here to define an object. Notice that the object's properties are referenced in the function's arguments.

```
function invoiceObject (custname, address, amount, duedate, custno) {
     this.custname = custname;
     this.address = address;
     this.amount = amount;
     this.duedate = duedate;
     this.custno = custno;
}
function OraclesUnpaidInvoice() {
     var OraclesUnpaidInvoice = new invoiceObject ("Oracle", "Redwood Shores,
CA", 5000, "April 25", "666Oracle");
}
```

In the preceding example, the *invoiceObject* object is defined by the *invoiceObject()* function. Once the object, along with its parameters, has been defined, the function *OraclesUnpaidInvoice()* creates a new invoice object with its own parameter values. In the example, the parameters for objects based on the *invoiceObject* are custname, address, amount, and custno. For *OraclesUnpaidInvoice*, the specific parameters are implemented and are associated with that particular *invoiceObject (e.g., Oracle, Redwood Shores, CA; 5000; etc.).* The keyword *this*, which will be seen later in the appendix, is an extremely useful keyword that describes the current object.

Properties

Now that you have been introduced to the objects available in JavaScript, you will see how to affect and interpret their properties. Following is an example of the syntax used to work with objects and their properties:

```
document.bgColor="FF00FF";
location.href evaluates to "http://www.browserbydesign.com";
```

Properties will be presented alphabetically within an alphabetical list of objects. The HTML and JavaScript (JS) examples follow each of the properties.

Area Object Properties

The area object is the JavaScript representation of the area tag used in client-side image maps. It uses the same properties as the link object.

hash

This property specifies the part of the URL address to the right of the hash mark (#). In the address ***http://www.x.com:80/doc.htm#test***, the *hash* property returns "***#test.***"

There is no corresponding HTML. It indicates an anchored reference within a document.

```
JS:   areaname.hash="#test";
```

host

This property specifies the domain name and port of the URL. In the address ***http:// www.x.com:80/some.htm#test***, the *host* property returns "***www.x.com:80***". There is no corresponding HTML.

```
JS:   areaname.host="www.x.com:80";
```

hostname

This property specifies the domain name of the URL. In the address ***http:// www.x.com:80/some.htm#test***, the *hostname* property returns "***www.x.com***". There is no corresponding HTML.

```
JS:   areaname.hostname="www.x.com";
```

href

This property specifies the entire URL. In the address ***http://www.x.com:80/ some.htm#test***, the *href* property returns "***http://www.x.com:80/some.htm#test*** ". There is no corresponding HTML.

```
JS:   areaname.href="http://www.x.com:80/some.htm#test"
```

pathname

This property specifies the pathname of the URL. In the address ***http:// www.x.com:80/test/some.htm#test***, the *pathname* property returns "***/test/some.htm***". There is no corresponding HTML.

```
JS:   areaname.pathname="/test/some.htm"
```

port

This property specifies the domain name of the URL. In the address ***http:// www.x.com:80/some.htm#test***, the ***port*** property returns "***:80***". There is no corresponding HTML.

```
JS:   areaname.port=":80"
```

protocol

This property specifies the protocol of the URL. In the address ***http://www.x.com:80/ some.htm#test***, the ***protocol*** property returns "***http:***". There is no corresponding HTML.

```
JS:   areaname.protocol="http:"
```

search

This property is a string beginning with a question mark (?) that specifies query information in the URL. The query information follows the question mark and its syntax is determined by the CGI program on the server where the query is directed.

```
HTML: <AREA COORDS="10,10,50,50" HREF="http:/www.xyx.com/quiz?q=12&a=blue"
NAME=firstLink>
JS:   firstLink.search="?q=12&a=blue";
```

target

This property designates the window or frame whose contents you want to change in response to a link or form request.

```
HTML: <AREA COORDS="10,10,50,50" HREF="1.htm" TARGET="MainFrame" NAME="MyArea">
JS:   MyArea.target evaluates to "MainFrame"
```

Array Object Properties

The Array object is new to Navigator 3.0. It is used to refer to more than one instance of a specific object. This can be used in conjunction with existing Navigator objects, such as images and links, as well as with user-defined objects (see the preceding example).

length

This property indicates the number of elements in an array. This could refer to anchors, links, or other element that is referred to using Array definition.

```
JS:   Arrays.length
```

Button Object Properties

The button object is the JavaScript representation of the button type form input tag.

name

This is used to reference the button object. Using the *name* property enables you to refer to an object by name, rather than using the full JavaScript hierarchy to refer to it.

HTML: <INPUT TYPE=BUTTON NAME=FirstButton>
JS: button.name evaluates to FirstButton

type

This property reflects the type attribute of the input tag. For buttons, the type attribute is button.

HTML: <INPUT TYPE=BUTTON NAME=FirstButton>
JS: FirstButton.type evaluates to BUTTON

value

This property reflects the value attribute of the input tag. For buttons, this refers to the text that appears on the button when displayed in the HTML page.

HTML: <INPUT TYPE=BUTTON NAME=FirstButton VALUE="Click Me">
JS: FirstButton.value evaluates to "Click Me"

Checkbox Object Properties

The Checkbox object is the JavaScript representation of the checkbox type form input tag.

checked

This is used with radio buttons and checkboxes. It indicates whether an option is selected. Unlike *defaultChecked*, this property refers to the state of the button at any moment, not just when the document is first opened.

HTML: <INPUT NAME=CheckMe TYPE=RADIO CHECKED>
JS: CheckMe.checked evaluates to True

defaultChecked

This is used with radio or checkbox form elements. It indicates that the form element has been checked or selected. The difference between this attribute and the *checked* attribute is that this determines the initial state of the form element. The default state for elements without this attribute is deselected.

```
HTML: <INPUT NAME=CheckMe TYPE=RADIO CHECKED>
JS:   CheckMe.defaultChecked evaluates to True
```

name

This is used to reference the checkbox object. Using the *name* property enables you to refer to an object by name, rather than using the full JavaScript hierarchy to refer to it.

```
HTML: <INPUT TYPE=CHECKBOX NAME=CheckMe>
JS:   checkbox.name evaluates to CheckMe
```

type

This property reflects the type attribute of the input tag. For the checkbox object, the type attribute is checkbox.

```
HTML: <INPUT TYPE=CHECKBOX NAME=CheckMe>
JS:   CheckMe.type evaluates to CHECKBOX
```

value

This property reflects the value attribute of the input tag. For the checkbox object, this refers to the information passed to the server based on the checkbox being selected.

```
HTML: <INPUT TYPE=CHECKBOX NAME=CheckMe VALUE="Selection A">
JS:   CheckMe.value evaluates to "Selection A"
```

Date Object Properties

The Date object is used to work with Date-type data.

prototype

This property is used to add properties to a Date object. There is no HTML equivalent.

```
JS:   MyDateObject.prototype.propertyName
```

Document Object Properties

The Document object is the JavaScript representation of the contents of the body tag.

alinkColor

This property determines the color of the text and borders of linked references while the mouse is clicked down on them. It accepts defined color names and hexadecimal numbers as valid values.

HTML: <BODY ALINK=FF0000>
```
JS:  document.alinkColor="FF0000";
```

anchors

The anchors array property specifies a named location that can be linked to by another document. This is an array property that uses an indexing method to refer to array elements on the page. As seen in the example, the indexing method defines the referenced element by referring to it. This is different from the link object that contains the HREF attribute. Both use the <A> tag.

HTML: <A NAME="AnchorText">Anchored Text</A>
```
JS:  document.anchors[0].name  evaluates to "AnchorText"
```

In examples where array objects are used, such as the anchors array property of the document object, the first indexed item is used as a reference. In this case, the first anchor tag in the document is named "***AnchorText***." The first indexed item in any array is referred to within the brackets following the array as number 0. The anchors array object has one property, length, which defines the number of anchors within a document.

applets

This is an array property that reflects the inclusion of Java applets within a document. The applets are referred to through the indexing method associated with array objects. The applets array object has one property, length, which defines the number of applets within a document.

HTML: <APPLET HEIGHT=100 WIDTH=100 NAME="FirstApp" CODE="somecode.class">
```
JS:  document.applets[0].name evaluates to "FirstApp"
```

bgcolor

This property reflects the background color of the HTML document. It accepts defined color names and hexadecimal numbers as valid values.

```
HTML:<BODY BGCOLOR=000000>
JS:   document.bgcolor="000000";
```

cookie

This property is used to read or write cookies on the client hard disk. Cookies are small text files that record information for future reference. This could include user preferences and other information for the server to use in future interaction with the user. There is no HTML equivalent.

```
JS:   document.cookie = "MyCookie=Large44D";
```

fgColor

This property defines the text color in the HTML document. It uses hexadecimal or special color names.

```
HTML: <BODY TEXT=000000>
JS:   document.fgColor=000000;
```

forms

This property is used to define forms within an HTML page. It uses either an indexed argument or the form name as an argument. The forms array object has one property, length, which defines the number of forms within a document. There is no corresponding HTML.

```
JS:   document.forms[0].element1.value="sometext";
```

images

This property is used to define images within an HTML page. It uses either an indexed argument or the image name as an argument. The images array object has one property, length, which defines the number of images within a document. There is no corresponding HTML.

```
JS:   document.images[0].src="http://www.browserbydesign.com/image.gif";
```

lastModified

This property represents the date that the document was last modified. It is read-only and has no HTML equivalent.

```
JS:  document.lastModified evaluates to July 31 12:00:00 1996
```

linkColor

This determines the color of linked text in the body of the HTML document for URLs that have not yet been visited.

HTML: <BODY LINK=FF0000>
```
JS:  document.linkColor="FF0000";
```

links

This is an array property that reflects the number of links in the document. There is no HTML equivalent. The links array object has one property, length, which defines the number of links within a document.

```
JS:  document.links[0]
```

location

This property is a string that specifies the complete URL of the document. This is a specific property of the document object, as opposed to the location object, which has its own properties. There is no corresponding HTML.

```
JS:  document.location evaluates to "http://www.pubnet.qc.ca/ben"
```

referrer

This property specifies the URL of the document that called the present document. There is no corresponding HTML equivalent.

```
JS:  document.referrer evaluates to "http://www.3pdesign.com"
```

title

This property represents the title of a document and is available to read only.

HTML: <TITLE>My Title</TITLE>
```
JS   document.title evaluates to "My Title"
```

vlinkColor

This property determines the text and border color of visited linked references within the HTML document. It accepts defined color names and hexadecimal numbers as valid values.

```
HTML: <BODY VLINK="#FF0000">
JS:   document.vlinkColor evaluates to "FF0000"
```

Form Object Properties

The form object is the JavaScript representation of the form tag from HTML.

action

This property references a specified URL that form contents will be sent to. This is usually a CGI program.

```
HTML: <FORM ACTION="http://domainname.com/cgi-bin">
JS: document.formName.action = "http://domainname.com/cgi-bin/myCgi";
```

elements

This array object is used with the Form object to describe form elements in a page. All input types are considered to be form elements. The individual form element is referred to by its indexed position or as a named object.

```
JS:   FirstForm.elements[0].value;
```

encoding

This property is used with forms or form elements. It indicates the type of encoding being used.

```
HTML: <FORM NAME=FirstForm ENCTYPE="multipart/form-data">
JS:   FirstForm.encoding evaluates to "multipart/form-data"
```

fileUpload

This property is used to enable the user to specify a file to load. It is new to Navigator 3.0. The file name to upload is provided by the user at runtime. The name parameter that is used with fileUpload is used for referencing the element, *not* for specifying the file to be uploaded.

```
HTML: <INPUT TYPE="file" NAME="UploadFile">
JS:   UploadFile.type evaluates to "file"
```

method

This determines how form field input information is processed. Possible values are get or post. Get is used to retrieve information, Post is used to send information.

```
HTML: <FORM NAME="TheForm" METHOD=POST>
JS:   TheForm.method="POST"
```

name

This property defines the name of the form.

```
HTML: <FORM NAME="FirstForm">
JS:   document.forms[0].name evaluates to "FirstForm"
```

target

This property designates the window or frame whose contents you want to change in response to a link or form request.

```
HTML: <FORM TARGET="MainFrame" NAME="FirstForm">
JS:   FirstForm.target evaluates to "MainFrame"
```

Frame Object Properties

From a JavaScript perspective, frames are windows. They share all the properties and methods of the window object. They do not have any event handlers associated with them. To include event handler functionality in a frame, the event handler would be included in the <BODY> tag of the document that is referred to by the SRC attribute of the <FRAME> tag.

defaultStatus

This indicates the message that appears in the status bar of the window when the document is first opened. There is no HTML equivalent.

```
JS:   window.defaultStatus = "Some text...";
```

frames

This array object property is used to define frames within an HTML page. The frame can be referenced by using the indexed number of its named reference. The frames array object has one property, length, which defines the number of child frames within a window. There is no corresponding HTML. A child frame is a frame contained within a frameset. The frameset document is considered the parent document.

```
JS:   window.frames.length evaluates to the number of frames within the window
```

opener

This property is new to Navigator 3.0. It refers to the window name of the calling document when a window is opened using the open method. There is no HTML equivalent.

JS: `window.opener="http://www.browserbydesign.com"`

parent

This property is used to describe a parent window within a framed page. The parent window is the one containing the frameset definition of the child window. There is no HTML equivalent.

JS: ***window.parent*** `evaluates to the parent window`

scroll

The scroll property is new to Navigator 3.0. It scrolls a window a specific number of pixels. Its arguments are number of pixels along the x and y axes.

JS: `window1.scroll(10,100) results in the window being scrolled 10 pixels to the right and 100 pixels down`

self

This property refers to the current window or frame. It is used to reduce ambiguity in code. There is no HTML equivalent.

JS: `self.status="Welcome to my Home Page.";`

status

This determines the text to display at the bottom of the Navigator window. There is no HTML equivalent.

JS: `window.status="Welcome to my home page"`

top

This property corresponds to the topmost ancestor window, which is its own parent. The property has three properties of its own: *defaultStatus*, *status*, and *length*. There is no HTML equivalent.

JS: ***top.frameName*** `evaluates to` ***FrameName*** `which is a child of the topmost window`

window

This property, which makes clear reference to the current window, is virtually synonymous in usage to *self*. It does not have a corresponding element in HTML.

```
JS:   window
```

Hidden Object Properties

The hidden object is the JavaScript representation of the hidden type form input tag.

defaultValue

This property determines the value of the form element when the document is first opened.

```
HTML: <INPUT TYPE=HIDDEN NAME=HideMe VALUE="some text">
JS:   HideMe.defaultValue evaluates to "some text"
```

name

This is used to reference the hidden object. Using the *name* property enables you to refer to an object by name, rather than using the full JavaScript hierarchy to refer to it.

```
HTML: <INPUT TYPE=HIDDEN NAME=HideMe>
JS:   hidden.name evaluates to HideMe
```

type

This property reflects the type attribute of the input tag. For hidden objects, the type attribute is hidden.

```
HTML: <INPUT TYPE=HIDDEN NAME=HideMe VALUE="some text">
JS:   HideMe.type evaluates to HIDDEN
```

value

This property reflects the value attribute of the input tag. For hidden objects, this refers to the text value assigned to the element using the VALUE attribute.

```
HTML: <INPUT TYPE=HIDDEN NAME=HideMe VALUE="some text">
JS:   HideMe.value evaluates to "some text"
```

History Object Properties

This object reflects the contents of the Go menu in Navigator.

length

This property reflects the number of sites in the history object that are visible under the Go menu.

```
JS:  history.length evaluates to an integer defining the number of pages
➥visited.
```

Image Object Properties

The image object is new to Navigator 3.0. It is the JavaScript representation of the image tag <IMG>. The image object is a property of the document object, like the images object. The primary difference between the images object, which is an array object, and the image object, is that the former uses indexing methods that are available to array objects. This can be seen in the following example:

```
document.images[0].src="somegif.gif"
```

If you were to do the same using the image object, you would probably use the name of the image object that you had used to define it, as seen here:

```
MyNamedImage = new Image([width],[height])
MyNamedImage.src = "somegif.gif"
```

The images object, like all array objects, has one property, length, which reflects the number of images in the document.

The preloading of images before they are actually needed for display is a particularly useful implementation of image creation and manipulation. For instance, if you wanted to design a page that had an image with multiple source files based on user interaction, you could make them load very quickly by creating a new image object and then placing it into your HTML page.

First, a function that contains statements that create the object and give it a source file needs to be executed. This can be done in the <BODY> tag using the *onLoad* event handler:

```
function onLoader() {
MyNamedImage = new Image(160,120)
MyNamedImage.src = "http://www.construct.net/deepBlueWorld.jpg"
}
```

Then, you include a second script that is associated with the event that you want to initiate the changing of the image. The image file will load very quickly because it had already been loaded into cache:

```
function ReplaceImage() {
document.images[0].src = MyNamedImage
}
```

If the above function was called by a mouse click or other event, the first image in the HTML document would be changed to the image defined by MyNamedImage.

border

This property determines the border width, as measured in pixels, that surrounds an image.

HTML: <IMG BORDER=5 SRC="some.gif">
JS: image.border = 5;

complete

This property determines whether an image is completely loaded. It is a read-only property and there is no HTML equivalent.

JS: imagename.complete

height

This property specifies the height of an image either in exact pixels or a percentage of the window height.

HTML: <IMG SRC="imageA.gif" NAME="imageA" HEIGHT=40>
JS: imageA.height evaluates to 40

hspace

This property specifies the horizontal space that surrounds an image and is measured in pixels.

HTML: <IMG SRC="imageA.gif" NAME="imageA" HSPACE=10>
JS: imageA.hspace evaluates to 10

length

This property belongs to the images object, not the image object. It reflects the number of images in a document. There is no HTML equivalent.

```
JS:  document.images.length evaluates to the integer number of images in the
 document.
```

lowsrc

This property is used to define a low-resolution image that is displayed in the page before the document specified by src is loaded.

```
HTML: <IMG SRC="some.gif" LOWSRC="someLowRes.gif" NAME="MyHiLoRes">
JS:   MyHiLoRes.lowsrc="someLowRes.gif"
```

src

This property is used to define the source file for a displayed image.

```
HTML: <IMG SRC="some.gif" LOWSRC="someLowRes.gif" NAME="MyHiLoRes">
JS:   MyHiLoRes.src="some.gif"
```

vspace

This property specifies the vertical space that surrounds an image and is measured in pixels.

```
HTML: <IMG SRC="imageA.gif" NAME="imageA" VSPACE=10>
JS:   imageA.vspace evaluates to 10
```

width

This property specifies the width of an image either in exact pixels or a percentage of the window width.

```
HTML: <IMG SRC="imageA.gif" NAME="imageA" WIDTH=40>
JS:   imageA.width evaluates to 40
```

Link Object Properties

The link object, as contrasted to the anchor object, includes an HREF attribute in the <A> tag definition. There is also a links array object, like the images and forms array objects, which has only one property, length, which reflects the number of links in the document. See the image object description for more information.

hash

This property specifies the part of the URL address to the right of the hash mark (#). In the address *http://www.x.com:80/doc.htm#test*, the *hash* property returns "#test".

There is no corresponding HTML. It indicates an anchored reference within a document.

```
JS:   linkName.hash="#test";
```

host

This property specifies the domain name and port of the URL. In the address ***http://www.x.com:80/some.htm#test***, the *host* property returns "***www.x.com:80***". There is no corresponding HTML.

```
JS:   linkName.host="www.x.com:80";
```

hostname

This property specifies the domain name of the URL. In the address ***http://www.x.com:80/some.htm#test***, the *hostname* property returns "***www.x.com***". There is no corresponding HTML.

```
JS:   linkName.hostname="www.x.com";
```

href

This property specifies the entire URL. In the address ***http://www.x.com:80/some.htm#test***, the *href* property returns "***http://www.x.com:80/some.htm#test*** ". There is no corresponding HTML.

```
JS:   linkName.href="http://www.x.com:80/some.htm#test"
```

length

This property belongs to the links object, not the link object. It reflects the number of links in a document. There is no HTML equivalent.

```
JS:   document.links.length evaluates to the integer number of links in the
document.
```

pathname

This property specifies the pathname of the URL. In the address ***http://www.x.com:80/test/some.htm#test***, the *pathname* property returns "***/test/some.htm***". There is no corresponding HTML.

```
JS:   linkName.pathname="/test/some.htm"
```

port

This property specifies the domain name of the URL. In the address ***http:// www.x.com:80/some.htm#test***, the ***port*** property returns "***:80***". There is no corresponding HTML.

```
JS:   linkName.port=":80"
```

protocol

This property specifies the protocol of the URL. In the address ***http://www.x.com:80/ some.htm#test***, the ***protocol*** property returns "***http:***". There is no corresponding HTML.

```
JS:   linkName.protocol="http:"
```

target

This property designates the window or frame whose contents you want to change in response to a link or form request.

```
HTML: <A HREF="1.htm" TARGET="MainFrame" NAME="First">
JS:   First.target evaluates to "MainFrame"
```

Location Object Properties

The location object is used to describe the URL of the window. It is a property of the window object.

hash

This property specifies the part of the URL address to the right of the hash mark (#). In the address ***http://www.x.com:80/doc.htm#test***, the hash property returns "#test". There is no corresponding HTML.

```
JS:   location.hash="#test";
```

host

This property specifies the domain name and port of the URL. In the address ***http:// www.x.com:80/some.htm#test***, the *host* property returns "***www.x.com:80***". There is no corresponding HTML.

```
JS:   location.host="www.x.com:80";
```

hostname

This property specifies the domain name of the URL. In the address ***http://www.x.com:80/some.htm#test***, the *hostname* property returns "***www.x.com***". There is no corresponding HTML.

```
JS:   location.hostname="www.x.com";
```

href

This property specifies the entire URL. In the address ***http://www.x.com:80/some.htm#test***, the *href* property returns "***http://www.x.com:80/some.htm#test***". There is no corresponding HTML.

```
JS:   location.href="http://www.x.com:80/some.htm#test"
```

pathname

This property specifies the pathname of the URL. In the address ***http://www.x.com:80/test/some.htm#test***, the *pathname* property returns "***/test/some.htm***". There is no corresponding HTML.

```
JS:   location.pathname="/test/some.htm"
```

port

This property specifies the domain name of the URL. In the address ***http://www.x.com:80/some.htm#test***, the ***port*** property returns "***:80***". There is no corresponding HTML.

```
JS:   location.port=":80"
```

protocol

This property specifies the protocol of the URL. In the address ***http://www.x.com:80/some.htm#test***, the ***protocol*** property returns "***http:***". There is no corresponding HTML.

```
JS:   location.protocol="http:"
```

search

This property is a string beginning with a question mark (?) that specifies query information in the URL.

```
HTML: <A HREF="http:/www.xyx.com/quiz?q=12&a=blue" NAME=firstLink>
JS:   firstLink.search="?q=12&a=blue";
```

Math Object Properties

The Math object extends the JavaScript language by providing constant values, in the form of properties, and conversion processes, in the form of methods. Constant values, such as pi, provide a shorthand way for engineers and other technical professionals to refer to important, often used mathematical values. Conversion processes, such as determining a square root, are performed by methods, which are featured later in this appendix.

E

This property gives Euler's constant as a value. This constant is used in differential calculus equations and is represented in math formulas as E. There is no HTML equivalent.

```
JS:   Math.E evaluates to 2.718282
```

LN2

This value corresponds to the natural logarithm of two, which is approximately 0.693. There is no HTML equivalent.

```
JS:   Math.LN2 evaluates to 0.693
```

LN10

This value corresponds to the natural logarithm of 10, which is approximately 2.302. There is no HTML equivalent.

```
JS:   Math.LN2 evaluates to 2.302
```

PI

This references the constant number that is equal to the ratio of the circumference of a circle compared to its diameter. There is no corresponding HTML.

```
JS:   Math.PI evaluates to 3.1416
```

SQRT1_2

This property represents the square root of one-half, approximately 0.707. There is no HTML equivalent.

```
JS:Math.SQRT1_2 evaluates to 0.707
```

SQRT2

This property represents the square root of two, approximately 1.414. There is no HTML equivalent.

```
JS:Math.SQRT2 evaluates to 1.414
```

mimeTypes Object Properties

The mimeTypes object is a property of the navigator object. It is used to determine whether a certain file type is supported.

description

The *description* property describes the file format type of the referenced MIME type.

```
JS:   navigator.mimeTypes[image/jpeg].description evaluates to "JPEG Image plug"
```

enabledPlugins

The *enabledPlugins* property reflects the plug-in that will display a file type. This was still being implemented as this book went to press.

type

This property provides the MIME type name of a specific file format, such as application/director or image/jpeg.

```
JS:   navigator.mimeTypes[4].type evaluates to "image/jpeg" (the number of the
mimeTypes element is arbitrary)
```

suffixes

The *suffixes* property lists the various suffixes of file names that will be recognized as being a specific MIME type.

```
JS:   navigator.mimeTypes[image/jpeg].suffixes evaluates to "jpeg, jpg, jpe,
jfif, pjpeg, pjp"
```

Navigator Object Properties

The navigator object is used by JavaScript to determine characteristics about the browser itself. Information such as the operating system and version number are associated with this object.

appCodeName

This is a read-only property that gives the code name of the browser that is being used.

```
JS:   navigator.appCodeName evaluates to Mozilla
```

appName

This is a read-only property that gives the name of the browser that is being used.

```
JS:   navigator.appName evaluates to Netscape
```

appVersion

This is a read-only property that gives the version number of the browser that is being used.

```
JS:   navigator.appVersion evaluates to 3.0b4
```

javaEnabled

This is a read-only property that is new to Navigator 3.0 and later. It returns true if the browser is Java-enabled. If the browser supports Java, but has been switched off by the user, the property returns false.

```
JS:   navigator.javaEnabled evaluates to True (or 1)
```

mimeTypes

The *mimeTypes* property is a read-only property that is new to Navigator 3.0 and later. It is an array property that reflects all the file formats supported by the browser. It also has one property, length, which gives the number of mimeTypes that are available to the browser.

```
JS:   navigator.mimeTypes.length evaluates to the number of MIME types supported
by the browser.
```

plugins

The plugins property is a read-only property that is new to Navigator 3.0 and later. It is an array property that reflects all the plug-ins presently installed for the browser. It also has one property, length, which gives the number of plug-ins that are available to the browser.

```
JS:   navigator.plugins.length evaluates to the number of plugins available to
the browser.
```

userAgent

This property is a string value that identifies the client browser to the host server. It is a read-only property and has no HTML equivalent. It includes the appCodeName, appVersion, and operating system information.

```
JS:   navigator.userAgent evaluates to Mozilla/3.0b5 (Win32;I)
```

Options Object Properties

The options object is the JavaScript representation of an option tag occurring within a select tag.

defaultSelected

This property determines the default state of an option object. It indicates that the option is selected when the document is first opened. Without this, the default is unselected.

HTML: `<OPTION VALUE="Moderate" SELECTED NAME="optionname">`
```
JS:   optionname.defaultSelected
```

index

This property reflects the index of an option within a select group. There is no corresponding HTML.

```
JS:   selectGroupName.options[indexNumber].
```

length

This property reflects the number of options within a select group. There is no HTML equivalent.

```
JS:   selectName.options.length evaluates to the number of options in the select
↪group
```

name

This property names the option. It is not displayed in the browser.

HTML: `<OPTION NAME="MyOption">`
```
JS:   selectName.options[0].name evaluates to "MyOption"
```

selected

This property determines whether an option in a select object has been selected.

HTML: `<OPTION SELECTED VALUE="Blue">Blue`
JS: `options[0].selected evaluates to TRUE`

selectedIndex

This property represents the option selected in a select object. It can be used with either the select object or the *options* array property of the select object. There is no HTML equivalent.

JS: `selectObject.options.selectedIndex evaluates to the selected option`

text

This property designates the text value of a selected option that is displayed in the browser.

HTML: `<OPTION SELECTED VALUE="TheBest">My Selection`
JS: `FormName.options[0].text evaluates to "My Selection"`

value

This property designates the value of a selected option. This value is used for the server and is not displayed in the browser.

HTML: `<OPTION SELECTED VALUE="TheBest">My Selection`
JS: `FormName.options[0].text evaluates to "TheBest"`

PASSWORD Object Properties

The PASSWORD object is the JavaScript representation of the password type form input tag.

defaultValue

This property determines the value of the form element when the document is first opened.

HTML: `<INPUT TYPE=PASSWORD NAME=MyPass VALUE="some text">`
JS: `MyPass.defaultValue evaluates to "some text"`

name

This is used to reference the password object. Using the *name* property enables you to refer to an object by name, rather than using the full JavaScript hierarchy to refer to it.

```
HTML: <INPUT TYPE=PASSWORD NAME=MyPass>
JS:   password.name evaluates to MyPass
```

type

This property reflects the type attribute of the input tag. For password objects, the type attribute is password.

```
HTML: <INPUT TYPE=PASSWORD NAME=MyPass VALUE="some text">
JS:   MyPass.type evaluates to PASSWORD
```

value

This property reflects the value attribute of the input tag. For password objects, this refers to the text value assigned to the element using the VALUE attribute.

```
HTML: <INPUT TYPE=PASSWORD NAME=MyPass VALUE="some text">
JS:   MyPass.value evaluates to "some text"
```

Plug-In Object Properties

The plug-in object is new to Navigator 3.0. It is a property of the navigator object.

description

The *description* property is provided by the plug-in to the browser. It describes the plug-in.

```
JS:   navigator.plugins[0].description evaluates to "Live3D Plugin Library"
```

fileName

This property reflects the plug-in file that interprets a MIME type. This is not the file that is being viewed, but the file that permits the file to be viewed.

```
JS:   navigator.plugins[0].filename evaluates to
"c:\atlas\program\program\plugins\npl3d32.dll"
```

length

This property is a read-only property that gives the number of plug-ins available to the browser.

```
JS:  navigator.plugins.length evaluates to the number of plugins installed
```

mimeTypes

This property is used to tell whether a plug-in supports a specific MIME type. It returns true if the MIME type is supported by the plug-in.

```
JS:  navigator.plugins[0].mimeTypes[application/director] evaluates to FALSE
```

name

This property is a read-only property that reflects the name of the selected plug-in.

```
JS:  navigator.plugins[0].name evaluates to "Live3D Plugin DLL"
```

Radio Object Properties

The Radio object is the JavaScript representation of the radio type form input tag.

checked

This is used with radio buttons and checkboxes. It indicates whether an option is selected. Unlike *defaultChecked*, this property refers to the state of the button at any moment, not just when the document is first opened.

```
HTML: <INPUT TYPE=RADIO CHECKED>
JS:  radiobuttonname.checked
```

defaultChecked

This is used with radio or checkbox form elements. It indicates that the form element has been checked or selected. The difference between this attribute and the *checked* attribute is that this determines the initial state of the form element. The default state for elements without this attribute is deselected.

```
HTML: <INPUT TYPE=RADIO CHECKED>
JS:  radiobuttonname.defaultChecked
```

name

This property names the radio button. It is not displayed in the browser.

```
HTML: <FORM>
        <INPUT TYPE="RADIO" NAME="option1">
        ...
      </FORM>
JS:   formName.elements[0].name evaluates to "option1"
```

type

This property reflects the type attribute of the input tag. For radio objects, the type attribute is radio.

```
HTML: <INPUT TYPE=RADIO NAME=MyRadio VALUE="some text">
JS:   MyRadio.type evaluates to RADIO
```

value

This property defines the value of radio form elements. This is a reflection of the VALUE attribute. It is displayed in the browser.

```
HTML: <INPUT TYPE=RADIO NAME=MyRadio VALUE="some text">
JS:   MyRadio.value evaluates to "some text"
```

Reset Object Properties

The reset object is the JavaScript representation of the reset type form input tag.

name

This property names the reset button. It is not displayed in the browser.

```
HTML: <INPUT TYPE="RESET" VALUE="Click to Refresh" NAME="ResetMe">
JS:   formName.elements[0].name evaluates to "ResetMe"
```

type

This property reflects the type attribute of the input tag. For reset objects, the type attribute is reset.

```
HTML: <INPUT TYPE="RESET" VALUE="Click to Refresh" NAME="ResetMe">
JS:   ResetMe.type evaluates to RESET
```

value

This property defines the text that appears on the reset button. This is a reflection of the VALUE attribute. It is displayed in the browser.

```
HTML: <INPUT TYPE="RESET" VALUE="Click to Refresh" NAME="ResetMe">
JS:   ResetMe.value evaluates to "Click to Refresh"
```

Select Object Properties

The select object is the JavaScript representation of the select tag. It appears in the browser as either a pull-down menu or as a list with a scroll bar (if necessary).

length

This property reflects the number of options within a select group. There is no HTML equivalent.

```
JS:   selectName.length evaluates to the number of options in the select group
```

name

This property names the select group. It is not displayed in the browser.

```
HTML: <SELECT NAME="MyGroup">
JS:   formName.elements[0].name evaluates to "MyGroup"
```

options

This is an array property that contains an entry for each option in a select object. It has the following properties: *defaultSelected, index, length, name, selected, selectedIndex, text,* and *value.*

```
HTML: <OPTION NAME="anyName" VALUE="None of the above">
JS:   selectName.options[0].value="None of the above"
```

selectedIndex

This property represents the option selected in a select object. It can be used with either the select object or the *options* array property of the select object. There is no HTML equivalent.

```
JS:   selectObject.options.selectedIndex evaluates to the selected option
```

type

This property is used if you need to use the MULTIPLE attribute of the <SELECT> tag.

```
HTML: <SELECT TYPE=MULTIPLE NAME=MultiSelect>
```

```
JS:  MultiSelect.type evaluates to MULTIPLE
```

String Object Properties

The String object is a built-in object that enables JavaScript to use text, or string, variables.

length

This property indicates the number of characters in a string object. There is no HTML equivalent.

```
JS:  string.length evaluates to the number of characters in the string
```

prototype

This property is used to add properties and methods to the String, Date, and User-Defined objects. There is no HTML equivalent.

```
JS:  StringObjectName.prototype.proporMethName = nameofExistingFunction
```

In this case, the function named *nameofExistingFunction* was created to give definition to the prototype property. All objects of the type StringObjectName will now have a property or method titled *proporMethName* associated with them that is based on the function *nameofExistingFunction*.

Submit Object Properties

The submit object is the JavaScript representation of the submit type form input tag.

name

This property names the submit button. It is not displayed in the browser.

```
HTML: <INPUT TYPE="SUBMIT" VALUE="Submission Time" NAME="TheSubmitButton">
JS:  formName.elements[0].name evaluates to "TheSubmitButton"
```

type

This property reflects the type attribute of the input tag. For submit objects, the type attribute is submit.

```
HTML: <INPUT TYPE="SUBMIT" VALUE="Submission Time"
NAME="TheSubmitButton">
JS:  TheSubmitButton.type evaluates to SUBMIT
```

value

This property defines the text that appears on the submit button. This is a reflection of the VALUE attribute. It is displayed in the browser.

```
HTML: <INPUT TYPE="SUBMIT" VALUE="Submission Time"
➥NAME="TheSubmitButton">
JS:   TheSubmitButton.value evaluates to "Submission Time"
```

Textarea Object Properties

The textarea object is the JavaScript representation of the textarea tag.

defaultValue

The *defaultValue* property defines the value of a textarea object as the page is first loaded. This is determined by the VALUE attribute of the <INPUT> tag. The difference between this attribute and the *value* attribute is that this determines the initial state of the form element. The default state for elements without this attribute is blank text.

```
HTML: <TEXTAREA VALUE="Text to appear" NAME="MyTextArea">
JS:   MyTextArea.defaultValue evaluates to "Text to appear"
```

name

This property names the text object. It is not displayed in the browser.

```
HTML: <TEXTAREA VALUE="Text to appear" NAME="MyTextArea">
JS:   formName.elements[0].name evaluates to "MyTextArea"
```

type

This property reflects the type attribute of the input tag. For text objects, the type attribute is text.

```
HTML: <TEXTAREA VALUE="Text to appear" NAME="MyTextArea">
JS:   MyTextArea.type evaluates to TEXTAREA
```

value

This property defines the text that appears in the textarea box. Unlike *defaultValue*, this property refers to the text that appears in the textarea box at any time, including when it is first loaded and any time that the text is changed.

```
HTML: <TEXTAREA VALUE="Text to appear" NAME="MyTextArea">
JS:   MyTextArea.value evaluates to "Text to appear"
```

Text Object Properties

The text object is the JavaScript representation of the text type form input tag.

defaultValue

The *defaultValue* property defines the value of a text object as the page is first loaded. This is determined by the VALUE attribute of the <INPUT> tag. The difference between this attribute and the *value* attribute is that this determines the initial state of the form element. The default state for elements without this attribute is blank text.

```
HTML: <INPUT TYPE="TEXT" VALUE="Text to appear" NAME="MyText">
JS:   MyText.defaultValue evaluates to "Text to appear"
```

name

This property names the text object. It is not displayed in the browser.

```
HTML: <INPUT TYPE="TEXT" VALUE="Text to appear" NAME="MyText">
JS:   formName.elements[0].name evaluates to "MyText"
```

type

This property reflects the type attribute of the input tag. For text objects, the type attribute is text.

```
HTML: <INPUT TYPE="TEXT" VALUE="Text to appear" NAME="MyText">
JS:   MyText.type evaluates to TEXT
```

value

This property defines the text that appears in the text box. Unlike *defaultValue*, this property refers to the text that appears in the text box at any time, including when it is first loaded and any time that the text is changed.

```
HTML: <INPUT TYPE="TEXT" VALUE="Text to appear" NAME="MyText">
JS:   MyText.value evaluates to "Text to appear"
```

User-Defined Object Properties

prototype

This property is used to add properties and methods to the String, Date, and User-Defined objects. There is no HTML equivalent.

```
JS:  UserDefinedObjectName.prototype.proporMethName = nameofExistingFunction
```

In this case, the function named *nameofExistingFunction* was created to give definition to the prototype property. All objects of the type UserDefinedObjectName will now have a property or method titled *proporMethName* associated with them that is based on the function *nameofExistingFunction*.

Window Object Properties

defaultStatus

This indicates the message that appears in the status bar of the window when the document is first opened. There is no HTML equivalent.

```
JS:  window.defaultStatus = "Some text...";
```

frames

This array object property is used to define frames within an HTML page. The frame can be referenced by using the indexed number of its named reference. The frames array object has one property, length, which defines the number of child frames within a window. There is no corresponding HTML. A child frame is a frame contained within a frameset. The frameset document is considered the parent document.

```
JS:  window.frames.length evaluates to the number of frames within the window
```

opener

This property is new to Navigator 3.0. It refers to the window name of the calling document when a window is opened using the open method. There is no HTML equivalent.

```
JS:  window.opener="http://www.browserbydesign.com"
```

parent

This property is used to describe a parent window within a framed page. The parent window is the one containing the frameset definition of the child window. There is no HTML equivalent.

JS: **window.parent** evaluates to the parent window

scroll

The scroll property is new to Navigator 3.0. It scrolls a window a specific number of pixels. Its arguments are number of pixels along the x and y axes.

JS: **window1.scroll(10,100) results in the window being scrolled 10 pixels to the right and 100 pixels down**

self

This property refers to the current window or frame. It is used to reduce ambiguity in code. There is no HTML equivalent.

JS: self.status="Welcome to my Home Page.";

status

This determines the text to display at the bottom of the Navigator window. There is no HTML equiavalent.

JS: window.status="Welcome to my home page"

top

This property corresponds to the topmost ancestor window, which is its own parent. The property has three properties of its own: *defaultStatus*, *status*, and *length*. There is no HTML equivalent.

JS: **top.frameName** evaluates to **FrameName** which is a child of the top most window

window

This property, which makes clear reference to the current window, is virtually synonymous in usage to *self*. It does not have a corresponding element in HTML.

JS: window.status="This appears in the status bar"

Methods and Built-in Functions

Methods, unlike properties, act as modifiers to objects. Where properties describe objects, methods and objects have an adverbial relationship. Functions are used to designate additional properties, which will apply to the object(s) with which they are associated in the function. Using an English parts of speech metaphor, the method takes the place of the verb; the object takes the place of the subject; the argument (which is contained within parentheses) takes the place of the direct or indirect object. An example is the alert() method of the window object. Its argument displays as text in a window created by the method. Consider the following contrast between speech and JavaScript:

The Math object calculates the square root of x.

```
Math.sqrt(x)
```

Here, the Math object is the subject, the sqrt() method performs the verb function, while x is used as the indirect object. Technically, methods are functions, and functions are statements. In usage; however, they perform very differently:

Statements: Direct the flow of the JavaScript.

Functions: Group statements together into units that can be regularly called without having to rewrite the statements you want performed.

Methods and built-in functions: Special functions that do not require statements within braces ({}). Because the function they perform is understood by JavaScript, all that is needed for the method to activate is an argument.

In the following example, the argument 16 is treated in a predefined manner to determine its square root:

```
Math.sqrt(16) evaluates to 4
```

Compare this to the PI property of the math object that, as seen here, functions as an object itself.

```
Math.PI*3 evaluates to 9.425
```

Objects and properties can often be thought of interchangeably, although at the end of the object chain, properties perform a task similar to adjectives in human languages. For example, the document object has the form property. Form is also considered an object with its own set of properties, some of which also have their own properties. At the furthest link of the chain, properties define their object with names, numeric values, or other expression types.

The following methods and built-in functions are available in JavaScript. They are listed alphabetically under the objects to which they belong.

Array Object Methods

join

This is a new property to Navigator 3.0. It is used to join the elements in an array into a single string. It uses a separator as an argument that is used to divide the strings into logical entities. If no character is entered, a comma (,) is used by default. There is no HTML equivalent. In the example below, the ArrayofNoise object was created, which has three elements. The join() method using the argument "and " results in the joining of the three using the argument to separate the elements.

```
JS:   ArrayofNoise = new Array("Loud","Heated","Electric")
JS:   ArrayofNoise.join("and ")evaluates to "Loud and Heated and Electric"
```

reverse

This method reverses the order of elements in an array. For example, if you have five elements, the fifth element becomes number zero, the first becomes number four (remember that indexing results in the first number starting at zero). There is no HTML equivalent.

```
JS:   MyArray = new Array("x","y","z")
JS:   MyArray.reverse() evaluates to "z","y","x"
JS:   MyArray evaluates to {"z", "y", "x"}
```

sort

This method sorts elements in an array as determined by its argument, which is generally a function. If no argument is given, the elements are sorted alphabetically. There is no HTML equivalent.

```
JS:   MyArray = new Array("a", "m", "b");
JS:   MyArray.sort();
JS:   MyArray evaluates to {"a", "b", "m"}
```

Button Object Methods

click

This method performs the same action as if you clicked the button. There is no HTML equivalent.

```
JS:   NoiseForm.Button1.click();
```

Checkbox Object Methods

click

This method toggles between being selected and deselected. There is no HTML equivalent.

```
JS:   NoiseForm.Checkbox1.click();
```

Date Object Methods

getDate

This method returns the day of the month for the specified date. Its value is between 1 and 31. There is no HTML equivalent.

```
JS:   MyDate=new Date("November 5, 1996 11:15:00")
JS:   DateObject.getDate(MyDate) evaluates to 5;
```

getDay

This method returns the day of the week for the specified date. Its value is between 0 and 6, representing Sunday through Saturday. There is no HTML equivalent. November 5 is on a Tuesday, which is represented by the number 2.

```
JS:   MyDate=new Date("November 5 November 5, 1996 11:15:00");
JS:   DateObject.getDay(MyDate) evaluates to 2;
```

getHours

This method returns the hour using the 24-hour clock of an event on a specified date. Its value is between 0 and 23, representing 12:00 AM to 11:00 PM. There is no HTML equivalent.

```
JS:   MyDate=new Date("November 5, 1996 11:15:00");
JS:   DateObject.getHours(MyDate) evaluates to 11;
```

getMinutes

This method returns the minutes of an event on a specified date. Its value is between 0 and 59. There is no HTML equivalent.

```
JS:   MyDate=new Date("November 5, 1996 11:15:00")
JS:   DateObject.getMinutes(MyDate) evaluates to 15
```

getMonth

This method returns the month of the year for the specified date. Its value is between 0 and 11, representing January through December. There is no HTML equivalent.

```
JS:   MyDate=new Date("November 5, 1996 11:15:00")
JS:   DateObject.getMonth(MyDate) evaluates to 10
```

getSeconds

This method returns the seconds of an event on a specified date. Its value is between 0 and 59. There is no HTML equivalent.

```
JS:   MyDate=new Date("November 5, 1996 11:15:00")
JS:   DateObject.getSeconds(MyDate) evaluates to 0
```

getTime

This method returns the number of milliseconds that have passed since January 1, 1970 00:00:00. It is often used to assign relative relationships between date objects.

```
JS:   MyDate=new Date("November 5, 1996 11:15:00");
JS:   mydate.getTime() evaluates to 847224900000
```

getTimezoneOffset

This method returns the time zone offset in minutes for the current locale. This regards daylight savings time, and is generally between +60 and –60.

```
JS:   mydate.getTimezoneOffset() evaluates to 0
```

getYear

This method returns the year for the specified date. You subtract 1900 from the value it returns to calcluate the year. Due to limitations, it cannot calculate years prior to 1904 or after 2037. There is no HTML equivalent.

```
JS:   MyDate=new Date("November 5, 1996 11:15:00")
JS:   DateObject.getYear(MyDate) evaluates to 96
```

parse

This built-in function returns the number of milliseconds since January 1, 1970 00:00:00 GMT for its string argument. It uses the built-in Date object, not a user-defined Date object. This is often used in conjunction wth the setTime method to establish comparative date values. There is no HTML equivalent.

```
JS:   MyDateObj.setTime(Date.parse("Jan 1, 1997"));
```

setDate

This method sets or resets the day of the month for a specified date. Valid values are between 1 and 31. There is no HTML equivalent.

```
JS:   DateObject.setDate(13);
```

setHours

This method sets or resets the hour using the 24-hour clock for an event on a specified date. Valid values are between 0 and 23, representing 12:00 AM to 11:00 PM. There is no HTML equivalent.

```
JS:   DateObject.setHours(10);
```

setMinutes

This method sets or resets the minutes for an event on a specified date. Valid values are between 0 and 59. There is no HTML equivalent.

```
JS:   DateObject.setMinutes(15);
```

setMonth

This method sets or resets the month of the year for a specified event. Valid values are between 0 and 11, representing January through December. There is no HTML equivalent.

```
JS:   DateObject.setMonth(8);
```

setSeconds

This method sets or resets the seconds for an event on a specified date. Valid values are between 0 and 59. There is no HTML equivalent.

```
JS:   DateObject.setSeconds(30);
```

setTime

This method sets or resets the number of milliseconds that have passed since January 1, 1970 00:00:00 for a particular event. It is generally used to assign relative relationships between date objects.

```
JS:   MyFuturePlan=new Date("December 31, 1999");
```

```
JS:   MyFriendsPlan=new Date();
JS:   MyFriendsPlan.setTime(MyFuturePlan.getTime());
```

setYear

This method sets or resets the year for a specified event. You subtract 1900 from the value it returns to calcluate the year. Due to limitations, it cannot calculate years prior to 1904 or after 2037. There is no HTML equivalent.

```
JS:   DateObject.setYear(97);
```

toGMTString

This method converts a Date object into a String object using the Internet GMT conventions. There is no HTML equivalent.

```
JS:   MyDate.toGMTString() evaluates to Tue, 05 Nov 1996 20:15:00 (Notice that
the book was written in California during daylight savings time. This explains
the 8 hour difference between the time selected and the time revealed by this
method.)
```

toLocaleString

This method converts a Date object into a String object using the current locale's conventions. The date format varies depending on the operating system. There is no HTML equivalent.

```
JS:   MyDate.toLocaleString();
```

UTC

This method returns the number of milliseconds that have passed since January 1, 1970 00:00:00 and its argument. The UTC method takes comma-delimited date parameters for its argument. There is no HTML equivalent.

```
JS:   MyDate = new Date(Date.UTC(97, 10, 1, 0, 0, 0));
JS:   MyDate evaluates to "October 1, 1997 00:00:00"
```

Document Object Methods

clear

This method clears the contents of a window. There is no HTML equivalent.

```
JS:   windowName.document.clear();
```

close

This method stops incoming data and forces data already received to be displayed. **Document: Done** is displayed in the status bar when this method is enacted. There is no HTML equivalent. In Navigator 3.0 and later, the user is asked to confirm when the window is closed.

```
JS:   MyString="Some Text.";
JS:   MyNamedWindow.document.open();
JS:   MyNamedWindow.document.write(MyString);
JS:   MyNamedWindow.document.close();
```

open

This method opens a stream for collecting the output of write and writeln methods. The method uses a two part MIME type as its argument. If none are provided, it assumes it is text/html. Valid arguments for this method are text/html; text/plain; image/gif; image/jpeg; image/x-bitmap; and two part plug-in descriptions, such as application/x-director. There is no corresponding HTML.

```
JS:   MyString="Some Text.";
JS:   MyNamedWindow=window.open();
JS:   MyNamedWindow.document.open();JS:
➥MyNamedWindow.document.write(MyString);
JS:   MyNamedWindow.document.close();
```

write

This method is used to write HTML expressions in a specified window. For event handlers, you must use the writeln method. There is no HTML equivalent.

```
JS:   MyString="face";
JS:   document.write("In your ", Mystring) evaluates to "In your face"
```

writeln

This method writes HTML expressions in a specified window. The difference between write and writeln is that the latter inserts a carriage return after the text. There is no HTML equivalent.

```
JS:   MyString="face";
JS:   document.writeln("In your ", Mystring)evaluates to "In your face";
```

Form Object Methods

reset

This method performs the same action as if you clicked on the reset button. There is no HTML equivalent.

```
JS:  Mydocument.CheatSheetForm.reset();
```

submit

This method performs the same action as if you clicked on the submit button. It is generally used to send information to and from the server. There is no HTML equivalent.

```
JS:  Mydocument.CheatSheetForm.submit();
```

Frame Object Methods

Technically speaking, the frame object is a window object. It therefore shares the properties and methods of the window object. Unlike the window object, the frame object cannot access event handlers. For this reason, event handlers such as *onLoad* are not available to the <FRAME> tag. They are contained within the <BODY> tag of the HTML document that occupies the frame.

alert

This method displays an Alert dialog box with a text message and an OK button. There is no HTML equivalent.

```
JS:  alert("I have something to say.");
```

blur

This method in Navigator 3.0 now applies to the *frame* and *window* objects, as well as form *elements*. Blurring a form element or window refers to removing it from the "*focus*". In the case of a textbox, it would be when you clicked into another form element or the HTML page itself. In the case of a window, it would be when you directed your computer to display the screen from another application. The browser no longer has the "*focus*" of the computer. There is no HTML equivalent.

```
JS:  formElementName.blur();
```

clearTimeout

This method cancels a timeout that was set using the setTimeout method. There is no HTML equivalent.

```
JS:   clearTimeout(aNamedTimer);
```

close

This method closes the active window. There is no HTML equivalent.

```
JS:   frameName.close();
```

confirm

This method displays a Confirm dialog box with a text message and OK and Cancel buttons. It uses a string object as its argument. If OK is selected, the method returns *true*; if Cancel is selected, it returns *false*. There is no HTML equivalent.

```
JS:   confirm("Are you sure you want to leave the Web site already?");
```

focus

This method in Navigator 3.0 now applies to the *frame* and *window* objects, as well as form *elements*. Focusing a form element or window means bringing the cursor or the window itself into an active state. In the case of a window, it would be when you directed your computer to display the browser after having viewed another application. The browser then has the *"focus"* of the computer. There is no HTML equivalent.

```
JS:   formElementName.focus();
```

open

This method opens a new browser window. It is able to control several features in the new window. Each of the parameters in its argument control a different feature. If you want to display a toolbar or hide one, you would set the window display "toolbars=yes" or "toolbars=no," respectively. Notice that no spaces are placed between the parameters. The first two parameters; URL, which gives the HREF, and the name of the window are required arguments. If you want to open a window that is not associated with an URL, use empty quotation marks (""). Naming the window enables you to target it from another window or frame. Values for each of the additional parameters can be set to yes or no, 1 or 0. They are not required arguments. There is no HTML equivalent. The method and its arguments are presented in the following example.

```
JS:   MyWindow=window.open("URL", "Window
Name",["toolbars=yes","location=yes","directories=yes","status=yes","menubar=yes",
➥"scrollbars=yes", "resizable=yes","width=PixelValue","height=PixelValue"]);
```

prompt

This method is used to prompt a visitor to your Web page to enter a response. It uses
two arguments: the message you want displayed, and an initial value for the prompt
box. The initial value, if blank, should be indicated by using empty quotation marks
(""). There is no HTML equivalent.

```
JS:   prompt("What name will you be using?", "");
```

setTimeout

This method evaluates an expression after a specified number of milliseconds have
passed. In the following example, MyTimer identifies the timer in order for the
clearTimeout method to cancel it.

```
JS:   MyTimer=setTimeout("alert('Time up!');",10000);
```

History Object Methods

back

This method performs the same function as history.go(-1). It reloads the previous
URL in the history object (the page you were just at). There is no HTML equivalent.

```
JS:   history.back();
```

forward

This method advances to the next URL in the history list. It performs the same act as
the forward button in the browser. There is no HTML equivalent. Both methods in
the following examples do the same thing.

```
JS:   history.forward();
JS:   history.go(1);
```

go

This method is used to navigate through the browser's current history. It uses an
integer or an URL as its argument. The current page is numbered zero (0); positive
numbers go forward in history, negative numbers go backward in history. If the
location argument is a string, **go** loads the nearest history entry whose URL contains

the location as a substring. URL matching is not case-sensitive. There is no HTML equivalent.

```
JS:  history.go(-1);
JS:  history.go("http://www.browserbydesign.com");
```

Location Object Methods

reload

This method is new to Navigator 3.0. It reloads the window's current document. There is no HTML equivalent.

```
JS:  location.reload();
```

replace

This method is new to Navigator 3.0. It replaces the present document with the one referred to as a parameter. There is no HTML equivalent.

```
JS:  location.replace("http://www.typo.com/");
```

Math Object Methods

abs

This method returns the absolute value of a number. The absolute value of a number is the distance between the number and zero. There is no HTML equivalent.

```
JS:  Math.abs(-23) evaluates to 23
```

acos

This method returns the arc cosine of a number in radians. There is no HTML equivalent.

```
JS:  Math.acos(.3) evaluates to 1.266
```

asin

This method returns the arc sine of a number in radians. There is no HTML equivalent.

```
JS:  Math.asin(.3) evaluates to 0.3047
```

atan

This method returns the arc tangent of a number in radians. There is no HTML equivalent.

JS: `Math.atan(.3)` evaluates to `0.3093`

atan2

This method is new to Navigator 3.0. It returns the angle (theta component) of the polar coordinate (r, theta) that corresponds to its argument: a specific cartesian coordinate. There is no HTML equivalent.

JS: `Math.atan2(4,3)` evaluates to `0.9273`

ceil

This method returns the least integer greater than or equal to a number. For numbers less than zero, it would be the next integer closer to zero, for those greater than zero, the next integer further from zero. There is no HTML equivalent.

JS: `ceil(93.4)` evaluates to `94`

cos

This method returns the cosine of a number. Its argument is a value that represents the size of an angle in radians. The number it generates is a value between −1 and 1. There is no HTML equivalent.

JS: `Math.cos(1.266)` evaluates to `0.300`

exp

This method returns the numeric value e^x, where e is Euler's constant, and x is its argument.

JS: `exp(1)` evaluates to `2.7183`

floor

This method returns the greatest integer less than or equal to a number. For numbers less than zero, it would be the next integer further from zero, for those greater than zero, the next integer closer to zero. There is no HTML equivalent.

JS: `Math.floor(-93.4)` evaluates to `-94`

log

This method returns the natural logarithm for a number. Its argument is any positive numeric value. There is no HTML equivalent.

```
JS:   Math.log(10) evaluates to 2.3026;
```

max

This method returns the greater of two numbers. There is no HTML equivalent.

```
JS:   Math.max(10,15) evaluates to 15;
```

min

This method returns the lesser of two numbers. There is no HTML equivalent.

```
JS:   Math.min(10,15) evaluates to 10;
```

pow

This method returns a number that uses a base number and an exponent. The base number is then raised to the power of the exponent (this is the number of times that you multiply a number by itself—2 raised to the power of 3 (the third power) equals 2 $\times 2 \times 2$). There is no HTML equivalent.

```
JS:   Math.pow(2,3) evaluates to  8
JS:   Math.pow(5,3) evaluates to 125
```

random

This method returns a random number between 0 and 1. There is no HTML equivalent.

```
JS:   Math.random() evaluates to 0.4829
```

round

This method returns the closest integer to a numeric expression. There is no HTML equivalent.

```
JS:   Math.round(45.49999) evaluates to  45
JS:   Math.round(45.50000) evaluates to 46
```

sin

This method returns the sine of a number. Its argument is a value that represents the size of an angle in radians. The number it generates is a value between –1 and 1. There is no HTML equivalent.

```
JS:   Math.sin(Math.PI/2) evaluates to 1
```

sqrt

This method returns the square root of its argument. There is no HMTL equivalent.

```
JS:   Math.sqrt(256) evaluates to 16
```

tan

This method returns the tangent of a number. Its argument is a value that represents the size of an angle in radians. The number it generates is a value between –1 and 1. There is no HTML equivalent.

```
JS:   Math.sin(Math.PI/4) evaluates to 0.9999
```

Password Object Methods

blur

The blur method refers to the instant when a form element is exited by the mouse or cursor. It is the opposite of the focus method, which refers to the instant that a form element is first entered. There is no HTML equivalent.

```
JS:   PasswordName.blur();
```

focus

Focusing a form element refers to the moment when you enter the element using the mouse or tab key. There is no HTML equivalent.

```
JS:   PasswordName.blur();
```

select

This method is used to select the contents of a form element. In the following example, the password input box named "MyPassword" has its contents selected with the JavaScript. There is no HTML equivalent.

```
HTML: <INPUT TYPE=password NAME="MyPassword">
JS:   MyPassword.select();
```

Plug-Ins Object Methods

refresh

The refresh method is new to Navigator 3.0. It enables you to update a browser to recognize a file format supported by a plug-in that has been downloaded while the browser is open. In this manner, the browser does not need to be closed and re-opened to recognize a file format type. If you use the parameter true, Navigator will update any file formats of that type that are in the document.

```
JS:    navigator.plugins.refresh(true)
```

Radio Object Methods

click

This method toggles between being selected and deselected. There is no HTML equivalent.

```
JS:    NoiseForm.RadioButton.click();
```

Reset Object Methods

click

This method performs the same action as if you clicked the reset button. There is no HTML equivalent.

```
JS:    NoiseForm.ResetButton.click();
```

String Object Methods

The methods for the *string* object are used primarily with the write() and writeln() methods of the document object. They enable you to specify the HTML text format-ting associated with the text that is the method's argument.

anchor

This method is used in conjunction with the *write* or *writeln* methods. It enables you to specify an anchor within a document that you are creating with JavaScript. The first line in the example below is added to create a *string* object for the method in the second line. The third line shows how it would appear in the HTML source code.

```
JS:    MyString="SomeText";
```

```
JS:  document.writeln(MyString.anchor("Anchored"));evaluates to HTML: <A
➥NAME="SomeText">Anchored</A>
```

big

This method is used in conjunction with the *write* or *writeln* methods. It renders its string object argument in a big font. In the following example, the first line defines a *string* object for the method in the following line. The third line shows how it would appear in the HTML source code.

JS: MyString="Twisted Conversation";
```
JS:  document.writeln(MyString.big());evaluates to HTML: <BIG>Twisted
➥Conversation</BIG>
```

blink

This method is used in conjunction with the *write* or *writeln* methods. It renders its string object argument in blinking text. In the following example, the first line defines a *string* object for the method in the following line. The third line shows how it would appear in the HTML source code.

JS: MyString="Blinking Mania";
```
JS:  document.writeln(MyString.blink());evaluates to HTML: <BLINK>Blinking
➥Mania</BLINK>
```

bold

This method is used in conjunction with the *write* or *writeln* methods. It renders its *string* object argument in a bolded typeface. In the example, the first line defines a *string* object for the method in the following line. The third line shows how it would appear in the HTML source code.

JS: MyString="Bold and Brash";
```
JS:  document.writeln(MyString.bold());evaluates to HTML: <BOLD>Bold and
➥Brash</BOLD>
```

charAt

This method designates a character within a string object. Its argument is indexed starting from 0 and defines the character in relation to its distance from the first character in the string. There is no HTML equivalent. In the example below, the third character, indicated by the argument (2), is selected (z). In the second example, the ninth character is selected. Remember to subtract 1 from the number to refer to its indexed position, because the first position is zero, not one.

```
JS:  MyString="Lazy Brown Dog.";
JS:  MyString.charAt(2) evaluates to "z"
JS:  MyString.charAt(8) evaluates to "w"
```

fixed

This method is used in conjunction with the *write* or *writeln* methods. It renders its string object argument in a fixed-pitch font. In the following example, the first line defines a *string* object for the method in the following line. The third line shows how it would appear in the HTML source code.

```
JS:  MyString="Fix this broken String";
JS:  document.writeln(MyString.fixed());evaluates to HTML: <TT>Fix this broken
➥String</TT>
```

fontcolor

This method is used to affect the color of the font and is used in conjunction with the *write* or *writeln* methods. It renders its *string* object with a hexadecimal color or special color name as its argument. In the following example, the first line defines a string object for the method in the following line. The third line shows how it would appear in the HTML source code.

```
JS:  MyString="What color is your umbrella?";
JS:  document.writeln(MyString.fontcolor("00FF00"));evaluates to HTML: <FONT
➥COLOR=00FF00>What color is your umbrella?</FONT>
```

fontsize

This method is used to affect the size of the font and is used in conjunction with the *write* or *writeln* methods. It renders its string object at a relative font size using an integer value between 1 and 7. In the example, the first line defines a *string* object for the method in the following line. The third line shows how it would appear in the HTML source code.

```
JS:  MyString="This font sure is big!";
JS:  document.writeln(MyString.fontsize(7));evaluates to HTML: <FONT SIZE=7>
➥This font sure is big!</FONT>
```

indexOf

This method returns the distance in characters that a character is from the first character in a string object. Its argument is indexed starting from 0 and defines the first character that meets the argument criteria. There is no HTML equivalent.

```
JS:   MyString="Lazy Brown Dog.";
JS:   MyString.indexOf("B") evaluates to 5
JS:   MyString.indexOf("L") evaluates to 0
```

italics

This method is used in conjunction with the *write* or *writeln* methods. It renders its string object argument in an italicized typeface. In the following example, the first line defines a string object for the method in the following line. The third line shows how it would appear in the HTML source code.

```
JS:   MyString="Italics provide emphasis";
JS:   document.writeln(MyString.italics());evaluates to HTML: <I>Italics provide
➥emphasis</I>
```

lastIndexOf

This method returns the distance that the last character that meets the argument criteria is from the first character in a string object. Its argument is indexed starting from 0. There is no HTML equivalent.

```
JS:   MyString="Lazy Brown Dog.";
JS:   MyString.lastIndexOf("o") evaluates to 12
```

link

This method is used in conjunction with the *write* or *writeln* methods. It enables you to specify a hyperlink within a document that you are creating with JavaScript. The first line in the following example is added to create a string object for the method in the second line. The third line shows how it would appear in the HTML source code.

```
JS:   MyString="SomeText";
JS:   MyURL="http://www.3pdesign.com";
JS:   document.writeln(MyString.link(MyURL));evaluates to HTML: <A HREF="http://
➥www.3pdesign.com" NAME="SomeText">Linked Text</A>
```

small

This method is used in conjunction with the *write* or *writeln* methods. It renders its string object argument in a small font. In the following example, the first line defines a string object for the method in the following line. The third line shows how it would appear in the HTML source code.

```
JS:  MyString="My little mouth";
JS:  document.writeln(MyString.small());evaluates to HTML: <SMALL>My
➥littlemouth</SMALL>
```

strike

This method is used in conjunction with the *write* or *writeln* methods. It renders its string object argument with a strike placed through the center of it. In the example, the first line defines a string object for the method in the following line. The third line shows how it would appear in the HTML source code.

```
JS:  MyString="Smoking in Public";
JS:  document.writeln(MyString.strike());evaluates to HTML: <STRIKE>My little
➥mouth</STRIKE>
```

sub

This method is used in conjunction with the *write* or *writeln* methods. It renders its string object argument in a subscript font. In the example, the first line defines a string object for the method in the following line. The third line shows how it would appear in the HTML source code.

```
JS:  MyString="Subbing it";
JS:  document.writeln(MyString.sub());evaluates to HTML: <SUB>My little mouth</
➥SUB>
```

substring

This method is used to display a portion of a string object. It uses two arguments: the first one determines which indexed character the substring begins with; the second one determines which indexed character it ends with. The first character is number 0, the second is number 1, and so on. There is no HTML equivalent.

```
JS:  MyString="Fargo to Hellington";
JS:  MyString.substring(3,12) evaluates to "go to Hell"
```

sup

This method is used in conjunction with the ***write*** or ***writeln*** methods. It renders its string object argument in a superscript font. In the example, the first line defines a string object for the method in the following line. The third line shows how it would appear in the HTML source code.

```
JS:  MyString="superscripting";
JS:  document.writeln(MyString.sup());evaluates to HTML: <SUP>superscripting</
➡SUP>
```

toLowerCase

This method returns the string value to lowercase. There is no HTML equivalent.

```
JS:  MyString="HTML"
JS:  MyString.toLowerCase() evaluates to "html"
```

toUpperCase

This method returns the string value to uppercase. There is no HTML equivalent.

```
JS:  MyString="html"
JS:  MyString.to UpperCase() evaluates to "HTML"
```

Submit Object Methods

click

This method performs the same action as if you clicked the submit button. There is no HTML equivalent.

```
JS:  NoiseForm.SubmitButton.click();
```

Text Object Methods

blur

The blur method refers to the instant when a form element is exited by the mouse or cursor. It is the opposite of the focus method, which refers to the instant that a form element is first entered. There is no HTML equivalent.

```
JS:  TextObjectName.blur();
```

focus

Focusing a form element refers to the moment when you enter the element using the mouse or tab key. There is no HTML equivalent.

```
JS:   TextObjectName.blur();
```

select

This method is used to select the contents of a form element. In the following example, the text object named "TextObjectName" has its contents selected with the JavaScript. There is no HTML equivalent.

```
HTML: <INPUT TYPE=password NAME="TextObjectName">
JS:   TextObjectName.select();
```

Textarea Object Methods

blur

The blur method refers to the instant when a form element is exited by the mouse or cursor. It is the opposite of the focus method, which refers to the instant that a form element is first entered. There is no HTML equivalent.

```
JS:   TextAreaObject.blur();
```

focus

Focusing a form element refers to the moment when you enter the element using the mouse or tab key. There is no HTML equivalent.

```
JS:   TextAreaObject.blur();
```

select

This method is used to select the contents of a form element. In the following example, the textarea object named "TextObjectName" has its contents selected with the JavaScript. There is no HTML equivalent.

```
HTML: <TEXTAREA NAME="TextAreaObject">
JS:   TextAreaObject.select();
```

Window Object Methods

alert

This method displays an Alert dialog box with a text message and an OK button. There is no HTML equivalent.

```
JS:   alert("I have something to say.");
```

blur

This method in Navigator 3.0.now applies to the *frame* and *window* objects, as well as form *elements*. Blurring a form element or window refers to removing it from the *"focus."* In the case of a window, it would be when you directed your computer to display the screen from another application. The browser no longer has the *"focus"* of the computer. There is no HTML equivalent.

```
JS:   formElementName.blur();
```

clearTimeout

This method cancels a timeout that was set using the setTimeout method. There is no HTML equivalent.

```
JS:   clearTimeout(aNamedTimer);
```

close

This method closes the active window. There is no HTML equivalent.

```
JS:   windowName.close();
```

confirm

This method displays a Confirm dialog box with a text message and OK and Cancel buttons. It uses a string object as its argument. If OK is selected, the method returns *true*; if Cancel is selected, it returns *false*. There is no HTML equivalent.

```
JS:   confirm("Are you sure you want to leave the Web site already?");
```

focus

This method in Navigator 3.0 now applies to the *frame* and *window* objects, as well as form *elements*. Focusing a form element or window refers to bringing the cursor or the window itself into an active state. In the case of a window, it would be when you directed your computer to display the browser after having viewed another application. The browser then has the *"focus"* of the computer. There is no HTML equivalent.

```
JS:  formElementName.focus();
```

open

This method opens a new browser window. It is able to control several features in the new window. Each of the parameters in its argument control a different feature. If you want to display a toolbar or hide one, you would set the window display "toolbars=yes" or "toolbars=no", respectively. Notice that no spaces are placed between the parameters. The first two parameters; URL, which gives the HREF, and the name of the window are required arguments. If you want to open a window that is not associated with an URL, use empty quotation marks (""). Naming the window enables you to target it from another window or frame. Values for each of the additional parameters can be set to yes or no, 1 or 0. They are not required arguments. There is no HTML equivalent. The method and its arguments are presented in the following example.

```
JS:  MyWindow=window.open("URL", "Window
Name",["toolbars=yes","location=yes","directories=yes","status=yes","menubar=yes",
➥"scrollbars=yes", "resizable=yes","width=PixelValue","height=PixelValue"]);
```

prompt

This method is used to prompt a visitor to your Web page to enter a response. It uses two arguments: the message you wish displayed, and an initial value for the prompt box. The initial value, if blank, should be indicated by using empty quotation marks (""). There is no HTML equivalent.

```
JS:  prompt("What name will you be using?", "");
```

setTimeout

This method evaluates an expression after a specified number of milliseconds have passed. In the following example, MyTimer identifies the timer in order for the clearTimeout method to cancel it.

```
JS:  MyTimer=setTimeout("alert('Time up!');",10000);
```

Built-in Functions

escape

This built-in function encodes non-alphanumeric characters, such as spaces, using hexadecimal ASCII values. The most typical instance is the encoding for the space character (%20). There is no HTML equivalent.

```
JS:   escape("the end") evaluates to "the&20end"
```

eval

This built-in function evaluates a string and returns a value. There is no HTML equivalent.

```
JS:   x=10; y=20; z=30;
JS:   eval("x + y + z +900") evaluates to 960
```

isNaN

This method is only available for Unix platforms. It evaluates an argument to determine if it is Not a Number(NaN). Its returned value is either true or false. There is no HTML equivalent.

```
JS:   var va = Math.sqrt(2);
JS:   isNan(va) evaluates to True

JS:   var va="a";
JS:   isNan(va) evaluates to False
```

parseFloat

This built-in function returns a floating point number from a string object. If the function encounters any characters that are not numerals, decimal points, positive or negative signs, or exponents, it returns a floating point number based on the characters up until that point in the string. This is a very useful method for converting string values into numeric values. There is no HTML equivalent.

```
JS:   MyString="3.14";
JS:   parseFloat(MyString) evaluates to 3.14;
JS:   parseFloat("3.14") evaluates to 3.14;
```

parseInt

This built-in function returns an integer in a specified base from a string object. A specified base would be base 2, base 16 (hexadecimal), or the default, base 10. If the input string begins with "0x", the method returns a base 16 integer; if the input string begins with "0", it returns a base 8 (octal) integer. All other non-specified input strings return base 10 integers. If the function encounters any characters that are not numerals, decimal points, positive or negative signs, or exponents, it returns the number based on the characters up until that point in the string. Notice in the example, that if the base cannot interpret the number (for example, the number 9 in base 8), it and all the characters following it are ignored. Use this function to perform hexadecimal conversions and other conversions as necessary. There is no HTML equivalent.

```
JS:   MyString="1079";
JS:   parseInt(MyString, 16) evaluates to 4217
JS:   parseInt(MyString, 8) evaluates to 71
JS:   parseInt(MyString, 7) evaluates to 7
JS:   parseInt(MyString) evaluates to 1079
```

unescape

This built-in function decodes hexadecimal ASCII values into alphanumeric characters. There is no HTML equivalent.

```
JS:   unescape("the&20end") evaluates to "the end"
```

Values, Variables, and Literals

Values

After being introduced to the *objects*, *properties*, and *methods* in JavaScript, the next thing to become familiar with are values, variables, and literals. When working with any programming language, it is important to remember to use appropriate value types for their syntactical usage. If you don't, you will have errors when calculations are attempted to be performed (consider 99 + "Melonhead" for instance, or 84 * "My Fair Lady"). In JavaScript, there are four types of value types available:

1. Numbers: Many languages have different types of number values. Integers and floating point number values (those requiring a decimal point) are often separated into different groups. In JavaScript, all real numbers belong to a single value type.

2. Logical: Like most programming languages, JavaScript is able to use logical, or Boolean values. Logical values are either true or false.

3. Strings: The string value enables you to store text in reusable variables. It also enables you to treat a string object in a concise manner that would not otherwise be possible.

4. Null: The null value accesses a special keyword of JavaScript that denotes a null value. This is equal to zero or no returned answer.

Different functions and methods require different value types for their arguments. It is not difficult to convert between the various value types. JavaScript is flexible enough to allow the changing of value types for variables within <SCRIPT> and </SCRIPT> tags. In other words, a variable named MyVariable could be a string value at one point, then changed to another value type merely with another declaration. Consider the following code:

```
MyVariable="Some text";
MyVariable=59;
```

In the first example, a string value is given, and MyVariable is operationalized as a string object. In the second line of code, MyVariable was operationalized as a numeric value. To convert a variable; however, takes an additional line or two of code. The methods to convert were introduced in the section on methods. These are:

```
Number to String:    Var MyVariable = "999";
String to Number:    Var MyString = "FF00AA";
    Var MyNumber = parseInt(Mystring, 16);
```

Logical values are constructed from either string or number values by making them equal to True or False, respectively. To see more about data type conversions, refer to the description for the *eval, parseInt,* and *parseFloat* built-in functions. These are each used to convert strings to numbers.

Variables

Closely related to values are variables. Variables are names that are used to hold values. Variables can be named using uppercase and lowercase alphabetic characters, digits 0–9, and the underscore character (_). The first character in a variable name must be a letter or the underscore character. JavaScript is case sensitive, which means that if a letter is in uppercase or lowercase, it must always be referred to using the uppercase or lowercase letter as appropriate. In other words, JavaScript distinguishes between x and X.

Variables can be either global or local in scope. Global means that all functions can use the same variable as a particular value. A global variable is declared before the first function definition in the <SCRIPT> tag. A local variable is only available to the function that contains it, and it is declared within a function definition. The following example illustrates the difference in the structural position of the two variable types.

```
<SCRIPT>
var globalvar1=5;
function fivetimestwo() {
     var localvar1 = 2  * globalvar1;
     alert ("Five times two is" + localvar1);
}

function fivetimesten() {
     var localvar2 = localvar1  * globalvar1;
     alert ("Five times ten is" + localvar2);
}
</SCRIPT>
```

In the preceding example, the *globalvar1* global variable is declared before any functions are defined. The *localvar1* local variable is declared within the *fivetimestwo()* function. The first function is capable of being executed because it is able to use the global variable and the local variable that is declared within the function. The *localvar2* local variable is declared within the *fivetimesten()* function. In the second function, an attempt is made to use the *localvar1* variable. This is not possible because it is declared locally within the first function. If the variable *localvar1* had been declared before the function *fivetimestwo()*, the function *fivetimesten()* could have used the value to return a value. As it is, the function does not execute because of the function's inability to recognize the *localvar1* variable.

Literals

The last of the elements to describe that you will be working with to supply information to functions and expressions are literals. There are several types of literals:

- ◆ Integer literals: Whole numbers such as 3 or 7;

- ◆ Floating point literals: Numbers expressed with a decimal point, such as 0.2 or 99.9999;

- ◆ Boolean literals: "true" or "false"

- ◆ String literals: Zero or more characters contained within single (') or double("") quotation marks;

- ◆ Special characters which include:

    - ◆ \b: Indicates a backspace

    - ◆ \f: Indicates a form feed

◆ \n: Indicates a new line

◆ \r: Indicates a carriage return

◆ \t: Indicates a tab character

◆ \": Indicates a quotation mark enclosed within a string, as in the following example:

```
JavaScript:  MyQuote="He said don\'t go home."
Result: He said don't go home.
```

Expressions and Operators

Now that you have been introduced to values, variables, and literals, expressions and operators will enable you to assign, affect, and determine their values. Expressions are sets of literals, variables, operators, and expressions that evaluate to a single string. That is to say, expressions return a single value: there is no ambiguity in an expression's result. *X=7* is a perfect example of such an unambiguous expression. There are three kinds of expressions available in JavaScript:

◆ Arithmetic: Evaluates to a number

◆ String: Evaluates to a character string

◆ Logical: Evaluates to either true or false

In addition to these three expression types, there are also conditional expressions (also call ternary operators). Conditional expressions use the Question mark (?) and use the following syntax:

```
(condition) ? value1: value2
```

If the condition is true, the expression has the value of **value1**; if not, it has the value of **value2**. All expression types use operators to work with *operands*. Operands are the values, variables, or literals used with operators to form an expression. Operators are generally separated into two main groups: assignment operators and standard operators. The first group of operators assign values to the left-hand side of the operator; standard operators are used to otherwise affect a value. Within standard operators, there are arithmetic, string, and logical operators.

The assignment operators are:

Operator	Value
x=y	x=y
x+=y	x=x+y
x-=y	x=x-y
x*=y	x=x*y
x/=y	x=x/y
x%=y	x=x%y

There are additional assignment operators available for bitwise operators that will be presented in the following section. Each of the operator types that are not used for assignment are broken into two categories: binary and unary. The former requires two operands, the latter requires a single operand.

Arithmetic Operators

The arithmetic operators include the standard operators, addition (+), subtraction (–), multiplication (*), and division (/). In addition to the standard arithmetic operators, the following operators are available in JavaScript.

Modulus (%) Operators

Modulus operators return the integer remainder from a division equation between two numbers. In other words, 10 divided by 3 equals 3, remainder 1. The equation *10%3*, therefore, returns 1.

Increment (++) Operators

Increment operators increase the value of a variable by 1. It is generally placed after the number, but is sometimes placed before. To increase a number, use *x++* syntax. In working with two numbers, the placement of the increment operator affects how the equation is performed. If it is placed before the operand, the left operand uses the value of the number after it has been incremented; if it is placed after the operand, it uses the unincremented value to perform the calculation. In the following examples, the default value of b is 5.

```
a=++b (a=6, b=6)
a=b++ (a=5, b=6)
```

Decrement (--) Operators

Decrement operators decrease the value of a variable by 1. To make a number decrease, use x -- syntax. In working with two numbers, the placement of the increment operator affects how the equation is performed. If it is before the operand, the left operand uses the value of the number after it has been incremented; if it is placed after the operand, it uses the unincremented value to perform the calculation. In the following examples, the default value of b is 5.

```
a=--b (a=4, b=4)
a=b-- (a=5, b=4)
```

Negation (–) Operators

Negation operators reverse the polarity of a numeric value. It is placed before the value $(X=-X)$.

Bitwise Operators

The bitwise operators support binary equations. Binary numbers use the base two numbering system, and are made up of the numbers one and zero. There are several types of bitwise operators: logical, shift, and assignment types.

Logical Operators

Before performing logical calculations, these operators convert the numeric values into binary numbers. When the number has been converted, comparisons are made between the numbers to see how they pass individual logical tests.

The three logical bitwise operators are **AND (&)**, **OR** (|), and **XOR (^)**. The AND operator returns a 1 for each bit if both operands are ones; the OR operator returns a one if either operand is a one; and the XOR operator returns a one if one, but not both, of the operands is a one. These work as follows:

   13 & 10 returns 8 (1101 & 1010 = 1000)

   13 | 10 returns 15   (1101 | 1010 = 1111)

   13 ^ 10 returns 7 (1101 ^ 1010 = 0111)

Shift Operators

Shift operators move the first operand in a binary number a specified number of positions left or right. Each position left or right will increase or decrease the number by a power of two. There are three shift operators:

◆ Left Shift (<<)

◆ Sign-Propagating Right Shift (>>)

◆ Zero-fill Right Shift (>>>)

The latter two function the same for positive values. The shift operators take two arguments, the numeric value to be shifted and the number of bit positions by which the first operand is to be shifted. These work as follows:

13 << 2 returns 52 (1101 becomes 110100)

13 >> 2 returns 3 (1101 becomes 11)

13 >>> 2 returns 3 (1101 becomes 11)

Assignment Operators

The bitwise assignment operators function the same way as the other assignment operators, described above. These are:

Operator	Value
a <<= b	a = a<<b
a >>= b	a = a>>b
a >>> = b	a = a>>>b
a&=b	a=a&b
a|=b	a=a|b
a^=b	a=a^b

Comparison Operators

The comparison operators are used to compare two values and return a true or false logical value. They are often used with conditional statements to test for values. The six available comparison operators are:

Operator	Description
Equal (==)	This operator returns true if its operands are equal. if(x==y) {statements...}
Not Equal (!=)	This operator returns true if its operands are not equal. if(x!=y) {statements...}
Greater Than (>)	This operator returns true if the left operand is greater than the right operand. if(x>y) {statements...}
Greater Than or Equal to (>=)	This operator returns true if the left operand is greater than or equal to the right operand. if(x>=y) {statements...}
Lesser Than (<)	This operator returns true if the left operand is lesser than the right operand. if(x<y) {statements...}
Lesser Than or Equal to (<=)	This operator returns true if the left operand is lesser than the right operand. if(x<=y) {statements...}

Logical Operators

Logical operators return Boolean values (for example, True or False). The logical operators available in JavaScript are:

AND (&&): This operator returns a true if both of its operands, which are logical expressions, are true.

Expresssion1 && Expresssion2

OR (||): This operator returns a true if either of its operands, which are logical expressions, arc true.

Expresssion1 || Expresssion2

NOT (!): This is a unary operator that reverses the condition of the expression with which it is used. In other words, if the expression was true, it becomes false; if false, it becomes true.

    !Expression1

String Operators

String values can be used with the comparison operators above, as well as with two arithmetic operators. These concatenate strings as demonstrated:

```
"Ringling "+"Brothers" evaluates to "Ringling Brothers";
MyString="This is";
MyString+=" "+ Math.cos(0) +" strange example.";

MyString evaluates to "This is 1 strange example."
```

typeof Operator

The typeof operator is new to Navigator 3.0. It is used to determine the value type of a programming element or reserved word. This can be seen in the example below:

typeof parse == "function"

typeof "typed text" == "string"

typeof Date == "object"

typeof true == "boolean"

Operator Precedence

When more than one operator is used in an expression, the order in which the individual operators are executed can affect the outcome of the expression. Consider the following:

17 = 5 + 4 * 3

When no parentheses are present, the operators follow a predetermined order of execution. As seen in the example, the multiplication operator has a higher level of precedence than the addition operator. From highest to lowest precedence, operators are executed as follows:

Operator Precedence

Operator Name	Operator
call, member	() []
negation/increment	! - ++ - -
multiply/divide	* /
addition/subtraction	+ -
bitwise shift	<< >> >>>
relational	< <= > >=
equality	== !=
bitwise-and	&
bitwise-xor	^
bitwise-or	|
logical-and	&&
logical-or	||
conditional	?
assignment	= += -= *= /= %= <<= >>= >>>= &= |= ^=
comma	,

Now that you have been introduced to operators, you can begin to create expressions utilizing values, variables, and operators. The final piece of the JavaScript puzzle to look into are statements and the flow control they provide.

Statements

Statements direct the flow of JavaScripts. Much of the power in JavaScript lies in its capability to perform complex functions through loop statements, object manipulation statements, and conditional statements. Many of the more complex JavaScripts make extensive use of statements. Using statements effectively will help you reduce the lines of code that you use, assist you in advanced applications such as designing animations, and give you a much higher degree of control over your JavaScript than otherwise possible.

In designing loop statements, a simple differentiation between loop types is extremeley helpful. You use *if...else* statements principally when testing conditions that are either true or false. In other words, there are only two possible conditions, such as *if(x>y)*. The value *x* is either greater than the value *y*, or not greater.

You use *for* statements to declare an initial condition of a variable, a test condition for the statement to be executed, and a statement that updates the value of the variable's condition. The loop then iterates a block of statements for the tested range of values. All values that meet the defined criteria will process the series of statements that follow the *for* statement.

The *while* loop is similar to the *for* statement in that all values that meet your defined criteria will process the series of statements that follow the *while* statement. The *while* loop, however, does not declare a variable's value. It merely tests a variable until a condition becomes true, then breaks out of the loop.

The following sections discuss the statements currently available in JavaScript.

Break Statements

Break statements interrupt *while* or *for* loops. When setting up loops to perform repeated actions, the break statement prevents the loop from being endless. Once a condition has been met, the loop is interrupted, or broken. The code remaining after the interrupted loop statement is then processed normally.

```
function breakme() {
    while (x>0) {
            if (x>3)
                    break;
            x++;
    }
    return x;
}
```

In the preceding example, the while loop is interrupted by the break when x becomes greater than 3. This enables you to interrupt a loop from becoming endless through selecting the criteria that enables values to pass.

Comment Statements

Every language has its own way of commenting text that you do not want to be executed. JavaScript uses the forward slash character (/) for this purpose. There are two ways to use the comment marks:

```
// single line comment
/* multiple line comment*/
```

The top statement is used for a single line of commented text; the bottom statement is generally used for two or more lines of commented text.

Continue Statements

Continue statements terminate while or for loops differently from the break statement, which stops them completely. In the case of the while loop, the test condition is returned to; in the case of the for loop, the updated value or expression is passed.

```
while(x<10) {
    x++;
    if (x==8)
            continue;
    a+=x;
}
```

In the preceding example, the while loop repeats while x is less than 10. When x is equal to 8, the continue statement breaks the while loop, and continues to execute any statements that were waiting for the while loop to close.

For Loops

For loops consist of three optional expressions (separated by semicolons and contained within parentheses) and a block of statements. For loop syntax is:

```
    for  ([initial expression]; [condition]; [update expression])  {state-
ments}
```

The initial expression can use the var statement to declare a variable if necessary.

```
for (x=5; x<10; x++) {statements}
```

For...In Statements

For...In statements treat a specified variable for each property of an object. For each property, JavaScript executes the specified statements.

```
for (var in obj)   {statements}
```

Functions

Functions are the statments that contain other statements for execution and are called by event handlers or other functions. Every function has a name, parameter(s) enclosed in parentheses, and a body of statement definition(s), as shown below:

```
function myFunction () {
    alert("Go home, now!")
}
```

If....Else Statements

The *if...then* format for JavaScript actually uses an *if...else* phrasing as follows:

```
if (condition) {
        statements
}   [else   {
        else statements
} ]
```

If a test condition is true, the statements are executed; if they are false, the else statements are executed. If statements may include nested if statements.

New Statements

New statements enable you to define a new instance of a defined object type. These objects are either built-in objects or user-defined objects. To create a new object you first have to define it. After being defined, you use the following syntax:

```
new myObject(parameter1,parameter2, ...)
```

Objects are defined using functions. See the discussion on user-defined objects earlier in this appendix.

Return Statements

Specifies the value to be returned by a function.

This Keyword

This keyword is not really a statement. It is often grouped with statements for lack of a better classification. It is very useful for describing objects in JavaScript with a shorthand method. Consider the following two lines of code.

```
document.MusicForm.elements[0].value="True";
this.value="True";
```

Both examples may refer to the same form element. Using *this* enables you to use shorthand when defining the object within which the function call is made. In other words, if your form element has an *onChange* event handler, and the value changes, you can use *this.value* to test for field entry.

Var Statements

Var statements declare variables. Variables may be declared by using the var statement or simply by assigning them a value. Consider the following:

```
var varname[=varvalue]          or          varname=varvalue
```

Both declarations do the same thing. It is considered good practice to include the *var* statement with variable declarations, although it is not generally required.

While Statements

Similar to the *for* loop, this statement evaluates an expression condition, and if true, executes statements. It repeats this process as long as the condition is true.

```
while (condition)    {statements}
```

With Statements

With statements establish an object as the default object for multiple statements.

```
with (object)   {statements}
```

Consider the following example:

```
with (MyWindow.document) {
    open();
    write("Not so much code used");
    close();
}
```

Using the with statement enables the code to take much less space than would otherwise have been the case.

JavaScript to Java Communication

When starting to program with any language or new technology, such as LiveConnect, it is important to know as much as possible about all the technologies involved. This section discusses two major technologies: Java and JavaScript. Because the previous portion of this book deals with JavaScript, and that technology is now familiar to you, this section does not rehash it. This section begins with an introduction to the Java programming language to introduce you to the other new technology. After the introduction, this section shows you the LiveConnect technology that enables the two languages, Java and JavaScript, to communicate with each other.

Introduction to Java

Java is an object-oriented programming language developed by Unix workstation giant Sun Microsystems. Modeled after C++, the Java language was designed to be a small, simple, and portable language that would have widespread use across platforms and operating systems. This multi-platform compatibility was accomplished at both the source and at the binary level by the use of bytecode. Java was originally developed as a language to create software that could run on many different kinds of devices, but it evolved into a vehicle for distributing executable content through the Web.

Today, Java applications make Web pages more interesting because the pages provide the user with immediate feedback and accept continuous user input through mouse or keyboard entries. Moreover, their platform independence makes them as easy to distribute as simple text, with all of the underlying complexity hidden from the user.

Java brings interactivity into widespread use on the Web. Java-enabled Web browsers can provide users with animation and interactive applications. You can write a Java applet that plays a game such as tic-tac-toe or hangman with visitors to your Web site, for example. Although this section is not meant to be a Java tutorial, it does present a short description of what the Java programming language means to the Web. This section also discusses the limitations imposed by both the Java programming language and currently available Java-enabled browsers, such as the Netscape Navigator. This section also provides an example of a simple Java program that introduces many of the Java fundamentals. Finally, this section reviews a simple example of a LiveConnect application that shows how to communicate between JavaScript and a Java application.

Introduction to Java Applets

Java applets are easily compiled Java programs run by using a Web browser that supports Java. An applet's function is limited only by your imagination. It can display graphics, play sounds, accept user input, and manipulate data just like any other program.

Java applets were not conceived for use on the Internet. Instead, they were designed for use with hand-held computing devices, or Personal Digital Assistants (PDAs). The basic properties of applets, however, make them a perfect fit for use on the Internet and the World Wide Web. Applets are very small and can be downloaded and run quickly. They can add new levels of functionality and interactivity to normal Web pages without the overhead of full blown applications. With the introduction of Just-in-Time (JIT) compilers for Web browsers, Java applets have begun to make a serious impact on the World Wide Web. The JIT compilers make Java applets execute much faster than previously possible because the Java bytecode—an intermediate stage for program code between text (source) and executable (fully compiled source)—is executed as it is being downloaded, eliminating the need for the entire applet to be downloaded before beginning execution.

Limitations Imposed by Programming in Java

As with any programming language, many drawbacks as well as boons exist. It is important to understand these drawbacks before you begin to design a LiveConnect system so that you can work around the limitations and use the strengths to your advantage. With the Java programming language, most of the drawbacks deal with security issues. Even with its shortcomings, Java is certainly the language of the Internet and will continue to grow as long as the public continues to show an interest in it.

Applets are downloaded from their home servers as bytecode, which makes them easily portable from platform to platform. The bytecode is platform independent, and is executed through a Java-capable Web browser. Because the bytecode is executed on a user's local machine, a certain level of security is needed to make certain that the integrity of the user's machine is not compromised by the Java program executing a virus on the user's system, or in some other way performing maliciously.

Java achieves a level of security through a verification process that ensures that the bytecode does not violate any Java language conventions. To perform verification, all Java methods and variables must be called by name. Calling methods by name enables verification of all the methods and variables in the bytecode before execution. Calling methods by name also ensures that an applet is not accessing memory areas that might contain the operating system, other applications, or other similarly sensitive areas. Limiting functions to call by name also has the advantage of eliminating memory pointers, one of the more commonly misunderstood and misused aspects of other programming languages. Although taking away the use of memory pointers may seem to spell doom for some of the more creative programmers in the world, Java more than makes up for the lack of pointers by eliminating the need for an application to clean up its memory when done with it.

As a further security measure, applets are also not given full access to the local machine's file system. Applets currently do not have any means to save files on to a user's local system. Also, applets cannot read files on a user's local system. This restriction severely limits the functionality of applets, but allowing applets access to the local file system would present a serious security problem for the Web-using public as a whole. If an applet could read files on a system, for example, it could send information from those files back to the applet's author, who could then scan them and come up with damaging information, such as getting credit card and bank numbers from an accounting program. If an applet could write files to a system, it could potentially introduce viruses, delete files, or worse. Rather than risk security, applets are prevented from accessing these sensitive files. Undoubtedly, file access would increase the functionality of applets; the end goal of the Java language designers should be to allow applets to read and save files, and thereby provide the fullest programming language functionality. Until a secure way of allowing access to the local file system is found, Java programmers must live with the limitation or find creative ways around the problem.

Another limitation of Java applets is that they are restricted from loading dynamic or shared libraries developed in other programming languages. Java can declare methods as being *native,* which allows the operating system's virtual machine to take advantage of other language libraries, such as those written in C or C++. Because these libraries cannot be security validated and would require access to the file system, however, applets cannot use dynamic link libraries. The ultimate goal is to optimize Java to the point where all the dynamic libraries could be written in Java, and thus eliminate the need for other language libraries. As the Java language grows and evolves, many of these limitations will be removed. For now, these limitations are the price for participating so closely in the early evolutionary life cycle of a new programming language.

Along the same lines as loading dynamic link libraries, Java also prevents programmers from running any kind of executable program on the user's system. This could prove potentially dangerous because a creative programmer can always get executable code on to a user's file system. Because of the impossibility of validating all files transmitted to a user's local system by a Web browser, Java makes it impossible to run a program on the user's system.

Browser Limitations

In addition to the limitations imposed by the Java language itself, the Web browser that executes applet bytecode also places some restrictions on Java applets. Understanding these limitations is important when designing an applet that will be controlled by JavaScript. A Web browser is a trusted application, meaning that a user has chosen to load that browser on his or her machine and trusts that it will not damage any files or the operating system. Java applets are untrusted applications. They are downloaded immediately upon access to a Web page and are executed on a machine without receiving the user's consent. The user might choose to use a Java-capable browser, and therefore imply consent, but the user does not have the opportunity to approve individual applets. As a result, Java-capable browsers have placed some restrictions on applets to ensure that they do not inadvertently violate system integrity.

The most important limitation placed on an applet by the Web browser is network connectivity. Applets are currently limited to network connections with their own host machines. This means your Java applet can communicate directly back to the Web server that it has been downloaded from, but it cannot contact any other servers on the Internet. The limitations on networking also comes back to the issue of security.

By restricting access to the applet's original host, applets are provided basic network functionality with a minimal security risk. If applets could contact any server on the Internet, applets could perform some potentially dangerous tasks.

If an applet could contact any server, it would be possible to make a connection to any e-mail server. An applet could then masquerade as your machine and send forged mail that would appear to be coming from you. Java developers continue to widely debate the issue of network connectivity for applets. The possibility still exists to write a number of applets that take advantage of network connections to their own servers, although it requires more work on the server side of the communication channel. Although restricting network connectivity imposes some limits on applets, those limits serve the interest of security. Certainly, as better security methods develop, network connectivity will increase and applets will become more functional.

Differences Between Java and C/C++

It is no secret that the Java language borrows liberally from the C and C++ programming languages. Because C++ is currently considered the language of choice for professional software developers, understanding what aspects of C++ Java inherits is important. Of possibly even more importance is what aspects of C++ Java does not support. Because Java is a new and emerging language, it was possible for the language architects to pick and choose which features from C++ to implement in Java. This section points out the differences between Java and C++. If you are a C++ programmer, you will be able to appreciate the differences between Java and C++. Even if you don't have any C++ experience, you can gain some insight into the Java language by understanding what C++ discrepancies it clears up in its implementation. Because C++ backwardly supports C, many of the differences pointed out here refer to C++, but apply to C as well.

The Preprocessor

All C/C++ compilers contain a stage of compilation known as the preprocessor. The C++ preprocessor performs an intelligent search and replace on all identifiers that have been declared with the #define or #typedef directives. Although most C++ language purists discourage the use of the preprocessor, most C++ programmers continue to use it. Most of the preprocessor definitions are stored in header files, which are companion files to the actual source code files. Java does not have a preprocessor. It provides similar functionality to that provided by the C++ preprocessor, but with far more control. Constant data members are used in place of the #define statement, and class definitions replace the use of the #typedef directive. Java source code is, therefore, more consistent and easier to read than C++ source code. Also, Java programs do not use header files. The Java compiler builds class definitions directly from the source code files, which contain both the class definitions and the method implementations.

Structures and Unions

In C++, three types of complex data exist: classes, structures, and unions. Java only implements the classes data type. Java forces programmers to use classes when the functionality of structures and unions is desired. Although this sounds like unnecessary work for the programmer, it ends up being more consistent because classes can easily imitate structures and unions. Java's designers wanted to keep the language simple; it made sense to eliminate undo redundancies.

Pointers

Most developers agree that the misuse and abuse of pointers cause the majority of bugs in C/C++ programs. Put bluntly, when you have pointers, you are given the ability to trash memory. C++ programmers use complex pointer arithmetic to create and maintain dynamic data structures. In return, C++ programmers spend a lot of time tracking down complex bugs caused by their complex code.

The Java language does not support pointers. Java provides similar functionality by making use of references. Java passes all arrays and objects by reference. This approach prevents many common errors caused by pointer errors. The pass by reference model also makes programming easier because programmers do not have to learn by the pointer mismanagement mishaps.

Functions

In C, code is organized into global subroutines accessible to a program. These routines are called functions. C++ added classes and class methods, which are functions associated with classes. C++ class methods and Java class methods are very similar. The one major difference is that because C++ must still support the C programming language, there is no reason that you cannot make global subroutines, or functions, that are accessible to the rest of the program.

Java has no concept of a function. Because it is a more pure object-oriented language than C++, Java forces programmers to tie their subroutines to a specific class. By forcing programmers to implement their functions inside of a class, Java also forces programmers to organize code better.

Strings

The C and C++ programming languages provide no native support for strings. In C and C++, strings are thought of as arrays of characters with a null termination character.

String is one of the basic data object types of the Java language. This provides numerous advantages over the C/C++ methodology. One advantage is that the implementation is not platform specific. Another advantage is that the Java String class always operates in a predictable manner. Another advantage, probably the most important, is that the Java String class performs run-time checking to prevent boundary overruns. Boundary overruns and a missing null terminator are the two most common problems associated with using the C/C++ methodology.

Operator Overloading

In C++, you can overload the binary operators to add functionality that supports your classes. Although the same functionality can be implemented in Java, the C++ convenience of operator overloading is still missing. Again, this missing convenience results from the aim of keeping the Java language as simple as possible.

Variable Arguments

Both C and C++ enable you to declare functions that take a variable number of arguments. Although this feature enables you to do a tremendous amount of work, it makes it virtually impossible for the compiler to type check the arguments, which could produce some nasty run-time errors. Java does not support any variable arguments, again for the sake of simplicity.

The Command Line

Just a couple of differences exist between the way that command-line arguments are handled between C/C++ and Java. First, in C/C++ the command line consists of two components: argc and argv. Argc specifies the number of arguments stored in argv. Argv is a pointer to an array of characters containing the actual arguments. In Java, there is only one parameter: args. Args is an array of strings that contains all the command-line arguments.

Another difference is that the first parameter in argv is the name of the actual program. This parameter is usually ignored because there are easier ways to obtain the name of the program. Java cleans up this procedure by passing only the arguments following the name that invoked the program. This provides a much simpler and elegant design.

Multiple Inheritance

Multiple inheritance is a C++ feature that enables you to derive a class from multiple parent classes. Although multiple inheritance is powerful, it is complicated to use correctly and is generally misused, leading to problems.

Java takes the multiple inheritance feature and provides no direct support for it. You are able to implement functionality similar to multiple inheritance by using the Java interfaces feature. Java interfaces provide object method descriptions, but contain no implementations.

Applet Basics

To create effective Java applets that can be controlled by JavaScript, you need to know how to create a Java applet. First, you need to understand the object-oriented nature of Java. Then, compare that understanding to the knowledge of JavaScript that you have obtained from the rest of this book. From such a comparison, you will obtain an excellent base from which to build enticing LiveConnect applications in which your JavaScript can control your Java applet.

The object-oriented nature of Java is instrumental in understanding a technical-standpoint definition of an applet. Because of the hierarchy of the Java classes, an applet is an extension of the Panel object in the Abstract Windows Toolkit (AWT). A panel is a subclass of the Container class, and as such can contain any Java language components, such as buttons, menus, and scroll bars.

Because an applet is actually a class, applets can be used to build other applets or full-blown applications. Just as your applets can be used within other applets, they also inherit features from the classes above them in the hierarchy.

Applets have four distinct stages in their lifetime. These stages are init(), start(), stop(), and destroy(). All these methods can be overwritten by the applet programmer to accomplish specific tasks during each stage in an applet's lifetime.

Here is a breakdown of the four stages:

♦ **init()**   The init stage consists of initializing any methods and variables the applet needs to function, such as loading images or reading parameters from an external file. The init() method is called when the applet is first loaded into the Web browser.

♦ **start()**   The start stage begins the primary functions of an applet. If an applet plays a sound, for example, the sound could start playing during the start stage. The start method is called when the init() method has finished and the applet is ready to execute.

♦ **stop()**   The stop stage can be used to stop any actions that might still be in progress from the start stage. A sound loop, for example, would need to be stopped when a person left the Web page containing a sound applet. The stop() method is called when a new page is loaded into the Web browser, or the Web browser is taken out of focus.

♦ **destroy()**   The destroy method is called automatically and completes any memory cleanup or garbage collection that needs to be done when an applet is destroyed. It can be overwritten, but this is not generally necessary because the Java garbage collector will clean up almost any memory that your application leaves allocated. The destroy method is called when you quit your Web browser.

Applet Java Code

All applets inherit the properties of the Panel object in the AWT and the Applet class attributes from java.applet.Applet. This is evident in the way that all Java applets are structured. In defining the initial applet,

```
public class Classname extends java.applet.Applet { }
```

the code shows how your applet class is a subclass of the Applet class. A number of methods are built into the Applet class to make developing applets easier, but they are beyond the scope of this book.

The idea of inheritance is fundamental to the structure of applets. Applets inherit the capability to contain user interface objects because all applets are Panels. Applets inherit a large part of their functionality from the Java Applet class.

Applet HTML

Currently, applets can be viewed on any platform. The Java world is continuing to expand, and soon Java will be available for more of the popular platforms. After your Java code has been compiled, it can be executed through any Java-capable browser. Applets require the following two components to execute:

◆ The compiled bytecode

◆ An HTML file containing an <APPLET> tag, basic applet information, and parameters

The compiled bytecode is the executable component of the applet created by any of a number of Java compilers.

To execute the code properly, the browser requires the HTML file. The HTML file is based on the <APPLET> tag, and is composed of the following basic structure:

```
<HTML>
     <APPLET CODEBASE=location of code CODE=filename.class WIDTH=100 HEIGHT=150
alt=alternate>
     <PARAM name="parameter"  value="accepted value">
     </APPLET>
</HTML>
```

The <APPLET> tag contains all of the information necessary to run your Java applet. The CODEBASE parameter contains the location of your executable code by specifying the base directory where your applet bytecode is stored. The CODE parameter contains the name of your applet class in the format of filename.class. The next parameters define the dimensions of your applet, specified by the WIDTH and HEIGHT parameters. The initial dimensions of the applet are given in pixels. The dimensions are so designated because the applet has to fit into the conventions of a HTML page layout. The <PARAM> tag defines the applet parameter name and the parameter's associated value. The <PARAM> tag is only necessary if the applet is designed to take parameters, and it can be repeated as many times as necessary to establish the parameter values for the applet. Here is a list of the tags and values that can be used in an applet HTML file:

◆ **<PARAM>**   The parameter tag also takes name and value options to specify the values for any parameters an applet accepts. The following are actual parameters to the <APPLET> tag, and are used to give the browser information about the Java applet itself:

◆ **<CODEBASE>**   The codebase is the base URL location of the Java bytecode. This enables you to have your code in a different directory than the page on which your applet appears.

◆ **<ALT>**   Identical to the HTML <ALT> tag, this tag enables you to provide an alternative image or text for Web browsers that are not Java-capable. Alternative options can also be specified by placing HTML code between the <APPLET> and </APPLET> tags.

◆ **<NAME>**   The <NAME> tag enables you to specify a symbolic name for an applet. The name is used as a reference so that other applets or JavaScript on the same page can communicate through a more intuitive name.

◆ **<ALIGN>**   Identical to the standard HTML <ALIGN> tag, this tag enables you to specify right, left, or center alignment of your applet window.

◆ **<VSPACE> and <HSPACE>**   These tags enable you to specify the amount of vertical and horizontal space around an applet when it is aligned to the left or right with the <ALIGN> tag.

◆ **<CODE>**   The code parameter is required with the <APPLET> tag. It specifies the location of the actual compiled applet. This location is relative to the <CODEBASE> tag. If no <CODEBASE> tag is specified, the Web browser generally looks in the same directory as where the HTML is located, and then in the directory from which the browser is running. The exact sequence depends on the Web browser that you are using; consult the documentation for your own Web browser.

◆ **<WIDTH>**   The <WIDTH> tag is used with the <APPLET> tag to specify the width of the window that should be opened when the applet is added to the page. It is required by the <APPLET> tag.

◆ **<HEIGHT>**   The <HEIGHT> tag is similar to width, specifying the height of the applet window. It is also required by the <APPLET> tag.

Hello World Example

The following code is the Java version of every programmer's typical first program, Hello World. This program writes the text "Hello World" to the browser screen.

```
1   import java.awt.Graphics;
2
3   public class HelloWorldApplet extends java.applet.Applet {
4
5       public void paint(Graphics g) {
6           g.drawString("Hello world!", 5, 25);
7   }
```

The preceding example is Java code in its simplest form, and is aimed at introducing new users to the syntax and simplicity of Java. As C++ programmers will notice, Java code looks very similar to C++. Line 1 tells the Java compiler that you will be using the Java windowing toolkit's graphics package in your applet.

Line 3 declares your applet as public and tells the compiler that your program is a subclass of the java.applet.Applet object.

Note All Java applets are derived from this base class; the syntax of this line will become very familiar to you.

Lines 5 and 6 override the standard Java applet's paint method enabling you to paint your own special message to the screen. You reference the Graphics object g, and call the drawString() method. The drawString() method takes three parameters. Parameter 1 is the string value that you want to draw on the screen. Parameter 2 is the number of lines down the screen to which you wish to start drawing the string. Finally, the third parameter is the number of columns to the right on the screen to which you want to start drawing the string.

This applet is meant to be very simple, and therefore provides an example to which even non-programmers can relate. A more complex example will be presented later in this appendix that incorporates Netscape's LiveConnect technology.

Now that you have seen how easy it is to write a Java applet on the Java side, let's take a look at the HTML needed to bring your first applet up in a Web browser.

Following is the HTML code for the Hello World example:

```
1   <HTML>
2   <HEAD>
3   <TITLE>Hello to Everyone!</TITLE>
```

```
4    </HEAD><BODY>
5    <P>My Java applet says:
6    <APPLET CODE="HelloWorldApplet.class" WIDTH=150 HEIGHT=25></APPLET>
7    </BODY>
8    </HTML>
```

Most of this HTML should look very familiar to you. The one interesting line is line 6. This tag is used to denote that an applet definition follows. Here is the complete syntax for the applet tag:

```
<APPLET
   [Codebase = path to directory containing class files]
   Code = name of the class file for this applet
   Width = width of the applet window in pixels >
   Height = height of the applet window in pixels
   [Alt = text to display if the browser is not Java-enabled]
   [Align = Left ¦ Right ¦ Center = where to align the applet in the browser
   ➥window]
   [Vspace = Vertical space to add around the applet window]
   [Hspace = Horizontal space to add around the applet window]
   [<PARAM Name= "parameter name 1" Value = "value of parameter 1">]
   [<PARAM Name= "parameter name 2" Value = "value of parameter 2">]
</APPLET>
```

Figure B.1 shows what the previous code looks like on-screen.

Figure B.1

Output of Hello World Java Applet and HTML.

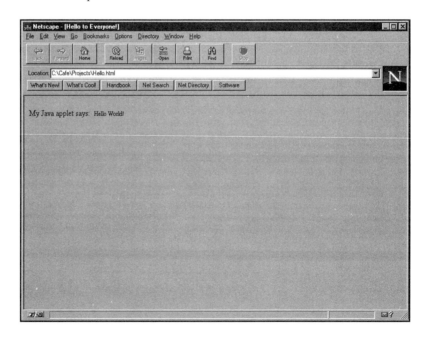

The only required parameters are the Code, Width, and Height. For this example, the name of the applet class is HelloWorldApplet.class, and the width and height of the applet are 150 and 25 respectively.

A More Complicated Example

The following code is a more complicated Java program that displays a graphic on the screen and plays a sound file at the same time. Although this is still a fairly simple Java applet, it does show off some of the more useful features of Java, namely its ease of using multimedia features such as graphics and sound.

Following is the Java code for the SightnSound example :

```
1    import java.awt.*;
2    import java.applet.*;
3    import java.lang.*;
4    import java.net.URL;
5
6    public class SightnSound extends java.applet.Applet   {
7         String graphicName;
8         Image imageFile;
9         String soundName;
10        AudioClip soundFile;
11
12       public String[][] getParameterInformation()   {
13            String[][] info={
14                {"graphic", "string",      "The image file to be displayed on
➡the screen."},
15                {"sound",   "string",      "The sound file to be played."},
16            };
17       return info;
18       }
19
20       public void init()   {
21            graphicName = getParameter("graphic");
22            soundName=getParameter("sound");
23            imageFile=getImage(getDocumentBase(),graphicName);
24            soundFile=getAudioClip(getDocumentBase(), soundName);
25       }
26
27       public void paint(Graphics g)    {
28            g.drawImage(imageFile, 0, 0, this);
```

```
29              }
30
31     public void start()    {
32           repaint();
33
34           //This could also be soundFile.play(); to play the sound once.
35           soundFile.loop();
36     }
37
38     public void stop()    {
39           soundFile.stop();
40     }
41 }
```

For this sample program, you use many more Java classes than you used in the Hello World sample. Lines 1–4 import quite a few classes. All the abstract window classes are imported in line 1, and then the applet classes are imported so that you can use the standard applet methods. Next you need to include the Java language classes for most of the data types. Finally in line 4, you import the java.net.URL class so that you can access files on the user's file system.

Next you declare your applet using the standard applet class definition:

```
public class SightnSound extends java.applet.Applet
```

Then in lines 7–10, you declare variables that will hold the names of the graphic and sound file as well as variables to hold the actual graphic and sound objects. In line 8, you use a new data type, an Image data type that holds the graphic that the Java applet will display. Similarly on line 10, you declare an AudioClip variable in which you store the actual sound file.

To make this a functional applet, SightnSound is designed to accept the image file and sound file from parameters specified in the <APPLET> tag. Parameters are a function of the user interface. They enable the user to specify changeable elements of an applet—in this case, the image and the sound for the applet. Lines 12 through 18 enable the applet to convert the parameters into variables to use internally. The information is passed from the HTML file to the applet. Then the applet stores that information in an array where it can be queried by other methods, such as getParameter(). By using getParameter(), the applet can use the user-provided file names to load the image file and the sound file.

In lines 20–25, the names of the image and sound file are read from the parameters in the HTML document into the Java applet. Then the actual image and sound file are loaded into their respective variables. Now that you have the image and sound files, you are ready to use them on your Web page.

In lines 27–29, you override the default paint method so that you can paint your image into the browser window by using the drawImage() method. The drawImage() method takes four parameters. The first parameter is an Image class that contains a valid graphics file. The next two parameters are the top right corner of the window in which you are going to display the graphic. The final parameter is the parent window for the graphic. The paint() method is overridden to utilize the drawImage() method of the Image object. When repaint() is called in start(), the update() method is automatically called, which in turn calls the paint() method. While in the start() method, you also start the sound playing.

The last thing that you need to do is override the stop() method for your applet. The stop() method is called at any time when either the user chooses to go to another URL or the user minimizes the Web browser. Within the stop() method, you want to stop your sound file from playing so that the user is not constantly reminded that your applet is running in the background.

Following is the HTML code for the SightnSound example:

Now that you have seen what a few lines of Java code can do, you are probably wondering how much more work it takes on the HTML side of the project. The answer is, not much. Take a look at the following HTML code.

```
1    <HTML>
2    <HEAD>
3    <TITLE>Hello Web Surfers</TITLE>
4    </HEAD>
5    <BODY>
6    <P>My second Java applet says:
7    <APPLET CODE="SightnSoundApplet.class"  WIDTH=300 HEIGHT=250>
8    <PARAM NAME="graphic" VALUE="graphic/hello.gif">
9    <PARAM NAME="sound" VALUE="sound/hello.au">
10   </APPLET>
11   </BODY>
12   </HTML>
```

The only difference between this HTML and the HTML for the HelloWorld applet is lines 8 and 9. These two lines define the graphic file and the sound file that your SightnSound Java applet are to use. Line 8 tells the applet to find the directory that it is running in, change to the graphic directory, and use the hello.gif file located there when displaying your Web page. Similarly, line 9 tells the applet to change to the sound directory and use the hello.au sound file located there as the sound to play in your applet. As you can tell from this example, Java does not make the HTML side of your Java projects any more difficult. This gives non-programmers the ability to use Java applets in their Web pages, even if they don't know how to write in Java.

Figure B.2 displays the output for the previous code.

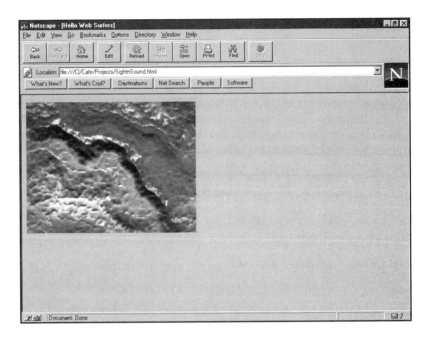

Controlling Java from JavaScript

Now that you have a basic understanding of how to program in Java, you can get to the real heart of this appendix—that is, Netscape's LiveConnect technology. LiveConnect extends the use of the Java programming language to other Netscape technologies like JavaScript, HTML, and plug-ins so that they can interact seamlessly with one another. LiveConnect links these different elements together and enables Java and JavaScript to script and control any object of another type: JavaScript, HTML, Java, or plug-ins. This enables richer, more complex applications to be developed on a Web page and produces truly compelling results. A mouse click can trigger a JavaScript; a Java applet can use an audio plug-in; a JavaScript can pass values to a Java applet. All of this becomes reality after you learn how to use the LiveConnect technology.

LiveConnect works because it is based on the platform-independent Java language object model. Using LiveConnect, each component on a Web page can expose its functionality via a Java object interface. Likewise, each component can call other functions in other objects regardless of their composition. A Java applet can, for example, use a method declared in a plug-in or a JavaScript. Likewise, a plug-in can call a JavaScript object or a method in a Java applet by using the Java object model.

You may be asking yourself why you would ever want to have all this interactivity, but you will quickly realize the benefits of being able to use all these technologies in a cohesive manner. An advantage of a JavaScript is that it can validate user data in fewer lines of code than Java or a plug-in. Another advantage of JavaScript is that creating user interface elements is a trivial task, but the same tasks in a Java applet would be more difficult. By the same token, an advantage of Java is that it can perform more complex algorithms more easily than a JavaScript. You can, therefore, create a simple JavaScript that handles receiving all of a user's data input and validation of that input. Then you can pass that data off to a Java applet to perform all of the complex data manipulation, whether it be interaction with a database or sorting a list of numbers. In this manner, you can use the best of both technologies to accomplish a task more quickly and in a more elegant fashion.

Through the information in this appendix, you will understand how the LiveConnect technology enables you to use two different technologies, Java and JavaScript, to make your Web pages more compelling (and give them the capability of offering Web surfers a more interactive media). The connection between Java and JavaScript is the first step in understanding LiveConnect. In the next appendix, you will be able to take the second step by understanding the connection between JavaScript and plug-ins. After completing these two chapters, you will have a thorough understanding of LiveConnect and have the ability to use the technology to turn your Web pages into one-of-a-kind masterpieces.

Netscape LiveConnect provides three ways for JavaScript to communicate with Java:

◆ JavaScript can control Java applets.

◆ JavaScript can control Java plug-ins.

◆ JavaScript can call Java methods directly from an HTML document.

This section discusses how you can use JavaScript to control Java applets. Such control enables you to create your own LiveConnect-enabled Web pages. By using JavaScript to control your Java applets, you gain unparalleled control over your Web pages. Just think, you can do all of the user interface for your applet in a JavaScript form, which takes only a few minutes. Then you create all of the real work functions in your Java applet. Add a few lines of JavaScript code to your HTML page, and suddenly your JavaScript is talking to your Java applet, passing parameters and variables back and forth. This enables you to create simple interactive applets as well as incredibly complex systems that could become one of the new generation of *Internet applications* (possibly replacing your old desktop applications).

Referencing Java Applets Within JavaScript

Each Java applet in a HTML document is accessed in JavaScript by referencing the document object in the following way:

```
document.appletName
```

where appletName is the value of the NAME attribute of the Java APPLET tag for the specific applet you would like to control. The following HTML, for example, launches an applet called "myApplet":

```
<APPLET CODE=Mytest.class NAME=myApplet WIDTH=100 HEIGHT=50>
    <PARAM NAME="string" VALUE="Test value" >
    <PARAM NAME="integer" VALUE=86>
</APPLET>
```

You can reference this applet in JavaScript in any of the following ways:

- ◆ **document.myApplet**   Referencing the myApplet object directly from within the document object.

- ◆ **document.applets["myApplet"]**   Referencing the document objects' applets array, using the "myApplet" offset. The applets array contains pointers to all of the applets in the current Web page. Each applet has an integer value associated with it that corresponds to its position in the applets array. The integer is relative to the applets position in the document.

- ◆ **document.applets[0]**   You can also reference the applet directly through the applets array. If it is the first applet in the document, for example, you refer to it as the zero element in the applets array.

Accessing Applets

All public variables declared in a Java applet, its ancestor classes, and packages are available in JavaScript. Static methods and properties declared in an applet are available to JavaScript as methods and properties of the applet object. You can get and set property values, and you can call methods that return string, numeric, and Boolean values.

All access to applets is done through the document object. Suppose, for example, that you have a WAV player applet, named "myWavPlayer", that exposes a start() and a stop() method. To start the applet though JavaScript, you make a method call such as:

```
document.myWavPlayer.start()
```

Suppose that your WAV player applet's start method takes two parameters. The first parameter is a Boolean that tells the applet whether it should continue to loop after it finishes. The second parameter is an integer that specifies the number of seconds to delay between the end of one playing of the WAV file and the start of the next playing. You would then call the start method just as you would call any other method in C++:

```
document.myWavPlayer.start(true, 5)
```

This tells your WAV player applet to continually loop until it is explicitly stopped, and to wait five seconds between each successive playing of the WAV file.

Adding JavaScript Control to a Java Applet

Enabling JavaScript to control your Java applet is a very simple process.

1. In your Java applet, declare the functions that you want visible to JavaScript as Public, as in the following:

    ```
    public void myFunction()
    ```

2. Recompile your Java applet.

3. Add appropriate function calls to your HTML, as in the following:

    ```
    document.myApplet.myFunction()
    ```

    where myApplet is the name given to the embedded applet and myFunction is the name of the Java function that you wish to call.

4. Make certain that your Java .class file is in the same directory as your HTML file.

5. Launch Netscape and watch your JavaScript and Java applet run!

That's all there is to the communication part of the LiveConnect system. The majority of the work is in creating the rest of the Java applet and the HTML Web page. The next section provides an example of a fairly simple LiveConnect system that enables you to control a Java alarm clock from your JavaScript.

Presentation of the Java Clock Applet

To get more acquainted with communication between a JavaScript and a Java applet, consider the following project. It is a simple alarm clock for which the user sets the time for the alarm to go off. All of the user interface and user input validation is handled by a few lines of JavaScript. The checking for whether the alarm should sound and the actual sounding of the alarm are handled by a Java applet. By writing a few lines of code in each component, you can create a fairly sophisticated package in a few minutes.

Source Listing—HTML

Before you look at the Java source code for the Java clock applet, take a look at the more familiar JavaScript code to get an idea of how little it takes on the JavaScript side to create an interface to your Java applet.

```
1    <HTML>
2    <HEAD>
3    <TITLE>Java Alarm Clock</TITLE>
4    <SCRIPT Language="JavaScript">
5    <!--
6    function processInput(myHour,myMinute,mySecond) {
7        //Convert from string to integer
8        myHour = parseInt(myHour)
9        myMinute = parseInt(myMinute)
10       mySecond = parseInt(mySecond)
11       //Validate user input
12       if ( (myHour > 23 ) || (myHour < 0) || (myMinute > 59) || (myMinute < 0) ||
13          (mySecond > 59) || (mySecond < 0) ) {
14          //Invalid input
15          alert("Invalid values used to set alarm clock.\n\n Please try again")
16       } else {
17          //Set the alarm
18          document.AlarmClockApplet.setAlarm(myHour,myMinute,mySecond)
19       }
20    }
21    //-->
22    </SCRIPT>
23    </HEAD>
24    <BODY>
25    <H1>Java Alarm Clock</H1>
26    <APPLET CODE="AlarmClock.class" NAME="AlarmClockApplet" HEIGHT=75
27    WIDTH=400>
28    <PARAM NAME="Hour" Value="6">
29    <PARAM NAME="Minute" Value="30">
30    <PARAM NAME="Second" Value="0">
31    <PARAM NAME="AudioFile" Value="wakeUp.au">
```

```
32   </APPLET>
33   <FORM NAME="AlarmForm">
34   Please enter alarm values below:<br>
35   Hour<INPUT TYPE="text" NAME="formHour" SIZE="2">
36   Minute<INPUT TYPE="text" NAME="formMinute" SIZE="2">
37   Second<INPUT TYPE="text" NAME="formSecond" SIZE="2">
38   <INPUT TYPE="button" VALUE="Change Alarm"
39   OnClick="processInput( AlarmForm.formHour.value,
     ↪AlarmForm.formMinute.value,
40     AlarmForm.formSecond.value)">
41   </FORM>
42   </BODY>
43   </HTML>
```

The start of the HTML document (lines 1–3) are standard HTML tags to set up the document. The processInput() method definition (line 6) sets up the function that will eventually call the Java applet. This function takes three parameters, one each for hours, minutes, and seconds.

The first process in the processInput function is to convert the string parameters, myHour, myMinute, and mySecond to integer values in preparation of sending these values to the Java applet. This conversion process is done in lines 7–10 using the JavaScript parseInt() function.

Because it is easier to validate values in JavaScript than in Java, you should perform your input value validation next. An example validation is performed in lines 12–13. Because this applet assumes military time, it will check to make certain that the hour is between 0 and 24. In the same manner, it checks to make certain that minutes and seconds are between 0 and 60. If the applet detects a validation error with one of the values, it alerts the user (line 15) and never passes control to the Java applet. Not only is performing the value validation in JavaScript easier, you also avoid the overhead of calling the Java applet with bad values, and thus increase the perceived speed of your Web page.

Now that you have your values converted to the correct data type and you know that the values are correct, you are finally ready to call your Java applet. Line 18 makes the all important function call to the Java applet. You start by referencing the JavaScript document object. From there you are able to reference any of the objects that appear in your HTML document. One of these objects is your Java applet, defined in lines 26–31.

After you have narrowed your object list down to a specific Java applet, you can narrow it down even further by referencing any of your applet's publicly declared functions. In this case, you will reference the setAlarm() function (see the AlarmClockApplet code later in this section for more detail). This function takes three integer values, one each for hours, minutes, and seconds. If you are familiar with object-oriented programming, this syntax will look familiar. The familiar syntax is one of the major advantages of LiveConnect. There is really no difficult syntax to learn, it is just a matter of using logic and planning to organize all of your objects so you can reference them.

The next thing to do is to set up your Java applet. Line 26 sets up the applet tag for your Java applet. In this case, the Java applet is called the AlarmClockApplet. You will always want to set up default values for your Java applet since it will not be very interesting if it has no values with which to start. In this case, the default values for the alarm are set for 6:30 a.m. (lines 28–30). The applet will play the *AudioFile* parameter whenever the alarm clock goes off (line 31).

After you have set up the function to call your Java program, you now need to set up the rest of your HTML document to provide the user interface for your Java program. In lines 33–37, the JavaScript form is set up so that you have text input boxes for hours, minutes, and seconds. This enables the user to change the time of the alarm clock. Of course you can't know when the user has finished typing the alarm clock time, so you need to add a button for the user to *set* the alarm (line 38).

The final interesting portion of this HTML document is what to do when the user clicks on your button. All you need to do is call your function that converts, validates, and passes information on to your Java applet. Lines 39–40 perform this action. Now that you understand the JavaScript portion of this applet, let's go on to the Java portion.

Source Listing—Java

```
1    import java.awt.Graphics;
2    import java.util.Date;
3    import java.applet.AudioClip;
4
5    public class AlarmClock extends java.applet.Applet implements Runnable {
6
7        Thread clockThread;
8        Date alarmTime = new Date();
9        AudioClip alarmSnd;
10
11    public void init() {
12        setAlarm( Integer.parseInt(getParameter("Hour")),
13                  Integer.parseInt(getParameter("Minute")),
14                  Integer.parseInt(getParameter("Second")) );
15        alarmSnd = getAudioClip(getCodeBase(),getParameter("AudioFile"));
```

```
16
17    }
18
19    public void start() {
20        if (clockThread == null) {
21            clockThread = new Thread(this, "Clock");
22            clockThread.start();
23        }
24    }
25    public void run() {
26        while (clockThread != null) {
27            repaint();
28            try {
29                clockThread.sleep(1000);
30            } catch (InterruptedException e){
31            }
32        }
33    }
34    public void setAlarm(int myHour,int myMinute,int mySecond) {
35        alarmTime.setHours(myHour);
36        alarmTime.setMinutes(myMinute);
37        alarmTime.setSeconds(mySecond);
38    }
39
40    public void paint(Graphics g) {
41        Date now = new Date();
42        g.drawString("Current time is  " + now.getHours() + ":" +
➥now.getMinutes() +
43            ":" + now.getSeconds(), 5, 10);
44        g.drawString("Alarm is set for " + alarmTime.getHours() + ":" +
45            alarmTime.getMinutes() + ":" + alarmTime.getSeconds(), 5, 30);
46        if ( (now.getHours()   == alarmTime.getHours()) &&
47            (now.getMinutes() == alarmTime.getMinutes()) &&
48            (now.getSeconds() == alarmTime.getSeconds()) )
49              alarmSnd.play();
50
51    }
52    public void stop() {
53        clockThread.stop();
54        clockThread = null;
55    }
56 }
```

This Java example uses many of the essential features of Java. Although all of the explanations are written for programmers of all levels, they do assume that you have a basic working knowledge of Java. If you are unable to follow them, you should refer to your Java documentation to clarify fundamental Java concepts.

The first thing that you must do is to import all of the necessary Java components for your Java applet to run (lines 1–3). Because you are going to be using graphic objects, you need to import java.awt.Graphics. The next objects that you need are the java.util.Date objects. You store the date information passed from the JavaScript code in Date objects. The final package that you need is the java.applet.AudioClip object. This object is used to store and play the sound clip when the alarm clock goes off.

Next you need to declare your applet (line 5):

```
public class AlarmClock extends java.applet.Applet implements Runnable
```

You must declare the class as public to use it in your HTML document. Like all applets, your AlarmClock applet is derived from java.applet.Applet. The Runnable interface may be new to many programmers. This interface enables your applet to run on a new thread separate from all other threads. This is a necessary evil because you want the alarm to have the capability of going off, even if the user is inputting information into the Alarm form. By using the Runnable interface, the alarm has the capability of sounding whether the user is entering information or just sitting and waiting. If you are familiar with the concept of timers in other languages, the Runnable interface is a similar concept.

Lines 7–9 set up your variables to use throughout the applet. Line 7 is the new thread on which the AlarmClock applet runs. Line 8 creates the Date object that holds all of the hour, minute, and second data for the alarm. Finally, you need to set up a variable to control your sound; this is the AudioClip object on line 9.

```
11    public void init() {
12        setAlarm( Integer.parseInt(getParameter("Hour")),
13                  Integer.parseInt(getParameter("Minute")),
14                  Integer.parseInt(getParameter("Second")) );
15        alarmSnd = getAudioClip(getCodeBase(),getParameter("AudioFile"));
16    }
```

The first method that you need is the one to initialize your Java applet. To accomplish this, use the init() method. In this case, call the setAlarm() method in your Java applet by using the default values read from the HTML document. This method is a perfect example of how compact your code can be. This example converts the string values read from the HTML document and passes the values to the setAlarm() method. Line 15 stores the audio clip into the alarmSnd class variable by reading the name of the audio file from the parameters in the HTML document. If the setAlarm() method looks familiar, you are correct. Look back to line 18 of the HTML document listing for the Alarm Clock example. More on this later when you get to the code for the setAlarm() method.

```
19    public void start() {
20        if (clockThread == null) {
21            clockThread = new Thread(this, "Clock");
22            clockThread.start();
23        }
24    }
```

The start() method is interesting because it shows how to set up and start a thread for your AlarmClock applet. You only want to start the thread once, so the check on line 20 is very important. You then store the newly created thread in the clockThread class variable so that you can manipulate it later.

```
25    public void run() {
26        while (clockThread != null) {
27            repaint();
28            try {
29                clockThread.sleep(1000);
30            } catch (InterruptedException e){
31            }
32        }
33    }
```

You are now ready to actually run the Clock applet. You want to make certain that the clock thread is not null (line 26), otherwise your applet will have problems. You don't want the applet to be checking to see if the alarm should go off every cycle of the computer clock, so you have the thread on which the Clock applet is running take a rest for 1000 milliseconds in between each check of the alarm time. Your clock thread, however, may be interrupted by another thread while sleeping. In such a case, it throws an InterruptedException.

Note | Now, because run() is not defined as throwing this exception, you must *hide* the fact by catching and handling the exception yourself. This is the reason for the try/catch pair on lines 28 and 30 respectively.

Line 27 forces a repaint to occur every time that an InterruptedException happens.

```
34    public void setAlarm(int myHour,int myMinute,int mySecond) {
35        alarmTime.setHours(myHour);
36        alarmTime.setMinutes(myMinute);
37        alarmTime.setSeconds(mySecond);
38    }
```

Now on to that familiar looking setAlarm() method. This is the implementation of the method that is called on line 18 of the HTML listing for the Clock applet. This method takes three integer values—one each for hours, minutes, and seconds—and uses them to set the time that the alarm goes off by modifying the times stored in the alarmTime Date object. This is the heart of the Java/JavaScript communication. Easy, right? That is the true power of the LiveConnect philosophy. It makes everything unassuming and easy to implement while hiding all of the complicated back-stage processing away from the programmer.

```
40    public void paint(Graphics g) {
41        Date now = new Date();
42        g.drawString("Current time is  " + now.getHours() + ":" +
                now.getMinutes() +
43            ":" + now.getSeconds(), 5, 10);
44        g.drawString("Alarm is set for " + alarmTime.getHours() + ":" +
45            alarmTime.getMinutes() + ":" + alarmTime.getSeconds(), 5, 30);
46        if ( (now.getHours()   == alarmTime.getHours()) &&
47            (now.getMinutes() == alarmTime.getMinutes()) &&
48            (now.getSeconds() == alarmTime.getSeconds()) )
49              alarmSnd.play();
50    }
```

The paint() method is where most of the logic for your simple Alarm clock applet takes place. First, on line 41 you create a new Date object that holds the current time. Then on lines 42–43 you print to the Netscape screen the current time in hours, minutes, and seconds. Next on lines 44–45 you print to the Netscape screen the alarm time in hours, minutes, and seconds. Now comes the all important step of determining whether it is time for the alarm to go off. Lines 46–48 compare the hours, minutes, and seconds from your now Date object to the hours, minutes, and seconds of your alarmTime Date object. If all three (hours, minutes, and seconds) match, then it is time to let the user know by playing the alarm sound.

```
52    public void stop() {
53        clockThread.stop();
54        clockThread = null;
55    }
```

The final method of the Alarm clock example is the stop() method. Normally this method is very bland. It does become an interesting sidebar, however, because you are using threads. With a threading Java applet, you must be careful about re-entry and processing multiple applets. When the operating system tells your applet to stop, therefore, not only do you have to tell the applet to stop, you have to tell your applet thread to stop also. And for good measure, you should set the thread to null to ensure that when you check for a null thread later on in your applet, you have a null value and the correct code is executed.

That's it for the Alarm clock example. This is a good first LiveConnect project because it is simple enough that first-time Java programmers will be able to understand, and accomplished Java programmers will be able to immediately pick out the portions of the Java and HTML that are non-standard, and therefore part of the LiveConnect functionality. You can also use this example as a framework for your own LiveConnect applications because it is so simple.

Controlling JavaScript from Java

Now that you have seen how you can pass data from a JavaScript to a Java applet, you can take a look at how you can go the other way around. To access JavaScript methods, properties, and data structures from your Java applet, you must first import the Netscape JavaScript package into your Java applet as shown in the following example:

```
import netscape.javascript.*
```

The package netscape.javascript defines the JSObject class and the JSException exception object, which enables access to all of the JavaScript functions and variables.

Just including the Netscape JavaScript package in your Java applet is not enough for anyone to use your Java applet methods and variable in a Web page. The author of the HTML page must explicitly permit an applet to access JavaScript by specifying the MAYSCRIPT attribute in the APPLET tag. This prevents an applet from accessing JavaScript on a page without the knowledge of the page author. If your Java applet tries to access JavaScript when the MAYSCRIPT attribute is not specified on the HTML page, an exception is raised. You should always provide an exception handler when dealing with the JavaScript object. To give the myApplet.class applet access to JavaScript on your page, for example, specify the following:

```
<APPLET CODE = "myApplet.class" WIDTH=200 HEIGHT=150 NAME="myApp" MAYSCRIPT>
```

Before your Java applet can access the JavaScript object, you must get a handle for the Netscape Navigator window. To do this, use the getWindow() method in the class netscape.javascript.JSObject.

If window is a previously declared variable of type JSObject, for example, the following code assigns a window handle to window:

```
public void init()
    {
    window = JSObject.getWindow(this);
    }
```

Accessing JavaScript Objects and Properties

Just as you can access Java applet public methods and variables from JavaScript, you can also access JavaScript objects and properties from Java. The getMember() method in the class netscape.javascript.JSObject enables you to access JavaScript objects and properties. Call getWindow() to get a handle for the JavaScript window, and then call getMember() to access each JavaScript object in a containership path in turn.

The following Java code enables you to access the JavaScript object document.testForm through the variable myForm, for example:

```
public void init()
    {
    window = JSObject.getWindow(this);
    JSObject doc = (JSObject) window.getMember("document");
    JSObject myForm = (JSObject) doc.getMember("testForm");
    }
```

Notice that JavaScript objects appear as instances of the class netscape.javascript.JSObject in Java. Values passed from Java to JavaScript are converted as described in the JSObject Package documentation available from the Netscape Web site or the LiveConnect SDK.

If the JavaScript object document.testForm.test is a check box, the following code enables you to access its checked property:

```
public void init()
    {
    window = JSObject.getWindow(this);
    JSObject doc = (JSObject) window.getMember("document");
    JSObject myForm = (JSObject) doc.getMember("testForm");
    JSObject check = (JSObject) myForm.getMember("test");
    Boolean isChecked = (Boolean) check.getMember("checked");
    }
```

Calling JavaScript Methods

The call() and eval() methods in the class netscape.javascript.JSObject enable you to call JavaScript methods. As with accessing JavaScript objects and properties, use getWindow() to get a handle for the JavaScript window, and then use call() or eval() to access a JavaScript method.

Use either of the following syntaxes to call JavaScript methods:

1. JSObject.getWindow().call("methodName", arguments)

2. JSObject.getWindow().eval("expression")

In the first form of this syntax, methodName is the name of the JavaScript method you want to call, and arguments is an array of arguments to pass to the JavaScript method. In the second form of the syntax, expression is a JavaScript expression that evaluates to a JavaScript method.

The following code uses call() to call the JavaScript alert method when a mouseUp event occurs, for example:

```
public void init()
    {
    JSObject window = JSObject.getWindow(this);
    }


public boolean mouseUp(Event e, int x, int y)
    {
    window.call("alert("Mouse Up from Call()");");
    return true;
    }
```

Similarly, the following code uses eval() to call the JavaScript alert method:

```
public void init()
    {
    JSObject window = JSObject.getWindow(this);
    }


public boolean mouseUp(Event e, int x, int y)
    {
    window.eval("alert("Mouse up from Eval()");");
    return true;
    }
```

Summary

As you can see, it does not take a lot of Java code to make some great enhancements to your Web pages. With a few short lines of code, you can add graphics and sound easily by just linking an applet to your pages with a few lines of HTML. Now that you have an idea about the basic workings of applets, you can move on to more advanced Java and LiveConnect applets.

Applets are the most common use of the Java language today. Applets are more complicated than many Java applications because they are executed and drawn inline within Web pages, but they can access the graphics, user interface, and event structure provided by the Web browser itself.

A few basic things to remember about Java applets are:

◆ All applets you develop by using Java inherit from the Applet class part of the java.applet package. The Applet class provides basic behavior for how the applet will integrate with and react to the browser and various forms of input from that browser and the person running it. By subclassing Applet, you have access to all that behavior.

◆ Applets have five main methods used for the basic activities an applet performs during its life cycle: init(), start(), stop(), destroy(), and paint(). Although you don't need to override all these methods, these are the most common methods you'll see repeated in many of the applets you will create in this book and in other sample programs.

◆ To run a compiled applet class file, you include it in an HTML Web page by using the <APPLET> tag. When a Java-capable browser comes across <APPLET>, it loads and runs the applet described in that tag. Note that to publish Java applets on the Web alongside HTML files, you do not need special server software; any Web server will work.

◆ Unlike applications, applets do not have a common line on which to pass arguments, so those arguments must be passed into the applet through the HTML file that contains it. You indicate parameters in an HTML file by using the <PARAM> tag inside the opening and closing <APPLET> tags. <PARAM> has two attributes: NAME for the name of the parameter, and VALUE for its value. Inside the body of the applet, you can then gain access to those parameters using the getParameter() method.

This appendix has just touched the surface of the Java programming language. Java is a full-featured programming language, and undoubtedly the subject of applet programming could fill an entire book of its own. Java is also constantly evolving. As the language becomes more complete, changes will be made. To learn about all of the necessary changes, updates, and features that could not be covered here, you should consult the official Sun documentation of the Java language. Most of the API and other Java-related documentation can be found at http://www.javasoft.com. Keep in mind that the Sun documentation is very technical and often requires an advanced understanding of Java, but as a technical reference source it can be invaluable.

◆ This appendix introduces you to Java programming basics. Specifically the limitations imposed by the Java programming language and the current World Wide Web browsers. This appendix provides background information to enable the beginning Java programmer to make informed design decisions while creating their LiveConnect projects.

◆ This appendix also introduces Java Applet basics that enable you to create your own Java Applets and embed them within your HTML page. This section includes several examples to get the beginning Java programmer off the ground. This appendix is very important for the beginning Java programmer because it enables the beginner to quickly get up to speed and create LiveConnect projects in which he or she controls the Java applets.

◆ You also receive instruction on how to control your Java applets with a JavaScript by using LiveConnect technology. This appendix includes an in depth look at a real LiveConnect project. This appendix strips LiveConnect to the bones and shows you how to actually use the LiveConnect technology to enable your JavaScripts to control your Java applets by using the shared Java object model.

◆ Finally, an introduction instructs on how you can control a JavaScript from a Java applet, which is as simple as controlling a Java applet from a JavaScript. This appendix is also a down-and-dirty, hands-on appendix in which you use the LiveConnect JavaScript object model to control your JavaScripts using Java.

APPENDIX C

Writing a Plug-In that Can Be Controlled by JavaScript

This appendix explains the use of the Netscape Navigator LiveConnect/Plug-In Software Development Kit (SDK) that enables third-party developers to extend the capabilities of Navigator by creating new Netscape plug-ins and enabling them with LiveConnect. Being LiveConnect-enabled means that they can be controlled by both Java and JavaScript.

By developing their own plug-ins, developers can provide integration with, and control over, a wide range of data types, protocols, and file formats from within Netscape Navigator. Because plug-ins can be written in C++, they can do anything available in that language, which opens up an area that was unavailable until now. With LiveConnect you can extend this even further by exposing portions of your plug-in so that you are able to control the plug-in from your JavaScript.

◆ This section introduces you to writing plug-ins for the Netscape Navigator. In particular, you will learn how to use the Netscape plug-in API together with the LiveConnect SDK to create JavaScript controllable plug-ins. This enables you to create some of the most user-interactive and compelling Web pages around.

◆ This section also introduces you to LiveConnect plug-in basics that enable you to create your own plug-ins and embed them within your HTML page. This section includes a sample application that takes you through all the steps involved in the creation of a LiveConnect-enabled plug-in.

◆ First you will learn how to set up your environment to write a Netscape plug-in. This is the first step to creating not only standard Netscape plug-ins, but also LiveConnect-enabled plug-ins.

  ◆ Next, you must decide which plug-in methods will be available to your JavaScript scripts. A little forward planning saves you much time in the future.

  ◆ Then, you will implement the Java interface that acts as buffer between your Netscape plug-in and your JavaScript code.

  ◆ Next, you are ready to implement your Java native methods. These native methods are the actual functions that you call from JavaScript and pass variables between your JavaScript and the native code contained in your plug-ins.

  ◆ Then, you need to implement the Netscape plug-in shell that acts as a buffer between your Java native methods and the Netscape Navigator window and object. You must do this so that the Netscape Navigator knows how to act when it sees your plug-in embedded in an HTML file.

  ◆ After you have everything planned out, you are ready to actually write the code contained in your plug-in. This will be standard C++ code that implements anything that you want.

  ◆ Finally, you must write the HTML code to show off your plug-in. This section introduces you to the <EMBED> tag used to tell your Web browser that you want to load a plug-in.

Introducing Plug-Ins

Plug-ins extend your Web browser to include a wide range of interactive and multimedia capabilities. Plug-ins are software modules merged into your Web browser and supplement the browser's capabilities.

Plug-ins offer a rich variety of functions and features to enhance and increase the functionality and compatibility of your browser. Plug-ins have been used as

◆ Multimedia objects, such as Live3D, Macromedia Shockwave, and LiveVideo

◆ Applications, such as calculators and information managers

◆ Utilities, such as OLE embedded objects and compression/decompression

The development of plug-in technology is constantly expanding beyond current applications, as demonstrated by the growing list of independent software vendors creating new and innovative plug-ins.

Plug-ins are usually installed by running a setup program supplied with the plug-in. Plug-ins reside on the user's local hard drive and are detected by the user's Web browser when it starts up. When the browser encounters a data type associated with a plug-in (either embedded in an HTML page or in a separate file), it loads the appropriate plug-in and gives it access to all or a part of the browser window. The plug-in remains active until the browser is terminated, or the plug-in's associated page or file is closed.

Discussing Plug-In Basics

Plug-ins are dynamic code modules, native to the specific platform on which Netscape Navigator runs. The primary goal of the plug-in API is to allow existing platform-dependent code to integrate with and enhance Navigator's core functionality by providing support for new data types. The plug-in API is designed to provide the maximum flexibility and be functionally equivalent across all platforms supported by Navigator.

Plug-ins are intended to complement many platform-specific architectures such as OLE and OpenDoc as well as platform-independent programming languages such as Java. OLE and OpenDoc are powerful, general-purpose component software systems, and components programmed in these languages are relatively complex and large. Netscape plug-ins are designed specifically to extend Netscape Navigator and are relatively simple and small. Java applets are secure and inherently cross-platform, but developing applets requires coding in a new language with new development tools. Netscape plug-ins can be written in C or C++ using existing development tools; this makes it easier to reuse existing code and platform-specific operating system capabilities.

With the plug-in API, plug-ins are capable of

◆ Registering one or more MIME types to be handled by the Netscape browser

◆ Obtaining data from Internet URLs

- ◆ Posting data to Internet URLs

- ◆ Drawing into a part of a Navigator window or frame

- ◆ Receiving keyboard and mouse events from the user

Plug-ins can be used one of two ways: either by being embedded in a Navigator window or by taking up the entire Navigator window. An embedded plug-in is part of a larger HTML document and is loaded by Navigator when the document is displayed. The plug-in is then visible as a rectangular window in the page. Embedded plug-ins are generally used for multimedia images that enhance or extend the text in the page. A full-page plug-in is not part of an HTML page, and is loaded by Navigator when the user opens a file of a MIME type registered by a plug-in, by clicking an URL to the file, dragging the file to the Navigator's icon, or opening the file from within Navigator. The loaded plug-in completely fills the Navigator window. Full-page plug-ins are commonly used for document viewers that take the place of HTML documents.

The part of the application window that does not display plug-in data remains familiar to the Netscape user because plug-ins rarely alter the user interface. In particular, the basic operations of Navigator, such as navigation, history, and opening files, apply to all pages regardless of which plug-ins are required to view a page.

 Scroll bars are not displayed for a full-page plug-in. If scroll bars are necessary in full-page mode, the plug-in must draw and maintain the scroll bars.

Using Plug-Ins and HTML

Embedded plug-ins are loaded by Navigator when the user encounters an HTML page that includes an embedded object with a MIME type registered by a plug-in. When loaded, an embedded plug-in is displayed as part of the browser window in a rectangular portion of the document. This is similar to how a GIF or JPEG image is embedded, except that the plug-in can be active and respond to user events (such as keyboard input and mouse clicks).

Plug-in objects are embedded in an HTML page by using the EMBED tag. The syntax of the EMBED tag is:

```
<EMBED attributes> ... </EMBED>
```

The following attributes are used with the EMBED tag:

HEIGHT="value" defines the horizontal location of the plug-in in the HTML page.

HIDDEN="value" indicates whether the plug-in is visible on the page. The value can be either true (the default value) or false.

PALETTE="value" indicates the mode of the plug-in's color palette. The value can be either foreground or background (the default).

PLUGINSPAGE="URL" indicates the location of instructions on installing the plug-in.

SRC="URL" optionally indicates the location of the plug-in data file. Either the SRC attribute or the TYPE attribute is required in an EMBED tag.

TYPE="type" optionally indicates the MIME type of the EMBED tag, which in turn determines which plug-in is loaded to handle this EMBED tag. Use TYPE instead of SRC for plug-ins that require no data or plug-ins that fetch all their data dynamically.

WIDTH="value" optionally defines the vertical location of the plug-in in the HTML page.

UNITS="value" defines the measurement unit used by the HEIGHT and WIDTH attributes. The value can be either pixels (the default) or en (half the point size).

In addition to these standard attributes, plug-ins may optionally have private attributes to communicate additional parameters between the HTML page and the plug-in code. Navigator ignores all HTML standard attributes when parsing the page, but passes all attributes to the plug-in, enabling the plug-in to examine the attribute list for any private attributes that may modify its behavior.

A plug-in that plays a Windows WAV file, for example, could have private parameters to determine whether the plug-in should automatically start playing the sound, and whether the audio player should quit when the sound is done, and whether to loop the sound until the user presses a button. Take a look at the following example EMBED tag:

```
<EMBED SRC="mysound.wav" WIDTH=100 HEIGHT=100 AUTOPLAY=true EXIT=true
LOOP=true>
```

Navigator would interpret the SRC tag to load the WAV file and determine the MIME type of the data. It would also interpret the WIDTH and HEIGHT values to make the plug-in window 100 pixels by 100 pixels. The Navigator browser would simply ignore the private attributes AUTOSTART and LOOP and pass them to the plug-in with the rest of the attributes. The plug-in could then scan its list of attributes to see if it should automatically start the WAV file, exit after the sound is played, or loop it until the user presses a button.

Understanding the Run-time Model

Plug-ins are dynamic code modules associated with one or more MIME types. When Netscape Navigator starts, it enumerates the available plug-ins, reads one or more string resources out of each plug-in file to determine the MIME types for that plug-in, and registers each plug-in with its MIME types.

When Navigator encounters data of a MIME type registered for a plug-in (either embedded in an HTML page or in a separate file), it loads the plug-in code into memory and creates a new instance of the plug-in. Netscape calls the plug-in API function NPP_Initialize() when the plug-in code is first loaded, and the function NPP_New() when the instance is created. There may be multiple instances of the same plug-in if multiple embedded objects are on a single page, or if several Netscape windows are open with each displaying the same MIME data type.

A plug-in instance is deleted when a user leaves the instances' page or closes the instances' window. Netscape will call the NPP_Destroy() function to inform the plug-in that it is being deleted. When the last instance of a plug-in is deleted, the plug-in code is unloaded from memory and Netscape calls the NPP_Shutdown() function. Plug-ins consume no resources if not referenced.

Using Windows and Events

All imaging and user interface events for a plug-in instance are handled differently depending on the platform on which they are being run. The plug-in API provides a native window handle within which an instance does its drawing. It accomplishes this via the API call NPP_SetWindow(), which passes the instance of an NPWindow object containing the native window handle. On Windows and Unix, each instance receives its own child window within the Navigator window hierarchy, and all imaging and event processing is relative to this window. On the Macintosh, however, the native window is shared between the instance and Navigator, so the instance must restrict its drawing to a specified area of the shared window, and must take care to always save, set up, and restore the shared drawing environment around any drawing operations. On the Macintosh, events are explicitly provided to the instance via the API NPP_HandleEvent().

Note that plug-ins do not block any API call from the Netscape client. There is no yield function from the plug-in to Netscape because many plug-ins may be active at once. If a plug-in involves substantial asynchronous work, it should use a separate thread or a timer as appropriate. In some cases, a plug-in may achieve this goal by communicating with an entirely separate application. If a plug-in makes API calls into Navigator, it should be prepared to handle re-entrant API calls back into the plug-in.

Using the LiveConnect/Plug-In SDK

The Netscape Navigator LiveConnect/Plug-In Software Development Kit (SDK) enables third-party developers to extend the capabilities of Navigator by creating new Netscape plug-ins and enabling them with LiveConnect. Being LiveConnect-enabled means they can be controlled by both Java and JavaScript.

By developing plug-ins, developers can provide integration with, and control over, a wide range of data types, protocols, and file formats from within Navigator. Some plug-ins add buttons and controls to the Netscape window, but many just display specified media types as embedded inline objects. Plug-ins have been used to display information, execute applications, support application-to-application communication, and provide links to other Web sites.

The LiveConnect SDK contains everything you need for developing a plug-in for the Netscape Navigator. It includes:

◆ The LiveConnect/Plug-In Developer's Guide

◆ Header and source files

◆ Source code examples

◆ Tools for LiveConnect development

Note The SDK is not identical across platforms. Although the basic plug-in functionality is supported on Windows, Macintosh, and Unix, there are some minor differences in the API's steps to creating a plug-in. Make certain, therefore, to follow directions for the appropriate environment.

Setting up to Write Plug-Ins

Creating a Navigator plug-in is a three-step process. First, you download and decompress the sample source code. Then, you make the necessary changes and write the required code in the files provided. Finally, you test your plug-in by creating an HTML document and viewing it in the Netscape Navigator.

The LiveConnect SDK includes complete step-by-step instructions for creating a plug-in. Because the process is slightly different depending on the platform you are working on, make certain to follow the steps for the appropriate environment.

Understanding the Netscape Navigator Startup Process

For users to access a plug-in, it must be located on their hard drive in the *plugins* subdirectory (Windows) or *Plug-ins* folder (Macintosh) in the same folder or directory as the Navigator application. Plug-ins can be installed through various methods, including manual installation (in which the user copies the plug-in to the appropriate directory by hand), automatic installation with an installation script provided with the plug-in, and Navigator's assisted installation feature. The assisted installation feature automatically activates when the user displays an HTML page containing embedded data requiring a plug-in not currently installed.

To view information about the currently installed plug-ins, the user can choose *About Plug-ins* from the Help menu (Windows and Unix) or Apple menu (Macintosh). Navigator displays a page listing all installed plug-ins and the MIME types they handle, as well as optional descriptive information supplied by the plug-in.

On Windows, installed plug-ins are automatically configured to handle the MIME types that they support. If multiple plug-ins handle the same MIME type, the last plug-in loaded handles the conflicting MIME type.

On Macintosh and Unix, in Navigator 3.0, the *Helpers* tab of the General Preferences window gives the user flexibility in configuring which MIME types are handled by which plug-ins or helper applications. *Helpers* displays a list of all handled MIME types and whether the type is saved to disk or is handled by Navigator, a plug-in, or a helper application. The user can select any MIME type in the list and click on the *Edit* button to change how the MIME type is handled, including selecting a different plug-in to handle the type from a pop-up menu of all plug-ins that support that type.

Calling a Plug-In Method from JavaScript

Not only can you call Java methods from a plug-in, but you can also define native methods that Java and JavaScript programs can call. *Native methods* is the name given to Java methods written in C, C++, or PASCAL code rather than in the Java programming language.

You may ask yourself why you would want to write native methods. The main reason is to be able to reuse lower-level functionality that could not be written directly in Java. Native methods can also be used when greater performance is required, such as in a sorting algorithm.

To Java and JavaScript programs, plug-ins appear as instances of the class netscape.plugin.Plugin. The Plugin class is described in the Netscape Packages documentation, which is available online on the Netscape Web site.

Actually, a plug-in designer can make three choices with respect to supplying a Java class for a plug-in:

   ◆ Don't supply a Java class

This causes the plug-in to be invisible to all Java applets. The plug-in can still call into Java, but has no object in the Java/JavaScript space that represents it, which renders the plug-in as just a plug-in. Neither Java applets nor JavaScripts have access to the plug-in.

◆ Supply the default class, Plugin

This should be done when the plug-in has a Java object associated with it, but otherwise doesn't define any additional methods in the Java/JavaScript space. This enables the plug-in to call methods in the Java class associated with the plug-in, but still renders the plug-in invisible to the rest of Java space.

◆ Supply a subclass of Plugin

This should be done when the plug-in wishes to expose additional functionality through the use of native methods. The subclassing of the Plugin class is the true use of LiveConnect and is the choice that is used in the example later in the next section. A lot of caveats are used in the creation of a Netscape plug-in. For a detailed explanation of these, you should look to the plug-in SDK documentation or Netscape's Web site.

Creating an Example Plug-in Controlled by JavaScript

The following source code listings provide an example plug-in that can be controlled with JavaScript. This plug-in plays Windows AVI files when you click on JavaScript buttons in an HTML page. Although this in itself is not a major accomplishment, the fact that the AVI plug-in can be controlled through a JavaScript interface shows off another feature of LiveConnect. For JavaScript to control the plug-in, the plug-in must provide a Java interface.

The Java file AviWatch.Java contains the Java interface for events coming from the AVI plug-in. Any object implementing this interface must register itself into the PlayAvi class to receive the notifications from the plug-in. The PlayAvi Java class is used to send AVI asynchronous events like OnStop or OnPositionChange using the AviWatch class as an interface. It also contains all the public function definitions that the program exposes to JavaScript.

The Avi.h and Avi.cpp files provide the code that does all the really hard work. These files contain some basic code to play and display AVI files. They implement an AVI class that can be used to display video for Windows files. This class calls back Java in two functions to notify when a stop or a position status change occurred.

Most of the lines of code highlighted in the following explanations are specific to the concept of JavaScript controlling a plug-in. Several other lines, where noted, are explained to make certain that you understand all the concepts in the code.

The Javah compiler is used to produce header files needed from your native methods. When running javah, you should pass it only the class name itself, and not the full file name, which ends with .class.

The avijava.cpp file contains all the external functions available to JavaScript. This is the main file in the communication channel between Java and the plug-in. In PlayAvi.Java, some native functions have been defined. The Javah compiler generates .c and .h files to represent that class (PlayAvi). These files declare the prototypes for the native methods. The files created by the Javah compiler contain the implementation for the native methods. The npshell.cpp and npshell.h files handle the entry points from the Netscape Navigator into the plug-in. This sample file shows a basic shell that can be used as a good starting point for other plug-ins. The Netscape SDK also provides several sample programs that make good starting points for your own plug-ins.

The plginwnd.cpp and plginwnd.h files implement a class that keeps the state information of the plug-in. The child window created by Netscape Navigator for the plug-in is sub-classed here. This plug-in handles left and right mouse clicks and paint messages, and has a set of AVI-specific calls.

AviWatch.Java

This file defines a Java interface for onStop and onPositionChange events to which the AVI plug-in will respond.

```
1    interface AviWatch {
2      public void onStop();
3      public void onPositionChange(int newPosition);
4    }
```

PlayAvi.Java

```
1    import netscape.plugin.Plugin;
2    import AviWatch;
3
4    public class PlayAvi extends Plugin {
5      private AviWatch watch;
6      public AviWatch getWatch() {
7            return watch;
8      }
9      public boolean advise(AviWatch o, int timeout) {
10           if (watch == null)
11                   watch = o;
12           else
13                   return false;
```

```
14              setTimeOut(timeout);
15              return true;
16      }
17      public native void setTimeOut(int timeout);
18      public native boolean play(boolean isAsync);
19      public native boolean stop(boolean isAsync);
20      public native boolean seek (boolean isAsync, int position);
21      }
```

Lines 5–8 create an AviWatch object used to send the AVI asynchronous onStop or onPositionChange events. The advise function in lines 9–16 provides the method by which objects interested in listening to the AVI plug-in must register. After registering, all objects that register with the PlayAvi object receive notification whenever onStop or onPositionChange events occur in the plug-in. Timeout defines the time that occurs between two onPositionChange events.

Lines 17–20 provide definitions to all of the functions in the plug-in callable from JavaScript. These functions are declared as *public*, so that they can be called by anyone, and they are declared as *native* to tell the compiler that they are implemented in non-Java code.

Avi.h

This file contains some basic function prototypes to functions that will play and display AVI files. It defines the AVI class used to display Video for Windows files.

```
1   #include <windows.h>
2   #include "npapi.h"
3
4   class Avi
5   {
6     private:
7           NPP       m_pluginInstance;
8           UINT      m_mDeviceID;
9           HWND      m_hMovieWnd;
10          BOOL      m_bLoop;
11          BOOL      m_bAutoStart;
12          BOOL      m_bPlaying;
13          UINT      m_uTimeOut;
14          UINT      m_uTimerID;
15
16    private:
17          static UINT      s_InstanceCount;
18
19    public:
20          Avi (BOOL autoStart, BOOL bLoop, NPP instance);
```

```
21          ~Avi ();
22
23          BOOL Open (HWND, LPCSTR);
24          void Close (void);
25          BOOL Play (void);
26          BOOL Stop (void);
27          BOOL Seek (ULONG);
28          DWORD GetLength (void);
29          DWORD GetPosition (void);
30          BOOL isPlaying() const { return m_bPlaying;}
31          void Update(void);
32          BOOL Realize (void);
33          void SetFrequency(UINT uTimer);
34          void OnStop();
35          void OnPositionChange();
36   };
37
38   class CRect : public RECT {
39     public:
40          CRect() {left = 0; top = 0; right = 0; bottom = 0;}
41          long Width() const {return right - left;}
42          long Height() const {return bottom - top;}
43          CRect& operator = (RECT rc) {left = rc.left, top = rc.top; right =
➥rc.right;
44                        left = rc.left; return *this;}
45   };
```

Only a few lines in this file have to do with the actual plug-in. Line 7 contains a definition to a pointer to the plug-in instance. The AVI class keeps this as a class variable so that any of the methods can interact with the plug-in. Line 17 contains a declaration for a variable to hold the timer information. Lines 38–44 are a simple rectangle class used when defining the window for the AVI.

Avi.cpp

This file contains the implementations to functions that will play and display AVI files. It implements the AVI class used to display Video for Windows files.

```
1    #include "avi.h"
2    #include <mmsystem.h>
3    #include <digitalv.h>
4    #include "resource.h"
5    #include "PlayAVI.h"
6    #include "AVIWatch.h"
```

```
7
8    extern HINSTANCE g_hDllInstance;
9    UINT Avi::s_InstanceCount = 0;
10
11   Avi::Avi (BOOL autoStart, BOOL bLoop, NPP Instance)
12   {
13     m_pluginInstance = Instance;
14     m_mDeviceID = 0;
15     m_hMovieWnd = 0;
16     m_bLoop = bLoop;
17     m_bAutoStart = autoStart;
18     m_bPlaying = FALSE;
19     m_uTimeOut = 0;
20     m_uTimerID = ++s_InstanceCount;
21   }
22
23   Avi::~Avi ()
24   {
25     Close();
26   }
27
28   BOOL Avi::Open (HWND hWnd, LPCSTR Filename)
29   {
30     DWORD RetCode;
31     MCI_DGV_OPEN_PARMS OpenParms;
32     MCI_DGV_WINDOW_PARMS WindowParms;
33
34     if (m_mDeviceID){
35     Close ();
36     }
37
38     OpenParms.dwCallback = 0;
39     OpenParms.wDeviceID = 0;
40     OpenParms.lpstrDeviceType = NULL;
41     OpenParms.lpstrElementName = (char*)Filename;
42     OpenParms.lpstrAlias = 0;
43     OpenParms.dwStyle = WS_CHILD | WS_VISIBLE;
44     OpenParms.hWndParent = hWnd;
45     if (RetCode = mciSendCommand(0, MCI_OPEN, (DWORD)
46          MCI_OPEN_ELEMENT | MCI_DGV_OPEN_PARENT |
47          MCI_DGV_OPEN_WS, (DWORD)(LPVOID)&OpenParms))
48     {
```

```
49   char szBuf[256];
50   char szError[128];
51   mciGetErrorString(RetCode, szBuf, 256);
52   ::LoadString(g_hDllInstance, MCI_ERROR_OPEN, szError, 128);
53   MessageBox(NULL, szBuf, szError , MB_OK);
54   return FALSE;
55   }
56   m_mDeviceID = OpenParms.wDeviceID;
57
58   WindowParms.dwCallback = 0;
59   WindowParms.hWnd = hWnd;
60   WindowParms.nCmdShow = SW_SHOW;
61   WindowParms.lpstrText = (LPSTR) NULL;
62   if (RetCode = mciSendCommand (m_mDeviceID, MCI_WINDOW,
63        MCI_DGV_WINDOW_HWND, (DWORD)(LPVOID)&WindowParms))
64   {
65   return FALSE;
66   }
67   m_hMovieWnd = WindowParms.hWnd;
68   if (m_bAutoStart)
69        ::PostMessage(m_hMovieWnd, WM_LBUTTONDOWN, 0, 0L);
70   return TRUE;
71   }
72
73   void Avi::Close (void)
74   {
75   if (m_mDeviceID)
76   mciSendCommand (m_mDeviceID, MCI_CLOSE, 0L, NULL);
77   m_bPlaying = FALSE;
78   m_mDeviceID = 0;
79   }
80
81   BOOL Avi::Play ()
82   {
83   DWORD RetCode, dwFlags = MCI_NOTIFY;
84   MCI_DGV_PLAY_PARMS PlayParms;
85   if (!m_mDeviceID)
86        return FALSE;
87   PlayParms.dwCallback = (DWORD)m_hMovieWnd;
88   PlayParms.dwFrom = PlayParms.dwTo = 0;
89   if (m_bLoop)
90        dwFlags = MCI_DGV_PLAY_REPEAT;
```

```
91    if (RetCode = mciSendCommand (m_mDeviceID, MCI_PLAY, dwFlags,
92       (DWORD)(LPVOID)&PlayParms))
93    {
94    char szBuf[256];
95    char szError[128];
96    mciGetErrorString(RetCode,szBuf,256);
97    ::LoadString(g_hDllInstance, MCI_ERROR_PLAY, szError, 128);
98    MessageBox(NULL, szBuf, szError /*"MCI Play Error"*/, MB_OK);
99    return FALSE;
100   }
101   if (m_uTimeOut)
102           SetTimer(m_hMovieWnd, m_uTimerID, m_uTimeOut, NULL);
103   m_bPlaying = TRUE;
104   return TRUE;
105   }
106
107 BOOL Avi::Stop (void)
108 {
109   if (m_mDeviceID && mciSendCommand (m_mDeviceID, MCI_STOP, 0L,
110      NULL))
111   {
112   return FALSE;
113   }
114   m_bPlaying = FALSE;
115   return TRUE;
116 }
117
118 BOOL Avi::Seek (ULONG dwSeekPosition)
119 {
120   MCI_SEEK_PARMS seekParams;
121   seekParams.dwTo = dwSeekPosition;
122   if (m_mDeviceID && mciSendCommand(m_mDeviceID, MCI_SEEK, MCI_TO,
123      (DWORD)(LPVOID)&seekParams))
124   {
125   return FALSE;
126   }
127
128   m_bPlaying = FALSE;
129   return TRUE;
130 }
131
132 DWORD Avi::GetLength (void)
```

```
133 {
134   MCI_STATUS_PARMS StatusParms;
135
136   StatusParms.dwItem = MCI_STATUS_LENGTH;
137   if (m_mDeviceID && mciSendCommand (m_mDeviceID, MCI_STATUS,
138       MCI_STATUS_ITEM, (DWORD)(LPVOID)&StatusParms))
139   {
140   return FALSE;
141   }
142   return StatusParms.dwReturn;
143 }
144
145 DWORD Avi::GetPosition (void)
146 {
147   MCI_STATUS_PARMS StatusParms;
148       StatusParms.dwItem = MCI_STATUS_POSITION;
149   if (m_mDeviceID && mciSendCommand (m_mDeviceID, MCI_STATUS,
150       MCI_STATUS_ITEM, (DWORD)(LPVOID)&StatusParms))
151   {
152   return FALSE;
153   }
154   return StatusParms.dwReturn;
155 }
156
157 void Avi::Update ()
158 {
159   MCI_DGV_UPDATE_PARMS UpdateParams;
160   BOOL result = FALSE;
161   char szErrorText[MAX_PATH];
162
163   szErrorText[0] = NULL;
164   UpdateParams.dwCallback = 0;
165   UpdateParams.hDC = ::GetDC(m_hMovieWnd);
166   if (m_mDeviceID)
167   mciSendCommand (m_mDeviceID, MCI_UPDATE,
168             MCI_DGV_UPDATE_HDC, (DWORD)(LPVOID)&UpdateParams);
169   ::ReleaseDC(m_hMovieWnd, UpdateParams.hDC);
170 }
171
172 BOOL Avi::Realize (void)
173 {
174   if (m_mDeviceID)
```

```
175            return !mciSendCommand (m_mDeviceID, MCI_REALIZE,
176              MCI_DGV_REALIZE_BKGD, NULL);
177   return FALSE;
178 }
179
180 void Avi::SetFrequency(UINT uTimer)
181 {
182   if (m_bPlaying && m_uTimeOut)
183          KillTimer(m_hMovieWnd, m_uTimerID);
184   m_uTimeOut = uTimer;
185   if (m_uTimeOut && m_bPlaying)
186           SetTimer(m_hMovieWnd, m_uTimerID, m_uTimeOut, 0);
187 }
188
189 void Avi::OnStop()
190 {
191   PlayAvi* javaAviInst;
192   JRIEnv* env;
193   AviWatch* observer = 0;
194   javaAviInst = (PlayAvi*)NPN_GetJavaPeer(m_pluginInstance);
195   if (javaAviInst) {
196          env = NPN_GetJavaEnv();
197          observer = javaAviInst->getWatch(env);
198   }
199   if (m_uTimeOut) {
200          KillTimer(m_hMovieWnd, m_uTimerID);
201          if (observer)
202                  observer->onPositionChange(env, GetPosition());
203   }
204   if (observer)
205          observer->onStop(env);
206   m_bPlaying = FALSE;
207 }
208
209 void Avi::OnPositionChange()
210 {
211   PlayAvi* javaAviInst;
212   JRIEnv* env;
213   AviWatch* observer = 0;
214   javaAviInst = (PlayAvi*)NPN_GetJavaPeer(m_pluginInstance);
215   if (javaAviInst) {
216   env = NPN_GetJavaEnv();
```

```
217          observer = javaAviInst->getWatch(env);
218   if (observer)
219          observer->onPositionChange(env, GetPosition());
220   }
221 }
```

The implementation of this class is fairly straightforward, although it is assumed that you have previous programming experience using the Windows MCI interface. Explanation of this interface is beyond the scope of this book. If you do not understand some portion of the MCI code, please refer to your Windows programming manual.

Most lines of code in this module are standard Windows API function calls (with a few exceptions). Lines 81–105 start the playing of the AVI file. This function immediately returns control back to the calling program. You must call back OnStop() when you want to stop the AVI file, which is handled in both the PluginWnd's PluginWndProc function as well as in the OnStop function on lines 189–207 of this file.

Lines 189–207 provide notification that a stop event occurred. Stop events originate from here and are passed on to the watching Java classes. Assume a Java class is listening for an event to happen. If no listener is passed to the Java class the OnStop event is not triggered. Line 194 loads the Java instance that represents the plug-in instance. In line 202, you find the listener (if any). Finally, on line 205, if a Java class is waiting for the event, trigger the event. For the Java class to receive the event, it must implement the AviWatch interface and register itself through the advise function in the PlayAvi Java class.

Lines 209–221 are basically a copy of the notification code for the OnStop event. This function provides the triggering of events for the onPositionChange event. That's all there is to it. By simply adding a few function calls to interface with the public Java classes, standard AVI functions can be used in your plug-in.

AviJava.cpp

This file contains most of the code in the Java to plug-in communication channel. The native functions that you defined in PlayAvi.Java are implemented in this file. All these functions are very straightforward and get an NPP instance to retrieve a PluginWindow object from which they get the AVI instance and call the method in which they are interested. The NPP instance is the main interface between the Netscape Navigator and the plug-in DLL.

```
1   #include "PlayAVI.h"
2   #include "AVIWatch.h"
3   #include "plginwnd.h"
4   #include "avi.h"
```

```
5
6   extern "C" JRI_PUBLIC_API(void)
7   native_PlayAvi_setTimeOut(JRIEnv* env, struct PlayAvi* self, jint timeout)
8   {
9    NPP instance = (NPP)self->getPeer(env);
10   PluginWindow* pPluginData = (PluginWindow*)instance->pdata;
11   pPluginData->GetAviStream().SetFrequency(timeout);
12  }
13
14  extern "C" JRI_PUBLIC_API(jbool)
15  native_PlayAvi_play(JRIEnv* env, struct PlayAvi* self, jbool isAsync)
16  {
17   NPP instance = (NPP)self->getPeer(env);
18   PluginWindow* pPluginData = (PluginWindow*)instance->pdata;
19   if (isAsync) {
20          ::PostMessage(*pPluginData, WM_COMMAND,
21            MAKEWPARAM(ID_VIDEO_PLAY, 0), 0);
22          return TRUE;
23   }
24   else
25          return pPluginData->GetAviStream().Play();
26  }
27
28  extern "C" JRI_PUBLIC_API(jbool)
29  native_PlayAvi_stop(JRIEnv* env, struct PlayAvi* self, jbool isAsync)
30  {
31   NPP instance = (NPP)self->getPeer(env);
32   PluginWindow* pPluginData = (PluginWindow*)instance->pdata;
33   if (isAsync) {
34          ::PostMessage(*pPluginData, WM_COMMAND,
35            MAKEWPARAM(ID_VIDEO_STOP, 0), 0);
36          return TRUE;
37   }
38   else
39          return pPluginData->GetAviStream().Stop();
40  }
41
42  extern "C" JRI_PUBLIC_API(jbool)
43  native_PlayAvi_seek(JRIEnv* env, struct PlayAvi* self, jbool isAsync, jint
➥position)
44  {
45   NPP instance = (NPP)self->getPeer(env);
```

```
46   PluginWindow* pPluginData = (PluginWindow*)instance->pdata;
47   if (isAsync) {
48          ::PostMessage(*pPluginData, WM_COMMAND,
49              MAKEWPARAM(ID_VIDEO_SEEK, 0), 0);
50          return TRUE;
51   }
52   else
53          return pPluginData->GetAviStream().Seek(position);
54   }
```

NpShell.cpp

This file contains all the functions that interface with the Netscape Navigator window and objects. Most of this file is part of the standard Netscape shell API interface.

```
1    #include <windows.h>
2    #include <string.h>
3    #include "npapi.h"
4    #include "npupp.h"
5    #include "plginwnd.h"
6    #include "avi.h"
7    #include "PlayAvi.h"
8    #include "AviWatch.h"
9
10   HINSTANCE g_hDllInstance = NULL;
11
12   BOOL WINAPI
13   DllMain( HINSTANCE  hinstDLL, DWORD  fdwReason, LPVOID  lpvReserved)
14   {
15    switch (fdwReason) {
16          case DLL_PROCESS_ATTACH:
17             g_hDllInstance = hinstDLL;
18             break;
19          case DLL_THREAD_ATTACH:
20          case DLL_PROCESS_DETACH:
21          case DLL_THREAD_DETACH:
22             break;
23    }
24    return TRUE;
25   }
26
27   NPError NPP_Initialize(void)
28   {
```

```
29   return NPERR_NO_ERROR;
30  }
31
32  void NPP_Shutdown(void)
33  {
34  }
35
36  jref NPP_GetJavaClass(void)
37  {
38    JRIEnv* env = NPN_GetJavaEnv();
39    use_netscape_plugin_Plugin(env);
40    use_AviWatch(env);
41    return use_PlayAvi(env);
42  }
43
44  NPError NP_LOADDS NPP_New(NPMIMEType pluginType, NPP instance, uint16
45  mode, int16 argc, char* argn[], char* argv[], NPSavedData* saved)
46  {
47    BOOL bAutoStart, bLoop;
48    PluginWindow * pluginData;
49    if (instance == NULL)
50    return NPERR_INVALID_INSTANCE_ERROR;
51    bAutoStart = FALSE;
52    bLoop = FALSE;
53    for (int idx =0; idx<argc; idx++) {
54    if (!strcmpi(argn[idx],"autostart")) {
55           if (!strcmpi(argv[idx],"true")) {
56                   bAutoStart = TRUE;
57           }
58    }
59    if (!strcmpi(argn[idx],"loop")) {
60           if (!strcmpi(argv[idx],"true")) {
61                   bLoop = TRUE;
62           }
63    }
64    }
65    pluginData = new PluginWindow (bAutoStart, bLoop, mode, instance);
66    instance->pdata = pluginData;
67    return NPERR_NO_ERROR;
68  }
69
70  NPError NP_LOADDS NPP_Destroy(NPP instance, NPSavedData** save)
```

```
71  {
72   PluginWindow * pluginData = (PluginWindow *)instance->pdata;
73   delete pluginData;
74   instance->pdata = 0;
75   return NPERR_NO_ERROR;
76  }
77
78  NPError NP_LOADDS NPP_SetWindow(NPP instance, NPWindow* window)
79  {
80   if (!window)
81   return NPERR_GENERIC_ERROR;
82   if (!instance)
83   return  NPERR_INVALID_INSTANCE_ERROR;
84   PluginWindow * pluginData = (PluginWindow *)instance->pdata;
85   if (pluginData) {
86          if (!window->window) {
87                  return NPERR_NO_ERROR;
88          }
89          if (!pluginData->GetWndProc()) {
90                  pluginData->SetWindow((HWND)window->window);
91          }
92          InvalidateRect(*pluginData, NULL, TRUE);
93          UpdateWindow(*pluginData);
94          return NPERR_NO_ERROR;
95   }
96    return NPERR_GENERIC_ERROR;
97  }
98
99  NPError NP_LOADDS NPP_NewStream(NPP instance, NPMIMEType type,
100 NPStream *stream, NPBool seekable, uint16 *stype)
101 {
102  if(!instance)
103  return NPERR_INVALID_INSTANCE_ERROR;
104  stream->pdata = instance->pdata;
105  *stype = NP_ASFILE;
106  return NPERR_NO_ERROR;
107 }
108
109 void NP_LOADDS NPP_StreamAsFile(NPP instance, NPStream *stream, const
110 char* fname)
111 {
112  if(fname == NULL || fname[0] == NULL)
```

```
113   return;
114   PluginWindow * pluginData = (PluginWindow *)instance->pdata;
115   Avi& aviPlayer = pluginData->GetAviStream();
116   aviPlayer.Open(*pluginData, fname);
117   aviPlayer.Update();
118   DWORD dwVer = GetVersion();
119   int iVer = (LOBYTE(LOWORD(dwVer))*100)+HIBYTE(LOWORD(dwVer));
120 }
121
122 int32 STREAMBUFSIZE = 0X0FFFFFFF; mode
123
124 int32 NP_LOADDS NPP_WriteReady(NPP instance, NPStream *stream)
125 {
126   return STREAMBUFSIZE;
127 }
128
129 int32 NP_LOADDS NPP_Write(NPP instance, NPStream *stream, int32 offset,
➥int32
130 len, void *buffer)
131 {
132   return len;
133 }
134
135 NPError NP_LOADDS NPP_DestroyStream(NPP instance, NPStream *stream,
136 NPError reason)
137 {
138   return NPERR_NO_ERROR;
139 }
140
141 void NP_LOADDS NPP_Print(NPP instance, NPPrint* printInfo)
142 {
143   if(printInfo == NULL)
144   return;
145   if (instance != NULL) {
146   PluginWindow* pluginData = (PluginWindow*) instance->pdata;
147           pluginData->Print(printInfo);
148   }
149 }
150
151 void NPP_URLNotify(NPP instance, const char* url, NPReason reason, void*
152 notifyData)
153 {
154 }
```

The Netscape plug-in API provides several templates for creating your own plug-ins. This file was created by one of the templates supplied by the Netscape API. You fill in the areas in which you want your program to act differently from the normal plug-in. In the case of the AVI plug-in, almost everything stays the same except for a few notable exceptions.

Line 38 is part of the standard template worth noting. This line retrieves the Java environment. You need this information pretty much for any JRI (Java Run-time Interface) function call. Lines 39–41 initialize the AviWatch class, the Plugin class and the PlayAvi class for use. Typically, you initialize any classes that define native methods, or whose methods you are going to use in your plug-in in this area. The actual functions are generated by the Javah compiler running on the Java classes representing this plug-in. Javah generates the files <Java class name>.h and <Java class name>.c (same for any additional class you may want to use).

Lines 44–68 create a new plug-in instance. Here you handle all the plug-in specific initialization. For this example, the plug-in takes a true/false value for both the AUTOSTART and LOOP parameters. Check the arguments passed to the plug-in to determine the plug-in style characteristics and set your class variables accordingly.

Pluginwnd.h

This file implements the class that keeps the state information of the plug-in. It is the main class from the Netscape Navigator standpoint, but from a Java standpoint this class is useless because all the AVI functionality is exposed from the AVI class.

```
1    #include <windows.h>
2    #include "npapi.h"
3    #include "avi.h"
4
5    #define ID_VIDEO_PLAY     5000
6    #define ID_VIDEO_STOP     5001
7    class PluginWindow
8    {
9      private:
10           HWND     _hPluginWnd;
11           WNDPROC _pfnDefault;
12           Avi *          _pAvi;
13           uint16         _mode;
14
15     private:
16           static LPSTR _ThisLookUp;
17
18     public:
```

```
19          static LRESULT CALLBACK PluginWndProc(HWND hWnd, UINT
20              Msg, WPARAM WParam, LPARAM lParam);
21
22  public:
23          PluginWindow(BOOL bAutoStart, BOOL bLoop, uint16 mode, NPP
24              instance);
25          ~PluginWindow();
26
27          void    SetWindow(HWND hWnd);
28          void    Print(NPPrint* printInfo) const;
29          Avi&    GetAviStream() const    {return *_pAvi;}
30          WNDPROC GetWndProc() const      {return _pfnDefault;}
31          operator      HWND() const {return _hPluginWnd;}
32          void          OnLButtonDown(UINT uFlags, LPPOINT pPoint);
33          void          OnRButtonDown(UINT uFlags, LPPOINT pPoint);
34          void          OnPaint();
35          void          OnPaletteChanged(HWND hFocusWnd);
36  };
```

Pluginwnd.cpp

This file again is derived from one of the template files that come with the Netscape plug-in SDK. As a result, only a few interesting areas are in the code. The main message loop is very familiar to anyone who has programmed in Windows before. The plug-in handles only a few Windows events, the left mouse button down, the right mouse button down, the paint message, the palette changed message, the notification from the Windows MCI when a stop has been called, and the play, stop, and seek commands from the public native functions.

```
1   #include "plginwnd.h"
2   #include "resource.h"
3
4   extern HINSTANCE g_hDllInstance;
5   LPSTR PluginWindow::_ThisLookUp = "this ptr";
6   LRESULT CALLBACK PluginWindow::PluginWndProc(HWND hWnd, UINT Msg,
7   WPARAM WParam, LPARAM lParam)
8   {
9     PluginWindow* pluginObj = (PluginWindow*)GetProp(hWnd,
10      PluginWindow::_ThisLookUp);
11
12    switch (Msg) {
13          case WM_LBUTTONDOWN:
14          {
```

```
15                      POINT p;
16                      p.x = LOWORD(lParam);
17                      p.y = HIWORD(lParam);
18                      pluginObj->OnLButtonDown(WParam, &p);
19          break;
20          }
21          case WM_RBUTTONDOWN:
22          {
23                      POINT p;
24                      p.x = LOWORD(lParam);
25                      p.y = HIWORD(lParam);
26                      pluginObj->OnRButtonDown(WParam, &p);
27          break;
28          }
29          case WM_PAINT:
30          {
31                      PAINTSTRUCT  PaintStruct;
32                      ::BeginPaint(hWnd, &PaintStruct);
33                      pluginObj->OnPaint();
34                      ::EndPaint(hWnd, &PaintStruct);
35          break;
36          }
37          case WM_PALETTECHANGED:
38                      pluginObj->OnPaletteChanged((HWND)WParam);
39          break;
40
41          case MM_MCINOTIFY:
42                      pluginObj->GetAviStream().OnStop();
43          break;
44          case WM_TIMER:
45                      pluginObj->GetAviStream().OnPositionChange();
46          break;
47          case WM_COMMAND:
48                      if (!HIWORD(WParam)) {
49                          switch LOWORD(WParam) {
50                              case ID_VIDEO_PLAY:
51                                      //pluginObj-
➥       >GetAviStream().Play();
52                                      pluginObj->OnLButtonDown(0, 0);
53                              return 0;
54                              case ID_VIDEO_STOP:
55                                      pluginObj->GetAviStream().Stop();
```

```
56                                    return 0;
57                                case ID_VIDEO_SEEK:
58                                        pluginObj-
➡                    >GetAviStream().Seek(lParam);
59                                        return 0;
60                                }
61                        }
62                default:
63                return CallWindowProc(pluginObj->GetWndProc(), hWnd, Msg, WParam,
64                    lParam);
65    };
66    return 0;
67  }
68
69  PluginWindow::PluginWindow(BOOL bAutoStart, BOOL bLoop, uint16 mode, NPP
70      instance)
71  {
72    _hPluginWnd = 0;
73    _pfnDefault = 0;
74    _mode = mode;
75    _pAvi = new Avi(bAutoStart, bLoop, instance);
76  }
77
78  PluginWindow::~PluginWindow()
79  {
80    delete _pAvi;
81    if (_pfnDefault) {
82            ::SetWindowLong(_hPluginWnd, GWL_WNDPROC,
83              (LONG)_pfnDefault);
84            ::RemoveProp(_hPluginWnd, PluginWindow::_ThisLookUp);
85    }
86  }
87
88  void PluginWindow::SetWindow(HWND hWnd)
89  {
90    _hPluginWnd = hWnd;
91    _pfnDefault = (WNDPROC)::SetWindowLong(hWnd, GWL_WNDPROC,
92      (LONG)PluginWindow::PluginWndProc);
93    ::SetProp(hWnd, PluginWindow::_ThisLookUp, (HANDLE)this);
94  }
95
96  void PluginWindow::Print(NPPrint* printInfo) const
```

```
97  {
98   if (printInfo->mode == NP_FULL) {
99   void* platformPrint = printInfo->print.fullPrint.platformPrint;
100  NPBool printOne = printInfo->print.fullPrint.printOne;
101        printInfo->print.fullPrint.pluginPrinted = FALSE;
102  }
103  else {
104  NPWindow* printWindow = &(printInfo->print.embedPrint.window);
105  void* platformPrint = printInfo->print.embedPrint.platformPrint;
106  HPEN hPen, hPenOld;
107  LOGBRUSH lb;
108  lb.lbStyle = BS_SOLID;
109  lb.lbColor = RGB(128, 128, 128);
110  lb.lbHatch = 0;
111  hPen = ::ExtCreatePen(PS_COSMETIC | PS_SOLID, 1, &lb, 0, NULL);
112  HDC hDC = (HDC)(DWORD)platformPrint;
113  hPenOld = (HPEN)::SelectObject(hDC, hPen);
114  BOOL r = ::Rectangle(hDC, (int)(printWindow->x), (int)(printWindow-
115  >y), (int)(printWindow->x + printWindow->width), (int)(printWindow-
116  >y + printWindow->height));
117  ::SelectObject(hDC, hPenOld);
118  ::DeleteObject(hPen);
119  }
120 }
121
122 void PluginWindow::OnLButtonDown(UINT uFlags, LPPOINT pPoint)
123 {
124  if (_pAvi->isPlaying()) {
125  _pAvi->Stop();
126  }
127  else {
128  DWORD dwPos, dwLen;
129  dwPos = _pAvi->GetPosition();
130  dwLen = _pAvi->GetLength();
131        _pAvi->Play();
132  }
133 }
134
135 void PluginWindow::OnRButtonDown(UINT uFlags, LPPOINT pPoint)
136 {
137  UINT uState;
138  char szMenuString[128];
139
```

```
140   HMENU hPopup = ::CreatePopupMenu();
141   if(hPopup == 0)  {
142   return;
143   }
144   if(_pAvi->isPlaying())
145           uState = MF_GRAYED;
146   else
147           uState = MF_ENABLED;
148   ::LoadString(g_hDllInstance, MENU_PLAY, szMenuString, 128);
149   ::AppendMenu(hPopup, uState, ID_VIDEO_PLAY, szMenuString);
150   ::LoadString(g_hDllInstance, MENU_PAUSE, szMenuString, 128);
151   ::AppendMenu(hPopup, !uState, ID_VIDEO_STOP, szMenuString);
152   ::ClientToScreen(_hPluginWnd, pPoint);
153   ::TrackPopupMenu(hPopup, TPM_LEFTALIGN ¦ TPM_RIGHTBUTTON,
154      pPoint->x, pPoint->y, 0, _hPluginWnd,  NULL);
155 }
156
157 void PluginWindow::OnPaint()
158 {
159   _pAvi->Update();
160 }
161
162 void PluginWindow::OnPaletteChanged(HWND hFocusWnd)
163 {
164   if(hFocusWnd != _hPluginWnd)    {
165           _pAvi->Realize();
166     }
167 }
```

In lines 122–133 of the plug-in code, the left mouse button down message is handled. If the AVI is playing, it is stopped; otherwise, the AVI is positioned to the location specified in the native method call, and the AVI is played.

In lines 135–155 of the plug-in code, the right mouse button down message is handled. In the case of your AVI plug-in, you want to give the user most of the same functionality as is available via its public interface. You add a pop-up context menu that enables the user to play or stop the AVI. It is simple to add this functionality because all the major functions are already declared public. It adds a nice usability touch to your plug-in so that power users will be able to get at your functionality quickly.

The palette handling, painting, and updating of the plug-in window is passed on to the AVI class. Because the AVI class must already handle the palette (due to its graphic nature), it is only natural to defer this functionality to this particular class.

Avi.html

This HTML document is the final piece in the JavaScript to plug-in communication channel. The document defines a form that will take the user input, validate the input, and pass the input to the plug-in via the Java interface. The majority of this HTML document will look familiar to you. Only the parts of the document that deal specifically with communication with the plug-in will be highlighted.

```
1    <HTML>
2    <HEAD>
3    <Title> Top Secret Video</Title>
4    <SCRIPT LANGUAGE="JavaScript">
5    <!--
6    function validate() {
7    if ((parseInt(document.myForm.frameNumber.value) > 31) ||
8       (parseInt(document.myForm.frameNumber.value) < 1)) {
9         alert("Invalid frame number entry. Please enter a number between 1
          and 31.")
10        document.myForm.frameNumber.value = "1"
11        document.myForm.frameNumber.focus()
12      }
13   }
14   //-->
15   </SCRIPT>
16   </HEAD>
17   <BODY BGCOLOR=#FFFFFF TEXT=#000000>
18   <CENTER>
19   <H1> Top Secret Video</H1>
20   <EMBED NAME="MartianAvi" SRC="Martian.avi" WIDTH=320 HEIGHT=200
21    AUTOSTART=TRUE LOOP=TRUE>
22   <FORM NAME=myForm>
23   <INPUT Type=Button Value=Play OnClick="document.MartianAvi.play(false)" >
24   <INPUT Type=Button Value=Stop OnClick="document.MartianAvi.stop(false)" >
25   <INPUT Type="Button" Value="Seek to frame" OnClick=
26      "document.MartianAvi.seek(false, parseInt(
27      document.myForm.frameNumber.value))">
28   <INPUT TYPE="text" NAME="frameNumber" VALUE="1" SIZE=2
29      onChange="validate()">
30   </FORM>
31   </CENTER>
32   </BODY>
33   </HTML>
```

In lines 6–12 we define a JavaScript function that will validate the user's input for the Seek To button. The input for this value must be between 1 and 31 because this is the number of frames in the sample AVI. You should change this value depending on your particular AVI file. Better yet, you could create another public function in your plug-in that would return the number of frames in your AVI file so the process would be dynamic.

Next you must use the <EMBED> tag to actually include the AVI plug-in. This is done in lines 20 and 21. The NAME of our plug-in will be MartianAvi, and the SOURCE file for the plug-in is Martian.avi. We set the AVI window to be 320 pixels wide by 200 pixels high. The AUTOSTART parameter, which we defined in the plug-in class is set to true. So when we load the HTML document, the AVI file will start playing immediately. The LOOP parameter is also set to true so that the AVI will continue to play until the user presses the Stop button on the form, or exits the page while in the Netscape browser.

Finally, you must define how the user is to communicate with your plug-in. In this case, we define a form on lines 21–30 that consists of three buttons: Start, Stop, and Seek To. The form also contains a text entry box so that the user can directly type a frame number to which the plug-in will then jump to directly.

The definition for the Play button is on line 23. Notice how the play method within the plug-in is called:

```
document.MartianAvi.play(false)
```

The first reference is to the HTML *document* object. Next, you reference the name you gave to the plug-in object in the <EMBED> tag, in this case MartianAvi. Finally, you reference the name of the public native function call that you want to call, including any parameters to send to the function. In this case, you do not want the play command to be run in asynchronous mode. On line 24, we define the Stop button in almost exactly the same manner that we define the Play button. The only difference is that you call the stop native method rather than the play method.

Lines 25–27 contain the definition for the Seek To button. This button differs slightly from the other two because it reads the value from the text field defined on line 28. The JavaScript script passes this integer value from the HTML through the Java interface and finally to the plug-in code to be processed. Now you have a fully functional AVI player that works inside your Netscape Navigator.

Figure C.1

An AVI plug-in controlled with JavaScript.

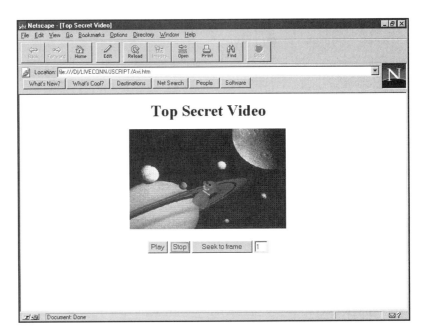

Summary

This appendix offered a quick introduction to Netscape plug-ins. You have seen what plug-ins can and can't do for your Web pages. Now that you have a basic understanding of Navigator plug-ins, you are ready to create your own plug-ins.

You have also created your first JavaScript controlled plug-in in this appendix. This sample provides a good starting point from which you can expand by adding your own functionality, or you can simply use this example as a base for your own plug-in. As an exercise to improve your understanding of plug-ins, try adding a rewind capability to your AVI class that will simply play your AVI in reverse. You need to add functionality to the AVI class, add another public native function to the Java interface, add another button to your HTML form, and last but not least, you will need to add a menu item to your pop-up context menu (initiated by pressing the right side of the mouse). If you are able to do this successfully, then you have a good basic knowledge of communication between Java, JavaScript, and plug-ins, and you are now well on your way to creating your own plug-ins.

Remember that the major factor in beginning to create plug-ins is getting your environment set up. Fortunately, Netscape has provided a plug-in SDK package that sets up most of your environment for you. This SDK package also provides several good templates for you to use when starting to create your own plug-ins. Visit the Netscape site to download the plug-in and LiveConnect SDKs.

Quick Reference: JavaScript Authoring Guide

While this entire book is about using JavaScript, this appendix was added as a quick reference. It is broken into two parts: JavaScript Basics and Language Concepts. For detailed explanations and useful examples, please see the appropriate chapters of the book.

PART I: JAVASCRIPT BASICS

Using JavaScript in HTML

JavaScript can be embedded in an HTML document in two ways:

◆ As statements and functions using the SCRIPT tag.

◆ As event handlers using HTML tags.

The SCRIPT tag

```
A script embedded in HTML with the SCRIPT tag uses the format:
<SCRIPT>
   JavaScript statements...
</SCRIPT>
```

The optional LANGUAGE attribute specifies the scripting language as follows:

```
<SCRIPT LANGUAGE="JavaScript">
   JavaScript statements...
</SCRIPT>
```

The HTML tag, <SCRIPT>, and its closing counterpart, </SCRIPT> can enclose any number of JavaScript statements in a document.

JavaScript is case-sensitive.

Example: A Simple Script

```
<HTML>
<HEAD>
<SCRIPT LANGUAGE="JavaScript">
document.write("Hello net.")
</SCRIPT>
</HEAD>
<BODY>
That's all, folks.
</BODY>
</HTML>
```

Code Hiding

Scripts can be placed inside comment fields to ensure that your JavaScript code is not displayed by old browsers that do not recognize JavaScript. The entire script is encased by HTML comment tags:

```
<!-- Begin to hide script contents from old browsers.
// End the hiding here. -->
```

Defining and Calling Functions

Scripts placed within SCRIPT tags are evaluated after the page loads. Functions are stored, but not executed. Functions are executed by events in the page.

It's important to understand the difference between defining a function and calling the function. Defining the function simply names the function and specifies what to do when the function is called. Calling the function actually performs the specified actions with the indicated parameters.

Example: A Script with a Function and Comments

```
<HEAD>
<SCRIPT LANGUAGE="JavaScript">
<!-- to hide script contents from old browsers
  function square(i) {
    document.write("The call passed ", i ," to the function.","<BR>")
    return i * i
  }
  document.write("The function returned ",square(5),".")
// end hiding contents from old browsers -->
</SCRIPT>
</HEAD>
<BODY>
<BR>
All done.
</BODY>
```

The HEAD tag

Generally, you should define the functions for a page in the HEAD portion of a document. Since the HEAD is loaded first, this practice guarantees that functions are loaded before the user has a chance to do anything that might call a function.

Example: A Script with Two Functions

```
<HEAD>
<SCRIPT>
<!--- hide script from old browsers

function bar() {
    document.write("<HR ALIGN='left' WIDTH=25%>")
}

function output(head, level, string) {
    document.write("<H" + level + ">" + head + "</H" + level + "><P>" + string)
}

// end hiding from old browsers -->
</SCRIPT>
</HEAD>

<BODY>
<SCRIPT>
<!--- hide script from old browsers
document.write(bar(),output("Make Me Big",3,"Make me ordinary."))
// end hiding from old browsers -->
</SCRIPT>
<P>
Thanks.
</BODY>
```

Quotes

Use single quotes (') to delimit string literals so that scripts can distinguish the literal from attribute values enclosed in double quotes. In the previous example, function bar contains the literal 'left' within a double-quoted attribute value. Here's another example:

```
<INPUT TYPE="button" VALUE="Press Me" onClick="myfunc('astring')">
```

Scripting Event Handlers

JavaScript applications in the Navigator are largely event-driven. Events are actions that occur, usually as a result of something the user does. For example, a button click is an event, as is giving focus to a form element. There is a specific set of events that Navigator recognizes. You can define Event handlers—scripts that are automatically executed when an event occurs.

Event handlers are embedded in documents as attributes of HTML tags to which you assign JavaScript code to execute. The general syntax is:

```
<TAG eventHandler="JavaScript Code">
```

where TAG is some HTML tag and eventHandler is the name of the event handler.

For example, suppose you have created a JavaScript function called compute. You can cause Navigator to perform this function when the user clicks on a button by assigning the function call to the button's onClick event handler:

```
<INPUT TYPE="button" VALUE="Calculate" onClick="compute(this.form)">
```

You can put any JavaScript statements inside the quotes following onClick. These statements get executed when the user clicks on the button. If you want to include more than one statement, separate statements with a semicolon (;).

In general, it is a good idea to define functions for your event handlers because:

◆ It makes your code modular—you can use the same function as an event handler for many different items.

◆ It makes your code easier to read.

Events apply to HTML tags as follows:

Focus, Blur, Change events: text fields, textareas, and selections

Click events: buttons, radio buttons, check boxes, submit buttons, reset buttons, links

Select events: text fields, textareas

MouseOver event: links

If an event applies to an HTML tag, then you can define an event handler for it. In general, an event handler has the name of the event, preceded by "on." For example, the event handler for the Focus event is onFocus.

Many objects also have methods that emulate events. For example, button has a click method that emulates the button being clicked. Note: The event-emulation methods do not trigger event-handlers. So, for example, the click method does not trigger an onClick event-handler. However, you can always call an event-handler directly (for example, you can call onClick explicitly in a script).

Example: A Script with a Form and an Event Handler Attribute

```
<HEAD>
<SCRIPT LANGUAGE="JavaScript">

function compute(form) {
   if (confirm("Are you sure?"))
      form.result.value = eval(form.expr.value)
   else
      alert("Please come back again.")
}

</SCRIPT>
</HEAD>

<BODY>
<FORM>
Enter an expression:
<INPUT TYPE="text" NAME="expr" SIZE=15 >
<INPUT TYPE="button" VALUE="Calculate" ONCLICK="compute(this.form)">
<BR>
Result:
<INPUT TYPE="text" NAME="result" SIZE=15 >
<BR>
</FORM>
</BODY>
```

Example: A Script with a Form and Event Handler Attribute within a BODY Tag.

```
<HEAD>
<SCRIPT LANGUAGE="JavaScript">
<!-- hide script from old browsers
function checkNum(str, min, max) {
    if (str == "") {
        alert("Enter a number in the field, please.")
        return false
    }
    for (var i = 0; i  "9") {
            alert("Try a number, please.")
            return false
        }
    }
```

```
var val = parseInt(str, 10)
    if ((val  max)) {
        alert("Try a number from 1 to 10.")
        return false
    }
    return true
}

function thanks() {
    alert("Thanks for your input.")
}
// end hiding from old browsers -->
</SCRIPT>
</HEAD>

<BODY>
<FORM NAME="ex5">
Please enter a small number:
<INPUT NAME="num"
    onChange="if (!checkNum(this.value, 1, 10))
            {this.focus();this.select();} else {thanks()}">
</FORM>
</BODY>
```

Tips and Techniques

This section describes various useful scripting techniques.

Updating Pages

JavaScript in Navigator generates its results from the top of the page down. Once something has been formatted, you can't change it without reloading the page. Currently, you cannot update a particular part of a page without updating the entire page. However, you can update a "sub-window" in a frame separately.

Printing

You cannot currently print output created with JavaScript. For example, if you had the following in a page:

```
<P>This is some text.
```

```
<SCRIPT>document.write("<P>And some generated text")</SCRIPT>
```

And you printed it, you would get only "This is some text", even though you would see both lines on-screen.

Using Quotes

Be sure to alternate double quotes with single quotes. Since event handlers in HTML must be enclosed in quotes, you must use single quotes to delimit arguments. For example

```
<FORM NAME="myform">
<INPUT TYPE="button" NAME="Button1" VALUE="Open Sesame!"
onClick="window.open('stmtsov.html', 'newWin', 'toolbar=no,directories=no')">
</FORM>
```

Alternatively, you can escape quotes by preceding them by a backslash (\).

Defining Functions

It is always a good idea to define all of your functions in the HEAD of your HTML page. This way, all functions will be defined before any content is displayed. Otherwise, the user might perform some action while the page is still loading that triggers an event handler and calls an undefined function, leading to an error.

Creating Arrays

An array is an ordered set of values that you reference through an array name and an index. For example, you could have an array called emp, that contains employees' names indexed by their employee number. So emp[1] would be employee number one, emp[2] employee number two, and so on.

JavaScript does not have an explicit array data type, but because of the intimate relationship between arrays and object properties, it is easy to create arrays in JavaScript. You can define an array object type, as follows:

```
function MakeArray(n) {
   this.length = n;
   for (var i = 1; i <= n; i++) {
     this[i] = 0 }
     return this
     }
}
```

This defines an array such that the first property, length, (with index of zero), represents the number of elements in the array. The remaining properties have an integer index of one or greater, and are initialized to zero.

You can then create an array by a call to new with the array name, specifying the number of elements it has. For example:

```
emp = new MakeArray(20);
```

This creates an array called emp with 20 elements, and initializes the elements to zero.

Populating an Array

You can populate an array by simply assigning values to its elements. For example:

```
emp[1] = "Casey Jones"
emp[2] = "Phil Lesh"
emp[3] = "August West"
```

and so on.

You can also create arrays of objects. For example, suppose you define an object type named Employees, as follows:

```
function Employee(empno, name, dept) {
   this.empno = empno;
   this.name = name;
   this.dept = dept;
}
```

Then the following statements define an array of these objects:

```
emp = new MakeArray(3)
emp[1] = new Employee(1, "Casey Jones", "Engineering")
emp[2] = new Employee(2, "Phil Lesh", "Music")
emp[3] = new Employee(3, "August West", "Admin")
```

Then you can easily display the objects in this array using the show_props function as follows:

```
for (var n =1; n <= 3; n++) {
   document.write(show_props(emp[n], "emp") + " ");
}
```

Using Navigator Objects

When you load a page in Navigator, it creates a number of objects corresponding to the page, its contents, and other pertinent information.

Every page always has the following objects:

◆ window: the top-level object; contains properties that apply to the entire window. There is also a window object for each for "child window" in a frames document.

◆ location: contains properties on the current URL

◆ history: contains properties representing URLs the user has previously visited

◆ document: contains properties for content in the current document, such as title, background color, and forms

The properties of the document object are largely content-dependent. That is, they are created based on the content that you put in the document. For example, the document object has a property for each form and each anchor in the document.

For example, suppose you create a page named simple.html that contains the following HTML:

```
<TITLE>A Simple Document</TITLE>
<BODY><FORM NAME="myform" ACTION="FormProc()" METHOD="get" >
```

Enter a value:

```
<INPUT TYPE=text NAME="text1" VALUE="blahblah" SIZE=20 >
```

Check if you want:

```
<INPUT TYPE="checkbox" NAME="Check1" CHECKED onClick="update(this.form)">
Option #1
<P>
<INPUT TYPE="button" NAME="Button1" VALUE="Press Me"
onClick="update(this.form)">
</FORM></BODY>
```

As always, there would be window, location, history, and document objects. These would have properties such as:

◆ location.href = "http://www.terrapin.com/samples/vsimple.html"

◆ document.title = "A Simple Document"

◆ document.fgColor = #000000

◆ document.bgColor = #ffffff

◆ history.length = 7

These are just some example values. In practice, these values would be based on the document's actual location, its title, foreground and background colors, and so on.

Navigator would also create the following objects based on the contents of the page:

◆ document.myform

◆ document.myform.Check1

◆ document.myform.Button1

These would have properties such as:

◆ document.myform.action = http://terrapin/mocha/formproc()

◆ document.myform.method = get

◆ document.myform.length = 5

◆ document.myform.Button1.value = Press Me

◆ document.myform.Button1.name = Button1

◆ document.myform.text1.value = blahblah

◆ document.myform.text1.name = text1

◆ document.myform.Check1.defaultChecked = true

◆ document.myform.Check1.value = on

◆ document.myform.Check1.name = Check1

Notice that each of the property references above starts with "document," followed by the name of the form, "myform," and then the property name (for form properties) or the name of the form element. This sequence follows the Navigator's object hierarchy, discussed in the next section.

Navigator Object Hierarchy

The objects in Navigator exist in a hierarchy that reflects the hierarchical structure of the HTML page itself. Although you cannot derive object classes from these objects, as you can in languages such as Java, it is useful to understand the Navigator's JavaScript object hierarchy. In the strict object-oriented sense, this type of hierarchy is known as an instance hierarchy, since it concerns specific instances of objects rather than object classes.

In this hierarchy, an object's "descendants" are properties of the object. For example, a form named "form1" is an object, but is also a property of document, and is referred to as "document.form1".

To refer to specific properties of these objects, you must specify the object name and all its ancestors. **Exception:** You are not required to include the window object.

See figure 5.1 or the inside front cover of this book for a visual depiction of the object hierarchy.

JavaScript and HTML Layout

To use JavaScript properly in the Navigator, it is important to have a basic understanding of how the Navigator performs layout. Layout refers to transforming the plain text directives of HTML into graphical display on your computer. Generally speaking, layout happens sequentially in the Navigator. That is, the Navigator starts from the top of the HTML file and works its way down, figuring out how to display output to the screen as it goes. So, it starts with the HEAD of an HTML document, then starts at the top of the BODY and works its way down.

Because of this "top-down" behavior, JavaScript only reflects HTML that it has encountered. For example, suppose you define a form with a couple of text input elements:

```
<FORM NAME="statform">
<input type = "text" name = "username" size = 20>
<input type = "text" name = "userage" size = 3>
```

Then these form elements are reflected as JavaScript objects document.statform.username and document.statform.userage, that you can use anywhere after the form is defined. However, you could not use these objects before the form is defined. So, for example, you could display the value of these objects in a script after the form definition:

```
<SCRIPT>
document.write(document.statform.username.value)
document.write(document.statform.userage.value)
</SCRIPT>
```

However, if you tried to do this before the form definition (i.e. above it in the HTML page), you would get an error, since the objects don't exist yet in the Navigator.

Likewise, once layout has occurred, setting a property value does not affect its value or its appearance. For example, suppose you have a document title defined as follows:

```
<TITLE>My JavaScript Page</TITLE>
```

This is reflected in JavaScript as the value of document.title. Once the Navigator has displayed this in layout (in this case, in the title bar of the Navigator window), you cannot change the value in JavaScript. So, if later in the page, you have the following script:

```
document.title = "The New Improved JavaScript Page"
```

it will not change the value of document.title nor affect the appearance of the page, nor will it generate an error.

Key Navigator Objects

Some of the most useful Navigator objects include document, form, and window.

Using the document Object

One of the most useful Navigator objects is the document object, because its write and writeln methods can generate HTML. These methods are the way that you display JavaScript expressions to the user. The only difference between write and writeln is that writeln adds a carriage return at the end of the line. However, since HTML ignores carriage returns, this will only affect pre-formatted text, such as that inside a PRE tag.

The document object also has onLoad and onUnload event-handlers to perform functions when a user first loads a page and when a user exits a page.

There is only one document object for a page, and it is the ancestor for all the form, link, and anchor objects in the page.

Using the form Object

Navigator creates a form object for each form in a document. You can name a form with the NAME attribute, as in this example:

```
<FORM NAME="myform">
<INPUT TYPE="text" NAME="quantity" onChange="...">
...
</FORM>
```

There would be a JavaScript object named myform based on this form. The form would have a property corresponding to the text object, that you would refer to as

```
document.myform.quantity
```

You would refer to the value property of this object as

```
document.myform.quantity.value
```

The forms in a document are stored in an array called forms. The first (topmost in the page) form is forms[0], the second forms[1], and so on. So the above references could also be:

```
document.forms[0].quantity
document.forms[0].quantity.value
```

Likewise, the elements in a form, such as text fields, radio buttons, and so on, are stored in an elements array.

Using the Window Object

The window object is the "parent" object for all other objects in Navigator. You can always omit the object name in references to window properties and methods.

Window has several very useful methods that create new windows and pop-up dialog boxes:

◆ open and close: Opens and closes a browser window

◆ alert: Pops up an alert dialog box

◆ confirm: Pops up a confirmation dialog box

The window object has properties for all the frames in a frameset. The frames are stored in the frames array. The frames array contains an entry for each child frame in a window. For example, if a window contains three child frames, these frames are reflected as window.frames[0], window.frames[1], and window.frames[2].

The status property enables you to set the message in the status bar at the bottom of the client window.

Using windows and frames

JavaScript lets you create and open windows for presenting HTML text, form objects, and frames. The window object is the top-level object in the JavaScript client hierarchy. Form elements and all JavaScript code exists in documents that are loaded into windows. By understanding how windows work, you can control and manipulate these windows.

Opening and Closing windows

A window is created automatically when a user launches Navigator, and a user can open a window by choosing New Web Browser from the Navigator's File menu. A user can close a window by choosing either Close or Exit from the Navigator's File menu. You can also open and close windows programmatically.

Opening a window

You can create a window with the open method. The following statement creates a window called msgWindow that displays the contents of the file sesame.html:

```
msgWindow=window.open("sesame.html")
```

The following statement creates a window called homeWindow that displays the Netscape home page:

```
homeWindow=window.open("http://www.netscape.com")
```

Windows can have two names. The following statement creates a window with two names. The first name, "msgWindow," is used when referring to the window's properties, methods, and containership; the second name, "displayWindow," is used when referring to the window as the target of a form submit or hypertext link.

```
msgWindow=window.open("sesame.html","displayWindow")
```

When you create a window, a window name is not required. But if you want to refer to a window from another window, the window must have a name.

When you open a window, you can specify attributes such as the window's height and width and whether the window contains a toolbar, location field, or scrollbars. The following statement creates a window without a toolbar but with scrollbars:

```
msgWindow=window.open
    ("sesame.html","displayWindow","toolbar=no,scrollbars=yes")
```

For details on these window attributes, see the open method.

Closing a window

You can close a window programmatically with the close method. You cannot close a frame without closing the entire parent window.

All of the following statements close the current window:

◆ window.close()

◆ self.close()

◆ // Do not use the following statement in an event handler

◆ close()

The following statement closes a window called msgWindow:

◆ msgWindow.close()

Using frames

A frame is a special type of window that can display multiple, independently scrollable frames on a single screen, each with its own distinct URL. Frames can point to different URLs and be targeted by other URLs, all within the same window. A series of frames makes up a page.

Creating a frame

You create a frame by using the <FRAMESET> tag in an HTML document. The <FRAMESET> tag is used in an HTML document whose sole purpose is to define the layout of frames that make up a page.

Example 1

The following statement creates the frameset shown in the previous diagram.

```
<FRAMESET ROWS="90%,10%">
    <FRAMESET COLS="30%,70%">
```

```
        <FRAME SRC=category.html NAME="listFrame">
        <FRAME SRC=titles.html NAME="contentFrame">
    </FRAMESET>
    <FRAME SRC=navigate.html NAME="navigateFrame">
</FRAMESET>
```

All frames have the same parent, even though some of the frames are defined within a separate frameset. This is because a frame's parent is its parent window, and a frame, not a frameset, defines a window.

Updating frames

You can update the contents of a frame by using the location property to set the URL, as long as you specify the frame hierarchy.

For example, suppose you are using the frameset described in Example 2 in the previous section. If you want users to be able to close the frame containing the alphabetic or categorical list of artists (in the frame listframe) and view only the music titles sorted by musician (currently in the frame contentFrame), you could add the following button to navigateFrame.

```
<INPUT TYPE="button" VALUE="Titles Only"
    onClick="top.frames[0].location='artists.html'">
```

When a user clicks this button, the file artists.html is loaded into the frame upperFrame; the frames listFrame and contentFrame close and no longer exist.

Referring to and Navigating Among Frames

Because a frame is a type of window, you refer to frames and navigate among frames the same as you do with a window.

Frame example

If the frameset in the previous section is designed to present the available titles for a music club, the frames and their HTML files could have the following content:

◆ category.html, in the frame listFrame, contains a list of musicians sorted by category.

◆ titles.html, in the frame contentFrame, contains an alphabetical list of each musician and the titles available for that musician.

◆ navigate.html, in the frame navigateFrame, contains hypertext links that let the user choose how the musicians are displayed in listFrame: in an alphabetical list or a categorical list. This file also defines a hypertext link that lets the user display a description of each musician.

◆ An additional file, alphabet.html, contains a list of musicians sorted alphabetically. This file is displayed in listFrame when the user clicks the link for an alphabetical list.

The file category.html (the categorical list) contains code similar to the following:

```
<B>Music Club Artists</B>
<P><B>Jazz</B>
<UL>
<LI><A HREF=titles.html#0001 TARGET="contentFrame">Toshiko Akiyoshi</A>
<LI><A HREF=titles.html#0006 TARGET="contentFrame">John Coltrane</A>
<LI><A HREF=titles.html#0007 TARGET="contentFrame">Miles Davis</A>
<LI><A HREF=titles.html#0010 TARGET="contentFrame">Dexter Gordon</A>
</UL>
<P><B>Soul</B>
<UL>
<LI><A HREF=titles.html#0003 TARGET="contentFrame">Betty Carter</A>
<LI><A HREF=titles.html#0004 TARGET="contentFrame">Ray Charles</A>
</UL>
```

The file alphabet.html (the alphabetical list) contains code similar to the following:

```
<B>Music Club Artists</B>
<UL>
<LI><A HREF=titles.html#0001 TARGET="contentFrame">Toshiko Akiyoshi</A>
<LI><A HREF=titles.html#0002 TARGET="contentFrame">The Beatles</A>
<LI><A HREF=titles.html#0003 TARGET="contentFrame">Betty Carter</A>
<LI><A HREF=titles.html#0004 TARGET="contentFrame">Ray Charles</A>
...
</UL>
```

The file navigate.html (the navigational links at the bottom of the screen) contains code similar to the following. Notice that the target for artists.html is "_parent". When the user clicks this link, the entire window is overwritten, because the top window is the parent of navigateFrame.

```
<A HREF="alphabet.html" TARGET="listFrame"><B>Alphabetical</B></A>
<A HREF="category.html" TARGET="listFrame"><B>By category</B></A>
<A HREF="artists.html" TARGET="_parent">
   <B>Musician Descriptions</B></A>
```

Referring to Windows and Frames

The name you use to refer to a window depends on whether you are referring to a window's properties, methods, and event handlers or are referring to the window as the target of a form submit or hypertext link.

Since the window object is the top-level object in the JavaScript client hierarchy, the window is essential for specifying the containership of objects in any window.

Referring to a Window's Properties, Methods, and Event Handlers

You can refer to the properties, methods, and event handlers of the current window or another window (if the other window is named) in any of the following ways:

◆ self or window. self and window are synonyms for the current window, and you can optionally use them to refer to the current window. For example, you can close the current window by calling either window.close() or self.close().

◆ top or parent. top and parent are also synonyms that can be used in place of the window name. top refers to the top-most Navigator window, and parent refers to a window containing a frameset. For example, the statement parent.frame2.document.bgColor="teal" changes the background color of the frame named frame2 to teal; frame2 is a frame in the current frameset.

◆ The name of a window variable. The window variable is the variable that is specified when a window is opened. For example, msgWindow.close() closes a window called msgWindow.

◆ However, when you open or close a window within an event handler, you must specify window.open() or window.close() instead of simply using open() or close(). Due to the scoping of static objects in JavaScript, a call to close() without specifying an object name is equivalent to document.close().

◆ Omit the window name. Because the existence of the current window is assumed, you do not have to reference the name of the window when you call its methods and assign its properties. For example, close() closes the current window.

Example: Referring to the Current Window

The following statement refers to a form named musicForm in the current window. The statement displays an alert if a check box is checked.

```
if (self.document.musicForm.checkbox1.checked) {
    alert('The checkbox on the musicForm is checked!')}
```

Example: Refer to Another Window

The following statements refer to a form named musicForm in a window named checkboxWin. The statements determine if a check box is checked, check the check box, determine if the second option of a select object is selected, and select the second option of the select object. Even though object values are changed in checkboxWin, the current window remains active: checking the check box and selecting the selection option do not give focus to the window.

To determine if a check box is checked:

```
if (checkboxWin.document.musicForm.checkbox2.checked) {
    alert('The check box on the musicForm in checkboxWin is checked!')}
```

To Check the check box:

```
checkboxWin.document.musicForm.checkbox2.checked=true
```

To determine if an option in a select object is selected:

```
if (checkboxWin.document.musicForm.musicTypes.options[1].selected)
    {alert('Option 1 is selected!')}
```

To select an option in a select object:

```
checkboxWin.document.musicForm.musicTypes.selectedIndex=1
```

Example: Refer to a Frame in Another Window

The following statement refers to a frame named frame2 that is in a window named window2. The statement changes the background color of frame2 to violet. The frame name, frame2, must be specified in the <FRAMESET> tag that creates the frameset.

```
window2.frame2.document.bgColor="violet"
```

Referring to a Window in a Form Submit or Hypertext Link

Use a window's name (not the window variable) when referring to a window as the target of a form submit or hypertext link (the TARGET attribute of a <FORM> or <A> tag). The window you specify is the window that the link is loaded into or, for a form, the window that server responses are displayed in.

Example: Second Window

The following example creates a hypertext link to a second window. The example has a button that opens a window named window2, then a link that loads the file doc2.html into the newly opened window, then a button that closes the window.

```
<P>
<INPUT TYPE="button" VALUE="Open window2"
  onClick="msgWindow=window.open('','window2','resizable=no,width=200,height=200')">
<P>
<A HREF="doc2.html" TARGET="window2"> Load a file into window2</A>
<P>
<INPUT TYPE="button" VALUE="Close window2"
   onClick="msgWindow.close()">
```

Example: Anchor in a Second Window

The following example creates a hypertext link to an anchor in a second window. The link displays the anchor named numbers in the file doc2.html in the window window2. If window2 does not exist, it is created.

```
<A HREF=doc2.html#numbers TARGET="window2">Numbers</A>
```

Example: Frame Name

The following example creates a hypertext link to an anchor in a frame. The link displays the anchor named abs_method in the file sesame.html in the frame named "contentFrame". The frame must be within the current frameset and the frame name must be defined in the NAME attribute of a <FRAME> tag.

```
<A HREF=sesame.html#abs_method TARGET="contentFrame">abs</A>
```

Example: Literal Frame Name

The following example creates a hypertext link to a file. The link displays the file named artists.html in the parent window of the current frameset. This link object appears in a frame within a frameset, and when the user clicks the link, all frames in the frameset disappear and the content of artists.html is loaded into the parent window.

```
<A HREF="artists.html" TARGET="_parent">
   <B>Musician Descriptions</B></A>
```

Navigating Among Windows

Many Navigator windows can be open at the same time. The user can move among these windows by clicking them to give them focus. You can give focus to a window programmatically by giving focus to an object in the window or by specifying the window as the target of a hypertext link. Although you can change an object's values in a second window, that does not make the second window active: the current window remains active.

The active window is the window that has focus. When a window has focus, it is brought to the front and changes in some visual way. For example, the window's title bar might change to a different color. The visual cue varies depending on the platform you are using.

Example: Giving Focus to an Object in Another Window

The following statement gives focus to a text object named city in a window named checkboxWin. Because the text object is gaining focus, checkboxWin also gains focus and becomes the active window. The example also shows the statement that creates checkboxWin.

```
checkboxWin=window.open("doc2.html")
...
checkboxWin.document.musicForm.city.focus()
```

Example: Give Focus to Another Window by Using a Hypertext Link

The following statement specifies window2 as the target of a hypertext link. When the user clicks the link, focus switches to window2. If window2 does not exist, it is created.

```
<A HREF="doc2.html" TARGET="window2"> Load a file into window2</A>
```

PART II: LANGUAGE CONCEPTS

Values

JavaScript recognizes the following types of values:

◆ numbers, such as 42 or 3.14159

◆ logical (Boolean) values, either true or false

◆ strings, such as "Howdy!"

◆ null, a special keyword denoting a null value

This relatively small set of types of values, or data types, enables you to perform useful functions with your applications. Notice that there is no explicit distinction between integer and real-valued numbers. Nor is there an explicit date data type in Navigator. However, the date object and related built-in functions enable you to handle dates.

Objects and functions are the other fundamental elements in the language. You can think of objects as named containers for values, and functions as procedures that your application can perform.

Datatype Conversion

JavaScript is a loosely typed language. That means that you do not have to specify the datatype of a variable when you declare it, and datatypes are converted automatically as needed during the course of script execution. So, for example, you could define a variable as follows:

```
var answer = 42
```

And later, you could assign the same variable a string value, for example:

```
answer = "Thanks for all the fish..."
```

Because JavaScript is loosely typed, this will not cause an error message.

In general, in expressions involving numeric and string values, JavaScript converts the numeric values to strings. For example, consider the following statements:

```
x = "The answer is " + 42
y = 42 + " is the answer."
```

The first statement will string "The answer is 42". The second statement will return the string "42 is the answer".

JavaScript provides several special functions for manipulating string and numeric values:

◆ eval attempts to evaluate a string representing any JavaScript literals or variables, converting it to a number.

◆ parseInt converts a string to an integer of the specified radix (base), if possible.

◆ parseFloat converts a string to a floating-point number, if possible.

Variables

You use variables to hold values in your application. You give these variables names by which you reference them, and there are certain rules to which the names must conform.

A JavaScript identifier or name must start with a letter or underscore ("_"); subsequent characters can also be digits (0-9). Letters include the characters "A" through "Z" (uppercase) and the characters "a" through "z" (lowercase). JavaScript is case-sensitive.

Some examples of legal names are:

◆ Number_hits

◆ temp99

◆ _name

Variable scope

The scope of a variable is where you can use it in a script. In JavaScript, there are two scopes that a variable can have:

◆ global: you can use the variable anywhere in the application.

◆ local: you can use the variable within the current function.

To declare a local variable inside a function, use the var keyword, for example:

```
var total = 0
```

To declare a global variable, declare the variable by assignment, that is simply assign the desired value to the variable (either in a function or outside a function), for example:

```
total = 0
```

It is good programming practice to declare global variables at the beginning of your script, so that functions will inherit the variable and its value.

Literals

Literals are the way you represent values in JavaScript. These are fixed values that you literally provide in your application source, and are not variables. Examples of literals include:

◆ 42

◆ 3.14159

◆ "To be or not to be"

Integers

Integers can be expressed in decimal (base 10), hexadecimal (base 16), or octal (base 8) format. A decimal integer literal consists of a sequence of digits (optionally suffixed as described below) without a leading 0 (zero).

An integer can be expressed in octal or hexadecimal rather than decimal. A leading 0 (zero) on an integer literal means it is in octal; a leading 0x (or 0X) means hexadecimal. Hexadecimal integers can include digits (0-9) and the letters a-f and A-F. Octal integers can include only the digits 0-7.

Floating Point Literals

A floating point literal can have the following parts: a decimal integer, a decimal point ("."), a fraction (another decimal number), an exponent, and a type suffix. The exponent part is an "e" or "E" followed by an integer, which can be signed (preceded by a "+" or "-"). A floating point literal must have at least one digit, plus either a decimal point or "e" (or "E"). Some examples of floating point literals are:

- 3.1415

- −3.1E12

- 1e12

- 2E−12

Boolean Literals

The boolean type has two literal values: true and false.

String Literals

A string literal is zero or more characters enclosed in double (") or single (') quotes. A string must be delimited by quotes of the same type; that is, either both single quotes or double quotes. The following are examples of string literals:

- "blah"

- 'blah'

- "1234"

- "one line \n another line"

Special Characters

You can use the following special characters in JavaScript string literals:

- \b indicates a backspace.

- \f indicates a form feed.

- \n indicates a new line character.

- \r indicates a carriage return.

- \t indicates a tab character.

Escaping Characters

You can insert quotes inside of strings by preceding them by a backslash. This is known as escaping the quotes. For example, var quote = "He read \"The Cremation of Sam McGee\" by R.W. Service"

```
document.write(quote)
```

The result of this would be

He read "The Cremation of Sam McGee" by R.W. Service

Expressions

An expression is any valid set of literals, variables, operators, and expressions that evaluates to a single value. The value may be a number, a string, or a logical value. Conceptually, there are two types of expressions: those that assign a value to a variable, and those that simply have a value. For example, the expression

x = 7

is an expression that assigns x the value 7. This expression itself evaluates to 7. Such expressions use assignment operators. On the other hand, the expression

3 + 4

simply evaluates to 7; it does not perform an assignment. The operators used in such expressions are referred to simply as operators.

JavaScript has the following kinds of expressions:

◆ Arithmetic: evaluates to a number, for example

◆ String: evaluates to a character string, for example "Fred" or "234"

◆ Logical: evaluates to true or false

The special keyword null denotes a null value. In contrast, variables that have not been assigned a value are undefined, and cannot be used without a run-time error.

Conditional Expressions

A conditional expression can have one of two values based on a condition. The syntax is

```
(condition) ? val1 : val2
```

If condition is true, the expression has the value of val1, otherwise it has the value of val2. You can use a conditional expression anywhere you would use a standard expression.

For example,

```
status = (age >= 18) ? "adult" : "minor"
```

This statement assigns the value "adult" to the variable status if age is eighteen or greater. Otherwise, it assigns the value "minor" to status.

Assignment Operators (=, +=, -=, *=, /=)

An assignment operator assigns a value to its left operand based on the value of its right operand. The basic assignment operator is equal (=), which assigns the value of its right operand to its left operand. That is, x = y assigns the value of y to x.

The other operators are shorthand for standard arithmetic operations as follows:

◆ x += y means x = x + y

◆ x -= y means x = x - y

◆ x *= y means x = x * y

◆ x /= y means x = x / y

◆ x %= y means x = x % y

There are additional assignment operators for bitwise operations:

◆ x <<= y means x = x << y

◆ x >>= y means x = x >> y

◆ x >>>= means x = x >>> y

◆ x &= means x = x & y

◆ x ^= means x = x ^ y

◆ x |= means x = x | y

Operators

JavaScript has arithmetic, string, and logical operators. There are both binary and unary operators. A binary operator requires two operands, one before the operator and one after the operator: operand1 operator operand2.

For example, 3 + 4 or x * y.

A unary operator requires a single operand, either before or after the operator: operator operand or operand operator.

For example x++ or ++x.

Arithmetic Operators

Arithmetic operators take numerical values (either literals or variables) as their operands and return a single numerical value.

Standard Arithmetic Operators

The standard arithmetic operators are addition (+), subtraction (-), multiplication (*), and division (/). These operators work in the standard way.

Modulus (%)

The modulus operator is used as follows:

var1 % var2

The modulus operator returns the first operand modulo the second operand, that is, var1 modulo var2, in the statement above, where var1 and var2 are variables. The modulo function is the remainder of integrally dividing var1 by var2. For example, 12 % 5 returns 2.

Increment (++)

The increment operator is used as follows:

var++ or ++var

This operator increments (adds one to) its operand and returns a value. If used postfix, with operator after operand (for example x++), then it returns the value before incrementing. If used prefix with operator before operand (for example, ++x), then it returns the value after incrementing.

For example, if x is 3, then the statement

y = x++

increments x to 4 and sets y to 3.

If x is 3, then the statement

y = ++x

increments x to 4 and sets y to 4.

Decrement (--)

The decrement operator is used as follows:

var-- or --var

This operator decrements (subtracts one from) its operand and returns a value. If used postfix (for example x--) then it returns the value before decrementing. If used prefix (for example, --x), then it returns the value after decrementing.

For example, if x is 3, then the statement

y = x--

decrements x to 2 and sets y to 3.

If x is 3, then the statement

y = --x

decrements x to 2 and sets y to 2.

Unary negation (-)

The unary negation operator must precede its operand. It negates its operand. For example,

x = -x

negates the value of x; that is if x were 3, it would become –3.

Bitwise Operators

Bitwise operators treat their operands as a set of bits (zeros and ones), rather than as decimal, hexadecimal, or octal numbers. For example, the decimal number 9 has a binary representation of 1001. Bitwise operators perform their operations on such binary representations, but they return standard JavaScript numerical values.

Bitwise Logical Operators

The bitwise logical operators work conceptually as follows:

◆ The operands are converted to 32-bit integers, and expressed a series of bits (zeros and ones).

◆ Each bit in the first operand is paired with the corresponding bit in the second operand: first bit to first bit, second bit to second bit, and so on.

◆ The operator is applied to each pair of bits, and the result is constructed bitwise.

The bitwise operators are:

◆ Bitwise AND & returns a one if both operands are ones.

◆ Bitwise OR | returns a one if either operand is one.

◆ Bitwise XOR ^ returns a one if one but not both operands are one.

For example, the binary representation of 9 is 1001, and the binary representation of 15 is 1111. So, when the bitwise operators are applied to these values, the results are as follows:

◆ 15 & 9 yields 9 (1111 & 1001 = 1001)

◆ 15 | 9 yields 15 (1111 | 1001 = 1111)

◆ 15 ^ 9 yields 6 (1111 ^ 1001 = 0110)

Bitwise Shift Operators

The bitwise shift operators are:

◆ Left Shift (<<)

◆ Sign-propagating Right Shift (>>)

◆ Zero-fill Right shift (>>>)

The shift operators take two operands: the first is a quantity to be shifted, and the second specifies the number of bit positions by which the first operand is to be shifted. The direction of the shift operation is controlled by the operator used.

Shift operators convert their operands to 32-bit integers, and return a result of the same type as the left operator.

Left Shift (<<)

This operator shifts the first operand the specified number of bits to the left. Excess bits shifted off to the left are discarded. Zero bits are shifted in from the right.

For example, 9<<2 yields 36, because 1001 shifted two bits to the left becomes 100100, which is 36.

Sign-propagating Right Shift (>>)

This operator shifts the first operand the specified number of bits to the right. Excess bits shifted off to the right are discarded. Copies of the leftmost bit are shifted in from the left.

For example, 9>>2 yields 2, because 1001 shifted two bits to the right becomes 10, which is 2. Likewise, -9>>2 yields -3, because the sign is preserved.

Zero-fill right shift (>>>)

This operator shifts the first operand the specified number of bits to the left. Excess bits shifted off to the right are discarded. Zero bits are shifted in from the left.

For example, 19>>>2 yields 4, because 10011 shifted two bits to the right becomes 100, which is 4. For positive numbers, zero-fill right shift and sign-propagating right shift yield the same result.

Logical Operators

Logical operators take logical (Boolean) values as operands. They return a logical value. Logical values are true and false.

And (&&)

Usage: expr1 && expr2

The logical "and" operator returns true if both logical expressions expr1 and expr2 are true. Otherwise, it returns false.

Or (||)

Usage: expr1 || expr2

The logical "or" operator returns true if either logical expression expr1 or expr2 is true. If both expr1 and expr2 are false, then it returns false.

Not (!)

Usage: !expr

The logical "not" operator is a unary operator that negates its operand expression expr . That is, if expr is true, it returns false, and if expr is false, then it returns true.

Short-Circuit Evaluation

As logical expressions are evaluated left to right, they are tested for possible "short circuit" evaluation using the following rule:

◆ false && anything is short-circuit evaluated to false.

◆ true || anything is short-circuit evaluated to true.

The rules of logic guarantee that these evaluations will always be correct. Note that the anything part of the above expressions is not evaluated, so any side effects of doing so do not take effect.

Comparison Operators (= =, >, >=, <, <=, !=)

A comparison operator compares its operands and returns a logical value based on whether the comparison is true or not. The operands may be numerical or string values. When used on string values, the comparisons are based on the standard lexicographical ordering.

The operators are:

◆ Equal (= =): returns true if the operands are equal

◆ Not equal (!=): returns true if the operands are not equal

◆ Greater than (>): returns true if left operand is greater than right operand. Example: x > y returns true if x is greater than y

◆ Greater than or equal to (>=): returns true if left operand is greater than or equal to right operand. Example: x >= y returns true if x is greater than or equal to y

◆ Less than (<): returns true if left operand is less than right operand. Example: x < y returns true if x is less than y

◆ Less than or equal to (<=): returns true if left operand is less than or equal to right operand. Example: x <= y returns true if x is less than or equal to y

String Operators

In addition to the comparison operators, which may be used on string values, the concatenation operator (+) concatenates two string values together, returning another string that is the union of the two operand strings. For example,

"my " + "string"

returns the string

"my string"

The shorthand assignment operator += can also be used to concatenate strings. For example, if the variable mystring is a string that has the value "alpha," then the expression

mystring += "bet"

evaluates to "alphabet" and assigns this value to mystring.

Operator Precedence

The precedence of operators determines the order they are applied when evaluating an expression. You can override operator precedence by using parentheses.

The precedence of operators, from lowest to highest is as follows:

comma ,

assignment = += -= *= /= %= <<= >>= >>>= &= ^= |=

conditional ?:

logical-or ||

logical-and &&

bitwise-or |

bitwise-xor ^

bitwise-and &

equality == !=

relational < <= > >=

bitwise shift << >> >>>

addition/subtraction + -

multiply/divide * / %

negation/increment ! ~ - ++ --

call, member () [] .

Objects and Properties

A JavaScript object has properties associated with it. You access the properties of an object with a simple notation:

```
objectName.propertyName
```

Both the object name and property name are case-sensitive. You define a property by assigning it a value. For example, suppose there is an object named myCar. You can give it properties named make, model, and year as follows:

```
myCar.make = "Ford"
myCar.model = "Mustang"
myCar.year = 69;
```

You can also refer to these properties using an array notation as follows:

```
mycar["make"] = "Ford
myCar["model"] = "Mustang"
myCar["year"] = 69;
```

This type of an array is known as an associative array, because each index element is also associated with a string value. To illustrate how this works, the following function displays the properties of the object, when you pass the object and the object's name as arguments to the function:

```
function show_props(obj, obj_name) {
    var result = ""
    for (var i in obj)
        result += obj_name + "." + i + " = " + obj[i] + "\n"
    return result;
}
```

So, the function call show_props(myCar, "myCar") would return the following:

myCar.make = Ford

myCar.model = Mustang

myCar.year = 67

You may also define properties using ordinal numbers, for example:

temp[0] = 34

temp[1] = 42

temp[2] = 56

These statements create three properties of the object temp, and you must refer to these properties as temp[i], where i is an integer between 0 and 2.

Functions and Methods

Functions are one of the fundamental building blocks in JavaScript. A function is a JavaScript procedure—a set of statements that performs a specific task.

A function definition consists of the function keyword, followed by

- ◆ the name of the function

- ◆ a list of arguments to the function, enclosed in parentheses, and separated by commas

- ◆ the JavaScript statements that define the function, enclosed in curly braces, {...}

In a Navigator application, you can use any functions defined in the current page. It is generally a good idea to define all your functions in the HEAD of a page. When a user loads the page, the functions will then be loaded first.

The statements in a function can include other function calls defined for the current application.

For example, here is the definition of a simple function named pretty_print:

```
function pretty_print(string) {
   document.write("<HR><P>" + string)
}
```

This function takes a string as its argument, adds some HTML tags to it using the concatenation operator (+), then displays the result to the current document.

Defining a function does not execute it. You have to call the function for it to do its work. For example, you could call the pretty_print function as follows:

```
<SCRIPT>
pretty_print("This is some text to display")
</SCRIPT>
```

The arguments of a function are not limited to just strings and numbers. You can pass whole objects to a function, too. The show_props function from the previous section is an example of a function that takes an object as an argument.

The arguments of a function are maintained in an array. Within a function, you can address the parameters passed to it as follows:

```
functionName.arguments[i]
```

where functionName is the name of the function and i is the ordinal number of the argument, starting at zero. So, the first argument passed to a function named myfunc would be myfunc.arguments[0]. The total number of arguments is indicated by the variable arguments.length.

A function can even be recursive, that is, it can call itself. For example, here is a function that computes factorials:

```
function factorial(n) {
  if ((n == 0) || (n == 1))
    return 1
  else {
    result = (n * factorial(n-1) )
    return result
  }
}
```

You could then display the factorials of one through five as follows:

```
for (x = 0; x < 5; x++) {
   document.write(x, " factorial is ", factorial(x))
   document.write("<BR>")
}
```

The results would be:

0 factorial is 1

1 factorial is 1

2 factorial is 2

3 factorial is 6

4 factorial is 24

5 factorial is 120

Functions with Variable Numbers of Arguments

You can call a function with more arguments than it is formally declared to accept using the arguments array. This is often useful if you don't know beforehand how many arguments will be passed to the function. You can use arguments.length to determine the number of arguments actually passed to the function, and then treat each argument using the arguments array.

For example, consider a function defined to create HTML lists. The only formal argument for the function is a string that is "U" if the list is to be unordered (bulleted) or "O" if the list is to be ordered (numbered). The function is defined as follows:

```
function list(type) {
   document.write("<" + type + "L>")                 // begin list
   for (var i = 1; i < list.arguments.length; i++)  // iterate through argu-
ments
      document.write("<LI>" + list.arguments[i])
   document.write("</" + type + "L>")               // end list
}
```

You can pass any number of arguments to this function and it will then display each argument as an item in the indicated type of list. For example, the following call to the function:

```
list("o", "one", 1967, "three", "etc, etc...")
```

Defining Methods

A method is a function associated with an object. You define a method in the same way you define a standard function. Then, use the following syntax to associate the function with an existing object:

```
object.methodname = function_name
```

where object is an existing object, methodname is the name you are assigning to the method, and function_name is the name of the function.

You can then call the method in the context of the object as follows: .

```
object.methodname(params);
```

Using this for Object References

JavaScript has a special keyword, this, that you can use to refer to the current object. For example, suppose you have a function called validate that validates an object's value property, given the object, and the high and low values:

```
function validate(obj, lowval, hival) {
   if ((obj.value < lowval) || (obj.value > hival))
      alert("Invalid Value!")
}
```

Then, you could call validate in each form element's onChange event handler, using this to pass it the form element, as in the following example:

<INPUT TYPE = "text" NAME = "age" SIZE = 3 onChange="validate(this, 18, 99)">

In general, in a method this refers to the calling object.

Creating New Objects

Both client and server JavaScript have a number of predefined objects. In addition, you can create your own objects. Creating your own object requires two steps:

◆ Define the object type by writing a function.

◆ Create an instance of the object with new.

To define an object type, create a function for the object type that specifies its name, and its properties and methods. For example, suppose you want to create an object type for cars. You want this type of object to be called car, and you want it to have properties for make, model, year, and color. To do this, you would write the following function:

```
function car(make, model, year) {
   this.make = make;
   this.model = model;
   this.year = year;
}
```

Notice the use of this to assign values to the object's properties based on the values passed to the function.

Now you can create an object called mycar as follows:

```
mycar = new car("Eagle", "Talon TSi", 1993);
```

This statement creates mycar and assigns it the specified values for its properties. Then the value of mycar.make is the string "Eagle", mycar.year is the integer 1993, and so on.

You can create any number of car objects by calls to new. For example,

```
kenscar = new car("Nissan", "300ZX", 1992)
```

An object can have a property that is itself another object. For example, suppose you 0 define an object called person as follows:

```
function person(name, age, sex) {
   this.name = name;
   this.age = age;
   this.sex = sex;
}
```

And then instantiate two new person objects as follows:

```
rand = new person("Rand McNally", 33, "M")
ken = new person("Ken Jones", 39, "M")
```

Then you can rewrite the definition of car to include an owner property that takes a person object, as follows:

```
function car(make, model, year, owner) {
   this.make = make;
   this.model = model;
   this.year = year;
   this.owner = owner;
}
```

To instantiate the new objects, use the following:

```
car1 = new car("Eagle", "Talon TSi", 1993, rand);
car2 = new car("Nissan", "300ZX", 1992, ken)
```

Notice that instead of passing a literal string or integer value when creating the new objects, the above statements pass the objects rand and ken as the arguments for the owners. Then if you want to find out the name of the owner of car2, you can access the following property:

```
car2.owner.name
```

Note that you can always add a property to a previously defined object. For example, the statement:

```
car1.color = "black"
```

adds a property color to car1, and assigns it a value of "black". However, this does not affect any other objects. To add the new property to all objects of the same type, you have to add the property to the definition of the car object type.

Defining Methods

You can define methods for an object type by including a method definition in the object type definition. For example, suppose you have a set of image GIF files, and you want to define a method that displays the information for the cars, along with the corresponding image. You could define a function such as:

```
function displayCar() {
   var result = "A Beautiful " + this.year
               + " " + this.make + " " + this.model;
   pretty_print(result)
}
```

where pretty_print is the previously defined function to display a string. Notice the use of this to refer to the object to which the method belongs.

You can make this function a method of car by adding the statement

```
this.displayCar = displayCar;
```

to the object definition. So, the full definition of car would now look like:

```
function car(make, model, year, owner) {
   this.make = make;
   this.model = model;
   this.year = year;
```

```
    this.owner = owner;
    this.displayCar = displayCar;
}
```

Then you can call this new method as follows:

```
car1.displayCar()
car2.displayCar()
```

This will produce output like this:

```
A Beautiful 1993 Eagle Talon TSi
A Beautiful 1992 Nissan 300ZX
```

Using Built-in Objects and Functions

The JavaScript Language contains the following built-in objects and functions:

- ◆ String object

- ◆ Math object

- ◆ Date object

- ◆ Built-in functions

These objects and their properties and methods are built into the language. You can use these objects in both client applications with Netscape Navigator and server applications with LiveWire.

Using the String Object

Whenever you assign a string value to a variable or property, you create a string object. String literals are also string objects. For example, the statement

```
mystring = "Hello, World!"
```

creates a string object called mystring. The literal "blah" is also a string object.

The string object has methods that return:

- ◆ a variation on the string itself, such as substring and toUpperCase

- ◆ an HTML formatted version of the string, such as bold and link

For example, given the above object, mystring.toUpperCase() returns "HELLO, WORLD!", and so does "hello, world!".toUpperCase().

Using the Math Object

The built-in Math object has properties and methods for mathematical constants and functions. For example, the Math object's PI property has the value of pi, which you would use in an application as

```
Math.PI
```

Similarly, standard mathematical functions are methods of Math. These include trigonometric, logarithmic, exponential, and other functions. For example, if you want to use the trigonometric function sine, you would write

```
Math.sin(1.56)
```

Note that all trigonometric methods of math take arguments in radians.

It is often convenient to use the with statement when a section of code uses several math constants and methods, so you don't have to type "Math" repeatedly. For example,

```
with (Math) {
    a = PI * r*r;
    y = r*sin(theta)
    x = r*cos(theta)
}
```

Using the Date Object

JavaScript does not have a date data type. However, the date object and its methods enable you to work with dates and times in your applications. The date object has a large number of methods for setting, getting, and manipulating dates. It does not have any properties.

JavaScript handles dates very similarly to Java. The two languages have many of the same date methods, and both languages store dates as the number of milliseconds since January 1, 1970 00:00:00.

NOTE: You cannot currently work with dates prior to 1/1/70.

To create a date object:

```
varName = new Date(parameters)
```

where varName is a JavaScript variable name for the date object being created; it can be a new object or a property of an existing object.

The parameters for the Date constructor can be any of the following:

◆ Nothing: creates today's date and time. For example, today = new Date().

◆ A string representing a date in the following form: "Month day, year hours:minutes:seconds." For example, Xmas95= new Date("December 25, 1995 13:30:00"). If you omit hours, minutes, or seconds, the value will be set to zero.

◆ A set of integer values for year, month, and day. For example, Xmas95 = new Date(95,11,25).

◆ A set of values for year, month, day, hour, minute, and seconds. For example, Xmas95 = new Date(95,11,25,9,30,0).

The Date object has a large number of methods for handling dates and times. The methods fall into these broad categories:

◆ "set" methods, for setting date and time values in date objects

◆ "get" methods, for getting date and time values from date objects

◆ "to" methods, for returning string values from date objects

◆ parse and UTC methods, for parsing date strings

The "get" and "set" methods enable you to get and set seconds, minutes, hours, day of the month, day of the week, months, and years separately. There is a getDay method that returns the day of the week, but no corresponding setDay method, because the day of the week is set automatically. These methods use integers to represent these values as follows:

◆ seconds and minutes: 0 to 59

◆ hours: 0 to 23

◆ day: 0 to 6 (day of the week)

◆ date: 1 to 31 (day of the month)

◆ months: 0 (January) to 11 (December)

◆ year: years since 1900

For example, suppose you define the following date:

```
Xmas95 = new Date("December 25, 1995")
```

Then

```
Xmas95.getMonth() returns 11, and Xmas95.getYear() returns 95.
```

The getTime and setTime methods are useful for comparing dates. The getTime method returns the number of milliseconds since the epoch for a date object.

For example, the following code displays the number of shopping days left until Christmas:

```
today = new Date()
nextXmas = new Date("December 25, 1990")
nextXmas.setYear(today.getYear())
msPerDay = 24 * 60 * 60 * 1000 ; // Number of milliseconds per day
daysLeft = (nextXmas.getTime() - today.getTime()) / msPerDay;
daysLeft = Math.round(daysLeft);
document.write("Number of Shopping Days until Christmas: " + daysLeft);
```

This example creates a date object named today that contains today's date. It then creates a date object named nextXmas, and sets the year to the current year. Then, using the number of milliseconds per day, it computes the number of days between today and nextXmas, using getTime, and rounding to a whole number of days.

The parse method is useful for assigning values from date strings to existing date objects. For example, the following code uses parse and setTime to assign a date to the IPOdate object.

```
IPOdate = new Date()
IPOdate.setTime(Date.parse("Aug 9, 1995"))
```

Using Built-in Functions

JavaScript has several "top-level" functions built-in to the language. They are:

- ◆ eval
- ◆ parseInt
- ◆ parseFloat

The eval Function

The built-in function eval takes a string as its argument. The string can be any string representing a JavaScript expression, statement, or sequence of statements. The expression can include variables and properties of existing objects.

If the argument represents an expression, eval evaluates the expression. If the argument represents one or more JavaScript statements, eval performs the statements.

This function is useful for evaluating a string representing an arithmetic expression. For example, input from a form element is always a string, but you often want to convert it to a numerical value.

The following example takes input in a text field, applies the eval function and displays the result in another text field. If you type a numerical expression in the first field, and click on the button, the expression will be evaluated. For example, enter "(666 * 777) / 3", and click on the button to see the result.

```
<SCRIPT>
function compute(obj) {
    obj.result.value = eval(obj.expr.value)
}
</SCRIPT>
<FORM NAME="evalform">

Enter an expression: <INPUT TYPE=text NAME="expr" SIZE=20 >

<BR>
Result: <INPUT TYPE=text NAME="result" SIZE=20 >
<BR>
<INPUT TYPE="button" VALUE="Click Me" onClick="compute(this.form)">
</FORM>
```

The eval function is not limited to evaluating numerical expressions, however. Its argument can include object references or even JavaScript statements. For example, you could define a function called setValue that would take two arguments: and object and a value, as follows:

```
function setValue (myobj, myvalue) {
  eval ("document.forms[0]." + myobj + ".value") = myvalue;
}
```

Then, for example, you could call this function to set the value of a form element "text1" as follows:

```
setValue(text1, 42)
```

The parseInt and parseFloat Functions

These two built-in functions return a numeric value when given a string as an argument.

ParseFloat parses its argument, a string, and attempts to return a floating point number. If it encounters a character other than a sign (+ or -), numeral (0-9), a decimal point, or an exponent, then it returns the value up to that point and ignores that character and all succeeding characters. If the first character cannot be converted to a number, it returns NaN (not a number).

The parseInt function parses its first argument, a string, and attempts to return an integer of the specified radix (base). For example, a radix of 10 indicates to convert to a decimal number, 8 octal, 16 hexadecimal, and so on. For radixes above 10, the letters of the alphabet indicate numerals greater than 9. For example, for hexadecimal numbers (base 16), A through F are used.

If parseInt encounters a character that is not a numeral in the specified radix, it ignores it and all succeeding characters and returns the integer value parsed up to that point. If the first character cannot be converted to a number in the specified radix, it returns NaN. ParseInt truncates numbers to integer values.

Additional JavaScript Resources: Resource Links, Reserved Words, and the Color Values Chart

Online Resources

The following sections contain resources to interesting and information-filled JavaScript sites. Some of these sites offer information and examples, while others give you the opportunity to ask questions and get help. Enjoy!

Netscape JavaScript Tutorial

http://home.netscape.com/comprod/products/navigator/version_2.0/script/script_info/tutorial/main.htm

Tutorial that walks you through using JavaScript to manipulate multi-frame documents. Good for beginners.

Introduction to JavaScript

http://gromit.webconn.com/java/javascript/intro/index.htm

Cool-looking site that has a lot of information about JavaScript, including running and embedding scripts, form elements, arrays, and working with windows and frames.

Verifying Form Input with JavaScript

http://gmccomb.com/javascript/valid.htm

Discusses forms on a Web page. Provides input validation examples and using the submit button. Note that you need Netscape 2.0 to successfully use the page.

Experiments with JavaScript

http://gmccomb.com/javascript/

Provides examples and tutorials on using JavaScript, including information on password protection, counting hits on your site, and creating a calendar with JavaScript.

JavaScript Index

http://www.c2.org/~andreww/javascript/

Includes sample JavaScript scripts, tutorials and unofficial documentation, links, and newsgroups. You'll find tons of good stuff here!

Ask the JavaScript Pro

http://www.inquiry.com/techtips/js_pro/

Geared toward all JavaScript users at all levels—beginners, intermediates, and gurus alike. Offers all kinds of information, including FAQs, discussion forums, and links to other Internet resources.

HTMLJive Info

http://www.cris.com/~raydaly/htmljive.html

HTML editor written in JavaScript.

JavaScript FAQ

http://www.freqgrafx.com/411/jsfaq.html

Great place for answers to your JavaScript questions. Includes known bugs and work-arounds, dealing with forms, arrays, windows and frames, and more.

Enhanced Cheat Sheet

http://www.intercom.net/user/mecha/java.html

Nifty little site with tips and instructions for building HTML pages.

JavaScript Frame

http://tanega.com/java/java.html

Friendly, straightforward site that offers tips and tricks, and basic how-to instructions for novices. Good spot for new ideas.

DryRoast JavaScript Page

http://tequila.randomc.com/JS/

Cool site that offers "home-grown" examples and links to other JavaScript sites. Also offers JavaScript tours. Good place to visit when you have a few minutes.

Danny Goodman's JavaScript Pages

http://www.dannyg.com/javascript/

Offers information on serverless database lookups, outline-style table of contents, and information on HTTP cookies.

JavaScript 411

http://www.freqgrafx.com/411/

Cool-looking site that offers tutorials, FAQs, and a library of JavaScript snippets. Makes you feel welcome, especially if you are a novice!

Programmer's File Editor Home Page

http://www.lancs.ac.uk/people/cpaap/pfe/

Programmer's File Editor (PFE) is a wonderful little freeware text editor that is powerful yet at the same time not overburdening. If you find yourself using Notepad to edit HTML files, you must get this program as a replacement.

Dippy Bird

http://www.dippybird.com/

Dippy Bird is a good site for JavaScript, LiveWire, Netscape plug-ins, and Java documentation in the search-friendly WinHelp online format.

Gamelan

http://www.gamelan.com

Gamelan serves as a directory and registry of Java and JavaScript resources. If you are looking for a particular Java or JavaScript code sample, development tool, or piece of documentation, Gamelan should be your first choice. No other site comes close to indexing as many Java programs as Gamelan does. Never being the Web site to sit still, Gamelan now hosts ActiveX controls.

Denise's JavaScript Page

http://www.loginet.com/users/d/denise/javascript.html

If you want to take a break from information overload at some of these JavaScript resource sites, check out Denise's JavaScript Page. You won't find a lot of JavaScript techno-babble, but you will have a good time.

Netscape's Secure JavaScript and LiveWire Newsgroups

snews://secnews.netscape.com/netscape.devs-livewire

snews://secnews.netscape.com/netscape.devs-javascript

If you are currently a member of Netscape's DevEdge program, you might want to take advantage of their secure newsgroups. These newsgroups can sometimes offer knowledgeable advice that you cannot get anywhere else.

LiveSoftware's JavaScript Examples Newsgroup

news://news.livesoftware.com/livesoftware.javascript.examples

If you are looking for a JavaScript newsgroup with infrequent flame wars and plenty of example code, this is the newsgroup for you.

JavaScript Resource Center

http://www.intercom.net/user/mecha/java/links.html

The JavaScript Resource Center keeps you in touch with JavaScript tutorials, newsgroups, and more than 50 links to cool personal and commercial JavaScript sites.

comp.lang.javascript Newsgroup

news:comp.lang.javascript

This newsgroup has very heavy traffic, and offers much of the information that the private Netscape newsgroup offers.

JavaScript Mailing List

http://www.inquiry.com/techtips/js_pro/maillist.html

This site makes it easy for you to subscribe to the JavaScript Mailing List. There is also a digest version of this mailing list that you can subscribe to here as well.

Reserved Words

The reserved words in this list cannot be used as JavaScript variables, functions, methods, or object names. Some of these words are keywords used in JavaScript; others are reserved for future use.

abstract	extends	int	super
boolean	false	interface	switch
break	final	long	synchronize
byte	finally	native	this
case	float	new	throw
catch	for	null	throws
char	function	package	transient
class	goto	private	true
const	if	protected	try
continue	implements	public	var
default	import	return	void
do	in	short	while
double	instanceof	static	with
else			

Color Values Chart

Color	Red	Green	Blue
aliceblue	F0	F8	FF
antiquewhite	FA	EB	D7
aqua	00	FF	FF
aquamarine	7F	FF	D4

Color	Red	Green	Blue
azure	F0	FF	FF
beige	F5	F5	DC
bisque	FF	E4	C4
black	00	00	00
blanchedalmond	FF	EB	CD
blue	00	00	FF
blueviolet	8A	2B	E2
brown	A5	2A	2A
burlywood	DE	B8	87
cadetblue	5F	9E	A0
chartreuse	7F	FF	00
chocolate	D2	69	1E
coral	FF	7F	50
cornflowerblue	64	95	ED
cornsilk	FF	F8	DC
crimson	DC	14	3C
cyan	00	FF	FF
darkblue	00	00	8B
darkcyan	00	8B	8B
darkgoldenrod	B8	86	0B
darkgray	A9	A9	A9
darkgreen	00	64	00
darkkhaki	BD	B7	6B
darkmagenta	8B	00	8B
darkolivegreen	55	6B	2F

Color	Red	Green	Blue
darkorange	FF	8C	00
darkorchid	99	32	CC
darkred	8B	00	00
darksalmon	E9	96	7A
darkseagreen	8F	BC	8F
darkslateblue	48	3D	8B
darkslategray	2F	4F	4F
darkturquoise	00	CE	D1
darkviolet	94	00	D3
deeppink	FF	14	93
deepskyblue	00	BF	FF
dimgray	69	69	69
dodgerblue	1E	90	FF
firebrick	B2	22	22
floralwhite	FF	FA	F0
forestgreen	22	8B	22
fuchsia	FF	00	FF
gainsboro	DC	DC	DC
ghostwhite	F8	F8	FF
gold	FF	D7	00
goldenrod	DA	A5	20
gray	80	80	80
green	00	80	00
greenyellow	AD	FF	2F
honeydew	F0	FF	F0

Color	Red	Green	Blue
hotpink	FF	69	B4
indianred	CD	5C	5C
indigo	4B	00	82
ivory	FF	FF	F0
khaki	F0	E6	8C
lavender	E6	E6	FA
lavenderblush	FF	F0	F5
lawngreen	7C	FC	00
lemonchiffon	FF	FA	CD
lightblue	AD	D8	E6
lightcoral	F0	80	80
lightcyan	E0	FF	FF
lightgoldenrodyellow	FA	FA	D2
lightgreen	90	EE	90
lightgrey	D3	D3	D3
lightpink	FF	B6	C1
lightsalmon	FF	A0	7A
lightseagreen	20	B2	AA
lightskyblue	87	CE	FA
lightslategray	77	88	99
lightsteelblue	B0	C4	DE
lightyellow	FF	FF	E0
lime	00	FF	00
limegreen	32	CD	32
lincn	FA	F0	E6

Color	Red	Green	Blue
magenta	FF	00	FF
maroon	80	00	00
mediumaquamarine	66	CD	AA
mediumblue	00	00	CD
mediumorchid	BA	55	D3
mediumpurple	93	70	DB
mediumseagreen	3C	B3	71
mediumslateblue	7B	68	EE
mediumspringgreen	00	FA	9A
mediumturquoise	48	D1	CC
mediumvioletred	C7	15	85
midnightblue	19	19	70
mintcream	F5	FF	FA
mistyrose	FF	E4	E1
moccasin	FF	E4	B5
navajowhite	FF	DE	AD
navy	00	00	80
oldlace	FD	F5	E6
olive	80	80	00
olivedrab	6B	8E	23
orange	FF	A5	00
orangered	FF	45	00
orchid	DA	70	D6
palegoldenrod	EE	E8	AA
palegreen	98	FB	98

Color	Red	Green	Blue
paleturquoise	AF	EE	EE
palevioletred	DB	70	93
papayawhip	FF	EF	D5
peachpuff	FF	DA	B9
peru	CD	85	3F
pink	FF	C0	CB
plum	DD	A0	DD
powderblue	B0	E0	E6
purple	80	00	80
red	FF	00	00
rosybrown	BC	8F	8F
royalblue	41	69	E1
saddlebrown	8B	45	13
salmon	FA	80	2
sandybrown	F4	A4	60
seagreen	2E	8B	57
seashell	FF	F5	EE
sienna	A0	52	2D
silver	C0	C0	C0
skyblue	87	CE	EB
slateblue	6A	5A	CD
slategray	70	80	90
snow	FF	FA	FA
springgreen	00	FF	7F
steelblue	46	82	B4

Color	Red	Green	Blue
tan	D2	B4	8C
teal	00	80	80
thistle	D8	BF	D8
tomato	FF	63	47
turquoise	40	E0	D0
violet	EE	82	EE
wheat	F5	DE	B3
white	FF	FF	FF
whitesmoke	F5	F5	F5
yellow	FF	FF	00
yellowgreen	9A	CD	32

GLOSSARY

A

applet a program written in Java that can be distributed as an attachment in a World Wide Web document and executed.

argument values separated by commas that are passed into the function. Also referred to as parameters.

array a set of two or more values in a particular order that you can refer to as one item through an index. For example, you could have an array named beer that contains different types of domestic beers to which you assigned numbers. If Samuel Adams was 1 and Killian's was 2, you then could refer to them as beer[1], beer[2], and so on.

assignment operator enables you to use assignment expressions to designate a value to a variable.

associative array provides a way in which each index element is associated with a string value that you can use to reference the array element; that is, a one-dimensional array of pairs.

AVS (address verification service) a security precaution that verifies the person using the credit card actually is the card holder. Merchants should not accept the transaction if one or more parts of the transaction do not match the verification.

B

bandwidth requiremen   refers to the amount of network traffic required by a certain system.

bank card acquirer   a financial institution that acts as a gateway between Internet merchants and the customer's bank card issuer.

batch   group of transactions that are settled, or reconciled, as a group rather than individual transactions and is provided by the acquirer.

block of statements   is made up of several statements that behave as a single statement. You introduce a block with a left brace ({) and end the block with the right brace (}).

C

C++   one of the most often used object-oriented languages. C++ is a superset of C developed primarily by Bjarne Stroustrup at AT&T Bell Laboratories in 1986. OLE (Object Linking and Embedding) Automation enables applications and components to expose data and functionality in a form that virtually any Windows application development language can access and use. OLE automation programs are most often controlled by scripts written in Visual Basic.

callback   a scheme used in event-driven programs where the program registers a callback handler for a certain event. The program does not call the handler directly but when the event occurs, the handler is called, possibly with arguments describing the event.

capture   the act of taking information from an authorized transaction and charging the authorized amount to the consumer's credit card.

CGI (Common Gateway Interface)   the interface used by servers to handle and interpret for information passed on to other programs on the server. Also is a standard for running external programs under a World Wide Web server.

client-side JavaScripts   JavaScript programs that run on your computer (an Internet client), which is running Netscape Navigator, and are interpreted by Netscape Navigator.

compiling   the act of converting a program from some source language (or programming language) to a destination machine language (object code) that can be interpreted by the computer. In JavaScript, this machine language is called bytecode. Bytecode is unique from most machine languages in that it is microprocessor independent.

cookie   a general mechanism that server-side connections can use to both store and retrieve information on the client side of the connection.

cpcmd (Card Processor Commands)   provides a command line interface to the card processor (ccpd), whereby all JavaScript and LiveWire functionality is bypassed. This utility provides a developer an interface to the card processing functions that use a command line, thus enabling users to integrate the utility into an existing CGI perl script.

D

DBMS (database management system)   a database system that enables you to control the organization, storage, and retrieval of data in fields, records, and files.

debugging   to attempt to determine the cause of the symptoms of malfunctions detected during testing or by users.

DER   Distinguished Encoding Rules used for encrypting and decrypting credit card information over the Internet.

direct substitution   a method that a server-side JavaScript can use to communicate with client-side JavaScript. Because a server-side JavaScript can dynamically create client-side JavaScript code, what the server-side JavaScript can do is directly substitute values to be passed to the client-side JavaScript as it is creating the code.

dot notation   enables you to indicate hierarchy and shows that an object is made up of two parts   the object to the left of the dot and the object to the right of the dot.

E

event handlers   scripts you define that enable you to link events (actions) to JavaScript functions in HTML.

expressions   a collection of variables, operators, and other expressions that return a single value.

external functions   functions that are written in other programming languages, such as C or C++, and are compiled into libraries and are available to you from the server.

F

file pointer   indicates the current position in a file.

floating point numbers   values that can include a fraction. The fraction can be expressed as a decimal number or an exponential number and can be positive or negative.

frames   rectangular areas that enable you to specify multiple, independent, scrollable regions within a display window. Users can scroll and resize frames at the discretion of the page creator.

frameset   a set of organized frames you use in an HTML document to display on one screen multiple, rectangular areas that are individually scrollable and have discrete URLs.

function   set of statements or block of code achieved by a program or section of code within a program. When the function is called, the code within that block executes. In JavaScript, when a function is contained within an object, it is referred to as a method.

H

HTML (HyperText Markup Language)   the programming language you use to create Web pages.

I

IDE (integrated development environment)   a system for supporting the process of writing software. Such a system can include a language-sensitive editor, a project management tool, and integrated support for compiling, linking, debugging, and running the software.

integer   a whole number that does not include any portion after the decimal point. Integers can be positive or negative numbers.

L

linking   the act of gathering the object code files of one or more separately compiled program modules, and binding them together into a complete executable program, resolving references from one module to another.

M

method   similar to a function in that it enables you to define the way in which you want the associated object to behave. The term method refers to both the named operation and the code that a specific class provides to perform that operation.

O

object   a software entity that is described both by its composition and its function. JavaScript uses objects to store and organize specific pieces of data.

object property   the variable in which you store the text that is on the button.

ODBC   Open DataBase Connectivity standard.

Operator   enables you to assign values to variables, changes variables, and perform calculations.

P

package   structure used in Java to categorize and group Java classes.

parameter   are values, separated by commas, that are passed into the function. Also referred to as arguments.

persistence functionality   where the server can take advantage of information gathered from a previous request.

platform independence   when your application is not dependent on any specific hardware platform.

plug-ins   files that contain data used to alter, enhance, or extend the operation of a parent application program.

precedence   refers to the order in which multiple operations are computed, which can determine the total value of an expression.

processing   refers to the way a browser reads plain text directives of HTML and then interprets the directives into on-screen graphical displays.

property   similar to a variable in that it contains or stores information an object needs to perform its specific task and is an element you can modify, such as color. In JavaScript, when a variable is contained within an object, it is referred to as a property.

Q

query   a way in which you can view, modify, and analyze data. Queries also are referred to as cursors or answer sets.

R

run-time   refers to program logic that is performed during the time of execution of a certain program. In the context of the preceding paragraph, the program that is executing is the client Web browser.

S

SET (Secure Electronic Transaction)   a protocol used to secure credit card transactions over open networks.

settling   the act of reconciling the transactions between the merchant and the acquirer. The batch settlement operation also requests that the acquirer transfer the money from the customer's account to the merchant's account.

slip   electronic, rather than paper, credit card slip used when performing monetary transactions over the Internet.

SQL (Structured Query Language)   (pronounced sequel) a language that provides a user interface to relational database management systems. SQL is the de facto standard, as well as being an ISO and ANSI standard. It often is embedded in other programming languages.

SSL (Secure Sockets Layer)   a protocol that uses channel encryption technology to protect information that is being transferred over the Web from consumer to merchant.

stateless server   a server that treats each request as an independent transaction, unrelated to any previous request.

T

trace   a method that developers use to put application output that is hidden from the end user, but is available during debugging.

U

URLs (Uniform Resource Locators)   addresses used for specifying objects on the Internet, such as files or newsgroups. URLs are used extensively on the World Wide Web. They are used in HTML documents to specify the target of a hyperlink.

user-defined property values   properties to which you assign property values specific to a client object.

V

variable   named piece of data to which you can refer when defining functions. You can change the value of a variable while the name of the variable remains the same. In JavaScript, when associated with an object, this is referred to as a property.

VRML (Virtual Reality Modeling Language)   a language that you use to display three-dimensional models.

INDEX I

REGISTRATION CARD

Inside JavaScript

Name _____ Title _____

Company _____ Type of business _____

Address _____

City/State/ZIP _____

Have you used these types of books before? ☐ yes ☐ no

If yes, which ones? _____

_____

How many computer books do you purchase each year? ☐ 1–5 ☐ 6 or more

How did you learn about this book? _____

Where did you purchase this book? _____

Which applications do you currently use? _____

_____

Which computer magazines do you subscribe to? _____

_____

What trade shows do you attend? _____

_____

Comments: _____

_____

_____

Would you like to be placed on our preferred mailing list? ☐ yes ☐ no

☐ **I would like to see my name in print!** You may use my name and quote me in future New Riders products and promotions. My daytime phone number is: _____

New Riders Publishing 201 West 103rd Street ◆ Indianapolis, Indiana 46290 USA

Fax to **317-581-4670** Orders/Customer Service **1-800-653-6156** Source Code **NRP95**

Fold Here

- -

PLACE
STAMP
HERE

NEW RIDERS PUBLISHING
201 W 103RD ST
INDIANAPOLIS IN 46290-9058